FALSTAFF

Major Literary Characters

CHELSEA HOUSE PUBLISHERS

Major Literary Characters

DAVID COPPERFIELD
Charles Dickens, *David Copperfield*

ROBINSON CRUSOE
Daniel Defoe, *Robinson Crusoe*

DON JUAN
Molière, *Don Juan*
Lord Byron, *Don Juan*

HUCK FINN
Mark Twain, *The Adventures of
    Tom Sawyer, Adventures of
    Huckleberry Finn*

CLARISSA HARLOWE
Samuel Richardson, *Clarissa*

HEATHCLIFF
Emily Brontë, *Wuthering Heights*

ANNA KARENINA
Leo Tolstoy, *Anna Karenina*

MR. PICKWICK
Charles Dickens, *The Pickwick Papers*

HESTER PRYNNE
Nathaniel Hawthorne, *The Scarlet Letter*

BECKY SHARP
William Makepeace Thackeray, *Vanity Fair*

LAMBERT STRETHER
Henry James, *The Ambassadors*

EUSTACIA VYE
Thomas Hardy, *The Return of the Native*

TWENTIETH CENTURY

ÁNTONIA
Willa Cather, *My Ántonia*

BRETT ASHLEY
Ernest Hemingway, *The Sun Also Rises*

HANS CASTORP
Thomas Mann, *The Magic Mountain*

HOLDEN CAULFIELD
J. D. Salinger, *The Catcher in the Rye*

CADDY COMPSON
William Faulkner, *The Sound and the Fury*

JANIE CRAWFORD
Zora Neale Hurston, *Their Eyes Were
    Watching God*

CLARISSA DALLOWAY
Virginia Woolf, *Mrs. Dalloway*

DILSEY
William Faulkner, *The Sound and the Fury*

GATSBY
F. Scott Fitzgerald, *The Great Gatsby*

HERZOG
Saul Bellow, *Herzog*

JOAN OF ARC
William Shakespeare, *Henry VI*
George Bernard Shaw, *Saint Joan*

LOLITA
Vladimir Nabokov, *Lolita*

WILLY LOMAN
Arthur Miller, *Death of a Salesman*

MARLOW
Joseph Conrad, *Lord Jim, Heart of
    Darkness, Youth, Chance*

PORTNOY
Philip Roth, *Portnoy's Complaint*

BIGGER THOMAS
Richard Wright, *Native Son*

CHELSEA HOUSE PUBLISHERS

Major Literary Characters

FALSTAFF

Edited and with an introduction by
HAROLD BLOOM

CHELSEA HOUSE PUBLISHERS
New York ◇ Philadelphia

Jacket illustration: Sir Ralph Richardson as Falstaff
at the Old Vic, London, 1946 (Springer/Bettmann Film Archive).

Chelsea House Publishers

Editor-in-Chief   Remmel T. Nunn
Managing Editor   Karyn Gullen Browne
Picture Editor   Adrian G. Allen
Art Director   Maria Epes
Manufacturing Manager   Gerald Levine

Major Literary Characters

Senior Editor   S. T. Joshi
Associate Editor   Richard Fumosa
Designer   Maria Epes

Staff for FALSTAFF

Picture Researcher   Jonathan Shapiro
Assistant Art Director   Noreen Romano
Production Manager   Joseph Romano
Production Coordinator   Marie Claire Cebrián

First Printing

1   3   5   7   9   8   6   4   2

Library of Congress Cataloging-in-Publication Data

Falstaff / edited and with an introduction by Harold Bloom.
        p.   cm.—(Major literary characters)
        Includes bibliographical references and index.
        ISBN 0-7910-0917-3.—ISBN 0-7910-0972-6 (pbk.)
        1. Shakespeare, William, 1564–1616—Characters—Falstaff.
        2. Falstaff, John, Sir (Fictitious character)   I. Bloom, Harold.
                II. Series.
                PR2993.F2F35   1991
                    822.3'3—dc20
                    90-27744
                        CIP

CONTENTS

THE ANALYSIS OF CHARACTER

Harold Bloom

"Character," according to our dictionaries, still has as a primary meaning a graphic symbol, such as a letter of the alphabet. This meaning reflects the word's apparent origin in the ancient Greek *charactēr*, a sharp stylus. *Charactēr* also meant the mark of the stylus' incisions. Recent fashions in literary criticism have reduced "character" in literature to a matter of marks upon a page. But our word "character" also has a very different meaning, matching that of the ancient Greek *ēthos*, "habitual way of life." Shall we say then that literary character is an imitation of human character, or is it just a grouping of marks? The issue is between a critic like Dr. Samuel Johnson, for whom words were as much like people as like things, and a critic like the late Roland Barthes, who told us that "the fact can only exist linguistically, as a term of discourse." Who is closer to our experience of reading literature, Johnson or Barthes? What difference does it make, if we side with one critic rather than the other?

Barthes is famous, like Foucault and other recent French theorists, for having added to Nietzsche's proclamation of the death of God a subsidiary demise, that of the literary author. If there are no authors, then there are no fictional personages, presumably because literature does not refer to a world outside language. Words indeed necessarily refer to other words in the first place, but the impact of words ultimately is drawn from a universe of fact. Stories, poems, and plays are recognizable as such because they are human utterances within traditions of utterances, and traditions, by achieving authority, become a kind of fact, or at least the sense of a fact. Our sense that literary characters, within the context of a fictive cosmos, indeed are fictional personages is also a kind of fact. The meaning and value of every character in a successful work of literary representation depend upon our ideas of persons in the factual reality of our lives.

Literary character is always an invention, and inventions generally are indebted to prior inventions. Shakespeare is the inventor of literary character as we know it; he reformed the universal human expectations for the verbal imitation of personality, and the reformation appears now to be permanent and uncannily inevitable. Remarkable as the Bible and Homer are at representing personages, their characters are relatively unchanging. They age within their stories, but their habitual modes of being do not develop. Jacob and Achilles unfold before us, but without metamorphoses. Lear and Macbeth, Hamlet and Othello severely modify themselves not only by their actions, but by their utterances, and most of all through *overhearing themselves,* whether they speak to themselves or to others. Pondering what they themselves have said, they will to change, and actually do change, sometimes extravagantly yet always persuasively. Or else they suffer change, without willing it, but in reaction not so much to their language as to their relation to that language.

I do not think it useful to say that Shakespeare successfully imitated elements in our characters. Rather, it could be argued that he compelled aspects of character to appear that previously were concealed, or not available to representation. This is not to say that Shakespeare is God, but to remind us that language is not God either. The mimesis of character in Shakespeare's dramas now seems to us normative, and indeed became the accepted mode almost immediately, as Ben Jonson shrewdly and somewhat grudgingly implied. And yet, Shakespearean representation has surprisingly little in common with the imitation of reality in Jonson or in Christopher Marlowe. The origins of Shakespeare's originality in the portrayal of men and women are to be found in the *Canterbury Tales* of Geoffrey Chaucer, insofar as they can be located anywhere before Shakespeare himself. Chaucer's savage and superb Pardoner overhears his own tale-telling, as well as his mocking rehearsal of his own spiel, and through this overhearing he is emboldened to forget himself, and enthusiastically urges all his fellow-pilgrims to come forward to be fleeced by him. His self-awareness, and apocalyptically rancid sense of spiritual fall, are preludes to the even grander abysses of the perverted will in Iago and in Edmund. What might be called the character trait of a negative charisma may be Chaucer's invention, but came to its perfection in Shakespearean mimesis.

The analysis of character is as much Shakespeare's invention as the representation of character is, since Iago and Edmund are adepts at analyzing both themselves and their victims. Hamlet, whose overwhelming charisma has many negative components, is certainly the most comprehensive of all literary characters, and so necessarily prophesies the labyrinthine complexities of the will in Iago and Edmund. Charisma, according to Max Weber, its first codifier, is primarily a natural endowment, and implies a primordial and idiosyncratic power over nature, and so finally over death. Hamlet's uncanniness is at its most suggestive in the scene of his long dying, where the audience, through the mediation of Horatio, itself is compelled to meditate upon suicide, if only because outliving the prince of Denmark scarcely seems an option.

Shakespearean representation has usurped not only our sense of literary character, but our sense of ourselves as characters, with Hamlet playing the part of the largest of these usurpations. Insofar as we have an idea of human disinterestedness, we tend to derive it from the Hamlet of Act V, whose quietism has about it a ghostly authority. Oscar Wilde, in his profound and profoundly witty dialogue, "The Decay of Lying," expressed a permanent insight when he insisted that art shaped every era, far more than any age formed art. Life imitates art, we imitate Shakespeare, because without Shakespeare we would perish for lack of images. Wilde's grandest audacity demystifies Shakespearean mimesis with a Shakespearean vivaciousness: "This unfortunate aphorism about art holding the mirror up to Nature is deliberately said by Hamlet in order to convince the bystanders of his absolute insanity in all art-matters." Of *Hamlet*'s influence upon the ages Wilde remarked that: "The world has grown sad because a puppet was once melancholy." "Puppet" is Wilde's own deconstruction, a brilliant reminder that Shakespeare's artistry of illusion has so mastered reality as to have changed reality, evidently forever.

The analysis of character, as a critical pursuit, seems to me as much a Shakespearean invention as literary character was, since much of what we know about how to analyze character necessarily follows Shakespearean procedures. His hero-villains, from Richard III through Iago, Edmund, and Macbeth, are shrewd and endless questers into their own self-motivations. If we could bear to see Hamlet, in his unwearied negations, as another hero-villain, then we would judge him the supreme analyst of the darker recalcitrances in the selfhood. Freud followed the pre-Socratic Empedocles, in arguing that character is fate, a frightening doctrine that maintains the fear that there are no accidents, that overdetermination rules us all of our lives. Hamlet assumes the same, yet adds to this argument the terrible passivity he manifests in Act V. Throughout Shakespeare's tragedies, the most interesting personages seem doom-eager, reminding us again that a Shakespearean reading of Freud would be more illuminating than a Freudian exegesis of Shakespeare. We learn more when we discover Hamlet in the Freudian Death Drive, than when we read *Beyond the Pleasure Principle* into *Hamlet*.

In Shakespearean comedy, character achieves its true literary apotheosis, which is the representation of the inner freedom that can be created by great wit alone. Rosalind and Falstaff, perhaps alone among Shakespeare's personages, match Hamlet in wit, though hardly in the metaphysics of consciousness. Whether in the comic or the modern mode, Shakespeare has set the standard of measurement in the balance between character and passion.

In Shakespeare the self is more dramatized than theatricalized, which is why a Shakespearean reading of Freud works out so well. Character-formation after the passing of the Oedipal stage takes the place of fetishistic fragmentings of the self. Critics who now call literary character into question, and who proclaim also the death of the author, invariably also regard all notions, literary and human, of a stable character as being mere reductions of deeper pre-Oedipal desires. It becomes

clear that the fortunes of literary character rise and fall with the prestige of normative conceptions of the ego. Shakespeare's Iago, who wars against being, may be
the first deconstructionist of the self, with his proclamation of "I am not what I am."
This constitutes the necessary prologue to any view that would regard a fixed ego
as a virtual abnormality. But deconstructions of the self are no more modern than
Modernism is. Like literary modernism, the decentered ego came out of the
Hellenistic culture of ancient Alexandria. The Gnostic heretics believed that the
psyche, like the body, was a fallen entity, mechanically fashioned by the Demiurge
or false creator. They held however that each of us possessed also a spark or
pneuma, which was a fragment of the original Abyss or true, alien God. The soul
or psyche within every one of us was thus at war with the self or pneuma, and only
that sparklike self could be saved.

Shakespeare, following after Chaucer in this respect, was the first and remains
still the greatest master of representing character both as a stable soul and a
wavering self. There is a substance that endures in Shakespeare's figures, and there
is also a quicksilver rendition of the unsettling sparks. Racine and Tolstoy, Balzac and
Dickens, follow in Shakespeare's wake by giving us some sense of pre-Oedipal
sparks or drives, and considerably more sense of post-Oedipal character and
personality, stabilizations or sublimations of the fetish-seeking drives. Critics like Leo
Bersani and René Girard argue eloquently against our taking this mimesis as the only
proper work of literature. I would suggest that strong fictions of the self, from the
Bible through Samuel Beckett, necessarily participate in both modes, the sublima-
tion of desire, and the persistence of a primordial desire. The mystery of Hamlet
or of Lear is intimately invested in the tangled mixture of the two modes of
representation.

Psychic mobility is proposed by Bersani as the ideal to which deconstructions
of the literary self may yet guide us. The ideal has its pathos, but the realities of
literary representation seem to me very different, perhaps destructively so. When
a novelist like D. H. Lawrence sought to reduce his characters to Eros and the
Death Drive, he still had to persuade us of his authority at mimesis by lavishing upon
the figures of The Rainbow and Women in Love all of the vivid stigmata of
normative personality. Birkin and Ursula may represent antithetical and uncanny
drives, but they develop and change as characters pondering their own pronounce-
ments and reactions to self and others. The cost of a non-Shakespearean representation is enormous. Pynchon, in The Crying of Lot 49 and Gravity's Rainbow,
evades the burden of the normative by resorting to something like Christopher
Marlowe's art of caricature in The Jew of Malta. Marlowe's Barabas is a marvelous
rhetorician, yet he is a cartoon alongside the troublingly equivocal Shylock. Pynchon's personages are deliberate cartoons also, as flat as comic strips. Marlowe's
achievement, and Pynchon's, are beyond dispute, yet they are like the prelude and
the postlude to Shakespearean reality. They do not wish to engage with our hunger
for the empirical world and so they enter the problematic cosmos of literary
fantasy.

No writer, not even Shakespeare or Proust, alters the available stock that we agree to call reality, but Shakespeare, more than any other, does show us how much of reality we could encounter if only we retained adequate desire. The strong literary representation of character is already an analysis of character, and is part of the healing work of a literary culture, which implicitly seeks to cure violence through a normative mimesis of ego, *as if it were stable,* whether in actuality it is or is not. I do not believe that this is a social quest taken on by literary culture, but rather that we confront here the aesthetic essence of what makes a culture *literary,* rather than metaphysical or ethical or religious. A culture becomes literary when its conceptual modes have failed it, which means when religion, philosophy, and science have begun to lose their authority. If they cannot heal violence, then literature attempts to do so, which may be only a turning inside out of the critical arguments of Girard and Bersani.

I conclude by offering a particular instance or special case as a paradigm for the healing enterprise that is at once the representation and the analysis of literary character. Let us call it the aesthetics of being outraged, or rather of successfully representing the state of being outraged. W. C. Fields was one modern master of such representation, and Nathanael West was another, as was Faulkner before him. Here also the greatest master remains Shakespeare, whose Macbeth, himself a bloody outrage, yet retains our imaginative sympathy precisely because he grows increasingly outraged as he experiences the equivocation of the fiend that lies like truth. The double-natured promises and the prophecies of the weird sisters finally induce in Macbeth an apocalyptic version of the stage actor's anxiety at missing cues, the horror of a phantasmagoric stage fright of missing one's time, of always reacting too late. Macbeth, a veritable monster of solipsistic inwardness but no intellectual, counters his dilemma by fresh murders, that prolong him in time yet provoke him only to a perpetually freshened sense of being outraged, as all his expectations become still worse confounded. We are moved by Macbeth, however estrangedly, because his terrible inwardness is a paradigm for our own solipsism, but also because none of us can resist a strong and successful representation of the human in a state of being outraged.

The ultimate outrage is the necessity of dying, an outrage concealed in a multitude of masks, including the tyrannical ambitions of Macbeth. I suspect that our outrage at being outraged is the most difficult of all our affects for us to represent to ourselves, which is why we are so inclined to imaginative sympathy for a character who strongly conveys that affect to us. The Shrike of West's *Miss Lonely-hearts* or Faulkner's Joe Christmas of *Light in August* are crucial modern instances, but such figures can be located in many other works, since the ability to represent this extreme emotion is one of the tests that strong writers are driven to set for themselves.

However a reader seeks to reduce literary character to a question of marks on a page, she will come at last to the impasse constituted by the thought of death, her death, and before that to all the stations of being outraged that memorialize her own drive towards death. In reading, she quests for evidences that are strong representations, whether of her desire or her despair. Such questings constitute the necessary basis for the analysis of literary character, an enterprise that always will survive every vagary of critical fashion.

EDITOR'S NOTE

This volume brings together a representative selection of the best criticism, old and new, that has been devoted to Shakespeare's Sir John Falstaff, as a major literary and dramatic character. I am indebted again to the erudition and acuity of S. T. Joshi. The critical extracts and essays are reprinted here in the chronological order of their original publication.

My introduction relates Falstaff's grand wit and sense of play to his freedom from the superego, as well as to his ceaseless agon, with time and with the interests of the state.

The critical extracts range through more than three centuries, and take us from John Dryden and Dr. Samuel Johnson through William Hazlitt, Swinburne, and George Bernard Shaw, on to crucial modern critics including William Empson and John Middleton Murry.

Maurice Morgann's great essay of 1777 leads off the critical essays, because so much of the subsequent major criticism of the sublime Falstaff can be read as a reply to this work, as well as to A. C. Bradley's essay of 1902, which follows Morgann here. My own favorite among all modern Shakespeare critics, Harold C. Goddard, comes next, with his superb defense of Shakespeare's greatest comic creation.

Time, the Falstaffian antagonist, is the central figuration in Peter J. Seng's analysis of the relations of the songs in *2 Henry IV* to Hal's rejection of Falstaff. Harold E. Toliver returns us to Morgann in a further consideration of his mentor in wit.

In Willard Farnham's meditation on the grotesque, Falstaff is seen as both an antique vice and an elf, while Michael Platt centers upon the death of Falstaff, fascinatingly compared to the death of the Biblical King David. Leo Salingar finds in the Shakespearean trope of "shadows" or doubles a prime emblem for Falstaff, after which Barbara Freedman offers a feminist reading of the Falstaff of *The Merry Wives of Windsor*.

A comprehensive discussion by the late C. L. Barber and Richard P. Wheeler emphasizes how Falstaff's aura of freedom pervades the *Henry IV* plays. In this volume's final essay, Paul M. Cubeta returns us to the death of Falstaff, showing us how the greatest of wits is master of the art of dying.

INTRODUCTION

In an earlier study (*Ruin the Sacred Truths,* 1989) I ventured the judgment that Shakespeare's Falstaff was a successful representation of what Freud thought impossible, a human being without a superego. Nietzsche, I remarked, had attempted just such a representation in his Zarathustra, and rather conspicuously had failed. What I forgot then, or more likely repressed, was that Freud had commented upon Falstaff in his *Jokes and Their Relation to the Unconscious* (1905). As a fierce Falstaffian, and a rather ambivalent Freudian, I rather dislike Freud on Falstaff, and I quote it here with some distaste:

> The grandiose humorous effect of a figure like that of the fat knight Sir John Falstaff rests on an economy in contempt and indignation. We recognize him as an undeserving gormandizer and swindler, but our condemnation is disarmed by a whole number of factors. We can see that he knows himself as well as we do; he impresses us by his wit, and, besides this, his physical misproportion has the effect of encouraging us to take a comic view of him instead of a serious one, as though the demands of morality and honor must rebound from so fat a stomach. His doings are on the whole harmless, and are almost excused by the common baseness of the people he cheats. We admit that the poor fellow has a right to try to live and enjoy himself like anyone else, and we almost pity him because in the chief situations we find him a plaything in the hands of someone far his superior. So we cannot feel angry with him and we add all that we economize in indignation with him to the comic pleasure which he affords us apart from this. Sir John's own humor arises in fact from the superiority of an ego which neither his physical nor his moral defects can rob of its cheerfulness and assurance.

Freud's economics of the psyche certainly are not Shakespeare's, and I am reminded again how much we need a Shakespearean reading of Freud and how little use is a Freudian reading of Shakespeare. The cheerfulness and assurance of the greatest wit in all literature do not stem from the superiority of his ego but from his freedom, specifically freedom of his ego from the superego. It is dangerous to condescend to Falstaff (as Freud does) because there is no greater wit in a literary representation than Shakespeare invested in Falstaff, the Falstaff of the *Henry IV* plays. Fundamentally, Freud thought that the comic spirit could flourish only when the superego mitigated its severities towards the battered ego. But what of the comedy that rises where there simply is no superego, no overdetermined need for punishment, no turning of the ego against itself? Where is the superego in the magnificent Falstaff? Is there any other literary character whatsoever who seems so free, free to play, free to mock the state, free to evade time? With a few honorable exceptions, Shakespeare's critics simply seem incapable of hearing what Falstaff says, and how he says it. Not even Hamlet is endowed by Shakespeare with more wit and intellect than Falstaff. It is Falstaff's cognitive strength that should astonish us. Nearly everything he says demands subsequent meditation on our part, and rewards our reveries with fresh insights that expand our understanding of far more than Falstaff himself. I am suggesting that the disreputable Falstaff—glutton, boozer, womanizer—is a teacher of wisdom, a hilarious teacher. When I was fifteen, I saw Ralph Richardson play Falstaff (with Laurence Olivier as Hotspur), and I have carried the image of Richardson's exuberant and inventive Falstaff in my head for forty-five years now, and find the image informing the text every time I reread or teach the *Henry IV* plays. Richardson's Falstaff was neither an adorable roisterer nor a kind of counter-courtier, eager for possibilities of power. Rather, he was a veteran warrior who had seen through warfare, discarded its honor and glory as pernicious illusions, and had decided that true life was play, both as we play on stage or in games, and as we play when we are children. Falstaff, wicked and old, has become a wise child again, which is the meaning of the magnificent apologia delivered by him to the Lord Chief Justice, when that embodiment of the state's sagacity reproves him for pretending to be young:

> My lord, I was born about three of the clock in the afternoon, with a white head and something a round belly. For my voice, I have lost it with hallowing and singing of anthems. To approve my youth further, I will not. The truth is, I am only old in judgment and understanding; and he that will caper with me for a thousand marks, let him lend me the money, and have at him!

Falstaff is of the company both of the heroic wits, Rosalind and Hamlet, and of the heroic vitalists, the Wife of Bath and the Panurge of Falstaffian Rabelais. He could also ride into the world of Sancho Panza and the Don, because in some sense he is their synthesis, fusing Sancho's ribald realism and the Don's faith in his own imagination and in the order of play. The Don's chivalric madness is shared by Hotspur, and not at all by Falstaff, but Cervantes is perhaps the only author except Chaucer, and Shakespeare himself, who could have imagined Sir John Falstaff. Hazlitt charmingly remarked that the Fat Knight "is perhaps the most substantial comic character that ever was invented," and certainly Falstaff is the patron of all fat men forever. There is a great deal more to him psychically than his wit, and yet wit is more central to him than to Rosalind or Hamlet. The formidable Rosalind has a gentleness that tempers her exuberance, while Hamlet, in his bewildering complexity, has in him a savagery nearly as strong as his skepticism. Falstaff's exuberance is primal and unstoppable, while he has nothing of Hamlet's savagery, or of Hal's. If there is a mystery to Falstaff, it is in his vexed relationship to Hal, which is hardly to be understood if we refuse to imagine its prehistory. L. C. Knights and other Formalists long ago shamed most critics out of considering the long foregrounds of Shakespearean protagonists, but I am no more a Formalist than I am an Historicist, and I am happy to puzzle out how the given has been constituted each time I start on one of the plays.

Hal's ambivalence towards Falstaff evidently passed into an exasperated negativity, almost a murderousness, long before the first part of *Henry IV* opens. A Formalist or an Historicist would say there was no such "long before," but no start is an authentic genesis after Genesis itself, and Shakespeare is much the greatest master of implied foregrounds that we ever will know. When we first encounter Falstaff and Hal, their dialogue is already the death's duel it rarely ceases to be, with the Prince of Wales almost perpetually attacking, and Sir John defending with deftness and a teacher's dignity, since he is aware that the rhetoric used against him by Hal remains always his own invention. The character of the future Henry V is fortunately hardly my concern here, since this cold opportunist, so admired by scholars, is precisely what Harold Goddard termed him: a hypocritical and ambitious politician, caring only for glory and for power, his father's true son. Hal is best categorized by his own despicable couplet:

I'll so offend, to make offence a skill;
Redeeming time when men think least I will.

Redemption of time is not exactly the Falstaffian project, as Hotspur tells us, when he asks if Hal and Falstaff's gang are coming to the battle:

Where is his son,
The nimble-footed madcap Prince of Wales,
And his comrades, that daffed the world aside
And bid it pass?

Thrusting the world aside, and telling it to pass, indeed is pure Falstaff, when one translates "the world" as Hotspur's exaltation of battle. However one wants to interpret Hal's Falstaffian phrase, it is difficult to improve upon Dr. Johnson's analysis of the relationship between Falstaff and Hal:

Yet the man thus corrupt, thus despicable, makes himself necessary to the Prince that despises him, by the most pleasing of all qualities, perpetual gaiety, by an unfailing power of exciting laughter, which is the more freely indulged as his wit is not of the splendid or ambitious kind but consists in easy escapes and sallies of levity, which make sport but raise no envy. It must be observed that he is stained with no enormous or sanguinary crimes, so that his licentiousness is not so offensive but that it may be borne for his mirth.

Johnson's ambivalence towards Falstaff only superficially resembles Hal's. Both despise Falstaff, on conventional grounds, but Johnson, afflicted by a vile melancholy, forgives Falstaff everything for his perpetual gaiety, which the great doctor so desperately sought in his companions. Hal, no melancholic, found something else in Falstaff, a teacher of wit and wisdom, but a teacher he no longer cares to need. We, the audience, find more in Falstaff, because Falstaff—more than any other character in Shakespeare, indeed in all literature—bears the Blessing, in the original Yahwistic sense of more life. Falstaff, in himself, is one of the enlargements of life, one of the intimations of a time without boundaries, of a desire that cannot be beggared by fulfillment.

It is another critical commonplace to assert that Falstaff undergoes a degeneration in moral sensibility in Part Two of *Henry IV*. His humor may be a touch coarser, I might admit, but his exuberance does not falter, and his intelligence remains triumphant. What a teacher instructs us in is at last himself, and the more attractive qualities manifested by the protagonist of *Henry V* are subtly traceable to the lesson of the master. Falstaff is more than equal to every event and to every antagonist. Hamlet's intellect has faith neither in language nor in itself; Falstaff's intellect molds language precisely to its ends, and retains a perfect confidence in the mind's triumph over every danger. Hal's obsessive need to prove Falstaff a coward tells us nothing about Falstaff, and almost too much about Hal.

Falstaff's rivals in Shakespeare are not many: Hamlet, Rosalind, and Cleopatra would complete the list unless we admit the intellectual villains, Iago and Edmund. All six of these have the rhetorical genius to overcome any disputant. Yet Falstaff stands apart from the others, because he is older than all of them, and younger than all of them, younger and older even than Cleopatra, who ends in absolute transcendence, whereas Falstaff ends in rejection and grief. The great wit has violated Freud's admonition, which is not to invest too much affection in any single person. Falstaff's tragedy (what else can we call it?) is one of misplaced love, but Shakespeare does not allow that to be our final sense of his grandest comic creation. Instead, we are given the great vision of the death of Falstaff in *Henry V*, which assures us that "he's in Arthur's bosom, if ever man went to Arthur's bosom. A' made a finer end and went away an it had been any christom child." Playing with flowers, and smiling upon his fingers' end, Sir John dies as a child, reminding us again of his total lack of hypocrisy, of what after all makes us love him, of what doubtless first drew the Machiavellian Hal to him. Freedom from the superego, authentic freedom, is the liberty to play, even as a child plays, in the very act of dying.

—H. B.

CRITICAL EXTRACTS

W. J.

I dare here speake it, and my speech mayntayne,
That Sir Iohn Falstaffe was not any way
More grosse in body, than you are in brayne.
But whether should I (helpe me nowe, I pray)
For your grosse brayne, you like I. Falstaffe graunt,
Or for small wit, suppose you Iohn of Gaunt?

—W. J., *The Whipping of the Satyre* (London, 1601)

JOHN DRYDEN

I am assur'd from diverse persons, that *Ben. Johnson* was actually acquainted with such a man, one altogether as ridiculous as he ⟨Morose in *The Silent Woman*⟩ is here represented. Others say it is not enough to find one man of such an humour; it must be common to more, and the more common the more natural. To prove this they instance in the best of Comical Characters, Falstaff: There are many men resembling him; Old, Fat, Merry, Cowardly, Drunken, Amorous, Vain, and Lying: But to convince these people I need but tell them, that humour is the ridiculous extravagance of conversation, wherein one man differs from all others. If then it be common or communicated to many, how differs it from other mens? or what indeed causes it to be ridiculous so much as the singularity of it? As for Falstaffe, he is not properly one humour, but a Miscellany of Humours or Images, drawn from so many several men; that wherein he is singular in his wit, or those things he sayes, *praeter expectatum*, unexpected by the Audience; his quick evasions when you imagine him surpriz'd, which as they are extreamly diverting of themselves, so receive a great addition from his person; for the very sight of such an unwieldy old debauch'd fellow is a Comedy alone.

—JOHN DRYDEN, *Of Dramatick Poesie: An Essay* (London: Henry Herringman, 1668), pp. 51–52

JEREMY COLLIER

In the mean time I shall take a Testimony or two from *Shakespear*. And here we may observe the admir'd *Falstaffe* goes off in Disappointment. He is thrown out of Favour as being a *Rake*, and dies like a Rat behind the Hangings. The Pleasure he has given, would not excuse him. The *Poet* was not so partial, as to let his Humour compound for his Lewdness. If 'tis objected that this remark is wide of the Point, because *Falstaffe* is represented in Tragedy, where the Laws of Justice are more strickly observ'd. To this I answer, that you may call *Henry* the Fourth and Fifth, Tragedies if you please. But for all that, *Falstaffe* wears no *Buskins*, his Character is perfectly comical from end to end.

—JEREMY COLLIER, *A Short View of the Immorality and Profaneness of the English Stage* (London: S. Keble, R. Sare, & H. Hindmarsh, 1698), p. 154

JOHN DENNIS

That this Comedy ⟨*The Merry Wives of Windsor*⟩ was not despicable, I guess'd for several Reasons: First, I knew very well, that it had pleas'd one of the greatest Queens that ever was in the World, great not only for her Wisdom in the Arts of Government, but for her knowledge of Polite Learning, and her nice taste of the Drama, for such a taste we may be sure she had, by the relish which she had of the Ancients. This Comedy was written at her Command, and by her direction, and she was so eager to see it Acted, that she commanded it to be finished in fourteen days; and was afterwards, as Tradition tells us, very well pleas'd at the Representation. In the second place, in the Reign of King *Charles* the Second, when People had an admirable taste of Comedy, all those men of extraordinary parts, who were the Ornaments of that Court; as the late Duke of *Buckingham*, my Lord *Normanby*, my Lord *Dorset*, my late Lord *Rochester*, Sir *Charles Sidley*, Dr *Frazer*, Mr *Savil*, Mr *Buckley*, were in Love with the Beauties of this Comedy. In the third place, I thought that after so long an acquaintance as I had with the best Comick Poets, among the Antients and Moderns, I might depend in some measure upon my own Judgment, and I thought I found here three or four extraordinary Characters, that were exactly drawn, and truly Comical; and that I saw besides in it some as happy touches as ever were in comedy: Besides I had observed what success the Character of *Falstaffe* had had, in the first place of *Harry* the Fourth. And as the *Falstaffe* in the Merry Wives is certainly superiour to that of the second part of *Harry* the Fourth, so is can hardly be said to be inferior to that of the first.

For in the second part of *Harry* the Fourth, *Falstaffe* does nothing but talk, as indeed he does nothing else in the third and fourth Acts of the first part. Whereas in the Merry Wives, he every where Acts, and that action is more Regular, and more in compass than it is in the first part of *Harry* the Fourth. 'Tis true, what he says in *Harry* the Fourth is admirable; but action at last is the business of the Stage.

The Drama is action itself, and it is action alone that is able to excite in any extraordinary manner the curiosity of mankind. What News, is the Question now adays ev'ry moment, but people by that question demand what is done, and not what is said upon the Great Stage of the World. In short, I defie any man to name me a Play that has ever succeeded without some sort of action or another. But I could if I pleased mention more than one, that has succeeded barely by the force of Action, without almost any thing else.

—JOHN DENNIS, *A Large Account of the Taste in Poetry, and the Causes of the Degeneracy of It* [1702], *The Critical Works of John Dennis*, ed. Edward Niles Hooker (Baltimore: Johns Hopkins University Press, 1939), Vol. I, pp. 279–80

NICHOLAS ROWE

She ⟨Queen Elizabeth⟩ was so well pleas'd with that admirable Character of *Falstaff*, in the two Parts of *Henry* the Fourth, that she commanded him to continue it for one Play more, and to shew him in Love. This is said to be the Occasion of his Writing *The Merry Wives of* Windsor. How well she was obey'd, the Play it self is an admirable Proof. Upon this Occasion it may not be improper to observe, that this part of *Falstaff* is said to have been written originally under the Name of *Oldcastle;* some of that Family being then remaining, the Queen was pleas'd to command him to alter it; upon which he made use of *Falstaff.* The presence Offence was indeed avoided; but I don't know whether the Author may not have been somewhat to blame in his second Choice, since it is certain that Sir *John Falstaff*, who was a Knight of the Garter, and a Lieutenant-General, was a Name of distinguish'd Merit in the Wars in *France* in *Henry* the Fifth's and *Henry* the Sixth's Times. What Grace soever the Queen confer'd upon him, it was not to her only he ow'd the Fortune which the Reputation of his Wit made.

—NICHOLAS ROWE, "Some Account of the Life, &c. of Mr. William Shakespear," *The Works of Mr. William Shakespear* (London: Jacob Tonson, 1709), Vol. I, pp. viii–ix

CORBYN MORRIS

These seem to me to be the different Powers and Effects of HUMOUR and WIT. However, the most agreeable Representations or Compositions of all others, appear not where they *separately* exist, but where they are *united* together in the same Fabric; where HUMOUR is the *Ground-work* and chief Substance, and WIT happily spread, *quickens* the whole with Embellishments.

This is the Excellency of the *Character* of Sir *John Falstaff;* the *Ground-work* is *Humour,* or the Representation and Detection of a bragging and vaunting *Coward* in *real Life;* However, this alone would only have expos'd the *Knight,* as a meer

Noll Bluff, to the Derision of the Company; And after they had once been gratify'd with his Chastisement, he would have sunk into Infamy, and become quite odious and intolerable: But here the inimitable *Wit* of Sir *John* come in to his Support, and gives a new *Rise* and *Lustre* to his Character; For the sake of his *Wit* you forgive his *Cowardice;* or rather, are fond of his *Cowardice* for the Occasions it gives to his *Wit.* In short, the *Humour* furnishes a Subject and Spur to the *Wit,* and the *Wit* again supports and embellishes the *Humour.*

At the *first* Entrance of the *Knight,* your good Humour and Tendency to *Mirth* are irresistibly excited by his jolly Appearance and Corpulency; you feel and acknowledge him, to be the fittest Subject imaginable for yielding *Diversion* and *Merriment;* but when you see him immediately set up for *Enterprize* and *Activity,* with his evident *Weight* and *Unweildiness,* your Attention is all call'd forth, and you are eager to watch him to the End of his Adventures; Your Imagination pointing out with a full Scope his future Embarrassments. All the while as you accompany him forwards, he *heightens* your Relish for his future Disasters, by his happy Opinion of his own Sufficiency, and the gay Vaunts which he makes of his Talents and Accomplishments; so that at last when he falls into a Scrape, your Expectation is exquisitely gratify'd, and you have the full Pleasure of seeing all his trumpeted Honour laid in the Dust. When in the midst of his Misfortunes, instead of being utterly demolish'd and sunk, he rises again by the superior Force of his *Wit,* and begins a *new* Course with fresh Spirit and Alacrity; This excites you the more to *renew* the Chace, in full View of his *second* Defeat; out of which he recovers again, and triumphs with new Pretensions and Boastings. After this he immediately starts upon a *third* Race, and so on; continually detected and caught, and yet constantly extricating himself by his inimitable *Wit* and *Invention;* this yielding a perpetual *Round* of Sport and Diversion.

Again, the genteel *Quality* of Sir *John* is of great Use in supporting his Character; It prevents his *sinking* too low after several of his Misfortunes; Besides, you allow him, in consequence of his *Rank* and *Seniority,* the Privilege to dictate, and take the Lead, and to rebuke others upon many Occasions; By this he is sav'd from appearing too *nauseous* and *impudent.* The good *Sense* which he possesses comes also to his Aid, and saves him from being *despicable,* by forcing your Esteem for his real Abilities.—Again, the *Privilege* you allow him of rebuking and checking others, when he assumes it with proper Firmness and Superiority, helps to *settle* anew, and *compose* his Character after an Embarrassment; And reduces in some measure the *Spirit* of the Company to a proper *Level,* before he sets out again upon a fresh Adventure;—without this, they would be kept continually *strain'd,* and *wound up* to the highest Pitch, without sufficient Relief and Diversity.

It may also deserve to be remark'd of *Falstaff,* that the *Figure* of his *Person* is admirably suited to the *Turn* of his *Mind;* so that there arises before you a perpetual *Allusion* from one to the other, which forms an incessant Series of *Wit,* whether they are in *Contrast* or *Agreement* together.—When he pretends to *Activity,* there is Wit in the *Contrast* between his *Mind* and his *Person,*—And *Wit* in their *Agreement,* when he triumphs in *Jollity.*

To compleat the whole,—you have in this Character of *Falstaff*, not only a free Course of *Humour*, supported and embellish'd with admirable *Wit*; but this *Humour* is of a Species the most *jovial* and *gay* in all Nature.—Sir *John Falstaff* possesses Generosity, Chearfulness, Alacrity, Invention, Frolic and Fancy superior to all other Men;—The *Figure* of his *Person* is the Picture of Jollity, Mirth, and Good-nature, and banishes at once all other Ideas from your Breast; He is happy himself, and makes you happy.—If you examine him further, he has no Fierceness, Reserve, Malice or Peevishness lurking in his Heart; His Intentions are all pointed at innocent Riot and Merriment; Nor has the Knight any inveterate Design, except against *Sack,* and that too he *loves.*—If, besides this, he desires to pass for a Man of *Activity* and *Valour,* you can easily excuse so harmless a *Foible,* which yields you the highest Pleasure in its constant *Detection.*

If you put all these together, it is impossible to *hate* honest *Jack Falstaff;* If you observe them again, it is impossible to avoid *loving* him; He is the gay, the witty, the frolicksome, happy, and fat *Jack Falstaff,* the most delightful *Swaggerer* in all Nature.—You must *love* him for your *own* sake,—At the same time you cannot but *love* him for *his own* Talents; And when you have *enjoy'd* them, you cannot but *love* him in *Gratitude;*—He has nothing to disgust you, and every thing to give you Joy;—His *Sense* and his *Foibles* are equally directed to advance your Pleasure; And it is impossible to be tired or unhappy in his Company.

This *jovial* and *gay* Humour, without any thing *envious, malicious, mischievous,* or *despicable,* and continually *quicken'd* and adorn'd with *Wit,* yields that peculiar Delight, without any *Alloy,* which we all feel and acknowledge in *Falstaff*'s Company.

—CORBYN MORRIS, *An Essay towards Fixing the True Standards of Wit,*
Humour, Raillery, Satire, and Ridicule (London: J. Roberts
& W. Bickerton, 1744), pp. 25–29

SAMUEL JOHNSON

But Falstaff unimitated, unimitable Falstaff, how shall I describe thee? Thou compound of sense and vice; of sense which may be admired but not esteemed, of vice which may be despised, but hardly detested. Falstaff is a character loaded with faults, and with those faults which naturally produce contempt. He is a thief, and a glutton, a coward, and a boaster, always ready to cheat the weak, and prey upon the poor; to terrify the timorous and insult the defenceless. At once obsequious and malignant, he satirises in their absence those whom he lives by flattering. He is familiar with the Prince only as an agent of vice, but of this familiarity he is so proud as not only to be supercilious and haughty with common men, but to think his interest of importance to the Duke of Lancaster. Yet the man thus corrupt, thus despicable, makes himself necessary to the prince that despises him, by the most pleasing of all qualities, perpetual gaiety, by an unfailing power of exciting laughter, which is the more freely indulged, as his wit is not of the splendid or ambitious kind, but consists in easy escapes and sallies of levity, which make sport but raise no envy. It must be observed that he is stained with no enormous or sanguinary crimes, so that his licentiousness is not so offensive but that it may be borne for his mirth.

The moral to be drawn from this representation is, that no man is more dangerous than he that with a will to corrupt, hath the power to please; and that neither wit nor honesty ought to think themselves safe with such a companion when they see Henry seduced by Falstaff.

—SAMUEL JOHNSON, *The Plays of William Shakespeare*
(London: J. & R. Tonson, 1768), Vol. 4, p. 355

ELIZABETH MONTAGU

Whether we consider the character of Falstaffe as adapted to encourage and excuse the extravagancies of the Prince, or by itself, we must certainly admire it, and own it to be perfectly original.

The professed wit, either in life or on the stage, is usually severe and satirical. But mirth is the source of Falstaffe's wit. He seems rather to invite you to partake of his merriment, than to attend to his jest; a person must be ill-natured, as well as dull, who does not join in the mirth of this jovial companion, who is in all respects the best calculated to raise laughter of any that ever appeared on a stage.

He joins the finesse of wit with the drollery of humour. Humour is a kind of grotesque wit, shaped and coloured by the disposition of the person in whom it resides, or by the subject to which it is applied. It is oftenest found in odd and irregular minds: but this peculiar turn distorts wit, and though it gives it a burlesque air, which excites momentary mirth, renders it less just, and consequently less agreeable to our judgments. Gluttony, corpulency, and cowardice, are the peculiarities of Falstaffe's composition, they render him ridiculous without folly, throw an air of jest and festivity about him, and make his manners suit with his sentiments, without giving to his understanding any particular bias. As the contempt attendant on these vices and defects is the best antidote against any infection that might be caught in his society, so it was very skilful to make him as ridiculous as witty, and as contemptible as entertaining. The admirable speech upon honour would have been both indecent and dangerous from any other person. We must every where allow his wit is just, his humour genuine, and his character perfectly original, and sustained through every scene, in every play, in which it appears.

—ELIZABETH MONTAGU, *An Essay on the Writings and Genius of Shakespeare*
(London: J. & H. Hughs, 1769), pp. 106–7

WILLIAM RICHARDSON

Thus Shakespeare, whose morality is no less sublime than his skill in the display of character is masterly and unrivalled, represents Falstaff, not only as a voluptuous and base sycophant, but totally incorrigible. He displays no quality or disposition which can serve as a basis for reformation. Even his abilities and agreeable qualities contribute to his depravity. Had he been less facetious, less witty, less dexterous, and less inventive, he might have been urged to self-condemnation, and so inclined to amendment. But mortification leads him to no conviction of folly, nor determines him to any change of life. He turns, as soon as possible, from the view given him of his baseness; and rattles as it were in triumph, the fetters of habituated and willing bondage.—Lear, violent and impetuous, but yet affectionate; from his misfortunes derives improvement. Macbeth, originally a man of feeling, is capable of remorse. And the understanding of Richard, rugged and insensible though he be, betrays his heart to the assault of conscience. But the mean sensualist, incapable of honorable and worthy thoughts, is irretrievably lost; totally, and for ever depraved. An important and awful lesson!

I may be thought perhaps to have treated Falstaff with too much severity. I am aware of his being a favorite. Persons of eminent worth feel for him some attachment, and think him hardly used by the King. But if they will allow themselves to examine the character in all its parts, they will perhaps agree with me, that such feeling is delusive, and arises from partial views. They will not take it amiss, if I say that they are deluded in the same manner with Prince Henry. They are amused, and conceive an improper attachment to the means of their pleasure and amusement. I appeal to every candid reader, whether the sentiment expressed by Prince Henry is not that which every judicious spectator and reader is inclined to feel.

I could have better spar'd a better man.

Upon the whole, the character of Sir John Falstaff, consisting of various parts, produces various feelings. Some of these are agreeable and some disagreeable; but, being blended together, the general and united effect is much stronger than if their impulse had been disunited: not only so, but as the agreeable qualities are brought more into view, for in this sense alone they can be said to prevail in the character; and as the deformity of other qualities is often veiled by the pleasantry employed by the poet in their display, the general effect is in the highest degree delightful.

—WILLIAM RICHARDSON, *Essays on Shakespeare's Dramatic Character
of Sir John Falstaff, and on His Imitation of Female Characters*
(London: J. Murray, 1789), pp. 54–56

AUGUST WILHELM VON SCHLEGEL

Falstaff is the crown of Shakspeare's comic invention. He has, without exhausting himself, continued this character throughout three plays, and exhibited him in every variety of situation; the figure is drawn so definitely and individually, that even to the mere reader it conveys the clear impression of personal acquaintance. Falstaff is the most agreeable and entertaining knave that ever was portrayed. His contemptible qualities are not disguised: old, lecherous, and dissolute; corpulent beyond measure, and always intent upon cherishing his body with eating, drinking, and sleeping; constantly in debt, and anything but conscientious in his choice of means by which money is to be raised; a cowardly soldier, and a lying braggart; a flatterer of his friends before their face, and a satirist behind their backs; and yet we are never disgusted with him. We see that his tender care of himself is without any mixture of malice towards others; he will only not be disturbed in the pleasant repose of his sensuality, and this he obtains through the activity of his understanding. Always on the alert, and good-humoured, ever ready to crack jokes on others, and to enter into those of which he is himself the subject, so that he justly boasts he is not only witty himself, but the cause of wit in others, he is an admirable companion for youthful idleness and levity. Under a helpless exterior, he conceals an extremely acute mind; he has always at command some dexterous turn whenever any of his free jokes begin to give displeasure; he is shrewd in his distinctions, between those whose favour he has to win and those over whom he may assume a familiar authority. He is so convinced that the part which he plays can only pass under the cloak of wit, that even when alone he is never altogether serious, but gives the drollest colouring to his love-intrigues, his intercourse with others, and to his own sensual philosophy. Witness his inimitable soliloquies on honour, on the influence of wine on bravery, his descriptions of the beggarly vagabonds whom he enlisted, of Justice Shallow, &c. Falstaff has about him a whole court of amusing caricatures, who by turns make their appearance, without even throwing him into the shade. The adventure in which the Prince, under the disguise of a robber, compels him to give up the spoil which he had just taken; the scene where the two act the part of the King and the Prince; Falstaff's behaviour in the field, his mode of raising recruits, his patronage of Justice Shallow, which afterwards takes such an unfortunate turn:—all this forms a series of characteristic scenes of the most original description, full of pleasantry, and replete with nice and ingenious observation, such as could only find a place in a historical play like the present.

Several of the comic parts of *Henry the Fourth* are continued in *The Merry Wives of Windsor*. This piece is said to have been composed by Shakspeare, in compliance with the request of Queen Elizabeth, who admired the character of Falstaff, and wished to see him exhibited once more, and in love. In love, properly speaking, Falstaff could not be; but for other purposes he could pretend to be so, and at all events imagine that he was the object of love. In the present piece accordingly he pays his court, as a favoured Knight, to two married ladies, who lay their heads together and agree to listen apparently to his addresses, for the sake of making him the butt of their just ridicule. The whole plan of the intrigue is therefore derived from the ordinary circle of Comedy, but yet richly and artificially inter-woven without another love affair. The circumstance which has been so much admired in Molière's *School of Women,* that a jealous individual should be made the constant confidant of his rival's progress, had previously been introduced into this play, and certainly with much more probability. I would not, however, be understood as maintaining that it was the original invention of Shakspeare: it is one of those circumstances which must almost be considered as part of the common stock of Comedy, and everything depends on the delicacy and humour with which it is used. That Falstaff should fall so repeatedly into the snare gives us a less favourable opinion of his shrewdness than the foregoing pieces had led us to form; still it will not be thought improbable, if once we admit the probability of the first infatuation on which the whole piece is founded, namely, that he can believe himself qualified to inspire a passion. This leads him, notwithstanding his age, his corpulency, and his dislike of personal inconveniences and dangers, to venture on an enterprise which requires the boldness and activity of youth; and the situations occasioned by this infatuation are droll beyond all description. Of all Shakspeare's pieces, this approaches the nearest to the species of pure Comedy: it is exclusively confined to the English manners of the day, and to the domestic relations; the characters are almost all comic, and the dialogue, with the exception of a couple of short love scenes, is written in prose. But we see that it was a point of principle with Shakspeare to make none of his compositions a mere imitation of the prosaic world, and to strip them of all poetical decoration: accordingly he has elevated the conclusion of the comedy by a wonderful intermixture, which suited the place where it was probably first represented. A popular superstition is made the means of a fanciful mystification of Falstaff; disguised as the Ghost of a Hunter who, with ragged horns, wanders about in the woods of Windsor, he is to wait for his frolicsome mistress; in this plight he is surprised by a chorus of boys and girls disguised like fairies, who, agreeably to the popular belief, are holding their midnight dances, and who sing a merry song as they pinch and torture him. This is the last affront put upon poor Falstaff; and with this contrivance the conclusion of the second love affair is made in a most ingenious manner to depend.

—AUGUST WILHELM VON SCHLEGEL, *Lectures on Dramatic Art and Literature*
[1809], tr. John Black [1816], rev. A. S. W. Morrison
(London: Henry G. Bohn, 1846), pp. 426–28

WILLIAM HAZLITT

If Shakespear's fondness for the ludicrous sometimes led to faults in his tragedies (which was not often the case) he has made us amends by the character of Falstaff. This is perhaps the most substantial comic character that ever was invented. Sir John carries a most portly presence in the mind's eye; and in him, not to speak it profanely, 'we behold the fulness of the spirit of wit and humour bodily.' We are as well acquainted with his person as his mind, and his jokes come upon us with double force and relish from the quantity of flesh through which they make their way, as he shakes his fat sides with laughter, or 'lards the lean earth as he walks along.' Other comic characters seem, if we approach and handle them, to resolve themselves into air, 'into thin air'; but this is embodied and palpable to the grossest apprehension: it lies 'three fingers deep upon the ribs,' it plays about the lungs and the diaphragm with all the force of animal enjoyment. His body is like a good estate to his mind, from which he receives rents and revenues of profit and pleasure in kind, according to its extent, and the richness of the soil. Wit is often a meagre substitute for pleasurable sensation; an effusion of spleen and petty spite at the comforts of others, from feeling none in itself. Falstaff's wit is an emanation of a fine constitution; an exuberance of good-humour and good-nature; an overflowing of his love of laughter and good-fellowship; a giving vent to his heart's ease, and over-contentment with himself and others. He would not be in character, if he were not as fat as he is; for there is the greatest keeping in the boundless luxury of his imagination and the pampered self-indulgence of his physical appetites. He manures and nourishes his mind with jests, as he does his body with sack and sugar. He carves out his jokes, as he would a capon or a haunch of venison, where there is *cut and come again;* and pours out upon them the oil of gladness. His tongue drops fatness, and in the chambers of his brain 'it snows of meat and drink.' He keeps up perpetual holiday and open house, and we live with him in a round of invitations to a rump and dozen.—Yet we are not to suppose that he was a mere sensualist. All this is as much in imagination as in reality. His sensuality does not engross and stupify his other faculties, but 'ascends me into the brain, clears away all the dull, crude vapours that environ it, and makes it full of nimble, fiery, and delectable shapes.' His imagination keeps up the ball after his senses have done with it. He seems to have even a greater enjoyment of the freedom from restraint, of good cheer, of his ease, of his vanity, in the ideal exaggerated description which he gives of them, than in fact. He never fails to enrich his discourse with allusions to eating and drinking, but we never see him at table. He carries his own larder about with him, and he is himself 'a tun of man.' His pulling out the bottle in the field of battle is a joke to shew his contempt for glory accompanied with danger, his systematic adherence to his Epicurean philosophy in the most trying circumstances. Again, such is his deliberate exaggeration of his own vices, that it does not seem quite certain whether the account of his hostess's bill, found in his pocket, with such an out-of-the-way charge for capons and sack with only one halfpenny-worth of bread, was not put there by himself as a trick to humour the jest upon his favourite propensities, and as a conscious caricature of himself. He is represented as a liar, a braggart, a coward, a glutton, etc. and yet we are not offended but delighted with him; for he is all these as much to amuse others as to gratify himself. He openly assumes all these characters to shew the humourous part of them. The unrestrained indulgence of his own ease, appetites, and convenience, has neither malice nor hypocrisy in it. In a word, he is an actor in himself almost as much as upon the stage, and we no more object to the character of Falstaff in a moral point of view than we should think of bringing an excellent comedian, who should represent him to the life, before one of the police offices. We only consider the number of pleasant lights in which he puts certain foibles (the more pleasant as they are opposed to the received rules and necessary restraints of society) and do not trouble ourselves about the consequences resulting from them, for no mischievous consequences do result. Sir John is old as well as fat, which gives a melancholy retrospective tinge to the character; and by the disparity between his inclinations and his capacity for enjoyment, makes it still more ludicrous and fantastical.

The secret of Falstaff's wit is for the most part a masterly presence of mind, an absolute self-possession, which nothing can disturb. His repartees are involuntary suggestions of his self-love; instinctive evasions of every thing that threatens to interrupt the career of his triumphant jollity and self-complacency. His very size floats him out of all his difficulties in a sea of rich conceits; and he turns round on the pivot of his convenience, with every occasion and at a moment's warning. His natural repugnance to every unpleasant thought or circumstance, of itself makes light of objections, and provokes the most extravagant and licentious answers in his own justification. His indifference to truth puts no check upon his invention, and the more improbable and unexpected his contrivances are, the more happily does he seem to be delivered of them, the anticipation of their effect acting as a stimulus to the gaiety of his fancy. The success of one adventurous sally gives him spirits to undertake another: he deals always in round numbers, and his exaggerations and excuses and 'open, palpable, monstrous as the father that begets them.' ⟨. . .⟩

The Merry Wives of Windsor is no doubt a very amusing play, with a great deal of humour, character, and nature in it: but we should have liked it much better, if any one else had been the hero of it, instead of Falstaff. We could have been contented if Shakespear had not been 'commanded to shew the knight in love.' Wits and philosophers, for the most part, do not shine in that character; and Sir John himself, by no means, comes off with flying colours. Many people complain of the degradation and insults to which Don Quixote is so frequently exposed in his various adventures. But what are the unconscious indignities which he suffers, compared with the sensible mortifications which Falstaff is made to bring upon himself? What are the blows and buffettings which the Don receives from the staves of the Yanguesian carriers or from Sancho Panza's more hard-hearted hands, compared with the contamination of the buck-basket, the disguise of the fat woman of Brentford, and the horns of Herne the hunter, which are discovered on Sir John's head? In reading the play, we indeed wish him well through all these discomfitures, but it would have been as well if he had not got into them. Falstaff in *The Merry Wives of Windsor* is not the man he left him. Instead of making a butt of others, he is made a butt of by them. Neither is there a single particle of love in him to excuse his follies: he is merely a designing, bare-faced knave, and an unsuccessful one.

—WILLIAM HAZLITT, *Characters of Shakespear's Plays*
(London: C. H. Reynell, 1817)

H. N. HUDSON

Falstaff's character is more complex than can well be digested into the forms of logical statement; which makes him a rather impracticable subject for analysis. He has so much, or *is* so much, that one cannot easily tell what he is. Diverse and even opposite qualities meet in him; yet they poise so evenly, blend so happily, and work together so smoothly, that no generalities can set him off; if we undertake to grasp him in a formal conclusion, the best part of him still escapes between the fingers; so that the only way to give an idea of him is to take the man himself along and show him; and who shall do this with "plump Jack"? One of the wittiest of men, yet he is not a wit; one of the most sensual of men, still he cannot with strict justice be called a sensualist; he has a strong sense of danger and a lively regard to his own safety, a peculiar vein indeed of cowardice, or something very like it, yet he is not a coward; he lies and brags prodigiously, still he is not a liar nor a braggart. Any such general descriptions applied to him can serve no end but to make us think we understand him when we do not.

If I were to fix upon any one thing as specially characteristic of Falstaff, I should say it is an amazing fund of good sense. His stock of this, to be sure, is pretty much all enlisted in the service of sensuality, yet nowise so but that the servant still overpeers and outshines the master. Then too his thinking has such agility, and is at the same time so pertinent, as to do the work of the most prompt and popping wit; yet in such sort as to give the impression of something much larger and stronger than wit. For mere wit, be it ever so good, requires to be sparingly used, and the more it tickles the sooner it tires; like salt, it is grateful as a seasoning, but will not do as food. Hence it is that great wits, unless they have great judgment too, are so apt to be great bores. But no one ever wearies of Falstaff's talk, who has the proper sense for it; his speech being like pure fresh cold water, which always tastes good because it is tasteless. The wit of other men seems to be some special faculty or mode of thought, and lies in a quick seizing of remote and fanciful affinities; in Falstaff's it lies not in any one thing more than another, for which cause it cannot be defined: and I know not how to describe it but as that roundness and evenness of mind which we call good sense, so quickened and pointed indeed as to produce the effect of wit, yet without hindrance to its proper effect. To use a snug idiomatic phrase, what Falstaff says always *fits all round*.

—H. N. HUDSON, "Falstaff," *Shakespeare: His Life, Art, and Characters*
(Boston: Ginn & Co., 1872 [4th ed. 1882]), Vol. I, pp. 84–85

EDWARD DOWDEN

Sir John, although, as he truly declares, "not only witty in himself, but the cause that wit is in other men," is by no means a purely comic character. Were he no more than this, the stern words of Henry to his old companion would be unendurable. The central principle of Falstaff's method of living is that the facts and laws of the world may be evaded or set at defiance, if only the resources of inexhaustible wit be called upon to supply by brilliant ingenuity whatever deficiencies may be found in character and conduct. Therefore Shakspere condemned Falstaff inexorably. Falstaff, the invulnerable, endeavours, as was said in a preceding chapter, to cor-uscate away the realities of life. But the fact presses in upon Falstaff at the last relentlessly. Shakspere's earnestness here is at one with his mirth; there is a certain sternness underlying his laughter. Mere detection of his stupendous unveracities leaves Sir John just where he was before; the success of his lie is of less importance to him than is the glory of its invention. "There is no such thing as totally demolishing Falstaff; he has so much of the invulnerable in his frame that no ridicule can destroy him; he is safe even in defeat, and seems to rise, like another Antæus, with recruited vigour from every fall." (Maurice Morgann) It is not ridicule, but some stern invasion of fact—not to be escaped from—which can subdue Falstaff. Perhaps Nym and Pistol got at the truth of the matter when they discoursed of Sir John's unexpected collapse:—

> NYM: The king hath run bad humours on the knight; that's the even of it.
> PISTOL: Nym, thou hast spoke the right;
> His heart is fracted and corroborate.

In the relation by Mrs Quickly of the death of Falstaff pathos and humour have run together and become one. "A' made a finer end and went away an it had been any christom child; a' parted even just between twelve and one, even at the turning o' the tide: for after I saw him fumble with the sheets, and play with flowers and smile upon his fingers' ends, I knew there was but one way; for his nose was as sharp as a pen, and a' babbled of green fields." Here the smile and the tear rise at the same instant. Nevertheless, the union of pathos with humour as yet extends only to an incident; no entire pathetic-humorous character has been created like that of Lear's Fool.

Pathetically, however, the fat knight disappears, and disappears for ever. The Falstaff of *The Merry Wives of Windsor* is another person than the Sir John who is "in Arthur's bosom, if ever man went to Arthur's bosom." The epilogue to the second part of *Henry IV.* (whether it was written by Shakspere or not remains doubtful) had promised that "our humble author will continue the story with Sir John in it." But our humble author decided (with a finer judgment than Cervantes in the case of his hero) that the public was not to be indulged in laughter for laughter's sake at the expense of his play. The tone of the entire play of *Henry V.* would have been altered if Falstaff had been allowed to appear in it. During the monarchy of a Henry IV. no glorious enthusiasm animated England. It was distracted by civil contention. Mouldy, Shallow, and Feeble were among the champions of the royal cause. Patriotism and the national pride of England could not under the careful policy of a Bolingbroke burst forth as one ascending and universal flame. At such a time our imagination can loiter among the humours and frolics of a tavern. When the nation was divided into various parties, when no interest was absorbing and supreme, Sir John might well appear upon his throne at Eastcheap, monarch by virtue of his wit, and form with his company of followers a state within the state. But with the coronation of Henry V. opens a new period, when a higher interest animates history, when the national life was unified, and the glorious struggle with France began. At such a time private and secondary interests must cease; the magnificent swing, the impulse and advance of the life of England occupy our whole imagination. It goes hard with us to part from Falstaff, but, like the king, part from him we must; we cannot be encumbered with that tun of flesh; Agin-court is not the battle-field for splendid mendacity. Falstaff, whose principle of life is an attempt to coruscate away the facts of life, and who was so potent during the Prince's minority, would now necessarily appear trivial. There is no place for Falstaff any longer on earth; he must needs find refuge "in Arthur's bosom."

—EDWARD DOWDEN, "The Humour of Shakspere," *Shakspere: A Critical Study of His Mind and Art* (London: H. S. King, 1875), pp. 365–68

ALGERNON CHARLES SWINBURNE

Singular as may seem the collocation of the epithet "moral" with the name "Falstaff," I venture to maintain my thesis; that in point of feeling, and therefore of possible moral elevation, Falstaff is as undeniably the superior of Sancho as Sancho is unquestionably the superior of Panurge. The natural affection of Panurge is bounded by the self-same limits as the natural theology of Polyphemus; the love of the one, like the faith of the other, begins and ends alike at one point;

> Myself,
> And this great belly, first of deities;

(in which line, by the way, we may hear as it were a first faint prelude of the great proclamation to come—the hymn of praise and thanksgiving for the coronation day of King Gaster; whose laureate, we know, was as lovingly familiar with the Polyphemus of Euripides as Shakespeare with his own Pantagruel.) In Sancho we come upon a creature capable of love—but not of such love as kills or helps to kill, such love as may end or even as may seem to end in anything like heartbreak. "And now abideth Rabelais, Cervantes, Shakespeare, these three; but the greatest of these is Shakespeare."

I would fain score yet another point in the fat knight's favour; "I have much to say in the behalf of that Falstaff." Rabelais, evangelist and prophet of the Resurrection of the Flesh (so long entombed, ignored, repudiated, misconstrued, vilified, by so many generations and ages of Galilean preachers and Pharisaic schoolmen)—Rabelais was content to paint the flesh merely, in its honest human reality—human at least, if also bestial; in its frank and rude reaction against the half brainless and wholly bloodless teachers whose doctrine he himself on the one hand, and Luther on the other, arose together to smite severally—to smite them hip and thigh, even till the going down of the sun; the mock sun or marshy meteor that served only to deepen the darkness encompassing on every side the doubly dark ages—the ages of monarchy and theocracy, the ages of death and of faith. To Panurge, therefore, it was unnecessary and it might have seemed inconsequent to attribute other gifts or functions than are proper to such intelligence as may accompany the appetites of an animal. That most irreverend father in God, Friar John, belongs to a higher class in the moral order of being; and he much rather than his fellow-voyager and penitent is properly comparable with Falstaff. It is impossible to connect the notion of rebuke with the sins of Panurge. The actual lust and gluttony, the imaginary cowardice of Falstaff, have been gravely and sharply rebuked by critical morality;

we have just noted a too recent and too eminent example of this; but what mortal ever dreamed of casting these qualities in the teeth of his supposed counterpart? The difference is as vast between Falstaff on the field of battle and Panurge on the storm-tossed deck as between Falstaff and Hotspur, Panurge and Friar John. No man could show cooler and steadier nerve than is displayed in either case—by the lay as well as the clerical namesake of the fourth evangelist. If ever fruitless but endless care was shown to prevent misunderstanding, it was shown in the pains taken by Shakespeare to obviate the misconstruction which would impute to Falstaff the quality of a Parolles or a Bobadil, a Bessus or a Moron. The delightful encounter between the jester and the bear in the crowning interlude of *La Princess d'Elide* shows once more, I may remark, that Molière had sat at the feet of Rabelais as delightedly as Shakespeare before him. Such rapturous inebriety or Olympian incontinence of humour only fires the blood of the graver and less exuberant humourist when his lips are still warm and wet from the well-spring of the *Dive Bouteille.*

—ALGERNON CHARLES SWINBURNE, *A Study of Shakespeare*
(London: Macmillan, 1880), pp. 108–11

GIUSEPPE VERDI

What can I tell you? For forty years now I have wanted to write a comic opera, and for fifty years I have known *The Merry Wives of Windsor.* However, the usual 'buts' which pop up everywhere have always prevented me from doing what I wanted. Now Boito has swept away all the 'buts', and has written me a lyrical comedy which is unlike all others.

I am enjoying myself writing the music. I have no plans for it, and I don't even know if I shall finish it . . . I repeat, I'm enjoying myself . . .

Falstaff is a deplorable creature who does all kinds of bad things, but in a diverting manner. He's a real character. There are so many different characters! The opera is completely comic!

Amen. . . .

—GIUSEPPE VERDI, Letter to Marquess Gino Monaldi (December 3, 1890),
Letters of Giuseppe Verdi, ed. and tr. Charles Osborne
(New York: Holt, Rinehart & Winston, 1971), p. 241

GEORGE BERNARD SHAW

Don Quixote and Mr Pickwick are recognized examples of characters introduced in pure ridicule, and presently gaining the affection and finally the respect of their authors. To them may be added Shakespear's Falstaff. Falstaff is introduced as a subordinate stage figure with no other function than to be robbed by the Prince and Poins, who was originally meant to be the *raisonneur* of the piece, and the chief figure among the prince's dissolute associates. But Poins soon fades into nothing, like several characters in Dickens's early works; whilst Falstaff develops into an enormous joke and an exquisitely mimicked human type. Only in the end the joke withers. The question comes to Shakespear: *Is* this really a laughing matter? Of course there can be only one answer; and Shakespear gives it as best he can by the mouth of the prince become king, who might, one thinks, have the decency to wait until he has redeemed his own character before assuming the right to lecture his boon companion. Falstaff, rebuked and humiliated, dies miserably. His followers are hanged, except Pistol, whose exclamation "Old do I wax; and from my weary limbs honor is cudgelled" is a melancholy exordium to an old age of beggary and imposture.

But suppose Shakespear had begun where he left off! Suppose he had been born at a time when, as the result of a long propaganda of health and temperance, sack had come to be called alcohol, alcohol had come to be called poison, corpulence had come to be regarded as either a disease or a breach of good manners, and a conviction had spread throughout society that the practice of consuming "a half-pennyworth of bread to an intolerable deal of sack" was the cause of so much misery, crime, and racial degeneration that whole States prohibited the sale of potable spirits altogether, and even moderate drinking was more and more regarded as a regrettable weakness! Suppose (to drive the change well home) the women in the great theatrical centres had completely lost that amused indulgence for the drunken man which still exists in some out-of-the-way places, and felt nothing but disgust and anger at the conduct and habits of Falstaff and Sir Toby Belch! Instead of *Henry IV* and *The Merry Wives of Windsor,* we should have had something like Zola's *L'Assommoir.* Indeed, we actually have Cassio, the last of Shakespear's gentleman-drunkards, talking like a temperance reformer, a fact which suggests that Shakespear had been roundly lectured for the offensive vulgarity of Sir Toby by some woman of refinement who refused to see the smallest fun in giving a knight such a name as Belch, with characteristics to correspond to it. Suppose, again, that the first performance of *The Taming of the Shrew* had led to a modern Feminist demonstration in the theatre, and forced upon Shakespear's consideration a whole century of agitatresses, from Mary Wollstonecraft to Mrs Fawcett and Mrs Pankhurst, is it not likely that the jest of Katharine and Petruchio would have become the earnest of Nora and Torvald Helmer?

            —GEORGE BERNARD SHAW, *The Quintessence of Ibsenism* [1891], *The Works of Bernard Shaw* (London: Constable, 1930), Vol. 19, pp. 137–39

WALTER RALEIGH

From his first entrance Falstaff dominates the play. The Prince tries in vain to be even with him: Falstaff, as Hazlitt has said, is the better man of the two. He speaks no more than the truth when he makes his claim: "I am not only witty in myself, but the cause that wit is in other men." All the best wit in the play is engineered and suggested by him; even the Prince, when he tries to match him, falls under the control of the prime inventor, and makes the obvious and expected retorts, which give occasion for a yet more brilliant display of that surprising genius. It is the measure of the Prince's inferiority that to him Falstaff seems "rather ludicrous than witty," even while all the wit that passes current is being issued from Falstaff's mint, and stamped with the mark of his sovereignty. The disparity between the two characters extends itself to their kingdoms, the Court and the Tavern. The one is restrained, formal, full of fatigues and necessities and ambitions; the other is free and natural, the home of zest and ease. There are pretences in both, but with what a difference! In the one there is real, hard, selfish hypocrisy and treachery; in the other a world of make-believe and fiction, all invented for delight. It is no wonder that Falstaff attracts to himself the bulk of our sympathies, and perverts the moral issues. One critic, touched to the heart by the casting-off of Falstaff, so far forgets his morality as to take comfort in the reflection that the thousand pounds belonging to Justice Shallow is safe in Falstaff's pocket, and will help to provide for his old age.

Yet the Prince, if he loses the first place in our affections, makes a brave fight for it. Shakespeare does what he can for him. He is valorous, generous, and high-spirited. When Falstaff claims to have slain Percy in single fight, he puts in no word for his own prowess:

> For my part, if a lie may do thee grace,
> I'll gild it with the happiest terms I have.

He has some tenderness, and a deeply conceived sense of his great responsibilities. Even his wit would be remarkable in any other company, and his rich vocabulary of fancy and abuse speaks him a ready learner. If his poetry tends to rhetoric, in his instinct for prose and sound sense he almost matches the admirable Rosalind—"To say to thee that I shall die, is true; but for thy love, by the Lord, no; yet I love thee, too." It is all in vain; his good and amiable qualities do not teach him the way to our hearts. The "noble change" which he hath purposed, and of which we hear so much, taints him in the character of a boon-companion. He is double-minded: he keeps back a part of the price. Falstaff gives the whole of himself to enjoyment, so that the strivings and virtues of half-hearted sinners seem tame and poor beside him. He bestrides the play like a Colossus, and the young gallants walk under his huge legs and peep about to find themselves honourable graves. In all stress of circumstance, hunted by misfortune and disgrace, he rises to the occasion, so that the play takes on the colour of the popular beast-fable; our chief concern is that the hero shall never be outwitted; and he never is.

There is more of Shakespeare in this amazing character than in all the poetry of *Richard II*. Falstaff is a comic Hamlet, stronger in practical resource, and hardly less rich in thought. He is in love with life, as Hamlet is out of love with it; he cheats and lies and steals with no hesitation and no afterthought; he runs away or counterfeits death with more courage than others show in deeds of knightly daring. The accidents and escapades of his life give ever renewed occasion for the triumph of spirit over matter, and show us the real man, above them all, and aloof from them, calm, aristocratic, fanciful, scorning opinion, following his own ends, and intellectual to the fingertips. He has been well called "a kind of military freethinker." He will fight no longer than he sees reason. His speech on honour might have been spoken by Hamlet—with what a different conclusion! He is never for a moment entangled in the web of his own deceits; his mind is absolutely clear of cant; his self-respect is magnificent and unfailing. The judgments passed on him by others, kings or justices, affect him not at all, while there are few of these others who can escape with credit from the severe ordeal of his disinterested judgment upon them. The character of Master Shallow is an open book to that impartial scrutiny. "It is a wonderful thing," says Falstaff, "to see the semblable coherence of his men's spirits and his: they, by observing of him, do bear themselves like foolish justices; he, by conversing with them, is turn'd into a justice-like serving-man." Yet, for all his clarity of vision, Falstaff is never feared; there is no grain of malevolence in him; wherever he comes he brings with him the pure spirit of delight.

How was a character like this to be disposed of? He had been brought in as an amusement, and had rapidly established himself as the chief person of the play. There seemed no reason why he should not go on for ever. He was becoming dangerous. No serious action could be attended to while every one was waiting to see how Falstaff would take it. A clear stage was needed for the patriotic and warlike exploits of King Harry; here was to be no place for critics and philosophers. Shakespeare disgraces Falstaff, and banishes him from the Court. But this was not enough; it was a part of Falstaff's magnanimity that disgrace had never made the smallest difference to him, and had often been used by him as a stepping-stone to new achievement. Even in banishment he was likely to prove as dangerous as Napoleon in Elba. There was nothing for it; in the name of the public safety, and to protect him from falling into bad hands, Falstaff must be put to death. So he takes his last departure, "an it had been any christom child," and King Harry is set free to pursue the life of heroism.

With the passing of Falstaff Shakespeare's youth was ended. All that wonderful experience of London life, all those days and nights of freedom and adventure and the wooing of new pleasures, seem to be embodied in this great figure, the friend and companion of the young. We can trace his history, from his first boyhood, when he broke Scogan's head at the court gate, to his death in the second child-hood of delirium. He was never old. "What, ye knaves," he cries, at the assault on the Gadshill travellers, "young men must live." "You that are old," he reminds the Chief Justice, "consider not the capacities of us that are young." The gods, loving him, decreed that he should die as he was born, with a white head and a round belly, in the prime of his joyful days.

He was brought to life again, by Royal command, in *The Merry Wives of Windsor;* but his devoted admirers have never been able to accept that play for a part of his history. The chambering and wantonness of amorous intrigue suits ill with his indomitable pride of spirit. It is good to hear the trick of his voice again; and his wit has not lost all its brightness. But he is fallen and changed; he has lived to stand at the taunt of one that makes fritters of English, and is become the butt of citizens and their romping wives. Worst of all, he is afraid of the fairies. Bottom the weaver never fell so low—"Scratch my head, Peaseblossom." Shakespeare has an ill conscience in this matter, and endeavours to salve it by a long apology. "See now," says Falstaff, "how wit may be made a Jack-a-lent, when 't is upon ill employment." But such an apology is worse than the offence. It presents Falstaff to us in the guise of a creeping moralist.

—WALTER RALEIGH, *Shakespeare* (London: Macmillan, 1907), pp. 187–91

ELMER EDGAR STOLL

As for Falstaff, he is not only subtilized but also sentimentalized! Mr Bradley does not mind saying that he for one is glad that Falstaff ran away on Gadshill; Monsieur Stapfer declares that morally he was no worse than you or I; Hazlitt, lost in sympathy with him on the blighting of his hopes at the succession, resentfully asserts that he was a better man than the Prince; and another critic, mentioned by Sir Walter Raleigh, 'takes comfort in the reflection that the thousand pounds belonging to Justice Shallow is safe in Falstaff's pocket, and will help to provide for his old age.' That is, the character is lifted bodily out of the dramatist's reach. Falstaff is a rogue, and as such people cannot like him: twice Morgann protests that in order to be comical at all he must be void of evil motive. Lying for profit and jesting for profit, the cheating and swindling of your unsophisticated admirers, gluttony, lechery, extortion, highway robbery, and cowardice—pray, what is funny about all these? Hence the profit has been turned to a jest, the misdemeanours to make-believe. Not otherwise, Hercules in the *Alcestis* was thought by Browning to get roaring drunk, not for his own private satisfaction but for that of the mourners—and there is another in a play who, in the good cause of human happiness, does not mind making a fool of himself! So it must be, when we take a character to our bosom out of an old play like a pet out of the jungle—we must extract his sting. This has by the critics been duly done, to Falstaff as to Shylock. Our 'white-bearded Satan' has had his claws pared.

For they that have not learned to think historically cannot stomach the pica-resque. It matters not to them that nearly all the professional comic characters of Elizabethan drama, as of all drama before it, have a vein of roguery in them—Sir Toby as well as Autolycus, the Clown as well as the Vice; or that in those days high and low were rejoicing in the roguery romances, English, French, or Spanish. Such people must have delighted in Falstaff as unreservedly as does the Prince in the play. That they did not take him for an innocuous mimic and merrymaker numerous allusions in the seventeenth century, as we have already seen, attest. And Hal loved him as Morgante loved Margutte, as Baldus loved Cingar, and Pantagruel—'all his life long'—loved Panurge, not for his humour only but for his lies and deviltry. They had their notions of 'a character' as we have ours. With endless variety of repetition Rabelais revels in notions of mendacity, drunkenness, gluttony, and lasciviousness, and in tricks of cheating and cruelty, as things funny almost in themselves. With what gusto he tells of the outrages perpetrated by Panurge on the watch, the difficult Parisian lady, and Dingdong and his flock, and of Friar John's slaying and curiously and expertly mutilating his thousands with the staff of the cross in the abbey close! And yet, frowning down the facts, the critics declare that Falstaff has no malice in him, and though he laments the repayment, has had no intention of keeping the stolen money, repays Quickly full measure and running over with his company, and after all does no mentionable injury to Shallow, who has land and beeves. 'Where does he cheat the weak,' cries Maginn, 'or prey upon the poor?' There is Quickly, poor, and weak at least before his blandishments, 'made to serve his uses both in purse and in person'; and there are Bullcalf, who has a desire to stay with his friends, and Mouldy, whose dame is old and cannot help herself, both swindled in the name of the King, as Wart, Feeble, and Shadow, the unlikeliest men, are wrongfully pressed into service. All this once was funny and now is base and pitiful, but why should we either shut our eyes to it or bewail it? Surely we cannot with Morgann make allowances for his age and corpulency (how that would have staggered an Elizabethan!) and corrupting associations; or with Maginn trace the pathos of his degradation, hope after hope breaking down; or with Swinburne discover the well of tenderness within him, his heart being 'fracted and corroborate,' not through material disappointment, but for wounded love. With this last the present Chief Secretary for Ireland (Augustine Birrell) is properly disgusted, though in being less sentimental he is hardly more Elizabethan in spirit as he calls him 'in a very real sense a terrible character, so old and so profane.' About as properly 'terrible' as was the nurse Sairey Gamp of late to an eminent literary critic writing for the *Times,* though truly it would have been a fearful thing to fall into the hands of the living Sairey. Yet Mr Birrell remembers Falstaff (where others have been but too glad to forget him) with Doll at the Boar's Head; and he reads an unexpurgated text. And if he does not look with the eyes of an Elizabethan, he looks honestly (though shamefacedly), with his own, and sees the old rogue and satyr in his heathen nakedness, not in the breeches that, like Volterra in the Sistine, the critics have hastened to make him.

Morals and sentiments alike, in the lapse of time, obliterate humour. Laughter is essentially a *geste social,* as Meredith and Professor Bergson have truly told us; and the immediate and necessary inference, which no doubt they themselves would have drawn, is that it languishes when the tickled *mores* change. The discussion of wit and humour and the examples of both in Castiglione's *Courtier* are illuminating. Much that was funny to the Elizabethans, or to the court of Urbino, or of the Grand Monarch, has since become pathetic, as in Shylock and Harpagon, Alceste and George Dandin; and 'disgusting' or even 'terrible,' as in Falstaff or Tartuffe. Of this we have just seen repeated instances, and of the process of critical emasculation which ensues. Even the form and fashion of the older humour have given offense. Most of the English critics apparently have not seen Falstaff on the stage, but those who have cannot recall him without a shudder. The roaring, the falling flat, and above all the padding—'a very little stuffing under the waistcoat,' one of them pleads, 'would answer all the requirements of the part.' And the padded bulk of his humour, as of his person—'out of all measure, out of all compass'— about his name being terrible to the enemy and known to all Europe, and Turk Gregory never doing such deeds, is so reduced by anachronizing Procrustean critics as to contain 'nothing but a light ridicule.' His ancestral ring seems to have been really of gold, not copper,—Morgann 'believes it was really of gold' just as he 'thinks he did not roar,' though 'probably a little too much alloyed with baser metal.' And his 'old ward,' like his 'manhood,' Prince Hal might have remembered if he would. What of the multitudinous knaves in buckram and Kendal green, or of the knight himself at Hal's age not an eagle's talon in the waist or an alderman's thumb-ring, or of the nine score and odd posts he foundered as he devoured the road to battle in Gaultree Forest? Even his laugh, which must have been big as his body, riotous as his fancy, lingering and reverberating as the repetitions of his tongue, has been taken away. 'The wit is from the head, not the heart. It is anything but fun.' If we are to depend on the bare text or stage-directions there is no laughter in Sir Toby either, or almost any other jovial soul in Shakespeare. In robbing these fat knights of their fun critical treason has well-nigh done its worst, though before that it robbed audiences (at the cost of truth though to the profit of morals) of the fun got from Shylock, Harpagon, Dandin, and Tartuffe. On the stage and in the study much of the comedy in Shakespeare and Molière has been drained out of them from the Romantic Revival unto this day, and yet we smile at the Middle Ages Christianizing the classics.

And yet people like Falstaff, however they may interpret or explain him, as I hope my reader still can. Men do, if not women; Englishmen do, if not for-eigners. It is partly, no doubt, because of the tradition that he is the supreme comic figure, and they have endeavoured and laboured to like him. But it is more because, however much in the centuries they have changed in morals, humour, and taste, Englishmen have not outlived their human nature—Shakespeare's art. Their pleasure in the picaresque they have not wholly lost: virtue cannot so in-oculate our old stock but we shall relish of it. Moreover, there is something in Falstaff's appeal that is immediate and perpetual; it lies not so much in his conduct as in his speech. He talks prose but is supremely poetic, and his is in many ways the most marvellous prose ever penned. It pulses with his vast vitality and irre-pressible spirit, it glows with the warmth of his friendliness and good humour, it sparkles with his fancy and wit. No prose or verse either is so heavily charged with the magnetism of a personality, or has caught so perfectly the accent and intonation of an individual human voice. It *is* a voice,—rich, full, and various. In dialogue or stage-direction there is nothing to indicate his laughter, but the words and phrases as they ripple and undulate in repetition amply suggest it or involve it. He rolls a jest as a sweet morsel upon his tongue,—food for powder, food for powder; they'll fill a pit as well as better. Tush, man, mortal men, mortal men! With that he laughs, and all the audience with him.

Englishmen cannot escape that strong infection, if Frenchmen and Germans, Spaniards and Italians may. Mézières, and perhaps most foreigners that read English no more readily than Spanish, prefer Sancho; and for a Spaniard possibly Sancho's speech may have an equal charm. The Squire, certainly, is tenderer, more naïve, more moral, than the Eastcheap knight. But to Englishmen he seems much less vivid and real, less alive in every phrase and syllable, less prodigiously entertaining. Falstaff is depicted with—and endowed with—a greater gusto.

He never bores you as Sancho with his proverbs sometimes does. He is voluble but never long-winded; he is the very spirit of comradeship, the genius of converse, always ready with something to say, which provokes an answer—which provokes a better answer in turn. He both speaks and also (as some clever ones do not) listens, both sways and is swayed, and knows the mutual precipitate exhilaration—as in song and dance—of good company. Conversation is to him a thing of infinite moment: in words, not in deeds, are, not all his delights, to be sure, but all his triumphs. Time is nothing to him—he is always for making a night of it, like the moral Dr Johnson, who therefore, no doubt, forgave him. And so it is that he is the life of the party, the king of companions, the prince of good fellows, though not good. There, in the idiom, lies embedded the contradiction which justifies the contradiction in Falstaff himself. We, too, after all, like Prince Hal and Mrs Quickly, take to a man because of his charm, if it be big enough, not because of his virtue; and as for Falstaff, we are bewitched with the rogue's company, even to the point of forgetting everything else, and like Mrs Quickly even momentarily attributing to him that one thing which (none should know so well as she) he lacketh:—'Well, fare thee well! I have known thee these twenty-nine years, come peascod-time; but an honester and truer-hearted man—well, fare thee well!' What a testimony and tribute, entirely fallacious! Or, as Hal, thinking him dead, puts it more soberly and truly, 'I could have better spared a better man.' Under the spell of his presence and speech Mrs Quickly forgets what he owes her, for his diet and by-drinkings, the shirts bought for him and the money lent him; and, did we not stop to think, we should do the same.

But it is not merely by Falstaff's speech that we are kept under his spell; it is by all Shakespeare's comic art in the play. Here is another case of *isolation,* of comic emphasis such as we have seen in Shylock, until at the end of the Second Part he meets with the rebuff from the King. Shakespeare does not insist on Falstaff's sins and vices; he subordinates them, as we have seen, to his comic effects,—does not let them become serious, 'terrible.' In what Maginn says there is half a truth— 'where does he cheat the weak or prey upon the poor?' His treatment of the travellers, and of Quickly, Bullcalf, Mouldy, Wart, Feeble, and Shallow, we are not suffered (or at least not expected) to take to heart or sternly remember against him. His boasting and lying is not a needless, silly, and chronic affair as it is with many braggart soldiers; it is the revival of enthusiasm after ignominious lapses, the glow of reaction after an escape. And his cowardice,—Morgann is right in insisting that it is not continual and contemptible like that of Parolles and Bobadill. That there is a difference between his and their evasions we have already noticed. In short, his roguery is not professional but human and incidental. No other coward is so attractive because none has such a variety of deportment, can in the presence of others put on such an air of dignity or pathos, or in the face of danger seem so philosophical and cool. He may run, roar, whimper, or fall flat upon the field, but so scared is he only for moments. When he hears the sheriff is at the door, he says to Prince Hal, 'If you will deny the sheriff, so; if not, let him enter'; and he debates the matter of his gracing a cart and the gallows to bring tears to the eyes of others, though there are none in his own. And again, when on the eve of the engagement, he cries, 'Hal, if thou see me down in the battle and bestride me, so; 'tis a point of friendship.' He has the manner; he can assume a virtue, though he has it not the next moment—'I would 'twere bedtime, Hal, and all well.' Yet the moment after (though for that moment only) he rallies, in soliloquy, the slender forces of manhood within him:—'Well, 'tis no matter; honour pricks me on.' It is a feint—a transport—a flash in the pan! 'Yea, but how if honour prick me off when I come on? How then?'

And his promptings of conscience and remorse touch us not too nearly. They are real but not too real. A quick shift of the burden to the villainous company he keeps, or a call for a bawdy song, ends them when in health; Quickly's deathbed comfort that there was no need of such thoughts yet, ends them forever. They had troubled him, though,—thoughts of honour, duty, religion; thoughts of his sins—his swearing, dicing, stealing, and lechery; thoughts of death—of God and Hell. 'Peace, good Doll!' he had said in his latter heyday; 'do not speak like a death's-head, do not bid me remember mine end.' He winces a little when he is reminded of them, they prick him a little on the battle-field, they for a moment at the last peer in at him upon his pillow. He is not perfectly 'free,' not, as Professor Bradley thinks, wholly happy or at his ease, or he would not be so funny or so human. He is, as we have seen, not exalted above name and fame and duty; and the droll and delightful thing about him is the quick way he has of dodging or overriding all such obstacles and stumbling-blocks to happiness in his path. He makes shift to rise superior to his debts and duties—to all immaterial things (which, as such, are immaterial to him)— but not to circumstances. He puts on a bold face as he receives the public rebuff at the hands of the king; and he jests on gamely, perhaps brazenly, as he gives Shallow the thin satisfaction of a formal acknowledgment, *coram* Pistol and Bardolph, of his debt of a thousand pounds, assures his creditor that the king will send for his indispensable friend 'soon at night,' and bids him 'fear no colours,' punning on the word. But he does not laugh at being cast off, we have noticed, till the welkin rings, as Mr Beerbohm would have him do, and as he would do, if Rötscher's, Bulthaupt's, and Professor Bradley's conception of him quite fitted. This, at last, is to him no laughing matter; and if he have a philosophy it is not adversity's sweet milk, which fortifies. He is planted on this earth, and cannot dispense with her favours; he is not the one (if really he had it) to live on honour, on 'air,' like a chameleon up a tree. And prison, in his old age, without creature comforts, or company, is quite too much for him. Not that he is heart-broken—'killed his heart,' we have seen, need not mean that—and though he had delighted in Prince Hal's company he on his death-bed does not remember him. Love he does not so much as crave love: Hal owes him his love, he once told him; and it pained and surprised the old fellow that Prince John, thought with no particular reason to do so, did not warm up to him:—'Good faith, this same young sober-blooded boy doth not love me.' He is not self-sufficient like a philosopher or a cat. Though not devoted himself, he likes the quality, insists on 'good fellowship,' and even on thieves being true one to another; he banks on it but all too fondly in the Prince. For he is by nature a guest, as Mr Beerbohm would say, not a host; to receive he has ever found more blessed than to give; and her guests he prays his hostess to cherish. But now the sun no longer shines; in the Fleet there is no cherishing; and while from duty he can dodge and sidle, he cannot from discomfort and cold fact. His comedy is at its period; reality, kept in the background, steps up and with disenchanting touch puts a stop to the merry make-believe; and Shakespeare is a tragic dramatist as well.

We may rightly complain of the King's priggish speech and harsh conduct; we may rightly complain perhaps that our comedy ends thus soberly; but both character and situation are true. The jig is up; the game of evasion could not last ever;—though afterwards, on his death-bed, he still contrived to evade the scruples which troubled him, and went away an it had been any christom child. But the facts, unlike the scruples and principles, that stood in the path of his happiness, he could not brush away, and he knew not how to laugh and face them. If Falstaff has, though much mirth, no philosophy, the poet has both; and Falstaff holds us under his spell not only in his own right but also in that of his maker.

—ELMER EDGAR STOLL, "Falstaff" [1914], *Shakespeare Studies: Historical and Comparative in Method* (New York: Macmillan, 1927), pp. 479–90

WYNDHAM LEWIS

Falstaff is a "man of wit and pleasure," and could generally be described as a very good specimen of a "man of the world." But the same thing applies to him as to Iago: the "man of the world" is never so dramatically and openly cynical as Falstaff, any more than he is so candid as Machiavelli. He is not dramatic at all. To come to one of the necessary conclusions in this connexion, if the *Machiavel* were an Englishman he would be like Falstaff. This laziness, rascality and "good fellow" quality, crafty in the brainless animal way, is the english way of being a "deepbrained Machiavel."

But Falstaff is a "'child," too, a *"naif,"* as Ulrici says. A worldly mixture of any strength is never without that ingredient. The vast compendium of worldly bluff that is Falstaff would have to contain that. It was like "'any christom child" that he "went away," Mistress Quickly says.

He is armed from head to foot with sly feminine inferiorities, lovable weaknesses and instinctively cultivated charm. He is a big helpless bag of guts, exposing himself boldly to every risk on the child's, or the woman's, terms. When he runs away or lies down he is more adorable than any hero "facing fearful odds."

His immense girth and stature lends the greatest point, even, to his character. He is a hero run hugely to seed: he is actually heavier and bigger than the heaviest and biggest true colossus or hero. He is in that respect, physically, a mock-hero. Then this childishness is enhanced by his great physical scale, so much the opposite of the child's perquisite of smallness. And because of this meaningless, unmasculine immensity he always occupies the centre of the stage, he is the great landmark in any scene where he is. It all means nothing, and is a physical sham and trick put on the eye. And so he becomes the embodiment of bluff and worldly practice, the colossus of the *little.*

—WYNDHAM LEWIS, "Falstaff," *The Lion and the Fox: The Role of the Hero in the Plays of Shakespeare* (New York: Harper & Brothers, 1927), pp. 226–27

JAMES BRANCH CABELL

When you departed this life, Sir John—at your country place, in Norfolk, in the November of 1459—none doubts that you died, as became a preeminently religious English gentleman, in the hope of a glorious resurrection. How very mercifully was hid from you the too speedy fulfilment of your aspirations! For you had looked to be revived by Dan Gabriel his dreadful and holy trumpet: in no wild fever dream could it by any chance have occurred to you that a lewd heathen goddess, the Muse of Comedy, would prove your awakener—and to an apotheosis how incredible, how sordid, how cruel, how delightful!

If I become exclamatory, Sir, it is because no considerate person can regard the unfairness of your doom without giving a loose to some natural emotion. For eighty and more years you had lived with piety and intelligence and honor, with a clear conscience and your due of worldly success. You had been an admired soldier during at least thirty-five of these years. Throughout some two or three campaigns, indeed, you had commanded all the English expeditionary forces in the French wars, winning as generalissimo the great battle of the Herrings, in which you fought against the combined armies of Scotland and France; you had been governor of Maine and Anjou; you were a knight of the Garter; and toward the end of your life (in a castle which covered no less than six acres of Norfolkshire) you thrived notably as a retired capitalist, as an extensive land-holder, as an open-handed philanthropist and, as a judicious patron of learning.

You have been yelped at, of course, by the envious, like any other prospering person; and a charge of military blunders you were once forced to repel—with entire success. Yet the sole failings more or less plausibly imputed to you appear to have been a certain rigor in your business dealings, as an unlenient creditor, and something of fanaticism in the practice of your religion. You inclined, in brief, to be a bit of a Puritan a good while before puritanism had been labelled. Such, then, was the honored and austere gentleman who died in the November of 1459, after thriftily subsidizing "'seven religious men" and "seven poor folk" to pray perpetually for his soul's welfare; and whom that bad baggage, Thalia, saw fit to revive prematurely, about a hundred and forty years later.

It skills not, Sir John, to repeat through what causes you were thrust up into a pillory originally meant for your colleague in arms, Lord Cobham. The point is that at this time, about 1599, a poet gave you new life upon earth, at a price which to a man of your known business principles, and of your painstaking respectability, might well have appeared exorbitant. Since with your other virtues you combined a gentleman's share of scholarship (as befitted a co-founder of St.

Mary Magdalen College) you will recall, no doubt, that of the great Greek captain Achilles it is recorded how, in Ades' dim realm, he declared to his former comrade, to wily Odysseus, that it was better to live in earth's sunlight as a slave than to be king over the shadowy nations of the dead. But I question if even this feebly whining Achilles (upon whose heroic nature death seems to have acted rather deleteriously) would have been content to live again as the Sir John Falstaff whom the last three centuries have known and—it is the bitter truth, Sir—have laughed at.

For the poet who revived you, Sir John, has left you not one shielding rag of gentility. He has set you a-stagger among us, an obscene gross belching tun-belly, out at the elbows, reeking of sack, gray with iniquity. Of the skilled and triumphant soldier this poet has made a faintheart; of the Puritan, a wencher; of the magnate, a wastrel; and of the staid business man, a Dionysiac choregus of all riot, immortality's darling. He has made of you, in brief, a calumny so engaging to human fancy that by no chance will mankind ever give up this counterfeit Falstaff in order to accord you, Sir, the respect and the praise which, living, you earned amply. Your case is outrageous; no man was ever libelled with more striking injustice; but your case is hopeless.

It is at all times the privilege of the artist to recreate history; provided only he has genius, he can elude punishment and compel belief: but I know of no instance in which this birthright has been abused more wantonly than when Shakespeare gave to the future his caricature of Sir John Falstaff. For Thackeray, or for Dumas, or for Maurice Hewlett—to cite but three prevaricators among thousands—when they libelled severally the Old Chevalier, or Catherine de Medici, or Mary Stuart, there was at least the excuse that the story they had in hand moved on the hinges of calumny. The events of their victims' lives and the nature of their victims' characters have been somewhat misrepresented, for utilitarian ends, for the plot's sake; and at worst, the sin is an affair of recoloring and of shifted emphases. But you, Sir John, have been endowed with all the vices you shunned; stripped of the many virtues which you practised faithfully throughout eighty and some years; and thrust into miry actions with which you had no more to do than had Aretino or King Arthur. As a member of the Protestant Episcopal Church, I cannot doubt that the soul of William Shakespeare is eternally damned for his parody of a devout Christian gentleman: and I doubt not, either, that upon holidays and the major saints' days you are permitted to peep in at his torments. It is your full due.

Yet, as a writer, I am conscious of some little sneaking complacency. Heaven made the flesh-and-blood Falstaff of the very best human material, turning out an exceptionally fine specimen of divine craftsmanship. By-and-by (through what exact causes we shall not ever know) a mere writer, the approved captain of my clan, made us another Falstaff after his own notions, a lewd and thoroughgoing and high-spirited libel, a gay trucidation of truth. And promptly the romance drove the reality out of the field of human beliefs. I educe a quaint moral which—to your somewhat puritanic ears, Sir John—it seems wiser not to express explicitly.

Yet do you take what lean comfort you may, Sir, from knowing that this slanderer has defamed not you alone . . . Indeed, one cannot but wonder over this Shakespeare whensoever one considers his never-failing absence of conscience in the presence of history. Caution may pardonably have prompted his maligning of King Richard the Third to a certain extent, when the granddaughter of that Tudor who stole England from the last Plantagenet still sat on the throne of England: but it does seem to be carrying caution too far, to accredit Richard with murdering virtually all members of the upper classes who died, whether by disease or due process of law or through any other cause, during his brief life, in addition to a few who survived him . . . And again, mere time-serving may have led Shakespeare to slander Macbeth in comparison with that Banquo who enjoyed the dubious honor of being the direct ancestor of King James the First. Nevertheless did Shakespeare, who had read his Holingshed's *Chronicles of Scotland* (in the edition of 1587) very well know that Macbeth had a quite tenable claim to the Scots throne; that he did not murder Duncan through treachery, but instead, with the assistance of Banquo, openly "slewe the king at Envernes, or, as some say, at Botgosuane"; and that afterward Macbeth reigned wisely and righteously for "XVII years over the Scottishmen," during which period "he accomplished many worthie actes right profitable to the common wealth." Such were the known and essential facts upon which the tragedy of *Macbeth*—to express matters as mildly as may be—does not dwell with untactful honesty.

Upon this playwright's wanton assassination of King Hamlet, that lordly Jutlander, in defiance of all history books, I have remarked in another place. Ah, but no less wickedly, Sir John, did this regicide deal with King Lear, fabling that the old gentleman died insane in a prison house, whereas in point of fact (as you will remember, Sir, who took a soldier's pride in your English history) stout Lear and his French army "fought with his enemies and reduced both his sons-in-law under his power"—thus winning back his England, and afterward reigning prosperously, even until he died of old age and was buried in the bed of a river. Before the Shakesperean version of Jeanne d'Arc (that same Pucelle against whom you fought with misguided valor, Sir, and whose martyrdom in Rouen's market-place you quite possibly witnessed) one can but observe that, unless the Roman Catholic Church has been sadly misled, this picture cannot well be the faithful likeness of a properly canonized saint. But before the man's version of Julius Cæsar one retires, in mere silent stupefaction.

I might cite you yet other instances, Sir John, of this poet's idle and lewd lying as to his betters. Let these few suffice to assure you of your many and great comrades in misfortune, of your fellow sufferers under the spew of his slanderings! And yet, wit ye well, Sir John, I educe that nothing whatever can be done about it.

This little Warwickshire calumnist had no conscience: that is granted. But he had genius, against which no other virtue may prevail.

I educe also, Sir John, that your own special and your far more respectable virtues have gone unrewarded. I educe that, for once, the memory of the just is not blessed. And I educe, in asking leave of you, that the innate depravity of man's nature is well attested by the fact that before your undeserved obloquy we stand charmed, and applaud the outrage delightedly. For Heaven made you good and great and successful: but art has made you amusing.

—JAMES BRANCH CABELL, "The Twelfth Letter: To Sir John Falstaff
of Caister in Norfolk," *Ladies and Gentlemen: A Parcel of Reconsiderations*
(New York: Robert M. McBride, 1934), pp. 171–80

WILLIAM EMPSON

It is as well to look at Falstaff in general for a moment, to show what this tender attitude to him has to fit in with. The plot treats him as a simple Punch, whom you laugh at with good-humour, though he is wicked, because he is always knocked down and always bobs up again. (Our attitude to him as a Character entirely depends on the Plot, and yet he is a Character who very nearly destroyed the Plot as a whole.) People sometimes take advantage of this to view him as a lovable old dear; a notion which one can best refute by considering him as an officer.

> I haue led my rag of Muffins where they are pepper'd: there's not three
> of my 150 left alive, and they for the Townes end, to beg during life.
>
> (Part I. v. iii.)

We saw him levy a tax in bribes on the men he left; he now kills all the weaklings he conscripted, in order to keep their pay. A large proportion of the groundlings consisted of disbanded soldiers who had suffered under such a system; the laughter was a roar of hatred here; he is 'comic' like a Miracle Play Herod. (Whereas Harry has no qualities that are obviously not W. H.'s.) And yet it is out of his defence against this, the least popularisable charge against him, that he makes his most unanswerable retort to the prince.

PRINCE: Tell me, Jack, whose fellows are these that come after?
FAL.: Mine, Hal, mine.
PRINCE: I never did see such pitiful rascals.
FAL.: Tut, tut; good enough to toss; food for powder, food for powder; they'll
    fill a pit as well as better; tush, man, mortal men, mortal men.

Mortal conveys both 'all men are in the same boat, all equal before God' and 'all you want is slaughter.' No one in the audience was tempted to think Harry as wicked as his enemy Hotspur, who deserved death as much as Lear for wanting to divide England. But this remark needed to be an impudent cover for villainy if the strength of mind and heart in it were not to be too strong, to make the squabbles of ambitious and usurping persons too contemptible.

On the other hand, Falstaff's love for the prince is certainly meant as a gap in his armour; one statement (out of so many) of this comes where the prince is putting his life in danger and robbing him of the (stolen) thousand pounds.

> I haue forsworne his company hourely any time this two and twenty yeares, and yet I am bewitcht with the Rogues company. If the Rascal haue not giuen me medecines to make me loue him, Ile be hang'd; it could not be else; I haue drunke Medecines.

He could continually be made to say such things without stopping the laugh at him, partly because one thinks he is pretending love to the prince for his own interest; 'never any man's thought keeps the roadway' as well as those of the groundlings who think him a hypocrite about it, but this phrase of mockery at them is used only to dignify the prince; the more serious Falstaff's expression of love becomes the more comic it is, whether as hopeless or as hypocrisy. But to stretch one's mind round the whole character (as is generally admitted) one must take him, though as the supreme expression of the cult of mockery as strength and the comic idealisation of freedom, yet as both villainous and tragically ill-used.

—WILLIAM EMPSON, "They That Have Power," *Some Versions of Pastoral* (London: Chatto & Windus, 1935), pp. 108–9

J. DOVER WILSON

Like all great Shakespearian characters Falstaff is a bundle of contradictions. He is not only Riot but also Repentance. He can turn an eye of melancholy upon us, assume the role of puritan sanctimony, and when it pleases him, even threaten amendment of life. It is, of course, *mock*-repentance, carried through as part of the untiring 'play extempore' with which he keeps the Prince, and us, and himself, entertained from beginning to end of the drama. And yet it is not mere game; Shakespeare makes it more interesting by persuading us that there is a strain of sincerity in it; and it almost completely disappears in Part II, when the rogue finds himself swimming on the tide of success. There is a good deal of it in Part I, especially in the earliest Falstaff scenes.

> But, Hal, I prithee, trouble me no more with vanity. I would to God thou and I knew where a commodity of good names were to be bought.
>
> Thou hast done much harm upon me, Hal—God forgive thee for it: before I knew thee, Hal, I knew nothing, and now am I, if a man should speak truly, little better than one of the wicked: I must give over this life, and I will give it over: by the Lord, an I do not, I am a villain. I'll be damned for never a king's son in Christendom.

One of his favourite poses is that of the innocent, beguiled by a wicked young heir apparent; he even makes it the burden of his apologia to the Lord Chief Justice at their first encounter. It serves too when things go wrong, when resolute men who have taken £1000 on Gad's Hill are left in the lurch by cowardly friends, or when there's lime in a cup of sack:

> There is nothing but roguery to be found in villainous man, yet a coward is worse than a cup of sack with lime in it. A villainous coward! Go thy ways, old Jack, die when thou wilt, if manhood, good manhood, be not forgot upon the face of the earth, then am I a shotten herring. . . . There lives not three good men unhanged in England, and one of them is fat, and grows old. God help the while! a bad world, I say. I would I were a weaver—I could sing psalms or anything.

But beside this talk of escaping from a wicked world and the toils of a naughty young prince, there is also the pose of personal repentance. At his first entry Poins hails him as Monsieur Remorse, an indication that this is one of his recognized roles among Corinthians and lads of mettle. And we may see him playing it at the opening of act 3, scene 3, when there is no Hal present to require entertaining.

> Well, I'll repent, and that suddenly, while I am in some liking. I shall be out of heart shortly, and then I shall have no strength to repent. An I have not forgotten what the inside of a church is made of, I am a peppercorn, a brewer's horse. The inside of a church! Company, villainous company, hath been the spoil of me.

Such passages, together with the habit of citing Scripture, may have their origin, I have said, in the puritan, psalm-singing, temper of Falstaff's prototype—that comic Lollard, Sir John Oldcastle in the old _Henry IV_. But, if so, the motif, adapted and developed in Shakespeare's hands, has come to serve a different end. In this play of the Prodigal Prince it is Hal who should rightly exhibit moods of repentance; and on the face of it, it seems quite illogical to transfer them to Falstaff, the tempter. Yet there are reasons why Hal could not be thus represented. In the first place, as already noted, repentance in the theological sense, repentance for sin, is not relevant to his case at all, which is rather one of a falling away from political virtues, from the duties laid upon him by his royal vocation. And in the second place, since Henry V is the ideal king of English history, Shakespeare must take great care, even in the days of his 'wildness', to guard him from the breath of scandal. As has been well observed by a recent editor: 'His riots are mere frolics. He does not get drunk and is never involved in any scandal with a woman.' And there is a third reason, this time one of dramatic technique not of morals, why the repentance of the Prince must be kept in the background as much as possible, viz. that as the only satisfactory means of rounding off the two parts, it belongs especially to the last act of the play.

Yet Monsieur Remorse is a good puppet in the property-box of the old morality, and may be given excellent motions in the fingers of a skilful showman, who is laying himself out, in this play especially, to make fun of the old types. Why not shape a comic part out of it, and hand it over to Falstaff, who as the heir of traditional medieval 'antics' like the Devil, the Vice, the Fool, Riot and Lord of Misrule, may very well manage one more? Whether or not Shakespeare argued it out thus, he certainly added the ingredient of melancholy, and by so doing gave a piquancy to the sauce which immensely enhances the relish of the whole dish. If only modern actors who attempt to impersonate Falstaff would realize it!

Falstaff, then, came to stand for the repentance, as well as the riotous living, of the Prodigal Son. And striking references to the parable, four of them, seem to show that his creator was fully aware of what he was doing. 'What, will you make a younker of me? shall I not take mine ease in mine inn but I shall have my pocket picked?' Sir John indignantly demands of Mistress Quickly, on discovering, or pretending to discover, the loss of his grandfather's seal-ring. The word 'younker' calls up a scene from some well-known representation of the parable, in picture or on the stage, a scene to which Shakespeare had already alluded in the following lines from *The Merchant of Venice:*

How like a younker or a prodigal
The scarféd bark puts from her native bay,
Hugged and embracéd by the strumpet wind!
How like a prodigal doth she return,
With over-weathered ribs and ragged sails,
Lean, rent, and beggared by the strumpet wind!

Equally vivid is Falstaff's description of the charge of foot he led into battle at Shrewsbury as so 'dishonourable ragged' that 'you would think that I had a hundred and fifty tattered prodigals, lately come from swine-keeping, from eating draff and husks'. And seeing that he calls them in the same speech 'slaves as ragged as Lazarus in the painted cloth, where the Glutton's dogs licked his sores', we may suppose that, here too, he is speaking right painted cloth, from whence he had studied his Bible; an inference which seems borne out by his third reference, this time from Part II. Having, you will remember, already honoured Mistress Quickly by becoming indebted to her for a hundred marks, that is for over £65, he graciously condescends to borrow £10 more from her. And when she protests that to raise the sum she must be fain to pawn both her plate and the tapestry of her dining-chambers, he replies: 'Glasses, glasses, is the only drinking—and for thy walls, a pretty drollery or the story of the Prodigal or the German hunting in waterwork is worth a thousand of these bed-hangers and these fly-bitten tapestries.' This is not just the patter of the confidence-trickster; Falstaff, we must believe, had a real liking for the Prodigal Son story, or why should that tactful person, mine Host of the Garter Inn, have gone to the trouble of having it painted, 'fresh and new', about the walls of the chamber that he let to the greasy philanderer who assumed the part of Sir John, in Windsor. Not being a modern critic, the good man could not know that his guest was an impostor.

—J. DOVER WILSON, *The Fortunes of Falstaff* (Cambridge: Cambridge University Press, 1943), pp. 32–35

R O B E R T   B .   H E I L M A N

In view of Smollett's constant reference to and quotation of Shakespeare in his novels and of his 'close reading of the Falstaff comedies' ⟨L. M. Ellison⟩, there is good reason to conclude that his treatment of Micklewhimmen in *Humphry Clinker* borrows heavily from the treatment of Falstaff in *I Henry IV,* II. iv. The main acts of cowardice differ, of course. When the inn at Harrogate catches fire, Micklewhimmen, an old Scotch lawyer who has gained much sympathy as a paralytic and victim of other ailments, comes charging down the passageway with a portmanteau on his shoulders and fights his way to the bottom of the crowded stairs, trampling over guests of both sexes. On the other hand, Falstaff and his robber-companions in II, ii, flee when they are assailed by Prince Hal and Poins. But there is strong evidence of borrowing in the supporting details—and especially in the theory by which Micklewhimmen justifies himself.

When Hal tells Falstaff about the trick played on him, Falstaff thus endeavours to account for his flight:

> . . . but beware instinct; the lion will not touch the true prince. Instinct is a grave matter; I was now a coward on instinct.

When Micklewhimmen is reproached for his violently inconsiderate escape, he explains:

> . . . I cannot claim any merit from the mode of my retreat. . . . there are two independent principles that actuate our nature. One is instinct, which we have in common with the brute creation, and the other reason. Noo, in certain great emergencies, when the faculty of reason is suspended, instinct takes the lead, . . . therefore, . . . I'm not accountable *in foro conscientiae* for what I did, while under the influence of this irresistible pooer.

Both men, besides using *instinct* identically, admit the discreditable conduct, compare men and beasts, and treat themselves as objects of a transcendent, morally neutral power.

Smollett continues to follow Shakespeare closely: like Falstaff, Micklewhimmen is twitted about his theory. Five times Hal playfully speaks about *instinct,* either referring directly to Falstaff's excuse or applying it to other matters; three times Micklewhimmen's associates make ironic application of his psychology, and Smollett himself adds a fourth comment. Very strikingly, Smollett even uses Shakespeare's method of making the coward become, in part, master of the situation—by sheer brazenness and hard-boiled casuistry, however, rather than by Falstaffian gaiety, resilience, and light-hearted carelessness of consequences.

That Smollett had Shakespeare's scene in mind is indicated also by more general similarities: like Falstaff, Micklewhimmen is a great eater and drinker; like Falstaff, he has a trick played upon him—Melford's public demonstration that his 'stomachic tincture' is claret; as Falstaff pretends to bravery, Micklewhimmen pretends to ill health. The novel is most emphatically reminiscent of the play in that each character is exposed in a special pretence of the moment: whereas Falstaff has hacked his sword and by making his nose bleed has made himself look like a bloody veteran of combat, Micklewhimmen groans, needs assistance, and wears a 'bloody napkin round his head'. In the one aspect in which the episode is Shakespearian in tone as well as in framework, Micklewhimmen grinningly accepts a challenge, lightly dances a Scotch measure, and thus tacitly admits the unreality of his injuries. Finally, the hold-up itself is apparently remembered and used by Smollett, who has *two* hold-ups just before his fire-scene; in the first of these the role of Martin, who drives off other hold-up men, is not unlike that of Hal in *I Henry IV*, ii. ii.

It is even possible that Micklewhimmen's dichotomy of reason and instinct may reflect part of the play. Before the exposé, Falstaff, while boasting of his exploit, is caught in a contradiction. '. . . tell us your reason', Hal demands of him, and Poins adds, '. . . your reason, . . . your reason'; in answering, Falstaff himself uses the word three times. Since Smollett knew Shakespeare chiefly by the acted plays, it is quite possible that the word *reason,* six times repeated, was echoed indistinctly in his memory as a part of the configuration of Falstaff images and hence, although in a changed form, came to the surface with the others.

The external facts which add weight to the supposition that Smollett was borrowing are Smollett's regular use of Shakespeare, the twelve Shakespeare references in *Humphry Clinker,* the consistent references to the Falstaff plays in other Smollett novels, and the fact that the Falstaff of the actor James Quin was Smollett's favourite Shakespearian character. Now Quin is lengthily described in *Humphry Clinker.* Of this well-known description, several details are worth noting here. Quin is a great eater and drinker, like Falstaff and Micklewhimmen; Jerry says to Quin, 'I would give a hundred guineas to see Mr. Quin act the part of Falstaff', and Quin says life 'would stink in his nostrils, if he did not steep it in claret'—the wine which is Micklewhimmen's hourly consolation for disability.

Smollett, however, did *not* borrow the Shakespearian spirit; in the main, Micklewhimmen is satirized, as Falstaff is not. A comparison with Smollett's sharp portrayal of the calculating lawyer sheds light on the innocuous humour and the essential childlikeness and irresponsibility of Falstaff.

—ROBERT B. HEILMAN, "Falstaff and Smollett's Micklewhimmen,"
Review of English Studies 22, No. 3 (July 1946): 226–28

JOHN MIDDLETON MURRY

Falstaff is completely alive in *Henry IV,* Part I. But we can say more than that. In that play, Falstaff is *primus inter pares;* he is the first and greatest, but he is the first and greatest among equals. Hotspur, being a character of history, with his fate appointed in the authorities, has to die: but if he could have been spared, he might have become another Falstaff for posterity. Of course, there could not be another Falstaff; but there could have been a rival to Falstaff—a character animated by a like fundamental irresponsibility; the antithesis of Falstaff, but his complement also; as careless in his pursuit of honour as Falstaff in his pursuit of pleasure. It is a curious relation that holds between the man who thought—

> It were an easy leap
> To pluck bright honour from the pale-faced moon,

and the other who said:

> Can honour set to a leg. No. Or an arm? No. . . . Honour hath no skill in surgery, then? No. What is honour? A word. What is that word honour? Air. A trim reckoning! Who hath it! He that died o' Wednesday. Doth he feel it? No. Doth he hear it? No. 'Tis insensible then? Yes, to the dead. But will it live with the living? No. Why? Detraction will not suffer it. Therefore, I'll none of it. Honour is a mere scutcheon; and so ends my catechism.

But though it is a strange one, the relation between these two exists. It is not a relation that would have been recognised by either of them in daily life. Hotspur would have despised Falstaff; and Falstaff, when safely out of reach of his sword, would have laughed at Hotspur. It is a relation of another kind.

For Hotspur, like Falstaff, is a character of the first order; in sheer imaginative reality he runs the fat knight very close. His scene with Lady Percy, his scene with Glendower, belong to the very highest manifestations of Shakespeare's creative power in his first unbroken period, when he seems to have been simply a force of nature in a sense in which perhaps only Homer and Tolstoy and Dickens have been forces of nature expressing themselves through the written word. We feel that the first part of *Henry IV* is naturally balanced and harmonious. It plays within a single world of Shakespeare's imagination. Falstaff is one denizen of it, Hotspur another; they breathe the same air, the same sunlight shines upon them, and we feel that if our vision were delicate enough we could see how the one creation implied the other, for we have a sense of them as necessary projections of the same moment in the same mood of the same genius. And what is true of these two heroes of the play holds good of the play altogether. There is an astonishing interdependence of the parts: they are irradiated by a shining atmosphere which unites them all, but which it would need much labour to define, for it is by nature almost beyond definition. But the word to describe it is 'lambent'; tongues of smiling flame play over everything. A point at which we can nearly capture the essence in a few lines is, perhaps, Prince Henry's casual remark:

> I am not yet of Percy's mind, the Hotspur of the North; he that kills me some six or seven dozen Scots at a breakfast, washes his hands, and says to his wife, 'Fie upon this quiet life! I want work.' 'Oh, my sweet Harry,' says she, 'how many hast thou killed to-day?' 'Give my roan horse a drench,' says he, and answers, 'Some fourteen,' an hour after. 'A trifle, a trifle.'

Intrinsically, it is perhaps not funnier than a dozen of the things that Falstaff says; but its effect in its place, following immediately upon the marvellous scene between Hotspur and his wife, is prodigious. This slant and smiling sunbeam, we feel, can be thrown upon anything. Hotspur throws it on the gentleman who came to demand his prisoners and on Glendower, Prince Harry on Hotspur, Falstaff on Prince Harry, and Shakespeare himself on the world.

But in the second part this magical condition—this champagne atmosphere—exists no longer. The second part contains, of course, many wonderful things, but this radiant naturalness is intermittent. Instead of being a play in which Falstaff is only a triumphant particular crystallisation of the general element, there is no general element at all—neither unity, nor atmosphere of unity. Against an irrelevant background of unsavoury history, Falstaff performs, and as often as not he has no heart at all in the performance. He is as often merely mechanical as he is inspired. This falling-off has been recognised by many; and condoned or excused or explained. It has been said, for instance, that between writing the first and the second parts of *Henry IV,* Shakespeare had come under the influence of Ben Jonson's inferior and mechanical conception of comedy. It is not likely on general grounds that a commanding genius, conscious of its powers, should be warped by the theories of a talent. To be influenced is one thing, to be inhibited is quite another. And as a matter of fact, it is precisely where the comedy of *Henry IV,* Part II, is in setting and externals most Jonsonian, that Shakespeare first becomes himself again. The tavern scene, where Falstaff dines with Mistress Quickly and Doll Tearsheet—a trick of name Shakespeare may very well have taken from Jonson—may offend our modern pretences of refinement; it is nevertheless superb—quite how superb we can only realise at the end, when it is plain that Shakespeare has achieved the miracle of carrying a thread of true sentiment clean through the scene without even a momentary discord.

And Falstaff is himself again in the scenes in which he is engaged in monstrously misusing the King's Press in Gloucestershire. It is when he is alone, with no other comic characters to bear him up, that it is most evident that the virtue has departed from him. His opening scene with the Lord Chief-Justice is a queer affair. Falstaff says some good things in the course of it: if it were taken away we should never know that 'he was born about three o'clock in the afternoon, with a white head and something a round belly'; and, certainly, we should never have guessed that he had lost his voice 'with hollaing and singing of anthems.' But for the most part the richness is departed. The fat knight's wit has become thin and verbal and boring: the stage-play is effective, but the substance of the talk is not. And when Falstaff plays the old, old comic trick of pretending not to hear the Lord Chief-Justice, we know that Shakespeare is getting through an uncongenial task by relying on his knowledge of stage technique. Falstaff never had to depend for his being upon such props before; nor did he ever descend so low as in his reply to the Lord Chief-Justice's rebuke:

> CH.-JUST.: There is not a white hair on your face but should have his effect of gravity.
> FALS.: His effect of gravy, gravy, gravy.

Let us hope that that is a gag of the Elizabethan clown which has found its way into the text. There is nothing quite so imbecile as that in the scene.

On the whole, it is not too much to say that in this second part of *Henry IV*

Falstaff is rather carried on than re-created. There is his great monologue on the virtues of sherris-sack; there are a few scattered sentences, of which the most famous perhaps is: 'I am not only witty in myself, but the cause that wit is in other men.' But in this play the wit in himself is conspicuous chiefly by its absence; the wit in other men of which he is the cause becomes only the more striking. For it is, to say the least, very peculiar that in his three most admirable scenes—the scene of his arrest for debt, the tavern scene with Quickly and Tearsheet and Pistol, and the recruiting scene in Gloucestershire, the only scenes in the play which are bathed in the true Falstaffian quality—Falstaff himself has little or nothing to say. In the first it is Mistress Quickly, in the second, Mistress Quickly and Pistol, in the third, Justice Shallow, who set the pace and give the tone. Sir John's presence is rather felt than manifested: the company is fit for him, we know that he is among it, and our imagination does the rest. Partly through the transferred vitality of his companions, partly in virtue of the radiant afterglow which persists from the first part and appears at the mention of his name, we incline to see him as the same Jack Falstaff, wrapped in the same rich clouds of glory. But he is not. He has his moments of indubitable inspiration; but he is in a decline. He is being kept alive, as it were, only by a transfusion of blood. He has become, in fact, something of a vampire, whose veins can be filled only by the sacrifice of fresh children of Shakespeare's creative imagination.

The disease and the heroic remedy point to a single conclusion. Shakespeare had begun to tire of Falstaff. He is no longer interested in him; he is, indeed, interested in anybody rather than him. To enable himself to go on writing comic scenes in which Falstaff can be kept afloat, in which an illusion of Falstaff's presence can be plausibly maintained, he has either to expand characters that existed in outline only, or to invent new ones. Thus in the tavern scene it is the richly-matured Mistress Quickly—first mother of that great succession of comic Cockney land-ladies and charwomen which touches the zenith again in Mrs. Gamp and descends into Samuel Butler's Mrs. Jupp in *The Way of All Flesh*—and Pistol (why, oh, why, is Pistol so funny, seeing that nine-tenths of his jokes are unintelligible?)—it is these two who carry the thing through. And even in Gloucestershire it is Shallow and Silence and the rich procession of Mouldies, Warts, Feebles, and Bullcalves who bear Sir John's banner high. Falstaff is no longer the executant, but the impresario. We remember his past triumphs and are content, and when he comes forward to the front of the stage to take his benefit with a monologue on the dangers of thin potations, we are ready for a moment to swear he is as good a man as ever he was. But our heart misgives us; we have a premonition that the end is near.

—JOHN MIDDLETON MURRY, "The Creation of Falstaff," *John Clare and Other Studies* (London: Peter Nevill, 1950), pp. 187–91

D. A. TRAVERSI

It is as a reaction against the precariousness increasingly felt to underlie the political values of these plays that Falstaff, Shakespeare's greatest comic character, makes his appearance. He undergoes, indeed, during the trilogy an evolution parallel to that implied in the growing sombreness of the later episodes. At the outset, in *Henry IV–Part I*, his function is evidently a critical one, not altogether different, though vastly developed, from that of Faulconbridge in *King John*. He serves, in a sense, as a connecting link between two worlds, the tavern world of comic incident and broad humanity in which he is obviously at home and the world of court rhetoric and political intrigue to which he also has access. So situated in two worlds and not entirely limited by either, Shakespeare uses him as a commentator who passes judgement on the events represented in the play in the light of his own super-abundant comic vitality. At one time, in his account of his own exploits at Eastcheap, he parodies the heroic boasting to which the more respectable characters in their weaker moments are given; at others, he provides a comic version of the moral lectures addressed by Henry IV, not without a strong hint of political calculation, to his son (II, iv) or comments bitingly at Shrewsbury (V, i, iii) on the true meaning of the word "honour" so freely invoked by dubious politicians to urge others to die in their interest. Working sometimes through open comment, sometimes through parody, his is a voice that lies outside the prevailing political spirit of the play, drawing its cogency from an insight that is the author's own and expressing itself in a flow of comic energy. Falstaff, we might say, represents in this first play of the three all the humanity which the politicians, bent on the attainment of success, seem bound to exclude. That humanity, as it manifests itself in these early tavern epi-sodes, is full of obvious and gross imperfections, and we should do wrong to slur over them or sentimentalize the humanity in any way; but the Falstaff of this play, while these imperfections are part of his nature, is not altogether limited by them. His lively intelligence, his real human understanding, his consistent refusal to be fobbed off by empty phrases are all characteristics that enable us to see in him the individual expression of the conscience of a great and perfectly serious artist.

The Falstaff of Part II is in many ways a very different person. He has under-gone, since the end of the previous play, an evolution parallel to that of the political figures who surround him, and as such proves once more Shakespeare's growing capacity to see his plays as wholes, to conceive expression and character as parts of an artistic unity greater than themselves. In the new play, dominated, as we have seen, by a sense of age and diseased impotence, fear and calculation assert them-selves openly at the expense of idealism, and success is sought without illusions but also without disguise. The trick by which Lancaster, in this his father's son, persuades the rebels at Gaultree Forest (IV, ii) to disband their armies so that he can lead them to execution is entirely typical of the new canons of political behaviour. Falstaff himself is subdued to the changed spirit. Finding his companions among aging dotards, he strips them mercilessly of their pretensions, penetrating with ruthless clarity of vision to the reality beneath:

> Lord, lord, how subject we old men are to this vice of lying. . . . I do remember him [Shallow] at Clement's Inn, like a man made after supper of a cheese-paring: when a' was naked, he was for all the world like a forked radish, with a head fantastically carved upon it with a knife.   (III, ii)

This new vision of Falstaff, in other words, is the product of experience coloured by an awareness of age. Death, disease, and the flesh now dominate his thoughts, so much so that the critics have detected the realistic, moral influence of Ben Jonson. No doubt that influence exists, but Shakespeare's emphasis is both individual and in tune with the rest of his play. It is not grotesque or farcical, even in the serious Elizabethan meaning of the word; it insists rather on tragic pathos and the corruption of human values by time and ill-living. Falstaff's memorable remark— "Peace, good Doll! do not speak like a death's head; do not bid me remember mine end"—strikes right across Jonson's simplified, intense effects and brings in the tragic note. It connects him with the dark feeling of the political scenes, a connection made yet more explicit by Poins's comment in the same scene: "Is it not strange that desire should so many years outlive performance?" These words join Falstaff's new burden of disease and concupiscence to the malady and disharmony common to Northumberland and the king. Here again a new sense of emotional unity is moulding the elements of poetry and drama in a way that anticipates the great tragedies.

Falstaff's attitude toward the political action around him undergoes a corresponding change. The criticism of "honour" in Part I is reinforced by a tragic sense of what now seems to be the normal condition of man. To the new emphasis there corresponds once more a changed external reality. The "food for powder," to use his own words, which he had formerly led into battle at Shrewsbury, now speak through Feeble, who has been pressed into serving a cause which has for him no meaning and who resigns himself to his fate in words that recall those once spoken to Falstaff at Shrewsbury: "a man can die but once; we owe God a death." The words are similar, but the attitude of Falstaff himself, confronted with all they imply, has changed. Whereas at Shrewsbury his reply to the Prince had been tinged with irony and wit, had implied an affirmation of the rights of life beyond the selfish calculations of politicians, this new Falstaff is content to allow those who have the means to buy their freedom from service and to accept Feeble's resignation to his fate: for such, and no other, is the nature of things, and necessity justifies all: "If the young dace be a bait for the old pike, I see no reason, in the law of nature, but I may snap at him. Let time shape, and there an end" (III, ii).

Shakespeare's growing conviction that the moral and political orders are barely to be reconciled finds its supreme expression in what has often been regarded as the most difficult scene of the play—that in which Prince Henry, newly crowned king, rejects his former companion. Here, as so often in Shakespeare, we must be careful not to simplify. There can be no doubt that the change noted in the conception of Falstaff is aimed, among other things, at making the rejection at once feasible and necessary. It is certainly no accident that he has been given a new burden of age, lechery, and disease, which fits in with the changed spirit of the play at the same time that it undoubtedly goes to justify his treatment at the hands of his friend. Henry, with the responsibilities he has just shouldered and the purposes he has in mind, could hardly do other than abandon Falstaff. When he denounces him as

So surfeit—swell'd, so old, and so profane,

he makes a true criticism, which an Elizabethan audience would not have found excessive; and the criticism is backed with the austerity of a great religious tradition when he adds

Make less thy body hence, and more thy grace.

Yet there is also another side of the picture to which we need to give its true weight. Though the king's words must be taken at their proper value, the same applies to Falstaff's repeated criticisms of the royal family, which can be traced back to the earliest scenes of the trilogy and are no less part of the truth. Henry's judgements, indeed, suffer persistently from being too easily made. The dismissal of past friendship invoked in his "I know thee not, old man," the tight-lipped implication of disgust in his advice to "leave gormandizing," the studied gesture to the gallery, "Presume not that I am the thing I was"—all these are as characteristic as the afterthought by which Falstaff, banished scarcely five minutes before, is arrested and thrown into prison by the returning ministers of the royal justice. There is no need, in short, to be sentimental on behalf of either the Prince or Falstaff. The "unpleasantness" detected by the critics in their relationships is a necessary part of the play. It springs from its most distinct individuality; it translates yet again into dramatic terms the "disease" which we have found hanging over the English state, and it relates all the divisions between age and youth, action and inaction, folly and calculation to a developing split in feeling which will become increasingly prominent in the later tragedies. The precise implications of this bitter contrast of aged dissolution and the controlled coldness so unnaturally attributed to youth require definition in terms of the great plays which follow.

—D. A. TRAVERSI, *An Approach to Shakespeare* (1938; rev. ed. Garden City, NY: Doubleday Anchor, 1956), pp. 30–35

W. H. AUDEN

At a performance, my immediate reaction is to wonder what Falstaff is doing in this play at all. At the end of *Richard II,* we were told that the Heir Apparent has taken up with a dissolute crew of "unrestrained loose companions." What sort of bad company would one expect to find Prince Hal keeping when the curtain rises on *Henry IV?* Surely, one could expect to see him surrounded by daring, rather sinister juvenile delinquents and beautiful gold-digging whores. But whom do we meet in the Boar's Head? A fat, cowardly tosspot, old enough to be his father, two down-at-heel hangers-on, a slatternly hostess and only one whore, who is not in her earliest youth either; all of them seedy, and, by any worldly standards, including those of the criminal classes, all of them *failures.* Surely, one thinks, an Heir Apparent, sowing his wild oats, could have picked himself a more exciting crew than that. As the play proceeds, our surprise is replaced by another kind of puzzle, for the better we come to know Falstaff, the clearer it becomes that the world of historical reality which a Chronicle Play claims to imitate is not a world which he can inhabit.

If it really was Queen Elizabeth who demanded to see Falstaff in a comedy, then she showed herself a very perceptive critic. But even in *The Merry Wives of Windsor,* Falstaff has not and could not have found his true home because Shakespeare was only a poet. For that he was to wait nearly two hundred years till Verdi wrote his last opera. Falstaff is not the only case of a character whose true home is the world of music; others are Tristan, Isolde, and Don Giovanni.

Though they each call for a different kind of music, Tristan, Don Giovanni, and Falstaff have certain traits in common. They do not belong to the temporal world of change. One cannot imagine any of them as babies, for a Tristan who is not in love, a Don Giovanni who has no name on his list, a Falstaff who is not old and fat, are inconceivable. When Falstaff says, "When I was about their years, Hal, I was not an eagle's talent in the waist; I could have crept into an alderman's thumb-ring"—we take it as a typical Falstaffian fib, but we believe him when he says, "I was born about three in the afternoon, with a white head and something of a round belly." ⟨. . .⟩

Reading *Henry IV,* we can easily give our full attention to the historical-political scenes, but, when watching a performance, attention is distracted by our eagerness to see Falstaff reappear. Short of cutting him out of the play altogether, no producer can prevent him stealing the show. From an actor's point of view, the role of Falstaff has the enormous advantage that he has only to think of one thing—playing to an audience. Since he lives in an eternal present and the historical world does not exist for him, there is no difference for Falstaff between those on stage and those out front, and if the actor were to appear in one scene in Elizabethan costume and in the next in top hat and morning coat, no one would be bewildered. The speech of all the other characters is, like our own, conditioned by two factors, the external situation with its questions, answers, and commands, and the inner need of each character to disclose himself to others. But Falstaff's speech has only one cause, his absolute insistence, at every moment and at all costs, upon disclosing himself. Half his lines could be moved from one speech to another without our noticing, for nearly everything he says is a variant upon one theme—"I am that I am."

Moreover, Shakespeare has so written his part that it cannot be played unsympathetically. A good actor can make us admire Prince Hal, but he cannot hope to make us like him as much as even a second-rate actor will make us like Falstaff. Sober reflection in the study may tell us that Falstaff is not, after all, a very admirable person, but Falstaff on the stage gives us no time for sober reflection. When Hal or the Chief Justice or any others indicate that they are not bewitched by Falstaff, reason might tell us that they are in the right, but we ourselves are already bewitched, so that their disenchantment seems out of place, like the presence of teetotalers at a drunken party.

—W. H. AUDEN, "The Prince's Dog" [1959], *The Dyer's Hand and Other Essays* (New York: Random House, 1962), pp. 183–86

JOHN WAIN

Like Hotspur, ⟨Falstaff⟩ is primarily a creature of the plot. The rival conceptions of honour would suffer from our ironic contemplation if he were not there to provide an irony we could never rise to. He says it all for us, and so much more that we could never have said for ourselves.

PRINCE: Say thy prayers, and farewell.

FALSTAFF: I would it were bed-time, Hal, and all well.

PRINCE: Why, thou owest God a death.

FALSTAFF: 'Tis not due yet: I would be loath to pay him before his day. What need I be so forward with him that calls not on me? Well, 'tis no matter; honour pricks me on. Yes, but how if honour pricks me off when I come on? how then? Can honour set to a leg? No. Or an arm? No. Or take away the grief of a wound? No. Honour hath no skill in surgery then? No. What is honour? a word. What is that word, honour? Air. A trim reckoning! Who hath it? he that died o' Wednesday. Doth he feel it? No. Doth he hear it? No. It is insensible, then? Yea, to the dead. But will it not live with the living? No. Why? Detractions will not suffer it. Therefore I'll none if it: honour is a mere scutcheon; and so ends my catechism.

With this, the range of human notions of honour is complete. Falstaff speaks for the common man, content with no more than a common share of honour. The common Englishman is capable of heroism, but not of heroic speeches. He can lay down his life for an ideal, but he cannot talk about laying down his life for an ideal. Nor can he bear to listen, for long, to anyone else talking about it. When the resounding oratory begins, he feels he is being cheated by someone. The leaders who can best rally and inspire him are those who confine themselves, as Churchill did, mainly to the expression of defiance.

That, roughly, is Falstaff's role in Part I of *Henry IV*. He provides the worm's eye view of honour, thus making a debate out of what would otherwise be a simple juxtaposition. And he provides fun—incomparable, glorious fun, never approached anywhere else in English literature. Even Chaucer, even Dickens, never come near the Falstaff scenes. If I forbear to comment on them, that is merely because there is nothing to be said from outside. With the exception of the mock-trial scene, of which we shall speak in a moment, they are pure gaiety and high spirits, without undertow or afterthought.

In Part 2, however, a change comes over the Falstaff scenes. As everyone has always noticed, the untroubled gaiety of Part I has gone. Falstaff is still magnificently himself—he bears no relation to the travesty Shakespeare was obliged to cook up in *The Merry Wives of Windsor*—but the landscape in which he gambols is a sadder one, its foliage nipped by a touch of frost. His role is now a sacrificial one. The Prince, his reputation already almost redeemed and his responsibilities almost upon him, returns briefly to the *demi-monde,* but with less than his old zest. He knows, and we know, that the party is nearly over. Time, the chief enemy of Falstaff's brand of irresponsible gaiety, is on everyone's mind. Even Falstaff himself has become conscious of his age. In the first Part, there were plenty of farcical references to it ('How long is't ago, Jack, since thou sawest thine own knee?', etc., etc.) but they were easily swept aside as part of the fun. Now, suddenly, the fact of his age is inescapable. When, in the first act, he offers the Lord Chief Justice the calm impertinence of, 'You that are old consider not the capacities of us that are young,' he gets a stern answer. 'Have you not a moist eye? a dry hand? a yellow cheek? a white beard? a decreasing leg? an increasing belly? is not your voice broken? your wind short? your chin double? your wit single? and every part about you blasted with antiquity?' To this formidable catalogue, Falstaff makes a flippant reply; but the charge is proven. He is old, and his age acts as a kind of super-fault which makes all his other faults inexcusable. Though in Part I there are plenty of joking references to whoring, in this part we actually see him with his whore, Doll Tearsheet. And suddenly the pathos of an old man's dependence on the affection of a bought girl is there, inescapably, before us.

> FALSTAFF: Thou dost give me flattering busses.
> DOLL: By my troth, I kiss thee with a most constant heart.
> FALSTAFF: I am old, I am old.
> DOLL: I love thee better than I love e'er a scurvy young boy of them all.
> FALSTAFF: What stuff wilt have a kirtle of? I shall receive money 'a Thursday; Shalt have a cap to-morrow. A merry song, come. 'A grows late; we'll to bed. Thou'lt forget me when I am gone.

We do not doubt that she loves him. But this only underscores the pathos. The Falstaff of Part I does not need to seek for love. He is the spirit of gaiety; all created life loves him. In Part 2, he is an old man who craves to stay in the sunshine a little longer.

It is not that Falstaff's character changes. It is rather that, as with Satan in *Paradise Lost,* we are shown progressively sadder and darker sides of the same character. The world of Part 2 is a drabber world, more realistically drawn. The scene, for instance, where Mrs. Quickly and Doll Tearsheet are arrested by the beadles, on what would nowadays be called 'a morals charge', is lurid enough to foreshadow the world of Mistress Overdone in *Measure for Measure,* or the hideous brothel in *Pericles.* Cursing and spitting, the two women are hauled away by leather-faced officials. To Doll's claim that she is pregnant, and Mrs. Quickly's vengeful cry of 'I pray God the fruit of her womb miscarry'—so that they can lodge a complaint of ill-treatment—the stolid beadle replies, 'If it do, you shall have a dozen of cushions again; you have but eleven now'. This is realism worthy of Zola, the cobweb-scrubbing realism of the post-Romantic novel.

We see the same disenchantment in the scene where Falstaff is misusing his commission as an officer by accepting bribes to release conscripted men. This was glanced at in Part I, where Falstaff gives a joking account of having 'misus'd the king's press damnably'. But, as with the whoring, to hear about it is one thing, to watch him engaged in it quite another. When Shallow's tenants present themselves to answer the call to arms, a whisper from Bardolph ('I have three pound to free

Mouldy and Bullcalf') is sufficient to get these two stalwart men waved aside with, 'for you, Mouldy, stay at home till you are past service:—and for your part, Bullcalf, grow till you come into it:—I will none of you'.

It is worth noticing here that Shakespeare's realism is not of the muck-raking kind that never admits to recognizing good qualities in human beings. The cowardice of Mouldy and Bullcalf is all too credible and understandable. So is the greedy opportunism of Falstaff, rejecting the two fittest men because they can afford to bribe him, and filling his muster with the least promising. But even in this *milieu* there is a flash of courage and manliness, such as everyday life generally provides. Francis Feeble, 'a woman's tailor', is good for a laugh, especially since the word 'tailor' was some sort of coarse joke in Elizabethan English; it meant, I understand, the sexual organ; hence Falstaff's reply to 'Shall I prick him?' with 'if he had been a man's tailor, he'd ha' pricked you.' But Feeble, with his comic name and his comic occupation, is a brave man.

> By my troth, I care not; a man can die but once; we owe God a death. I'll ne'er bear a base mind. An't be my destiny, so; an't be not, so. No man's too good to serve's prince; and let it go which way it will, he that dies this year is quit for the next.

Falstaff's image is badly tarnished by the time we have sat through these scenes. It was all very well for comfortable Victorian men of letters to smile indulgently at Falstaff's misuse of the press. But Shakespeare's audience included many who had suffered, or might suffer in the future, from this kind of injustice. Falstaff's swindling of Justice Shallow is another matter; he is implicated in the general grab for money and advantage; he is servile to Falstaff because he thinks Falstaff will be a royal favourite. He lends him a thousand pounds because he has grasped that 'a friend at court is better than a penny in purse'. The England we are visiting here is no picture-postcard island of sturdy yeomen and pretty thatched roofs. It is a place where money talks, where poor men are ill-treated and the law abused.

Falstaff, in his turn, sees Shallow not only as a source of revenue but as excellent copy. 'I will devise matter enough out of this Shallow to keep Prince Harry in continual laughter the wearing-out of six fashions'. He follows this with a remark that is one of the keys to the play.

'O, it is much that a lie with a slight oath, and a jest with a sad brow, will do with a fellow that never had the ache in his shoulders.'

In those words, Falstaff's life lies open to the cruel daylight. His joking description to Doll Tearsheet of Hal as 'a good shallow young fellow' was, it seems, no joke. If he is using Shallow, he is also using Hal. Shallow is vulnerable because he is provincial, senile and foolish. Hal is vulnerable because he knows nothing of life. He 'never had the ache in his shoulders', never knew the heaviness and weariness of everyday existence. And so to tickle him with a jest is to manipulate him.

Falstaff is wrong, and from the start we have known him to be wrong. But now, increasingly, his wrongness matters. He is fixed on a collision course which will smash him against Hal's granite royalty. He makes self-destructive error after error. His calculation is suddenly revealed as shoddy and superficial. On the news of the king's death, he rides day and night to be at Hal's coronation, arriving travel-stained and ungroomed, as a piece of deliberate staging. ('It shows my earnestness of affection.') With horrified fascination, we watch him offer himself up for sacrifice. But when the axe falls, it is enough to make one turn away one's eyes.

> FALSTAFF: My King! My Jove! I speak to thee, my heart!
> KING HENRY V: I know thee not, old man. Fall to thy prayers.
> How ill white hairs become a fool and jester!
> I have long dreamt of such a kind of man,
> So surfeit-swell'd, so old, and so profane;
> But, being awak'd, I do despise my dream.

Once again it is Falstaff's age that counts most against him. In five lines, it is thrown in his teeth three times. In the first line he is 'old', in the second he has 'white hairs', in the fourth he is 'old' again. The new king passes on, and Falstaff is left standing in the street, with Shallow at his side demanding his thousand pounds back on the spot. A few minutes later, by what seems a deliberate piece of cruelty (for, as Dr. Johnson pointed out, he has committed no new offence), he is arrested and carried off to the Fleet prison. He has paid for Hal's wild oats; the score is settled, and it is Falstaff who has settled it.

On that dreadful occasion, Falstaff makes no plea for himself. He is given no chance to do so. But, perhaps unable to be as unfair to him as Hal must inevitably be, Shakespeare has already given him a chance to speak up in his own defence. Back in Part I (Act II, Scene iv), Hal and Falstaff act out a little comedy for the amusement of their tavern companions. They take it in turns to guy King Henry reproving his son. When Hal acts the part of his father, he utters a special warning against associating with 'that swoll'n parcel of dropsies, that huge bombard of sack, that stuff'd cloakbag of guts'. Falstaff, impersonating Hal, makes a moving plea, in the course of which he soars upward from his familiar prose to conclude with three lines of stately verse—a sure sign, in Shakespeare, that lofty matter is at hand.

> FALSTAFF: That he is old—the more the pity—his white hairs do witness it; but that he is—saving your reverence—a whoremaster, that I utterly deny. If sack and sugar be a fault, God help the wicked! If to be old and merry be a sin, then many an old host that I know is damn'd: if to be fat be to be hated, then Pharaoh's lean kine are to be loved. No, my good lord: banish Peto, banish Bardolph, banish Poins; but, for sweet Jack Falstaff, kind Jack Falstaff, true Jack Falstaff, valiant Jack Falstaff—and therefore more valiant, being, as he is, old Jack Falstaff—banish not him thy Harry's company, banish not him thy Harry's company. Banish plump Jack, and banish all the world.
> PRINCE: I do, I will.

Immediately after Hal's quietly menacing words, we have the stage-direction 'A knocking heard'. We know that knocking. It is the hand of the cold reality which tells us we must search our pockets and pay up. It is the knocking on the gate in *Macbeth*. Or the knocking of Aeneas on the chamber door of Troilus and Cressida, when he comes to bear the news that Cressida must leave. 'Banish plump Jack, and banish all the world' is exactly the challenge Hal must take up. And when, finally, he says of his father 'in his tomb lie my affections,' the fullness of his meaning is precisely that this has been accomplished.

—JOHN WAIN, "The Sword and the Crown," *The Living World of Shakespeare: A Playgoer's Guide* (New York: St. Martin's Press, 1964), pp. 53–59

ROSALIE L. COLIE

⟨. . .⟩ Shakespeare offers us in the *Henry IV* plays a splendid creation, Sir John Falstaff, very different from the real and legendary Sir John Oldcastle, sometime companion to Prince Henry. *Why* this Falstaff? Some of the answer lies in the sources of the narrative. In the chronicles and onstage young Henry V had been fixed into a certain shape—a knobby, irregular, inconsistent shape, to be sure, but a shape firm enough to demand fairly strict *mimesis*. His madcap youth, his subservience to his father before and after the deathbed episode with the crown, his exemplary conduct as healer of national breaches and victor over foreign dangers were all fully established: Henry V was "this star of England," the fulfilment of Respublica's long-thwarted hopes. It was difficult to find in the sources the resources to give this English princeling depth of character; some other means had to be found—so Falstaff was evolved as foil to a prince for whom there were insufficient conventional guidelines.

The prince was very "given," in the factual ways of the literary *milieux* in which Shakespeare found him, the chronicles, chronicle-poems (*Mirror for Magistrates* and Daniel's *Civill Wars*), and a morality chronicle-play (*The Famous Victories*). For Falstaff the opposite is the case: brilliant studies have identified some of the many literary streams which conjoined to feed his substantial shape. We recognize in him the braggart soldier, the parasite, and the *buffone* of Latin comedy, *commedia erudita*, and *commedia dell' arte;* we recognize in him (as does the English Hal) the Vice of the morality play, *Mundus* with his *Infans*, Gluttony, Appetite, Riot, and the rest of the temptations besetting this important prodigal son: we recognize in him the Lord of Misrule and Carnival of folkish and medieval festivals; we recognize in him, too, the *Roi des sots* of medieval *sottie*, the court-jester accompanying a ruler, and the complex, critical, paradoxical ways of the Renaissance fool. We recognize in this *puer senex* who insists on the privileges, both of youth and of age, in a particular person: Falstaff. Paradoxically, then, this remarkable mixture of generic characters and stereotypes, this man made of whole cloth (buckram) who seems to be, literarily at least, "all the world," is far more mimetically "real" than the actual young man of history whose companion he is.

And what an extraordinary, exceptional exemplar he is of all these types!—a *miles gloriosus* whose brags are transparent, even arranged to suit the prince's expectation, who, when faced with a "real" braggart soldier from the repertory, Pistol, fearlessly drives him offstage; a parasite not just upon a powerful status-figure but also, *literally,* upon a hostel-keeper and a bawd; a Riot, a Master of the Revels, whose chief reveler knows throughout the game that it must one day end for good; a fool whose folly mocks himself as surely as it mocks king and royal justice; a devil whose temptations to this heir-apparent turn out to be as unavailing with that chill and distanced young man as Satan's importuning of Christ in the wilderness. Like Erasmus' Folly, Falstaff keeps us all off-balance—all save the prince, who knows even before the play begins that the revels must be ended and their master turned out of the game. In a final turning, perhaps owing something to the traditions of the morality-play, this *chevalier sans cheval,* this riotous glutton, this fool is shown to be off-balance too, surprised by the forms of worldliness his tender lambkin now displays.

By both the morality reading and the Machiavellian reading, the *Henry IV* plays are a mirror of princes, a study in rulers' regimen, where we watch a young man learning to rule his nation, growing into his kingship, building his character into its ultimate calling. But much of this character-building is Shakespeare's, who shows us an increasingly able Hal simply by putting him in relation to various symbolic characters in the play; from these arrangements we see where Hal starts. He is characteristically "between": between Falstaff, the festive mock-king, and grim, lamenting, businesslike Henry IV; between Falstaff, a braggart soldier forced into the field, and another glorious soldier, the overheroic Hotspur, who throws his cause away for the "honour" Falstaff has the good sense to reject; between Falstaff, careless of his master's cause and of human life ("tush, man, mortal men, mortal men"), and Prince John of Lancaster, so careful of polity that he cares not for his pledged word or for human life; between Falstaff, openly flaunting his cheating, and that intransigent servant of the king, the Lord Chief Justice. These pairings serve to identify for us a prince who, though he does not really develop in the play, is seen responding to more and more situations; even more important are those situations in which Hal is, as it were, bounced off Falstaff himself. From these we learn, unexpectedly, how like the two are. They share real distaste for responsibility. Though Hal bites the biter Falstaff in the Gadshill episode, they are alike in the pleasure they take in deviancy, alike in their different parodies of the highborn robberies in the kingdom at large. Their joint misrule speaks to England's condition: the jests at Eastcheap (for all their underworld character), furthermore, have an innocence which the king and the plotters have long since forfeited. Both Hal and Falstaff are Machiavellian, manipulating others (Mistress Quickly, Francis, Poins) and each other, enigmatically in the buckram exchange after Gadshill, tolerantly in the judgment-scene and in Hal's permitting Falstaff to steal his honor in Hotspur's death. Though the plays make quite clear that Hal once crowned has no intention of condoning Falstaff, from Hal's first soliloquy, *via* Falstaff's impressment of men and dealings with Justice Shallow and Mistress Quickly, to the morality harshness of "I know thee not, old man," they also unequivocally show Hal's enjoyment of Falstaff and, before the prince's final departure to labor in his vocation, his *need* for a figure of diversion, to take the sting out of his own rebellion against rank, to provide outlet for his dissatisfactions with the quality of life at his father's court. What Falstaff offers Prince Hal is not only the symbolic freedoms of youth, but also a chance to practice at being human.

Shifting the level of discussion from the play itself to the making of the play, we can see how Shakespeare found refuge from a ticklish literary problem in the accomplishments of his profession. From his models, those static chronicles and poems from which he took his story, he had little to go on to make of his prince a credible personality, as he had so brilliantly managed with Richard II; neither had he in Hal's life a steady progression toward ever-greater success, a dramatic paradigm such as that offered by Richard's magnificent fall from fortune. The *schemata* to hand were simply insufficient to make this real king into a dramatic character; so the playwright had to turn elsewhere, to other dramatic contexts, and to make from the jumble of *schemata* available to him a figure (out of whole cloth, wholly out of cloth) allied with and foil to the Lusty Juventus who will, like his medieval forebear, ultimately redeem the time he spent in alehouse anarchy, as well as the time wasted in a misgoverned nation.

To think of Falstaff in connection with these denatured types is in part to denature him to his earthy reality, so convincing is the illusion that this particular character is a real individual. Not for nothing did Prince Hal want to pass the time till Falstaff should arrive, nor Queen Elizabeth want him back (at least, on the stage) after his banishment. This unmetaphored figure for the world ("all the world"), the flesh ("Ribs," "Tallow," belly), and the devil ("old white-bearded Satan"), this voluntary anti-courtly fool forcing the problematics of public life upon us as upon the prince, gives form, in his very bulk and anarchic denial of all forms, to the dialectic which propels Hal out of Eastcheap to Shrewsbury and, finally, to Westminster and the responsibilities of Respublica. Quite simply, as we can see, though nature influences art, art influences art more: Shakespeare's success in making a "realer" person out of the art-generated Falstaff than of the actual Henry Plantagenet is a primary example of the Aristotelian notion that poetry is more powerful than history.

—ROSALIE L. COLIE, "Introduction," *Shakespeare's Living Art*
(Princeton: Princeton University Press, 1974), pp. 18–22

VINCENT GODEFROY

Verdi establishes at once the essential nature of his John Falstaff, Cavaliere, by the display of unflappable self-control he assumes in the face of the complaints and brawls of lesser people. Boito has managed a deft reduction of Shakespeare's sprawling start, telescoping Shallow and Slender and Doctor Caius; removing Evans, Simple, and Page; relegating the Host to a mute, and postponing the appearance of Anne Page, whom he will transfer to the Ford family. Falstaff is revealed affixing his seal to the two letters which are going to cause such a furore in sleepy Windsor. His movements are deliberate yet relaxed, while the orchestra leads off with a tremendous C major chord and at once proceeds to trundle a restless progression that heralds the approach of trouble. The angry Caius bursts in, hell-bent on having things out with him, the opening theme supporting his fury. Stephen Williams read into this apoplectic motif 'the bumping of casks over a cellar floor'—a picturesque analogy. But though it starts the opera rolling with a hefty shove, the ingenuity lies in Falstaff's monumental indifference to the outraged doctor's clatter. This is expressed by a steadily rising theme through four octaves. The direction *un poco meno animato* suggests the pervasion of a steadying influence, the effortless superiority of the titled aristocrat quelling the squabbles with a disdainful look. But the titled aristocrat is Falstaff, and the steady mounting motif, whether spread along the strings or woodwind, exudes just that hint of wariness with which the fumes of alcohol infiltrate into mind and limbs. Falstaff is master of himself, but only just; sufficiently, however, to deceive us into supposing that he may be on the side of the Establishment.

His magisterial role, together with Bardolph's impudent evidence, exasperates Doctor Caius into a pompous declaration of good intent. This is in fact Slender's, 'Ile nere be drunk whilft I liue againe, but in honest, ciuill, godly company.' The subsequent 'antiphonal' *Amen* of Bardolph and Pistol is clearly what he deserves and is a bonus of Boito's, with Verdi chuckling as he indulges in a few musical jokes derived from Shakespeare's text and deliciously embellished. But when Caius has departed unrevenged and deflated, a noticeable change comes over Falstaff. He is mentally unbuttoning himself and conceding to his cronies a sort of bucolic intimacy. Drily reading the landlord's account he is suddenly heard to linger ecstatically over the memory of the pheasants and anchovies. The fact that his purse is found to be virtually empty does not dispel his growing mellowness, as he sidles into a lethargically bibulous tune in which he recalls the pleasures of tavern-crawling. But as he rolls deeper into the melody he breaks it up with sudden disgust at the cost of keeping Bardolph in liquor. All this comes from *Henry IV* and both librettist and composer add perceptibly to the breadth of their portrait. But Boito, in his efforts to pepper his poem with local flavour, clearly reveals himself as no numismatist.

The apparent dissolution of Falstaff's tune is justified by his rising contempt for Bardolph which ends (naturally) in a call to the host for another bottle. It is only a few minutes since he last called for one. As Hal observed, 'O Villaine, thy Lippes are scarce wip'd, since thou drunk'st last.'

A sense of well-being pervades him. The 'fat paunch', the 'whoreson round man', now surveys his rotundity with self-admiration.... 'A goodly portly man yfaith, and a corpulent, of a chearfull Looke, a pleasing Eye, and a most noble Carriage.' Verdi delineates his vital statistics by sandwiching his vocal line between piccolo and cello. The effect, like a cartoon or line-drawing, fairly depicts the whole gross, carnal, vain monstrosity that the dramatist has built up in pages of loaded prose. The effect both preens and ridicules; and the means are so simple that one can only marvel at their ingenuity. As his complacency waxes, a derisory fanfare sustains his declamation, culminating in the famous 'Immenso Falstaff' of his irreverent cronies, ringing with almost Tamburlainean bravado. The subject of their acclamation, sensing a superb conclusion to the bickering, waxes confidential at once. So Falstaff enters the third stage of his opening sequence, detailing the scheme which he was hatching before the curtain rose.

A jaunty exchange with his minions leads up to his admission that in order to balance his budget he is planning to seduce two wealthy married ladies. The music fairly oozes self-satisfaction as he slips liltingly into a brief, voluptuous dream and then tries to persuade Bardolph and Pistol of his physical desirability. Another tune seems to develop, but is frittered away in a superbly egotistical fantasy in which he deludes himself that Alice Ford will accept him as a lover. His falsetto imitation of her surrender is both daring and challenging; but the very buffoonery of it releases us from supposing him to be serious about anything but the financial advantage that may accrue. As he switches to Meg Page the orchestra trips along with what might be the suppressed amusement of his henchmen. But once hooked by his own imaginings he pursues them, hinting that there should be plenty of money waiting to be scooped up, and capping it all by preening himself lyrically over his well-preserved sexuality. Under a sustained *mezza voce* high F sharp the complacent orchestra weaves a pattern of bon-vivant ripeness. Falstaff has reached the apex of his adventurous design. Warmed by the bottles of sack and his apparent charisma in the presence of his lesser colleagues, he gives peremptory orders for the delivery of his love-letters. When they refuse to participate, he is astounded at their infidelity; and having despatched Robin the page-boy in their stead, he turns on them with the supreme lecture that is the opera's most famous passage.

Boito's contribution must be commended unreservedly. The monologue starts with an adaptation of the scene in the second act of the play in which Falstaff berates Pistol ('you'll not beare a Letter for mee you roague? you stand vpon your honor'). This leads straight into his comparison between his own noble manipulation of conscience and the disreputable claims of his loathsome servants. This is close to Shakespeare's, 'I, I, I my selfe sometimes, leauing the feare of heauen on the left hand, and hiding mine honor in my necessity, am faine to shuffle: to hedge, and to lurch, and yet, you Rogue. . . .' Even those three *I*s are here, leading into one of those complacent fragments of self-satisfied melody like the 'So che se andiam la notte' of a few minutes back.

Thereon Boito sails into Falstaff's dissertation on honour delivered to the Prince before the battle of Shrewsbury. This literary bonus ensures that the operatic Falstaff waxes beyond the mere antics of a conventional comedy. Like a boat suddenly unfurling its spinnaker he burgeons with splendid rotundity. Verdi ingeniously peppers the whole monologue with felicitous instrumental comments that add spice to the text without ever obscuring it. For this is meant to be heard, syllable by syllable. Very subtle is the imperceptible switch from diatribe to reverie, as Falstaff wanders in pursuit of his catechism on honour and forgets the presence of Bardolph and Pistol. His distaste for them is amply reflected in the four-trombone echo of the snarled 'ladri!', the murky swirl of the strings under 'cloache d'ignominia,' and the great bass trill that rounds off his mounting exasperation at their arrogance. This trill is unexpectedly followed by a more delicate rebound on woodwind only. A new thought has struck Sir John, and this is the transition. Now he is in *Henry IV,* but at first he is still addressing his minions. Then, floating on the wind of his own rhetorical questions, which he answers himself, he becomes momentarily oblivious of them and their iniquities, until he has dismissed honour in a triumphant conclusion ('therefore I'll none of it'). The 'catechism' is over, and suddenly he remembers his forgotten congregation. With what may be the disintegrated fragment of a cabaletta Verdi indulges in a brief, riotous crescendo to round off the scene, in which by successive stages we have seen Falstaff as decayed gentleman, potential roysterer, unprincipled schemer, and equivocal philosopher. Not many actor-baritones get such a chance in their opening scene. Indeed, he has earned a brief respite.

—VINCENT GODEFROY, "Immenso Falstaff," *The Dramatic Genius of Verdi: Studies of Selected Operas* (London: Victor Gollancz, 1977), Vol. 2, pp. 300–303

JAMES L. CALDERWOOD

Falstaff appears to bespeak an old tendency toward sensual verbal indulgence in Shakespeare, a tendency that he has been punishing and symbolically killing off—or at least badly wounding—throughout a series of early plays, most recently in *Richard II.* There is much to be said for this. What was earlier a lyric self-indulgence on Shakespeare's part, a playful poetic interest in words for their own supple sakes and a tardiness in getting on with the action of the play, seems now to have corporealized itself in the suety shape of Falstaff. As wordplay in general involves a densening of the phonic substance of speech, so Falstaff the verbal improviser and embodiment of language games represents the full fleshing out of the word. He has been at a great feast of languages and has fed well on epithets, puns, sententia, inkhorn terms, bombast, slang, and all manner of styles from the biblical to the euphuistic to the mock-heroic to the fishwife screech. He seems almost to have swallowed the whole text of *Love's Labour's Lost.* So surfeit swelled with words, he bestrides the path of dramatic action in *Henry IV* like a colossus—or would do so if he were allowed on that path.

But Shakespeare, who is sufficiently cavalier with history to invent Falstaff in the first place and give him such prominence, is true to time at least in this: within the two plays he relegates Falstaff to a side-world, or a side-board, boxed off from recorded doings. Falstaff is to history as Academe and the Capulets' orchard are to the extramural world of affairs in those plays. It is not of course that Falstaff never acts but simply that his actions are not allowed to intrude into history. The one claim he makes to affect history—his "killing" of Hotspur—must of necessity be a lie; and it is precisely when he attempts to insert himself into history, at Hal's coronation, that he must be rejected.

So Falstaff, who feeds on language no less than on capons and sack, who appropriates the word for his own lying uses, seems a perfect embodiment, a final profane reincarnation of Shakespeare's impulse to create verbal worlds sufficient unto themselves, self-contained, self-absorbed, outside and largely indifferent to the mainstream of dramatic action. So stuffed with speech is he that doing is beyond him, he can only *be*—for there is an inevitable inertia to the word in itself as opposed to the inherently kinetic thrust of action. Not that Falstaff cherishes words for their own aesthetic selves. On the contrary, he is the "user" of words par excellence. But he uses them as his body does sack and capons. Through the metabolism of his wit they are transformed into the lying instruments of his most immediate corporeal needs. As an inveterate improviser Falstaff can use words only in the present; he cannot enlist them in the service of future action. He has no plans or programs. In short, he cannot plot, he can only extemporize to evade the plots of others, like Hal and Poins, or simply those of the world at large, which from his point of view seems increasingly ill-disposed toward white-haired old knights scoured almost to nothing with perpetual motion in behalf of the state.

Given all this, then, how has Shakespeare profited from his earlier dramatic efforts? Is he not merely wantoning again, or this time roistering, with words at the expense of action and plot—and indeed doing it so hilariously well that Falstaff is in danger of swallowing up the play much as the word-games did in *Love's Labour's Lost* (so that in *2 Henry IV* Shakespeare must have Hal play Mercade and dismiss the holiday of words in favor of an everyday of history)? Well, there is, as I've said, much to support such a view, and in later chapters I shall try to talk along these lines. But from another standpoint Shakespeare's treatment of Falstaff represents an advance upon his treatment of the scholars of Navarre, the lovers of Verona, or the late English king. For while Falstaff is using the word for his short-range selfish purposes Shakespeare is using Falstaff for his long-range artistic ones. That is, though Falstaff is isolated from the history plot in terms of action, he nevertheless participates in it verbally because his words reveal him to us as a burlesque low-life metaphor for Henry IV.

This point is a familiar one and needs no laboring here. Psychoanalytic critics like J. I. M. Stewart and Ernst Kris began seeing Falstaff as a father-substitute—a sacrificial stand-in for Bolingbroke—years ago. What needs stressing here is not the fact of Falstaffian burlesque but its relevance to the linguistic issues discussed earlier. Shakespeare's use of Falstaff as a metaphor for the king follows logically from his having dramatized in *Richard II* the discovery of the metaphor within the name. Moreover, it is by means of metaphor that the word emerges from isolation and comes into its dramatic own. In its very doubleness of focus, that is, metaphor enables the word to reach beyond itself to engage with actions elsewhere, so that Falstaff need not lumber bodily into the main historical plot in order to play a part in it. Merely by heaving himself onto his joint-stool throne in the kingdom of the Boar's Head Tavern, fisting his leaden-dagger sceptre, and commencing in his King

Cambyses tone, "Harry, I do not only marvel where thou spendest thy time" (*I Hen. IV*, 2.4.439), Falstaff casts his broad shadow of verbal parody forward into 3.2 of the main plot where Henry—pompous as Falstaff in his regal mood and rendered complacently tutorial by the success of his self-serving political strategies ("Thus did I keep my person fresh and new,/My presence, like a robe pontifical,/ Ne'er seen but wondered at" etc.)—reveals himself to be as much a self-constituted, play-acting, inauthentic monarch as his bombastic low-life counterpart. To Hal's scornful critique of Falstaff's performance—"Dost thou speak like a king?" (2.4.476)—Falstaff's answer might well be "As much like a king as Bolingbroke, and with as much legal justification."

In *I Henry IV*, then, it is not Falstaff who plays the role of Richard II—the role of the man whose poetic speech makes direct claims on the world but proves powerless in the event. That role devolves on Glendower, the poet-seer who issues commands to the devil and calls spirits from the vasty deep but who cannot liberate himself, in Hotspur's derisive view, from the categories of liar and pompous ass. Shakespeare is well beyond Richard now, and beyond poetic isolation. His concern is with the political word and how it makes its way in the world of action and history where Glendower, secluded in Wales and rapt in private dreams and prophecies that warn him away from history, never ventures.

—JAMES L. CALDERWOOD, *"Henry IV:* The Ascendance of the Lie,"
Metadrama in Shakespeare's Henriad: Richard II *to* Henry V
(Berkeley: University of California Press, 1979), pp. 41–46

JEANNE ADDISON ROBERTS

In spite of the variables and ambiguities, some real evidence of the nature of Falstaff is discernible in the text ⟨of *The Merry Wives of Windsor*⟩, and it helps to account for the division of the critics. Some mediation between them may be attempted. We must ask on the basis of text: Is Falstaff in this play a social menace who brings on himself a well-deserved punishment? Or is he a nearly innocent victim, entrapped by the scheming wives and used by society for its own rather devious ends? Is he a villain or a scapegoat?

The text shows us inescapably that he is both and that Shakespeare has carefully fostered in his audience both their sense of social justice and their sympathy with the misfit. The result is a very delicately balanced ambiguity, easy to shatter and difficult to maintain. The text of the play is constantly modifying its own signals. The idea of Falstaff's identical letters to the two wives is outrageous, but the tone of the letters is appealingly blunt and straightforward. Falstaff's agreeing to act as pander for "Mr. Brook" is preposterous, but it seems positively harmless in comparison with Ford's elaborate scheme to trap his own wife. The Falstaff of the buck basket is deservedly ridiculous, while the half-drowned old man pouring down sack to counteract the Thames water is hilarious, but pathetic.

Such conflicting signals may be discerned throughout the play. In the final scene they are especially important, however, and worth examining in some detail.

The setting of the last scene is Windsor Forest between twelve midnight and one o'clock. We have been prepared for the scene by Mistress Page in ominous and foreboding terms:

> There is an old tale goes, that *Herne* the Hunter,
> (Sometime a keeper heere in Windsor Forrest)
> Doth all the winter time, at still midnight,
> Walke round about an Oake, with great rag'd-hornes,
> And there he blasts the tree, and takes the cattle,
> And make milch-kine yeeld blood, and shakes a chaine
> In a most hideous and dreadfull manner.   [4. 4. 28–35 (2150–56)]

Page has added (4. 4. 39–40 [2161–62]) that many people still fear to walk at night by Herne's Oak. Even in Shakespeare's day Windsor Forest was more of a park than a forest—a fitting place to mediate between the town and the wild woods. This very fact tends to neutralize the effect of terrors and evil enchantments evoked by the Pages. The neutralization is immediately furthered in the play by the addition of the information that on this night the supernatural element will be provided by "fairies" in the form of Nan Page and numerous children. Hardly a horrifying prospect.

But the oak tree does legitimately suggest divinity of a more serious kind. Traditionally in mythology it is associated with strength, with shelter, with awesome size, and frequently with gods. Underneath this oak, as under the oak where Oliver finds regeneration in *As You Like It* (4. 3. 99–120), we may expect to find a scene appropriate both to divine judgment and to mercy and forgiveness.

In the mind of Falstaff, too, the oak tree suggests the supernatural—in this case superhuman fertility and virility—qualities which from the point of view of society are sometimes a blessing and sometimes a curse. The oak tree in classical times was sacred to Jove. Shakespeare's knowledge of this fact is manifest in *As You Like It* (3. 2. 236), when Rosalind praises "Jove's tree" for dropping such fruits as Orlando, who has been found lying under an oak. It is thus no accident that Falstaff's initial soliloquy (5. 5. 15 [2482–96]) is addressed partly to Jove, hero of many famous amorous adventures. Falstaff clearly sees himself as Jove's successor in sexual prowess as well as Jove's imitator in his bestial disguise.

Already, then, the audience has complex expectations evoked by the setting. It partakes of the forest, where anything can happen, as well as of the more socially regulated town. Mistress Page says quite appropriately of Falstaff's horns: "Do not these faire yoakes/Become the Forrest better than the Towne?" (5. 5. 108–10 [2590–91]). The time is midnight—the hour of ghosts and mysteries and amorous dalliance. And the site is dominated by a large oak tree—suggestive of Herne the Hunter (who is thought of as a menace to the countryside), but also conjuring up the possibility of divine presence. The tree elicits thoughts of fertility, but if we accept Page's description, it is "blasted," suggesting age. Like Falstaff himself at this moment, the tree is an image of both virility and decay. It is both ominous and reassuring. Under it we might expect to find both villains and victims.

As immediate in its impact as the setting is the visual image of the horned Falstaff. Like the setting, this image combines the wildness of the forest (horns) with the civilization (human form) of the town. The first problem in attempting to analyze the connotations of the horns is to establish how they ought to look. Pictures of performances of this scene vary widely. According to the Quarto stage direction, Falstaff should appear not only with horns, but "wearing a buck's head"; however, this phrase may refer to an entire head or antlers only. At least two artists (William Nelson Gardiner in 1798 and John Thurston in 1812) show Falstaff with the face of a deer as well as the horns—a bit like Bottom in his ass's head. Certainly the costume ought to include horns and asslike ears (actually found in some varieties of deer e.g. the American mule deer), because when Falstaff says "I do perceive that I am made an ass," Ford replies "Ay, and an ox too: both the proofs are extant" (5. 5. 120–21 [2602–3]). Ford's comment seems to refer to ass ears and ox horns. The shape of the horns should surely not be the many-branched antlers most familiar to Americans, but probably the horns of the English fallow deer—leaflike at the end, with a single main branch and one or two curved, oxlike offshoots near the forehead.

One's first impression would be the ludicrous sight of the fat old horned man, with the hint of ox and ass. But the horns would also reinforce the connection between Falstaff and the tree. That this is not a farfetched association is indicated by Jaques's advice in *As You Like It* (4. 2. 4–5) to set on the head of the deerslayer the horns of the deer as "a branch of victory." Both Falstaff and the tree suggest strength, the supernatural, and virility diminished by age. Other connotations evoked by Falstaff would include most obviously the suggestion of cuckoldry, but also the more generalized sexual virility—the aggressive sexuality of the stag in rutting season. This is emphasized when Mistress Ford greets her "lover" inquiringly as, "(my Deere?) My male-Deere?" and he responds passionately to his "Doe with the blacke Scut" (5. 5. 16–18 [2497–99]). John M. Steadman has established a likely connection between Falstaff and Actaeon, the hunter who was turned into a deer by Diana when he accidentally came upon her while she was bathing and who was later torn apart by his own dogs. There remains also the memory of the menace of Herne the Hunter. All these associations can be linked to Falstaff the villain, the threat to the social institutions of the city—most particularly the threat to marriage. But, although the threat is there, the audience's awareness of it is strongly modified by their perception of absurdity and by their knowledge of the wives' well-organized plan to "dishorn the spirit."

In addition I would argue that, although suggestions of threat are undeniably present, the image of the horned Falstaff is highly ambiguous; the view of the man as victim subtly overshadows any sense of his villainy. As victim he arouses pity and perhaps fear, becoming finally the scapegoat whose sacrifice reunites society.

The ambiguity may be clearly seen in the horn image itself. Shakespeare's fondness for horn-jokes is well-known, and surely there is a humorous use of the image in this scene—the would-be cuckolder is ironically wearing horns himself. That Shakespeare does associate deer's horns with cuckoldry is apparent in a reference in *All's Well That Ends Well* (1. 3. 54–55) to cuckolds who may "jowl horns together like any deer i'th'herd." That it was also an association likely to be in the minds of his audience is suggested by lines given to a deer in a 1651 edition of Aesop:

> Where is the Beast that can,
> Or the Cornuted Man
> Shew such a horney Forrest on his Head?

There is later in the same speech a specific link with Actaeon when the deer adds "Nor were Actaeons branches fairer spread."

The connection of Actaeon with cuckoldry has been discussed by both Bullough and Steadman. In Shakespeare there are only three references to Actaeon by name, two in *The Merry Wives* and one in *Titus Andronicus;* in all three cases the idea of his horns is specifically associated with cuckoldry. Cuckoldry, however, involves both a cuckold and cuckolder. The former is usually an object of derision, while the latter is a potential threat to society. Actaeon is ambiguous; he suggests both parties. The horns identify him with the cuckold, the foolish victim; but the fact that they grew at the sight of Diana's nude body suggests a virility which would make him a potential cuckolder, a threat. To further complicate the picture, his fate is shocking and apparently unjustified. Ovid explicitly calls Actaeon a victim of circumstance. The ambiguous quality of the story of the unfortunate hunter and his terrible fate is sharply focused in two quotations by Don Cameron Allen in his book *Mysteriously Meant.* Allen quotes Bersuire, a moralizer of Ovid, as saying, *"In malo* Actaeon is a usurer; *in bono* he is Christ." Allen also quotes Salmeron's attack on early seventeenth-century allegorizers who see crucifixion in Actaeon's fate. Whether such allegories were approved or not, the possibility exists, then, of seeing in the horned figure of Actaeon a scapegoat being sacrificed for society, as well as the possibility of seeing him as a figure of fun or a villain.

If the reference to the deerlike Actaeon is ambiguous, so indeed is the reference to the deer. Deer can be dangerous animals. George Turberville says that during the rutting reason their "heads are venomous" and that they are more dangerous than boar. Overwhelmingly, however, the connotation of deer in Shakespeare is not of lust or of aggression or of danger, but rather of the hunted animal, the pathetic victim. Of forty-four generic references to deer in Shakespeare, only five allude to the animal as amorous or threatening, while twenty-seven contain the words *blood* or *kill* or *hunt* or conjure up in some way pictures of the deer as a victim. There are "kill'd deer," "chas'd deer," "strooken deer," "timorous deer," "murther'd deer," "frighted deer," "poor deer," "stalled deer," and "poor dappled fools"—none of which sound very ominous.

Whether Shakespeare himself felt sympathy for the hunted deer cannot be proven by reference to Jaques's famous sentimental moralization of the wounded deer (2. 1. 29–66), but the passage does prove that Shakespeare was well aware that such feelings might occur in the minds of his audiences. To identify Falstaff in the forest with a deer rather than with a goat, or a donkey, or a boar is to invite the audience's pity for an essentially defenseless man. Our surviving pictures showing stage representations of the final moments of Falstaff's punishment—with the horned head near the earth and the great body prone, surrounded by small nagging figures—are strikingly like the pictures in Turberville's *The Noble Art of Venerie* of the deer felled and surrounded by hounds just before the kill. For the people of Windsor such a scene is the logical end of their sport: it represents "poetic justice" in the control and rebuke of lechery with Falstaff reduced to an ox (i.e., a castrated beast of burden) and an ass (i.e., a fool). A "period to the jest" has been reached by publicly shaming the villain. But for the onlookers in the theater there is surely a pang of sorrow for the deer.

That the wives themselves may have some sense of pity is indicated by Mistress Page's words to her husband: "I pray you come, hold up the jest no higher" (5. 5. 106 [2588]). But they do not heed their own advice. They continue to taunt Falstaff as "a hodge-pudding," a "bag of flax," a "puft man," and "Old, cold wither'd, and of intollerable entrailes" (5. 5. 152–54 [2636–39]).

It is too much. The audience, already very delicately balanced in their awareness of Falstaff as both villain and victim, begin to turn against the townspeople. Only just in the nick of time does Page cut off the persecutions and include Falstaff in the group with his words: "Yet be cheerfull Knight: thou shalt eat a posset to night at my house" (5. 5. 171–72 [2655–56]). The way for harmony, forgiveness, and laughter has been prepared by the group's uniting in the attack on Falstaff the outsider, but the final fugue of social reconciliation is possible only when Falstaff is recognized as an essential element of, and possibly even a savior of, that very society he threatens. It is perhaps not pushing analogy too far to say that as the illicitly killed deer of the first scene becomes the "hot venison pasty" over which the initial quarrel is resolved, so in the end another kind of illicit deer provides the basis for the final resolution.

There is one final irony in the working out of this scene, one more startling double vision. Hugh Evans, the Welsh priest, presides over Falstaff's humiliation, and the indications are strong that the man who sets out to "dis-horn the spirit" is himself wearing horns. He has said originally that he will come "like a Jacke-an-Apes" (4. 4. 67 [2193]), but the stage direction of Q says that he enters "as a Satyr." Mistress Ford refers to the "Welch-Devill Hugh" (5. 3. 12 [2459]), and Falstaff says toward the end, "Am I ridden with a Welch Goate?" (5. 5. 138 [2622]). The conclusion seems justified that it is not Falstaff alone who appears as a merging of beast and man. It is not Falstaff alone who suggests both the human order of the town and the lechery of woodland spirits. It is not Falstaff alone who mingles the innocent and the diabolical. When Page says, "'No man means evill but the devill, and we shal known him by his hornes" (5. 2. 12–13 [2443–44]), we take it as a clear preview of Falstaff, but the sight of Sir Hugh in his goat's horns must stir up some doubt. Goat's horns are more suggestive of lust and deviltry than are the horns of a deer. At the very moment that Sir Hugh is righteously rebuking Falstaff for being "given to fornications, and to taverns, and sack and wine and metheglins, and to drinkings and swearings and starings, pribbles and prabbles," the audience is both amused and faintly disquieted by his obliviousness to the horns on his own head. This ironic juxtaposition of horns cannot be an accident. Gently but surely Shakespeare is reminding us once again of the infinite ambiguity of human behavior.

The most important critical constant which emerges from the study of this character is the continuing fascination of the series of linguistic symbols known as Falstaff. Clearly for the most diverse groups of critics it has been richly evocative and has brought meaningful patterns into widely differing contexts. Part of Falstaff's "greatness," like Hamlet's, seems to lie in the ability of concrete images to attract and assimilate projections of a great variety of feelings from audiences. If the character is indeed a mirror held up to nature, it is clearly a mirror which can be seen over a very wide range and in many different lights. If the character is rather a lamp, it is a lamp which has illuminated different areas at different times, casting a brighter light for some than for others, and frequently leaving details obscure. And whether mirror or lamp, or both, or neither, the series of symbols is to be cherished for its enduring value—a value which seems to owe something to concreteness and something to ambiguity.

Having said all this, I will admit that I myself draw some further conclusions. Falstaff, incomparable as he is, is part of a developing plan and not an end in himself. The Falstaff of *The Merry Wives* is a comic device used for an important purpose in a rather complex play. The sequence of humiliations in this play is part of the progress of the three Falstaff plays, and in all of them the character is essentially the same man. The most important "problem" is why the Windsor Falstaff has been such a problem. My own view of the play is epitomized by Giuseppe Verdi's adaptation of it in his opera *Falstaff*, composed in 1890–92, which reveals a precociously modern obliviousness to any inconsistency in the title character.

Verdi maintains the comic brilliance of Falstaff without ever permitting the focus on the individual to throw out of balance the sense of the community. The librettist has drawn freely on *Henry IV* as well as *The Merry Wives* for lines which show Falstaff's wit, bravado, practicality, and essential self-centeredness. The man is a threat to the families in Windsor and the stability of society, but he is also an endlessly fertile source of amusement and delight. He never steals the whole show, however, and this is clearly due in large part to the music. We are told by Francis Toye that the composer was determined that all the parts "must be of equal importance." And it is notable that there is only one aria in the score.

As a result, Falstaff, although alternately—even simultaneously—outrageous and pathetic, is always part of the ensemble. He evokes sympathy in his downfall as an individual, but at the same time he arouses uneasiness as a threatening member of the community, and it is clear that he must be controlled. Even the process of controlling him turns out to be functional. In punishing him the group seems to release its own hostilities, variously directed, and to compose for itself a new harmony. This social reconciliation is brilliantly celebrated in the final fugue, which is all the more poignant because of Falstaff's important contribution to it.

No matter how clear to me this view of the importance of the play in itself and as part of a larger pattern is, however, I am forced by my own observations of the critical history to recognize that I, too, am a prisoner of my age and my presuppositions. My conclusions, therefore, are offered not as definitive, but as one more small contribution to the ever-expanding cumulative portrait of the Windsor Falstaff. Having attempted to deal with critical views of *The Merry Wives* as a whole, and with the problems of the Windsor Falstaff, we are now ready to return to the effort to show the relationships of this play to some of Shakespeare's other work.

—JEANNE ADDISON ROBERTS, "Character: The Windsor Falstaff,"
Shakespeare's English Comedy: The Merry Wives of Windsor in Context
(Lincoln: University of Nebraska Press, 1979), pp. 110–18

EDWARD PECHTER

Falstaff ⟨. . .⟩ is a role-player, but his mode contrasts completely with Hal's. "We play for advantage, but we play for pleasure, too," as Lanham puts it (*The Motives of Eloquence*), and though he is not thinking of *Henry IV,* his words describe precisely the difference between the two figures. Falstaff's performances have essentially no motive beyond (in the words of Thomas F. Van Laan) "the high degree of pleasure he obviously derives from shaping and executing the . . . different parts he gets a chance to play." (And from entertaining his audience as well, one ought to add.) They certainly are not intended to be believed, or to be judged by their reflection of any truth outside their own realization. Maurice Morgann was right in his observation that the sheer extravagance of Falstaff's monstrous inventions precludes our sense that he is trying to convince anybody. Even the confirming details that we hear about later—the hacked swords, the blood-beslubbered garments—take their place as stage props, contributing more to heighten his performance as a performance than to persuade us of its validity as reportage. Similarly, in his histrionics at the end of the scene, "Give me a cup of sack to make my eyes look red, *that it may be thought* I have wept" (379–81), the emphasized words play to the audience's consciousness of aesthetic effect, and undermine verisimilitude. Actual belief and dramatic belief inhabit parallel but untouching universes:

> FALSTAFF: A plague upon such backing, give me them that will face me! Give me
> a cup of sack: I am a rogue if I drunk today.
> PRINCE: O villain! Thy lips are scarce wiped since thou drunk'st last.
> FALSTAFF: All is one for that. *(He drinketh.)* A plague of all cowards, still say I.

Hal has him dead to rights here, and the bland insouciance of "all is one for that" is not one of Falstaff's wittier ripostes. And yet it works. Whether or not Falstaff has actually drunk a moment earlier has nothing to do with the histrionics of the situation. Thirsty Falstaff, deprived all day of liquid sustenance, fits the role he is playing here of beleaguered and deserted virtue. Hal has missed the point in insisting upon the lie; Falstaff, he nothing affirms, and therefore never lieth.

Inconsistency and contradiction are at the heart of Falstaff's role-playing. For Hal, with his relentlessly single-minded pursuit of kingship, this is unnatural lying, but for Falstaff, whose mode of action denies the validity of a unitary selfhood, this is the source of delightful variety. As Van Laan says, "Falstaff's is a world for playing roles for pleasure, as many as possible, and the more innovative the better" (*Role-Playing in Shakespeare*). Apart from Falstaff himself, the *locus classicus* for this mode of action in terms of the sheer exhilaration it affords is Bottom, condoling as lover, out-Erclesing Ercles, masking Thisbe in a monstrous little voice, and finally stealing Snug's part: "Let me play the lion too. I will roar that I will do any man's heart good to hear me. I will roar that I will make the Duke say, 'Let him roar again; let him roar again.'" What Bottom wants, Falstaff seems to achieve: not just the individual pleasures of a number of recognizable roles—Vice, Fool, *buffone, laudator temporis acti,* flaming youth, deserted old man, Lord of Misrule, zealous puritan, *miles gloriosus,* Henry, Hal, etc.—or even the collective pleasure of all of them, but the boundless joy of access to any one of them at any time, or all of them at once. "In a word, he is an actor in himself almost as much as upon the stage," as Hazlitt said, and the freedom he enjoys is, to take the title of Michael Goldman's latest book, "the actor's freedom."

But it is the audience's freedom as well; that is the point I would emphasize. The question of our relationship to Falstaff has been hopelessly muddled with a false historicity, a catalogue of confident assertions about a reification called "the Elizabethan audience," its politics, ethics, religion, sexuality, world view, psychology. But the only thing that can be said with anything approaching absolute conviction about an Elizabethan audience is that it was constituted of human beings who liked plays enough to choose to attend them, that it *was* an audience. And the condition of being an audience, then as now, involves a prior abandoning, at least temporarily, of the conditions of actual existence, an escaping from the responsibility of a serious and single selfhood, in order to enjoy and participate in the performance of a fiction. An audience's freedom is obviously restricted as compared to the actor's since we merely participate in what he (with the playwright behind him) initiates. In a way, however, the audience is freer than the actor; there is no Quince limiting us to a single role. On the contrary, the conventional imperative of the audience's situation is to extend itself into a responsive sympathy with all the roles. The boundless possibilities that we sense in Falstaff not only characterize the pleasures of this particular play—"inclusiveness," "amplitude," "abundance"; they constitute an essentially animating principle of all the theatrical experience.

Threatening Falstaff, then, Hal threatens us as well, during the two-knaves-in-buckram bit as during the play as a whole. Hal's directorial speech at Gad's Hill (II.ii.88–91) is a characteristically relentless assertion of temporal hierarchy ("week . . . month . . . for ever") and moral purpose ("argument . . . laughter . . . jest," the last term probably meaning "noble exploit," since "laughter" had already exhausted the sense of joke). Although his meaning may not be totally clear here, his intention hangs heavily over Falstaff's performance in II.iv. His humor will be upheld only for a while, and then there will be an end to it, a balancing of the books, a conclusive shaping of the experience. When, after a number of false stops and temporary escapes, Hal and Poins move in, armed with the irrefutable plainness of mathematics, upon Falstaff, exhausted on his chair, the pause seems to anticipate his inevitable concession and the falsification of our hopes.

But it does not:

> By the Lord, I knew ye as well as he that made ye. Why, hear you, my masters, was it for me to kill the heir-apparent? should I turn upon the true prince? Why, thou knowest I am as valiant as Hercules: but beware instinct—the lion will not touch the true prince; instinct is a great matter. I was now a coward on instinct: I shall think the better of myself, and thee, during my life—I for a valiant lion, and thou for a true prince. But by the Lord, lads, I am glad you have the money. Hostess, clap to the doors! Watch tonight, pray tomorrow!— Gallants, lads, boys, hearts of gold, all the titles of good fellowship come to you! What, shall we be merry, shall we have a play extempore?
>
> (II.iv.263–76)

With astonishingly unexpected versatility, Falstaff shifts roles—contradictorily, of course, but all is one for that—and snatches victory from the jaws of defeat. The triumph of his spontaneous inventiveness over Hal's single-minded purposiveness is one that we share, for the speech, beginning slowly with a smile, as the idea first suggests itself, then feeding on its own energy, mounts as Falstaff rises from his chair to a climax of abundant happiness that includes us as well in the embrace of the last words: "What, shall we be merry, shall we have a play extempore?" "Play extempore" describes not only the spontaneous inventiveness by which Falstaff eludes Hal's purposive morality, but our own escape, in going to the theater, from the responsibilities of—to use Jonas Barish's phrase—"the concept of an absolute identity." Like so many of the memorable moments in Shakespeare, this is one of expansive self-consciousness for an audience, for the words constitute an energizing revelation of where—and thus of what and who—we are.

And yet, not altogether so. Though Falstaff is felt to embody an essentially animating principle of dramatic experience, and though, like Bottom, there is no play without him, still there is no play merely with him either. This is what we are made to recognize as Hal, playing Quince so to speak, disposes with authorial or directorial intelligence of the question that Falstaff proposes:

> FALSTAFF: What, shall we be merry, shall we have a play extempore?
> PRINCE: Content, and the argument shall be thy running away.
> FALSTAFF: Ah, no more of that, Hal, and thou lovest me.   (275–79)

The pretended agreement of "Content" fools no one, least of all Falstaff, who sags visibly and audibly. The play extempore, as Falstaff means it, has already been played. The play extempore, as Hal envisages it, has an argument, an insistent, unspontaneous moral framework, a beginning, middle, and end; Hal's plays are always *in* tempore. So Hal wins after all, here and for the balance of the scene.

Though Falstaff initiates the plays at the end of the scene, it is Hal who clearly controls them (the conventional critical designation of these as plays extempore rather misses or at least blurs the point), and it is Hal who has their last words, after Falstaff's memorable plea not to be banished: "I do," he says, and pauses. "I will" (475).

"I do, I will" is another characteristic example of Hal's temporal control, his integration of past and future. And once again we are made to sense the implications of Hal's purposive mode of playing for the structure of the play itself: "I do" belongs to the play within the play, "I will" to the play, and to the pressure of Hal's character upon it, pushing it relentlessly toward an upbeat moral ending. Shakespeare has carefully engineered "I do, I will" to initiate a pause in the action, as richly resonant as the one preceding Falstaff's "By the Lord, I knew ye," about which the audience may well be reminded. Now, however, the pause signifies the victory of the lean prince and the fat knight. For when Bardolph reenters to explain the knocking ("O my lord, my lord, the sheriff with a most monstrous watch is at the door" [476–77]), the play signals a shift in direction. As the door, clapped to by the hostess according to the stage direction in Falstaff's "play extempore" speech earlier, is now opened, as the tavern world is invaded by the forces of the public order, the play in effect conforms itself to Hal's version of experience, and for the first time seems decisively to define its own structure as a creature of Hal's and not Falstaff's imagination. "A while" is over; "anon" has come. "Play out the play!" cries Falstaff. "I have much to say in the behalf of that Falstaff" (478–79). But the time allotted to "the play," as Falstaff means it, has expired.

As for Falstaff, so for us; our revels now are, if not quite ended, at least ending. Gone now is our giddying absorption in playing extempore, replaced by a sense of the play's temporariness and dependence, its ultimate subservience to the containing actuality of experience. If we seek a formula to locate ourselves, it would be something like this:

$$\text{(for Falstaff)} \qquad\qquad \text{(for audience)}$$
$$\frac{\text{Play within the play}}{\text{Play}} \quad = \quad \frac{\text{Play}}{\text{Life}}$$

But no formula can quite do justice to the complexity of feelings we are made to experience at this particular moment in the action. It is a reasuring moment from one point of view. By affirming its mimetic status and its moral function, the play provides a basis for self-defense against the godly brethren of Shakespeare's time who keep complaining about the idle, purposeless escapism of the theater; and it satisfies our own need, as partly their descendants, to perceive high seriousness in the drama. So much for *dulce*, back now to *utile:* "If all the year were playing holidays,/To sport would be as tedious as to work" (I.ii.199–200). From another point of view, however, we sense not a consolation, but a threat. We have enjoyed an exhilarated condition of privilege, the access to a seemingly infinite variety of self-validating roles. We have known what it feels like to be anything we can be called, to realize any identity we can project (or participate in imaginatively): squires of the night's body as well as thieves of the day's beauty, with all the punning permutations—all is one for that. But no more now; from this condition we shall be banished. The play here becomes a self-consuming artifact in both of Stanley Fish's senses, at once undermining its own validity as a play, and ours as an audience.

—EDWARD PECHTER, "Falsifying Men's Hopes: The Ending of *I Henry IV*,"
Modern Language Quarterly 41, No. 3 (September 1980): 221–26

SUKANTA CHAUDHURI

The growth of Shakespeare's distinctive view of man appears principally in *Hamlet*, the dark comedies, and the tragedies following them; but it is with his most brilliant comic creation that the story may be said to begin. Seldom even in Shakespeare are the human and the heroic thrown into sharper opposition than in the two parts of *Henry IV*. Critics tend to blur this opposition in one of two ways: either by proposing, with various degrees of erudite unsubtlety, that we should not waste sympathetic laughter on Falstaff; or else suggesting that such sympathy, while legitimately evoked by the play as it stands, represents a failure of Shakespeare's intentions. The former approach shows an insensitivity to dramatic texture that need hardly be taken seriously, in site of its advocacy by eminent scholars; while the latter view demands that we should ignore the most striking elements of the play while assessing it. It seems safer to interpret the play by the full formal evidence, without reference to the insoluble problem of intentions. If this is honestly done, one may detect a subtle treatment of human values which should not be ironed out by critical simplification.

Formally, the play appears to present the traditional duality in man. The heroic king-figure is opposed by the gross and unheroic form of Falstaff; it is *feritas* against *divinitas*, temptation against triumph, even (if we like) sin against grace. The action of the play represents the rejection of the lower elements to vindicate the royal or heroic ideal. So far, the pattern is that of an orthodox allegory that we may interpret at the political, moral, or theological level; and some interpreters feel no need to go further.

But it is the most patent truth about the play that at point after point, our intuitive response to this opposition is quite the reverse. Shakespeare confuses our responses so that such a simple moral interpretation is impossible. Many elements in the balance are transferred to the unorthodox side, so that an ideal may be divorced from the power needed to realize it, or a vice compounded with an indispensable human faculty. This is much more complex than mere antinomianism or inversion of values; but it does mean that the simple royal ideal is rejected for good. The dramatic sympathy attaches in great measure to the gross, unheroic aspect of man.

Nor is this sympathy born of pity or humility. For who can deny that the figure of Falstaff is an embodiment of energy and vitality? Of imagination too, for Falstaff opens up a new poetic dimension in all he talks about, be it Diana's foresters, or the lantern in Bardolph's poop, or 'a fork'd radish, with a head fantastically carved upon it with a knife'. This is a dimension that the kingly ideal leaves out of account, or rather rejects consciously: but it is with no sense of distaste that Shakespeare incorporates it in the spirit of Falstaff. Rather, it whets new appetites, suggests new possibilities of experience that will not be denied. 'Banish plump Jack, and banish all the world.'

What Falstaff *achieves* with this comprehensive power is of course a different question. But he shows an undeniable zest and acumen that we feel must leaven any true achievement. Neither gout, pox, nor white hairs can quite constitute an ironic negation of this energy. Rather, it coexists with them. In fact, it joyfully seizes upon them as matter through which it may declare itself the more strongly: 'valiant Jack Falstaff—and therefore more valiant, being, as he is, old Jack Falstaff . . .' (Pt. I, II. iv. 459–61). A comprehensive and satisfying humanity must incorporate many elements of the Falstaffian image. It must be built up through a full admission of the gross, the enfeebling, the intractable—even the sinful, because the vital energy of man is seen to lie in indivisible compound with these.

We are obviously approaching the Sceptical concept of man that we had noted at the outset in Montaigne, and the somewhat different Scepticism of Rabelais as well. But this generic resemblance conceals a radical difference between Shakespeare and the French authors, which may best be summed up by saying that what provides Montaigne and Rabelais with their crowning concepts of man are in Shakespeare only Falstaff's views, a mere starting-point for Shakespeare's own. Montaigne's celebration of humanity—more correctly, his preoccupation with it— was based on a sense of the littleness of man and the impossibility of a broader apprehension of things. It conceived of man as essentially linked to his body and markedly affected by his appetites: '. . . on the loftiest throne in the world, we are still sitting only on our own rump.' (*Essais,* III. 13, *De l'experience.*) This is a very Falstaffian sentiment. Indeed, Falstaff would surely evince a far more vehement, though not unenvious, contempt for elevated stations. Was not King Henry like a singing-man of Windsor, and did not the Hostess's eldest son resemble the Lord Chief Justice? 'God help the while! a bad world, I say.' But as this very vehemence may make us suspect, this Sceptical view of man is not the total theme of the play. Rather, it is checked and corrected within the total context in a way that I shall presently demonstrate.

The resemblance to Rabelais is a more immediate problem, for 'Rabelaisian' and 'Falstaffian' are commonly taken as synonyms. But I believe there is a notable difference between the two authors. To appreciate this, however, we must begin further back and treat the whole question of Falstaff's Scepticism (by no means the same thing as Shakespeare's own). We can hardly expect a systematic negation of the fields of knowledge one by one; but many of man's cherished methods and ideas are exploded.

Falstaff's demolition of honour is indeed too well-known to need mention; but the passage is worth quoting for another reason:

What is honour? A word. What is in that word? Honour. What is that honour?
Air. A trim reckoning! Who hath it? He that died o' Wednesday. Doth he feel
it? No. Doth he hear it? No. 'Tis insensible, then? Yea, to the dead.
(Pt. I, V. i. 133–7)

It is not only honour that is negated here, but the method of instruction through
catechism. Logical processes are similarly reduced to absurdity:

PRINCE: Sir John stands to his word—the devil shall have his bargain; for he was
never yet a breaker of proverbs; he will give the devil his due.
POINS: Then art thou damn'd for keeping thy word with the devil.
PRINCE: Else he had been damn'd for cozening the devil.   (Pt. I, I. ii. 113–19)

Christian morals are parodied, more daringly, a little earlier:

Why, Hal, 'tis my vocation, Hal; 'tis no sin for a man to labour in his vocation.
(Pt. I, I. ii. 101–2)

and much later as well:

Care I for the limb, the thews, the stature, bulk, and big assemblance of a man!
Give me the spirit, Master Shallow.   (Pt. II, III. ii. 251–3)

False figures of rhetoric are unblushingly exploited:

PRINCE: Sirrah, do I owe you a thousand pound?
FALSTAFF: A thousand pound, Hal! A million. Thy love is worth a million: thou
owest me thy love.   (Pt. I, III. iii. 135–7)

In a word, intellectual methods are totally exploded, reduced to jests and
playthings. And it is because they are so reduced that Falstaff can utilize them to
provide an ironic rationale for his own actions:

Counterfeit? I lie, I am no counterfeit: to die is to be a counterfeit; for he is but
the counterfeit of a man who hath not the life of a man; but to counterfeit
dying, when a man thereby liveth, is to be no counterfeit, but the true and
perfect image of life indeed.   (Pt. I, V. iv. 114–19)

And again:

I disprais'd him before the wicked—that the wicked might not fall in love with
thee; in which doing, I have done the part of a careful friend and a true
subject; . . .   (Pt. II. II. iv. 308–10)

Needless to say, Falstaff is not convinced by his own logic, nor does he expect
anyone else to be. He is merely concerned with self-preservation, indulgence of his
appetites, and instinctive defence of his misdoings. He does not see the need to
satisfy any higher ideal of conduct, as he is fully convinced of the hollowness of all
such values and ideals. And as a final mock at these rejected values, he tosses
fragments of them into his speeches, as a dog trots about with a plaything that is
'dead'.

The same cynicism lies behind Falstaff's consciously overdone mendacity. Of course he does not expect to be believed; and to many readers, his unblushing fictions are simply proof of his exuberant imagination. But unless I am much mistaken, they show also a cynical contempt for both fact and opinion that must not be overlooked because of the gay abandon that clothes it. As Bradley says, 'There is nothing serious in any of them [the lies] except the refusal to take anything seriously.' Or, in Harbage's stronger indictment, 'His seems to be the larger guilt of having no principles.' If people do not believe Falstaff, he does not care. They will at least know that he insists on having his own way, without discipline or altruism. This is the libertine spirit at its most sterile.

The Falstaffian spirit now begins to show in a new and less flattering light. His pristine, irrational vitality hides an essential cynicism, a sense of the futility of all values and the impossibility of achievement. The Falstaffian energy may be necessary leaven for all human activity; but in Falstaff himself, it remains frustrated for lack of any object or direction. In a truer sense than he knows, 'pregnancy is made a tapster, and his quick wit wasted in giving reckonings' (Pt. II, I. ii. 160–2).

Falstaff's buoyancy exists in curious combination with an innate defeatism:

> If I become not a cart as well as another man, a plague on my bringing up! I hope I shall as soon be strangled with a halter as another.
>
> (Pt. I, II. iv. 479–81)

In the last analysis, Falstaff's picture of life is very bleak, and he looks forward to no future at all. He can thus accept war casually, as an exercise in killing the regulation number of men.

> . . . food for powder, food for powder; they'll fill a pit as well as better: . . .
>
> (Pt. I, IV. ii. 63–4)

His account of his own virtue merely reveals that it is impossible for him to be virtuous—perhaps impossible for any man:

> I was as virtuously given as a gentleman need to be; virtuous enough: swore little, dic'd not above seven times a week, went to a bawdy-house not above once in a quarter—of an hour, paid money that I borrowed—three or four times . . .   (Pt. I, III. iii. 14–18)

In fact, he is resigned to an endemic sense of sin:

> Thou knowest in the state of innocency Adam fell; and what should poor Jack Falstaff do in the days of villainy?   (Pt. I, III. iii. 164–6)

To know the world is to fall. For Falstaff, the ideal of a comprehensive life seems incompatible with virtue:

> Before I knew thee, Hal, I knew nothing; and now am I, if a man should speak truly, little better than one of the wicked.   (Pt. I, I. ii. 90–2)

In a word, Falstaff is a sceptic not only in the technical or philosophic sense but the popular one as well. He views the world without apparent gloom, but with a degree of levity and cynicism unthinkable for the contemplative philosopher essaying to establish a tenable code of life in the absence of absolute values. Unlike Falstaff, such a philosopher would not be able to borrow ten pounds from the Hostess in full assurance that he cannot repay an earlier hundred marks; nor seize any man's horse to greet the young king at his coronation; nor, of course, misuse the King's press damnably. Falstaff does all this, and with aplomb too; but he has to pay for it by consciously divorcing himself from all norms that might have upheld his actions. There is nothing he can look to beyond the pursuit of his immediate satisfaction.

Nowhere does Falstaff's defeatism show itself more clearly than in his attitude to the flesh. Here at long last we may take up the question of his contrast with Gargantua and Pantagruel. In Rabelais, we have a celebration of the appetites; drink and sex provide a direct solution to Sceptical bewilderment. Of Rabelais indeed one may say that he takes the duality of soul and body, god and beast, and solves it simply by aggrandizing the latter element to heroic proportions. Shakespeare's solution is less simple.

For Falstaff the flesh is indeed both origin and receptacle of the joys of life; but at the same time, it is a burden and a weariness, a perpetual reminder of human frailty. His bulk enfeebles him in the most literal sense. Witness his trials on Gad's Hill when Poins hides his horse: 'Have you any levers to lift me up again, being down?' As for the moral impediment:

> POINS: . . . Jack, how agrees the devil and thee about thy soul, that thou soldest
> him on Good Friday last for a cup of Madeira and a cold capon's leg?
> (Pt. I, I. ii. 110–12)

'Thou seest I have more flesh than another man, and therefore more frailty.' The appetites are not taken as heroic. They are seen to be imperfections, and Falstaff gets a sort of resigned, indolent pleasure in contemplating this imperfection in himself. This is not to deny that he empties his cup of sack with the profoundest satisfaction to his throat; but this is compounded with a sense of his frailty in drinking it. Paradoxically, it is a comforting sense, indicating the frailty and futility of life generally, which justifies him in indulging his own weaknesses.

I wonder if this paradox cannot be substantiated by another: nowhere in the two parts of the play can we find a single speech where Falstaff directly states these motives for drinking. Rather, he argues more than once that 'If sack and sugar be a fault, God help the wicked!' Above all, he delivers in Part II his celebrated eulogy of the ennobling properties of sherris-sack (IV. iii. 103ff.) It is, of course, the style and context of these speeches that turn the apparent praise of drink into ironic banter, the usual hollow reasons trotted out with easy cynicism to gloss over indefensible addiction. The first-quoted speech is part of an ironic display of one-sided rhetoric and a parody of contemporary literary style. The second speech parodies contemporary medical methods. They show less true faith in the virtuous powers of sack than mere lack of faith in an ideal of abstention.

I have tried to define the limits of the Falstaffian ideal from the basic premises of the ideal itself, not the darker elements that are thought, with some justice, to overshadow it in Part II. In so far as Falstaff challenges the inadequacy of the orthodox order, his more comprehensive ethos seems feasible and attractive; but it achieves nothing, and its comprehensiveness finally proves to be sadly spurious. His topsy-turvydom holds meaning only as a temporary aberration from the norm.

The problem is that while Falstaff declines in stature, these normative values, as embodied in the royal ideal, do not acquire a compensating validity. This is what makes *Henry IV*—or the 'second tetralogy' of History Plays as a whole—so uncertain in dramatic effect. We are presented with two opposite, incompatible approaches to life: ethical alternatives that seem to cancel each other out.

—SUKANTA CHAUDHURI, "Falstaff and the King," *Infirm Glory: Shakespeare and the Renaissance Image of Man* (Oxford: Clarendon Press, 1981), pp. 122–29

COPPÉLIA KAHN

To conclude this anatomy of Shakespearean cuckoldry, let me evoke the curious and comic figure of Falstaff in *The Merry Wives of Windsor,* lurking impatiently by the great oak in Windsor Park at midnight, a buck's head with spreading antlers planted on his shoulders. Tricked into an assignation with Mistress Ford, he is discovered according to plan, and conclusively exposed, mocked, and rejected as a would-be cuckolder. It might seem that Shakespeare violates convention here, by putting the despised horns on the cuckolder's head instead of the cuckold's. But a closer look reveals, I believe, that the poet has gathered up into the horned Falstaff all the ambivalence of cuckoldry as a product of misogyny, patriarchal marriage, and the double standard. Falstaff's antlers are richly multivalent.

They are associated first with virility as divine power. Falstaff's soliloquy puts forth this ancient idea in a comic vein because the fat, excited, sweating knight is so obviously human rather than divine as he would like to be:

> Now, the hot-blooded gods assist me! Remember, Jove, thou wast a bull for thy Europa; love set on thy horns. O powerful love, that in some respects makes a beast a man; in some other, a man a beast. You were also, Jupiter, a swan for the love of Leda. O omnipotent love, how near the god drew to the complexion of a goose! . . . When gods have hot backs, what shall poor men do? For me, I am here a Windsor stag, and the fattest, I think, i' th' forest. Send me a cool rut-time, Jove, or who can blame me to piss my tallow?
>
> (5.5.2–15)

The speech traces Jove's declension from bull (an animal worshipped almost universally from prehistoric times for its fertilizing power) to swan to goose, the emblem of folly, thus setting the keynote of grandeur mixed with folly, god with beast, love with lust, which resonates through the scene. In man's sexual behavior these distant opposites meet and clash.

Second, when Falstaff is "dis-horned" by Ford and Page, and publicly humiliated, he becomes the scapegoat in whom the disruptive force of lust is embodied and symbolically rejected, whose sacrifice serves, as Jeanne Addison Roberts argues, "to draw the social group together and to create a new harmony." The play abounds in sexual rivalries, notably, Falstaff against the wives and the husbands; the wives against their husbands, particularly Mistress Ford against her jealous mate; Caius, Slender, and Fenton all vying for Anne Page's hand; and "Master Brooks" against Master Ford. The community of Windsor is based on marriage, and its domestic tranquillity is threatened not only by Falstaff the opportunistic outsider, but also by its own internal tensions; by making him the scapegoat of lust and sexual competition, the community cleanses itself of them. In this context, Falstaff's horns, which are specifically antlers, are most strongly associated with the deer as pathetic victim, that animal's typical role in Shakespeare. Falstaff is punished more than he deserves, for everyone's sexual license as well as his own, and when in the final speech of the play Ford says to Falstaff that "Master Brooke shall lie with Mistress Ford tonight," a transfer of potency and sexual rights is suggested, from the would-be cuckolder to the rightful possessor of his wife's sexual favors, her husband Master Ford alias Brooke. Thus sexuality is returned to its proper well-ordered sphere within marriage.

Finally, the stag-horned Falstaff in the forest recalls the figure of Actaeon, the hunter turned into a stag as punishment for inadvertently seeing Diana naked as she bathed. Actaeon is a common cant term for cuckold; in fact, it crops up when cuckoldry is first mentioned in the play. Pistol, warning Ford that Falstaff intends to seduce his wife, says,

> Prevent,
> Or go like Sir Actaeon he,
> With Ringwood at thy heels!
> O, odious is the name!   (2.1.115–117)

Why should Falstaff wear the cuckold's horns, then, when he is the cuckolder who conventionally goes scot-free? Poetic justice offers one answer, for Falstaff gets the horns he intended to give the husbands. This exchange of horns suggests an equality, and an identity, between the cuckolder and his victim that is reinforced when Falstaff says, "My horns I bequeath your husbands" (5.5.26–27) in the mistaken expectation of cuckolding them. The iconography of Actaeon as explicated by Renaissance mythographers also suggests a certain bond between cuckolder and cuckold: a common dilemma of desire as mediated by marriage. Whitney, following tradition, provides this interpretation of Actaeon as an emblem of the bestial transformation of man caused by the ravages of sexual desire:

> . . . those who do pursue
> Theire fancies fonde and thinges unlawful crave

Like brutish beastes appeare unto the viewe . . .
. . . . soe theire affections base
Shall them devoure, and all theire deedes deface.

As Actaeon was torn apart by his hounds, who mistook their master for their prey, so Falstaff is parodically pinched by fairies and deprived of his horns, his potency. This mockery of his desire, however, resembles the mockery of the cuckold's virility expressed *in* his horns, even though horns are removed in Falstaff's case and implanted in the cockold's.

As the horned cuckolder, he embodies the plight of all men, which is corollary to the double standard and the sexual property in woman allotted to them by patriarchal marriage. The double standard grants free sexual activity to men only, but marriage, by making their honor and virility depend on their wives' chastity, turns that sexual freedom into a threat. It makes every husband a potential cuckold, and gives every man, married or not, the opportunity to "plume his will" by cuckolding his friend. Cuckoldry, like rape, is thus an affair between men, rather than between men and women or husbands and wives, though men blame women for betraying them. The horned Falstaff, then, is an emblem of Everyman as both cuckold and cuckolder, victim and offender; "the savage yoke" of marriage subjugates all men. Falstaff's horns as an emblem of virility are mocked as virility is mocked by the peculiar institution of marriage, which makes men monsters of jealousy and monsters as cuckolds, beasts in lust and beasts in that their wives and other men can lead them by the nose as easily as asses.

—COPPÉLIA KAHN, " 'The Savage Yoke': Cuckoldry and Marriage," *Man's Estate: Masculine Identity in Shakespeare* (Berkeley: University of California Press, 1981), pp. 147–50

JONATHAN HALL

If Rabelais's giants are left aside, the two greatest carnival Fat Men of Renaissance literature, Falstaff and Sancho Panza, are both the product of reflection upon the contradictions which they mediate. The simple association of Falstaff with folk origins, and more directly with the figure of Vice in the morality plays, is by no means a new idea. But his comic function in *The Merry Wives of Windsor* is more straightforward than in *Henry IV*. In the comedy it is directly related to the world of carnival reversal, and to the old somewhat inconsequential breakdown of sexual identity and of the distinction between human and animal. The plot affirms a carnival utopianism insofar as the unmasking of Falstaff in the name of social order (represented by parental will) turns out to be precisely the defeat of the oppressive and deceitful within that order. The moon, the oak, the fairies, the superstitious fictions themselves, all turn out to have sway. This 'poetic' comedy consists in the defeat of the normal. Falstaff's presence enables the triumph of ambiguous interchangeability. The history play, however, tells of another outcome.

Frazer and many others have shown that the European carnival had its roots in ritual and the cyclical conception of time. However, it is necessary to state clearly that the affirmation of cyclical renewal, in its carnival form, was not pure ritual. In fact, it often parodied ritual to a great extent. Also it did not merely blot out history but provided a means of dealing with it. Mircea Eliade illuminatingly argues that the cyclical view of time served to protect men from the 'terror of history' which arises from an awareness of history's linearity. This striking phrase is a chapter title in his book on the cyclical conception of time. Eliade's book offers a historical schema in which the conception of linear history is superimposed upon the earlier cyclical versions of time. But his own account is not purely linear, because the emergence of the concept of linear time in the period from the late Middle Ages until the seventeenth century is in part a repetition of the earlier imposition of Judaic eschatology upon more primitive cyclical conceptions. The main interest of his argument is not in the old idea that cyclical time gives way to linear time, but in the notion that the cyclical persists in a transformed way within the linear. As a form of resistance to the 'terror of history', it is then the dialectical counterpart of linear history; it becomes a form of heightened awareness of the linearity that it resists. In this sense, the carnival represented in cultural practice a complex interaction of an awareness of history and a relativizing refusal of it. This complemented the resistance to hierarchical order discussed earlier. The conjunction has a great bearing on Shakespeare's use of carnival motifs in *Henry IV*.

Henry IV (Parts 1 and 2) is a historical play in a much deeper sense than in that of being a mere chronicle. The rift between Prince Henry and Falstaff is momentous because it transcends the terms in which Prince Henry himself understands it. The action of the play is concerned with the emergence of the new linear historical outlook, with its stern national purposiveness. In part this is pitted against feudal divisiveness, but it also struggles against the relativistic, cyclical concept of time with its concomitant denial of the new heroic ethic. Falstaff is the embodiment of those values which offer protection, in Eliade's striking phrase, against the 'terror of history'. His ultimate casting-off is therefore deeply serious, particularly for a pre-Puritan audience. (It might be called 'the death of parody'!) It is remarkable how Falstaff is first introduced as the carnivalistic denier of time:

> PRINCE: What a devil hast thou to do with the time of the day? Unless hours were cups of sack and minutes capons, and clocks the tongues of bawds, and dials the signs of leaping-houses and the blessed sun himself a fair hot wench in flame-coloured taffeta, I see no reason why thou shouldst be so superfluous to demand the time of the day.   (I, ii, 6–11)

The sexual transformation of the sun leads on to reversals under the governance of the moon in the ensuing dialogue. This is Falstaff's domain, and in this context he brings up the carnival theme of the reversal of official justice:

> FALSTAFF: . . . but, I prithee, sweet wag, shall there be gallows standing in England when thou art king, and resolution thus fubb'd as it is with the rusty curb of old father antic, the law? Do not thou, when thou art king, hang a thief.

PRINCE: No; thou shalt.

FALSTAFF: Shall I? O rare! By the Lord, I'll be a brave judge!

PRINCE: Thou judgest false already: I mean thou shalt have the hanging of the
thieves, and so become a rare hangman.   (I, ii, 56–66)

The same carnival theme recurs in the governorship of Sancho Panza and the elevation of Azdak (as well as in many other places, of course). Here the citation of the reversal in dialogue (rather than its actual enactment) gives it a muted but significant ambiguity. Falstaff claims as part of his sway the abolition of execution, whereas Prince Henry reinstates it. If Henry is participating verbally in a carnivalesque reversal, he is nonetheless making judgements alien to the carnival. It is from this alien standpoint that he judges Falstaff to be false. Thus the play does not simply operate on a series of contrasts between the historical scenes and the carnivalized ones; the ambivalent dialogue between Prince Henry and Falstaff brings the concerns of historical awareness within the carnival. As we have said already, this in itself is consistent with the carnival; but what is new is that in the end the new historical consciousness breaks the efficacy of the old modes of dealing with disaster. It is on this sinister note that the most overtly carnivalized scene of the whole play ends, the scene in the Boar's Head Inn which parodies royal authority but at the same time anticipates the actual banishment of Falstaff. This scene ends with the old carnival Lenten motif of the struggle of the Fat and the Thin, ending not in renewal but in the end of the world as understood in the 'old' manner (for Falstaff's age is as strongly emphasized as his fatness and sensuality):

FALSTAFF: If to be old and merry be a sin, then many an old host that I know
is damn'd; if to be fat be to be hated, then Pharaoh's lean kine are to be
loved. No, my good lord: banish Peto, banish Bardolph, banish Poins; but
for sweet Jack Falstaff, kind Jack Falstaff, true Jack Falstaff, valiant Jack
Falstaff . . . banish not him thy Harry's company. *Banish plump Jack, and
banish all the world.* [my emphasis]

PRINCE: I do, I will.   (II, iv, 454–64)

If Julius Caesar's preference for fat men simply refers to the carnival motif (and certainly the lean unleash the 'terror of history' together with its new possibilities for tragic heroism in that play), here Shakespeare does more than refer to the theme; he foregrounds it, placing it at the centre of a play about the emergence of purposive, linear historical consciousness. The capacity for greatness is measured against a terrible loss, which has little to do with sympathy for Falstaff as a 'character'. *Henry IV, Part I* ends with yet another carnival scene, the resurrection of the Fat Man from his 'death' and the re-enactment of the struggle with the Thin, as Falstaff stabs the already dead Hotspur. For the ethics of heroism this is mere lying, but Falstaff's words stand affirmatively against such ethics:

FALSTAFF: 'Sblood 'twas time to counterfeit, or that hot termagant Scot had paid
me scot and lot too. Counterfeit? I lie, I am no counterfeit: to die is to be

> a counterfeit; for he is but the counterfeit of a man who hath not the life
> of a man; but to counterfeit a dying, when a man hereby liveth, is to be
> no counterfeit, *but the true and perfect image of life indeed.* [my em-
> phasis]   (V. iv. 113–18)

Falstaff here speaks for the logic of the carnival. But his denial of the heroic and the
historical is itself ultimately denied by Prince Henry, and at least partly by Shakespeare. If the comedy unreservedly celebrates the values of the carnival as they
triumph, the history play measures the impotence of values that resist only through
words, and words moreover which now begin to appear as mere deceit. In the
new world of royal absolutism the carnivalesque is at most poetic metaphor.

So Shakespeare's *Henry IV* does not simply employ the carnival motifs within
a historical play. The play is not historical in the mere sense of being about past
events, however momentous they were. It is more importantly about a major
historical development enacted within its own present discourse, namely the divorce of the popular and traditional carnival outlook (with its relativizing, comic,
bodily anti-heroism and cyclical view of life) from the linear, historical and heroic
purposiveness of the new forms of royal power and ideology. The dialogue between Prince Henry and Falstaff exists to give full dramatic measure to the break.
Thus the carnivalesque in Shakespeare's play is not in simple continuity with the
past. The carnival motifs function with a new vigour in the literary work by pointing
to the historical impossibility of their actual continuance. Re-expressed in terms of
modern ideology, the historical break dramatized by Shakespeare conveys the total
separation of the utopian from the historical. In Shakespeare's version of history
there is therefore a serious loss as well as a triumph, and perhaps the tragedies can
also be understood historically as dramatic explorations of the implications of
unredeemable linear historical time.

> —JONATHAN HALL, "Falstaff, Sancho Panza and Azdak: Carnival and History,"
> *Comparative Criticism* 7 (1985): 131–34

TERRY EAGLETON

If the self in Shakespeare is divided between desire and position, then characters
who have scant regard for the latter are likely to escape a potentially tragic disunity.
Sir John Falstaff of *Henry IV* is more at home with drunks than dukes, and so
represents a danger to political stability apparent at once in his body and speech.
His body is so grossly material that he can hardly move; his language so shifty that
it resists all truth. Within the single figure of Falstaff, both body and language are
pressed to a self-parodic extreme. He falls 'below' social order in being too sheerly,
stubbornly himself, a brazen hedonist who refuses to conform the body's drives to
social decorum. Yet he also falls 'beyond' that order in his fantastical speech, as
hollow as his body is full, which can spin twelve rogues in buckram suits out of two

in as many lines. Falstaff can turn the brute materiality of the body against the airy abstractions of ruling-class rhetoric:

> Can honour set a leg? No. Or an arm? No. Or take away the grief of a wound? No. Honour hath no skill in surgery, then? No. What is honour? A word. What is in that word? Honour. What is that honour? Air. (1.V.i.130–4)

But he is himself one of Shakespeare's most shameless verbal mystifiers, divorcing word from deed in his pathological boasting, recklessly erasing distinctions in his metaphorical excess:

> FALSTAFF: . . . 'Sblood, I am as melancholy as a gib cat or a lugg'd bear.
> PRINCE: Or an old lion, or a lover's lute.
> FALSTAFF: Yea, or the drone of a Lincolnshire bagpipe.
> PRINCE: What sayest thou to a hare, or the melancholy of Moor Ditch?
> (1.I.ii.71–6)

If Falstaff appeals to the sensuous facts of the body to deflate ideological illusions, he also has a remarkably cavalier way with such facts:

> FALSTAFF: Give me a cup of sack; I am a rogue if I drunk today.
> PRINCE: O villain! thy lips are scarce wip'd since thou drunk'st last.
> FALSTAFF: All is one for that.

Both aspects of Falstaff—reductive materialism and verbal licence—belong to the carnivalesque, the satiric comedy of the people; but it is interesting to note their incongruity. Social order is subverted simultaneously from two opposed directions: by that which is purely and materially itself, the self-pleasuring body which refuses to be inscribed by social imperatives; and by that which is never at one with itself at all, the iconoclastic idiom of those who run verbal rings round their solemnly prosaic opponents. Unlike the comsummately self-conscious Henry and Hal, Falstaff is in one sense an indifferent actor, playing only himself, at ease within his own voluminous space and incapable of deferring or dissembling his appetites; yet in the tavern drama he shifts fluently between the parts of Hal and Henry, with the infinite opportunism of one who is both all and nothing.

—TERRY EAGLETON, "Language: *Macbeth, Richard II, Henry IV,*"
William Shakespeare (Oxford: Basil Blackwell, 1986), pp. 15–16

CRITICAL ESSAYS

Maurice Morgann

THE DRAMATIC CHARACTER OF FALSTAFF

The ideas which I have formed concerning the Courage and Military Character of the Dramatic Sir *John Falstaff,* are so different from those which I find generally to prevail in the world, that I shall take the liberty of stating my sentiments on the subject; in hope that some person as unengaged as myself, will either correct and reform my error in this respect; or, joining himself to my opinion, redeem me from, what I may call, the reproach of singularity.

I am to avow then, that I do not clearly discern that Sir *John Falstaff* deserves to bear the character so generally given him of an absolute Coward; or, in other words, that I do not conceive *Shakespeare* ever meant to make Cowardice an essential part of his constitution. ⟨. . .⟩

It will scarcely be possible to consider the Courage of *Falstaff* as wholly detached from his other qualities: But I write not professedly of any part of his character, but what is included under the term, *Courage;* however I may incidentally throw some lights on the whole.—The reader will not need to be told that this Inquiry will resolve itself of course into a Critique on the genius, the arts, and the conduct of *Shakespeare:* For what is *Falstaff,* what *Lear,* what *Hamlet,* or *Othello,* but different modifications of *Shakespeare's* thought? It is true that this Inquiry is narrowed almost to a single point: but general criticism is as uninstructive as it is easy: *Shakespeare* deserves to be considered in detail;—a task hitherto unattempted.

It may be proper, in the first place, to take a short view of all the parts of *Falstaff's* Character, and then proceed to discover, if we can, what *Impressions,* as to Courage or Cowardice, he had made on the persons of the Drama: After which we will examine, in course, such evidence, either of *persons* or *facts,* as are relative to the matter; and account as we may for those appearances, which seem to have led to the opinion of his Constitutional Cowardice.

The scene of the robbery, and the disgraces attending it, which stand first in

From *An Essay on the Dramatic Character of Sir John Falstaff* (London: T. Davies, 1777), pp. 1–2, 15–47, 166–85.

the Play, and introduce us to the knowledge of *Falstaff*, I shall beg leave (as I think this scene to have been the source of much unreasonable prejudice) to *reserve* till we are more fully acquainted with the whole character of *Falstaff*; and I shall therefore hope that the reader will not for a time advert to it, or to the jests of the *Prince* or of *Poins* in consequence of that unlucky adventure.

In drawing out the parts of *Falstaff*'s character, with which I shall begin this Inquiry, I shall take the liberty of putting Constitutional bravery into his composition; but the reader will be pleased to consider what I shall say in that respect as spoken hypothetically for the present, to be retained, or discharged out of it, as he shall finally determine.

To me then it appears that the leading quality in *Falstaff*'s character, and that from which all the rest take their colour, is a high degree of wit and humour, accompanied with great natural vigour and alacrity of mind. This quality so accompanied, led him probably very early into life, and made him highly acceptable to society; so acceptable, as to make it seem unnecessary for him to acquire any other virtue. Hence, perhaps, his continued debaucheries and dissipations of every kind.— He seems, by nature, to have had a mind free of malice or any evil principle; but he never took the trouble of acquiring any good one. He found himself esteemed and beloved with all his faults; nay *for* his faults, which were all connected with humour, and for the most part, grew out of it. As he had, possibly, no vices but such as he thought might be openly professed, so he appeared more dissolute thro' ostentation. To the character of wit and humour, to which all his other qualities seem to have conformed themselves, he appears to have added a very necessary support, *that* of the profession of a *Soldier*. He had from nature, as I presume to say, a spirit of boldness and enterprise; which in a Military age, tho' employment was only occasional, kept him always above contempt, secured him an honourable reception among the Great, and suited best both with his particular mode of humour and of vice. Thus living continually in society, nay even in Taverns, and indulging himself, and being indulged by others, in every debauchery; drinking, whoring, gluttony, and ease; assuming a liberty of fiction, necessary perhaps to his wit, and often falling into falsity and lies, he seems to have set, by degrees, all sober reputation at defiance; and finding eternal resources in his wit, he borrows, shifts, defrauds, and even robs, without dishonour.—Laughter and approbation attend his greatest excesses; and being governed visibly by no settled bad principle or ill design, fun and humour account for and cover all. By degrees, however, and thro' indulgence, he acquires bad habits, becomes an humourist, grows enormously corpulent, and falls into the infirmities of age; yet never quits, all the time, one single levity or vice of youth, or loses any of that chearfulness of mind, which had enabled him to pass thro' this course with ease to himself and delight to others; and thus, at last, mixing youth and age, enterprize and corpulency, wit and folly, poverty and expence, title and buffoonery, innocence as to purpose, and wickedness as to practice; neither incurring hatred by bad principle, or contempt by Cowardice, yet involved in circumstances productive of imputation in both; a butt and a wit, a humourist and a man of humour, a touchstone and a laughing stock, a jester and a jest, has Sir *John Falstaff,* taken at that period of his life in which we see him, become the most perfect Comic character that perhaps ever was exhibited.

It may not possibly be wholly amiss to remark in this place, that if Sir *John Falstaff* had possessed any of that Cardinal quality, Prudence, alike the guardian of virtue and the protector of vice; that quality, from the possession or the absence of which, the character and fate of men in this life take, I think, their colour, and not from real vice or virtue; if he had considered his wit not as *principal* but *accessary* only; as the instrument of power, and not as power itself; if he had had much baseness to hide, if he had had less of what may be called mellowness or good humour, or less of health and spirit; if he had spurred and rode the world with his wit, instead of suffering the world, boys and all, to ride him;—he might, without any other essential change, have been the admiration and not the jest of mankind:—Or if he had lived in our day, and instead of attaching himself to one Prince, had renounced *all* friendship and *all* attachment, and had let himself out as the ready instrument and Zany of every successive Minister, he might possibly have acquired the high honour of marking his shroud or decorating his coffin with the living rays of an Irish at least, if not a British Coronet: Instead of which, tho' enforcing laughter from every disposition, he appears, now, as such a character which every wise man will pity and avoid, every knave will censure, and every fool will fear: And accordingly *Shakespeare,* ever true to nature, has made *Harry* desert, and Lancaster censure him:—He dies where he lived, in a Tavern, broken-hearted, without a friend; and his final exit is given up to the derision of fools. Nor has his misfortunes ended here; the scandal arising from the misapplication of his wit and talents seems immortal. He has met with as little justice or mercy from his final judges the critics, as from his companions of the Drama. With our cheeks still red with laughter, we ungratefully as unjustly censure him as a coward by nature, and a rascal upon principle: Tho', if this were so, it might be hoped, for our own credit, that we should behold him rather with disgust and disapprobation than with pleasure and delight.

But to remember our question—*Is Falstaff a constitutional coward?*

With respect to every infirmity, except that of Cowardice, we must take him as at the period in which he is represented to us. If we see him dissipated, fat,—it is enough;—we have nothing to do with his youth, when he might perhaps have been modest, chaste, *'and not an Eagle's talon in the waist'.* But *Constitutional Courage* extends to a man's whole life, makes a part of his nature, and is not to be taken up or deserted like a mere Moral quality. It is true, there is a Courage founded upon *principle,* or rather a principle independent of Courage, which will sometimes operate in spite of nature; a principle, which prefers death to shame, but which always refers itself, in conformity to its own nature, to the prevailing modes of honour, and the fashions of the age.—But Natural courage is another thing: It is independent of opinion; It adapts itself to occasions, preserves itself under every shape, and can avail itself of flight as well as of action.—In the last war, some Indians of America perceiving a line of Highlanders to keep their station under every disadvantage, and under a fire which they could not effectually return, were so miserably mistaken in our points of honour as to conjecture, from observation on the habit and stability of those troops, that they were indeed the women of England, who wanted courage to run away.—That Courage which is founded in nature and constitution, *Falstaff,* as I presume to say, possessed;—but I am ready to allow, that the principle already mentioned, so far as it refers to reputation only, began with every other Moral quality to lose its hold on him in his old age; that is, at the time of life in which he is represented to us; a period, as it should seem, approaching to *seventy.*—The truth is that he had drollery enough to support himself in credit without the point of honour, and had address enough to make even the preservation of his life a point of drollery. The reader knows I allude, tho' something prematurely, to his fictitious death in the battle of Shrewsbury. This incident is generally construed to the disadvantage of *Falstaff:* It is a transaction which bears the external marks of Cowardice: It is also aggravated to the spectators by the idle tricks of the Player, who practises on this occasion all the attitudes and wild apprehensions of fear; more ambitious, as it should seem, of representing a Caliban than a *Falstaff;* or indeed rather a poor unweildy miserable Tortoise than either.—The painful Comedian lies spread out on his belly, and not only covers himself all over with his robe as with a shell, but forms a kind of round Tortoise-back by I know not what stuffing or contrivance; in addition to which, he alternately lifts up, and depresses, and dodges his head, and looks to the one side and to the other, so much with the piteous aspect of that animal, that one would not be sorry to see the ambitious imitator calipashed in his robe, and served up for the enter-tainment of the gallery.—There is no hint for this mummery in the Play: Whatever there may be of dishonour in *Falstaff*'s conduct, he neither does or says any thing on this occasion which indicates terror or disorder of mind: On the contrary, this very act is a proof of his having all his wits about him, and is a stratagem, such as it is, not improper for a buffoon, whose fate would be singularly hard, if he should not be allowed to avail himself of his Character when it might serve him in most stead. We must remember, in extenuation, that the executive, the destroying hand of *Douglas* was over him: *'It was time to counterfeit, or that hot termagant Scot had paid him scot and lot too.'* He had but one choice; he was obliged to pass thro' the ceremony of dying either in jest or in earnest; and we shall not be surprized at the event, when we remember his propensities to the former.—Life (and especially the life of *Falstaff*) might be a jest; but he could see no joke whatever in dying: To be chopfallen was, with him, to lose both life and character together: He saw the point of honour, as well as every thing else, in ridiculous lights, and began to renounce its tyranny.

But I am too much in advance, and must retreat for more advantage. I should not forget how much opinion is against me, and that I am to make my way by the mere force and weight of evidence; without which I must not hope to possess myself of the reader: No address, no insinuation will avail. To this evidence, then, I now resort. The Courage of *Falstaff* is my Theme: And no passage will I spare from which any thing can be inferred as relative to this point. It would be as vain as injudicious to attempt concealment: How could I escape detection? The Play is in every one's memory, and a single passage remembered in detection would tell, in the mind of the partial observer, for fifty times its real weight. Indeed this argument would be void of all excuse if it declined any difficulty; if it did not meet, if it did not challenge opposition. Every passage then shall be produced from which, in my opinion, any inference, favourable or unfavourable, has or can be drawn;— but not methodically, not formally, as texts for comment, but as chance or convenience shall lead the way; but in what shape soever, they shall be always distinguishingly marked for notice. And so with that attention to truth and candour which ought to accompany even our lightest amusements I proceed to offer such proof as the case will admit, that *Courage* is a part of *Falstaff*'s *Character,* that it belonged to his constitution, and was manifest in the conduct and practice of his whole life.

Let us then examine, as a source of very authentic information, what Impressions *Sir John Falstaff* had made on the characters of the Drama; and in what estimation he is supposed to stand with mankind in general as to the point of Personal Courage. But the quotations we make for this or other purposes, must, it is confessed, be lightly touched, and no particular passage strongly relied on, either in his favour or against him. Every thing which he himself says, or is said of him, is so phantastically discoloured by humour, or folly, or jest, that we must for the most part look to the spirit rather than the letter of what is uttered, and rely at last only on a combination of the whole.

We will begin then, if the reader pleases, by inquiring what Impression the very Vulgar had taken of *Falstaff*. If it is not that of Cowardice, be it what else it may, that of a man of violence, or *a Ruffian in years,* as Harry calls him, or any thing else, it answers my purpose; how insignificant soever the characters or incidents to be first produced may otherwise appear;—for these Impressions must have been taken either from personal knowledge and observation; or, what will do better for my purpose, from common fame. Altho' I must admit some part of this evidence will appear so weak and trifling that it certainly ought not to be produced but in proof Impression only.

The *Hostess Quickly* employs two officers to arrest *Falstaff:* On the mention of his name, one of them immediately observes, *'that it may chance to cost some of them their lives, for that he will stab'*—'Alas a day', says the hostess, *'take heed of him, he cares not what mischief he doth; if his weapon be out, he will foin like any devil; He will spare neither man, woman, or child.'* Accordingly, we find that when they lay hold on him he resists to the utmost of his power, and calls upon *Bardolph,* whose arms are at liberty, to draw. *'Away, varlets, draw Bardolph, cut me off the villain's head, throw the quean in the kennel.'* The officers cry, *a rescue, a rescue!* But the Chief Justice comes in and the scuffle ceases. In another scene, his wench *Doll Tearsheet* asks him *'when he will leave fighting ****** and patch up his old body for heaven'.* This is occasioned by his drawing his rapier, on great provocation, and driving *Pistol,* who is drawn likewise, down stairs, and hurting him in the shoulder. To drive *Pistol* was no great feat; nor do I mention it as such; but upon this occasion it was necessary. *'A Rascal bragging slave,'* says he, *'the rogue fled from me like quicksilver.'* Expressions, which as they remember the cowardice of *Pistol,* seem to prove that *Falstaff* did not value himself on the adventure. Even something may be drawn from *Davy, Shallow*'s serving man, who calls *Falstaff,* in ignorant admiration, the *man of war.* I must observe here, and I beg the reader will notice it, that there is not a single expression dropt by these people, or either of *Falstaff*'s followers, from which may be inferred the least suspicion of Cowardice in his character; and this is I think such an *implied negation* as deserves considerable weight.

But to go a little higher, if, indeed, to consider *Shallow*'s opinion be to go *higher:* It is from him, however, that we get the earliest account of *Falstaff.* He *remembers him a Page to Thomas Mowbray, Duke of Norfolk: 'He broke',* says he, *'Schoggan's head at the Court-Gate when he was but a crack thus high.'* Shallow, throughout, considers him as a great Leader and Soldier, and relates this fact as an early indication only of his future Prowess. *Shallow,* it is true, is a very ridiculous character; but he picked up these Impressions somewhere; and he picked up none of a contrary tendency.—I want at present only to prove that *Falstaff* stood well in the report of common fame as to this point; and he was now near seventy years of age, and had passed in a Military line thro' the active part of his life. At this period common fame may be well considered as the *seal* of his character; a seal which ought not perhaps to be broke open on the evidence of any future transaction.

But to proceed. *Lord Bardolph* was a man of the world, and of sense and observation. He informs *Northumberland,* erroneously indeed, that *Percy* had beaten the King at Shrewsbury. *'The King',* according to him, *'was wounded; the Prince of Wales and the two Blunts slain, certain Nobles,* whom he names, *had escaped by flight; and the Brawn Sir John Falstaff was taken prisoner.'* But how came *Falstaff* into this list? Common fame had put him there. He is singularly obliged to Common fame.—But if he had not been a Soldier of repute, if he had not been brave as well as fat, if he had been *mere brawn,* it would have been more germane to the matter if this lord had put him down among the baggage or the provender. The fact seems to be, that there is a real consequence about Sir *John Falstaff* which is not brought forward: We see him only in his familiar hours; we enter the tavern with *Hal and Poins;* we join in the laugh and *take a pride to gird at him:* But there may be a great deal of truth in what he himself writes to the Prince, that tho' he be *'Jack Falstaff with his Familiars, he is* Sir John *with the rest of Europe'.* It has been remarked, and very truly I believe, that no man is a hero in the eye of his valet-de-chambre; and *thus* it is, we are witnesses only of *Falstaff*'s weakness and buffoonery; our acquaintance is with *Jack Falstaff, Plump Jack,* and *Sir John Paunch;* but if we would look for *Sir John Falstaff,* we must put on, as *Bunyan* would have expressed it, the spectacles of observation. With respect, for instance, to his Military command at Shrewsbury, nothing appears on the surface but the Prince's familiarly saying, in the tone usually assumed when speaking of *Falstaff, 'I will procure this fat rogue a Charge of foot;'* and in another place, *'I will procure thee Jack a Charge of foot; meet me to-morrow in the Temple Hall.'* Indeed we might venture to infer from this, that a Prince of so great ability, whose wildness was only external and assumed, would not have procured, in so nice and critical a conjuncture, a Charge of foot for a known Coward. But there was more it seems in the case: We now find from this report, to which *Lord Bardolph* had given full credit, that the world had its eye upon *Falstaff* as an officer of merit, whom it expected to find in the field, and whose fate in the battle was an object of Public concern: His life was, it seems, very material indeed; a thread of so much dependence, that *fiction,* weaving the fates of Princes, did not think it unworthy, how coarse soever, of being made a part of the tissue.

We shall next produce the evidence of the Chief Justice of England. He inquires of his attendant, *'if the man who was then passing him was* Falstaff; *he who was in question for the robbery'.* The attendant answers affirmatively, but reminds his lord *'that he had since done good service at Shrewsbury';* and the Chief Justice, on this occasion, rating him for his debaucheries, tells him *'that his day's service at Shrewsbury had gilded over his night's exploit at Gads Hill'.* This is surely more than Common fame: *The Chief Justice* must have known his whole character taken together, and must have received the most authentic information, and in the truest colours, of his behaviour in that action.

But, perhaps, after all, the Military men may be esteemed the best judges in points of this nature. Let us hear then *Coleville* of the dale, *a Soldier, in degree a Knight, a famous rebel, and 'whose betters, had they been ruled by him, would have sold themselves dearer':* A man who is of consequence enough to be gaurded by *Blunt* and *led to present execution.* This man yields himself up even to the very Name and Reputation of *Falstaff. 'I think',* says he, *'you are Sir John Falstaff, and in that thought yield me.'* But this is but one only among the men of the sword; they shall be produced then by *dozens,* if that will satisfy. Upon the return of the King and Prince Henry from Wales, the prince seeks out and finds *Falstaff* debauching in a tavern; where *Peto* presently brings an account of ill news from the North; and adds, *'that as he came along he met or overtook a dozen Captains, bare-headed, sweating, knocking at the taverns, and asking every one for* Sir John Falstaff'. He is followed by *Bardolph,* who informs *Falstaff* that *'He must away to the court immediately; a dozen Captains stay at door for him.'* Here is Military evidence in abundance, and *Court evidence* too; for what are we to infer from *Falstaff's* being sent for to Court on this ill news, but that his opinion was to be asked, as a Military man of skill and experience, concerning the defences necessary to be taken. Nor is *Shakespeare* content, here, with leaving us to gather up *Falstaff's better character* from inference and deduction: He comments on the fact by making *Falstaff* observe that *'Men of merit are sought after: The undeserver may sleep when the man of action is called on.'* I do not wish to draw *Falstaff's* character out of his own mouth; but this observation refers to the fact, and is founded in reason. Nor ought we to reject, what in another place he says to the Chief Justice, as it is in the nature of an appeal to his knowledge. *'There is not a dangerous action',* says he, *'can peep out his head but I am thrust upon it.'* The Chief Justice seems by his answer to admit the fact. *'Well, be honest, be honest, and heaven bless your expedition.'* But the whole passage may deserve transcribing.

'Ch. Just. *Well, the King has severed you and Prince Henry. I hear you are going with Lord John of Lancaster, against the Archbishop and the Earl of Northumberland.'*

'*Fals. Yes, I thank your pretty sweet wit for it; but look you pray, all you that kiss my lady peace at home, that our armies join not in a hot day; for I take but two shirts out with me, and I mean not to sweat extraordinarily: If it be a hot day, if I brandish any thing but a bottle, would I might never spit white again. There is not a dangerous action can peep out his head but I am thrust upon it. Well I cannot last for ever.—But it was always the trick of our English nation, if they have a good thing to make it too common. If you will needs say I am an old man you should give me rest: I would to God my name were not so terrible to the enemy as it is. I were better to be eaten to death with a rust than to be scour'd to nothing with perpetual motion.'*

'*Ch. Just. Well be honest, be honest, and heaven bless your expedition.'*

Falstaff indulges himself here in humourous exaggeration;—these passages are not meant to be taken, nor are we to suppose that they were taken, literally;—but if there was not a ground of truth, if *Falstaff* had not had such a degree of Military reputation as was capable of being thus humourously amplified and exaggerated, the whole dialogue would have been highly preposterous and absurd, and the acquiescing answer of the *Lord Chief Justice* singularly improper.—But upon the supposition of *Falstaff*'s being considered, upon the whole, as a good and gallant Officer, the answer is just, and corresponds with the acknowledgment which had a little before been made, '*that his day's service at Shrewsbury had gilded over his night's exploit at Gads Hill.—You may thank the unquiet time,* says the Chief Justice, *for your quiet o'erposting of that action':* agreeing with what *Falstaff* says in another place;—'*Well God be thanked for these Rebels, they offend none but the virtuous: I laud them, I praise them.'*—Whether this be said in the true spirit of a Soldier or not, I do not determine; it is surely not in that of a mere Coward and Poltroon.

It will be needless to shew, which might be done from a variety of particulars, that *Falstaff* was known, and had consideration at Court. *Shallow* cultivates him in the idea that *a friend at Court is better than a penny in purse: Westmorland* speaks to him in the tone of an equal: Upon *Falstaff*'s telling him, that he thought his lordship had been already at Shrewsbury, *Westmorland* replies,—'*Faith Sir John, 'tis more than time that I were there, and you too; the King I can tell you looks for us all; we must away all to night.'*—'*Tut,* says Falstaff, *never fear me, I am as vigilant as a cat to steal cream.'*—He desires, in another place, of my lord John of Lancaster, '*that when he goes to Court, he may stand in his good report.'* His intercourse and correspondence with both these lords seem easy and familiar. '*Go,'* says he to the page, '*bear this to my Lord of Lancaster, this to the Prince, this to the Earl of Westmorland, and this* (for he extended himself on all sides), *to old Mrs. Ursula',* whom it seems, the rogue ought to have married many years before.—But these intimations are needless: We see him ourselves in the *Royal Presence;* where, certainly, his buffooneries never brought him; nor was the Prince of a character to commit so high an indecorum, as to thrust, upon a solemn occasion, a mere Tavern companion into his father's Presence, especially in a moment when he himself deserts his looser character, and takes up that of *a Prince indeed.*—In a very important scene, where *Worcester* is expected with proposals from *Percy,* and wherein he is received, is treated with, and carries back offers of accomodation from the King, the King's attendants upon the occasion are *the Prince of Wales, Lord John of Lancaster, the Earl of Westmorland, Sir Walter Blunt, and Sir John Falstaff.*—What shall be said to this? *Falstaff* is not surely introduced here in vicious indulgence to a mob audience;—he utters but one word, a buffoon one indeed, but aside and to the Prince only. Nothing, it should seem, is wanting, if decorum would here have permitted, but that he should have spoken one sober sentence in the Presence (which yet we are to suppose him ready and able to do if occasion should have required; or his wit was given him to little purpose) and Sir *John Falstaff* might be allowed to pass for an established Courtier and counsellor of state. *'If I do grow great,* says he, *I'll grow less, purge and leave sack, and live as a nobleman should do.'* Nobility did not then appear to him at an unmeasurable distance; it was, it seems, in his idea, the very next link in the chain.

But to return. I would not demand what could bring *Falstaff* into the Royal Presence upon such an occasion, or justify the Prince's so public acknowledgment of him, but an established fame and reputation of Military merit? In short, just the like merit as brought Sir *Walter Blunt* into the same circumstances of honour.

But it may be objected that his introduction into this scene is a piece of indecorum in the author. But upon what ground are we to suppose this? Upon the ground of his being a notorious Coward? Why this is the very point in question, and cannot be granted: Even the direct contrary I have affirmed, and am endeavouring to support. But if it be supposed upon any other ground, it does not concern me; I have nothing to do with *Shakespeare*'s indecorums in general. That there are indecorums in the Play I have no doubt: The indecent treatment of *Percy*'s dead body is the greatest:—the familiarity of the insignificant, rude, and even ill disposed *Poins,* with the Prince, is another;—but the admission of *Falstaff* into the Royal Presence (supposing, which I have a right to suppose, that his Military character was unimpeached) does not seem to be in any respect among the number. In camps there is but one virtue and one vice; Military merit swallows up or covers all. But, after all, what have we to do with indecorums? Indecorums respect the propriety or impropriety of exhibiting certain actions; not their *truth* or *falshood* when exhibited. *Shakespeare* stands to us in the place of *truth* and *nature:* If we desert this principle we cut the turf from under us; I may then object to the robbery and other passages as indecorums, and as contrary to the truth of character. In short we may rend and tear the Play to pieces, and every man carry off what sentences he likes best.—But why this inveterate malice against poor *Falstaff?* He has faults enough in conscience without loading him with the infamy of Cowardice; a charge, which, if true, would, if I am not greatly mistaken, spoil all our mirth.—But of that hereafter.

It seems to me that, in our hasty judgment of some particular transactions, we forget the circumstances and condition of his whole life and character, which yet deserve our very particular attention. The author, it is true, has thrown the most advantageous of these circumstances into the *back ground,* as it were, and has brought nothing *out of the canvass* but his follies and buffoonery. We discover however, that in a very early period of his life he was familiar with *John* of *Gaunt;* which could hardly be, unless he had possessed much personal gallantry and accomplishment, and had derived his birth from a distinguished at least, if not from a Noble family.

It may seem very extravagant to insist upon *Falstaff*'s birth as a ground from which, by an inference, Personal courage may be derived, especially after having acknowledged that he seemed to have deserted those points of honour, which are more peculiarly the accompanyments of rank. But it may be observed that in the Feudal ages rank and wealth were not only connected with the point of honour, but with personal strength and natural courage. It is observable that Courage is a quality, which is at least as transmissible to one's posterity as features and complexion. In these periods men acquired and maintained their rank and possessions by personal prowess and gallantry; and their marriage alliances were made, of course, in families of the same character: And from hence, and from the exercises of their youth, we must account for the distinguished force and bravery of our antient Barons. It is not therefore beside my purpose to inquire what hints of the origin and birth of *Falstaff, Shakespeare* may have dropped in different parts of the Play; for tho' we may be disposed to allow that *Falstaff* in his old age might, under particular influences, desert the point of honour, we cannot give up that unalienable possession of Courage, which might have been derived to him from a noble or distinguished stock.

But it may be said that *Falstaff* was in truth the child of invention only, and that a reference to the Feudal accidents of birth serves only to confound fiction with reality: Not altogether so. If the ideas of Courage and *birth* were strongly associated in the days of *Shakespeare,* then would the assignment of high birth to *Falstaff* carry, and be intended to carry along with it, to the minds of the audience the associated idea of Courage, if nothing should be specially interposed to dissolve the connection;—and the question is as concerning this intention, and this effect. ⟨. . .⟩

Let it not be here objected that *Falstaff* is universally considered as a Coward;—we do indeed call him so; but that is nothing, if the character itself does not act from any consciousness of this kind, and if our Feelings take his part, and revolt against our understanding.

As to the arts by which *Shakespeare* has contrived to obscure the vices of *Falstaff,* they are such, as being subservient only to the mirth of the Play, I do not feel myself obliged to detail.

But it may be well worth our curiosity to inquire into the composition of *Falstaff*'s character—Every man we may observe, has two characters; that is, every man may be seen externally, and from without;—or a section may be made of him, and he may be illuminated from within.

Of the external character of *Falstaff,* we can scarcely be said to have any steady view. *Jack Falstaff* we are familiar with, but *Sir John* was better known, it seems, *to the rest of Europe,* than to his intimate companions; yet we have so many glimpses of him, and he is opened to us occasionally in such various points of view, that we cannot be mistaken in describing him as a man of birth and fashion, bred up in all the learning and accomplishments of the times;—of ability and Courage equal to any situation, and capable by nature of the highest affairs; trained to arms, and possessing the tone, the deportment, and the manners of a gentlemen;—but yet these accomplishments and advantages seem to hang loose on him, and to be worn with a slovenly carelessness and inattention: A too great indulgence of the qualities of humour and wit seems to draw him too much one way, and to destroy the grace and orderly arrangement of his other accomplishments;—and hence he becomes strongly marked for one advantage, to the injury, and almost forgetfulness in the beholder, of all the rest. Some of his vices likewise strike through, and stain his Exterior;—his modes of speech betray a certain licentiousness of mind; and that high Aristocratic tone which belonged to his situation was pushed on, and aggravated into unfeeling insolence and oppression. *'It is not a confirmed brow,'* says the Chief Justice, *'nor the throng of words that come with such more than impudent sauciness from you, can thrust me from a level consideration:'* *'My lord,'* answers *Falstaff,* *'you call honourable boldness impudent sauciness. If a man will court'sie and say nothing, he is virtuous: No my lord, my humble duty remembered, I will not be your suitor. I say to you I desire deliverance from these officers, being upon hasty employment in the King's affairs.'* *'You speak',* replied the Chief Justice, *'as having power to do wrong.'*—His whole behaviour to the Chief Justice, whom he despairs of winning by flattery, is singularly insolent; and the reader will remember many instances of his insolence to others: Nor are his manners always free from the taint of vulgar society;—*'This is the right fencing grace, my lord,'* (says he to the Chief Justice, with great impropriety of manners) *'tap for tap, and so part fair:'* *'Now the lord lighten thee,'* is the reflection of the Chief Justice, *thou art a very great fool,'*—Such a character as I have here described, strengthened with that vigor, force, and alacrity of mind, of which he is possessed, must have spread terror and dismay thro' the ignorant, the timid, the modest, and the weak: Yet is he however, when occasion requires, capable of much accomodation and flattery;—and in order to obtain the protection and patronage of the great, so convenient to his vices and his poverty, he was put under the daily necessity of practising and improving these arts; a baseness, which he compensates to himself, like other unprincipled men, by an increase of insolence towards his inferiors.—There is also a natural activity about *Falstaff,* which for want of proper employment, shews itself in a kind of swell or bustle, which seems to correspond with his bulk, as if his mind had inflated his body, and demanded a habitation of no less circumference: Thus conditioned he rolls (in the language of *Ossian*) like a *Whale of Ocean,* scattering the smaller fry; but affording, in his turn, noble contention to *Hal* and *Poins;* who, to keep up the allusion, I may be allowed on this occasion to compare to the Thresher and the Sword-fish.

To this part of *Falstaff*'s character, many things which he does and says, and which appear unaccountably natural, are to be referred.

We are next to see him *from within:* And here we shall behold him most

villainously unprincipled and debauched; possessing indeed the same Courage and
ability, yet stained with numerous vices, unsuited not only to his primary qualities,
but to his age, corpulency, rank, and profession;—reduced by these vices to a state
of dependence, yet resolutely bent to indulge them at any price. These vices have
been already enumerated; they are many, and become still more intolerable by an
excess of unfeeling insolence on one hand, and of base accommodation on the
other.

But what then, after all, is become of *old Jack?* Is this the jovial delightful
companion—*Falstaff,* the favourite and the boast of the Stage?—by no means. But
it is, I think however, the *Falstaff* of Nature; the very stuff out of which the *Stage
Falstaff* is composed; nor was it possible, I believe, out of any other materials he
could have been formed. From this disagreeable draught we shall be able, I trust,
by a proper disposition of light and shade, and from the influence and compression
of external things, to produce *plump Jack,* the life of humour, the spirit of pleasantry, and the soul of mirth.

To this end, *Falstaff* must no longer be considered as a single independent
character, but grouped, as we find him shewn to us in the Play;—his ability must be
disgraced by buffoonery, and his Courage by circumstances of imputation; and
those qualities be thereupon reduced into subjects of mirth and laughter:—His
vices must be concealed at each end from vicious design and evil effect, and must
thereupon be turned into incongruities, and assume the name of humour only;—his
insolence must be repressed by the superior tone of *Hal* and *Poins,* and take the
softer name of spirit only, or alacrity of mind;—his state of dependence, his temper
of accomodation, and his activity, must fall in precisely with the indulgence of his
humours; that is, he must thrive best and flatter most, by being extravagantly
incongruous; and his own tendency, impelled by so much activity, will carry him
with perfect ease and freedom to all the necessary excesses. But why, it may be
asked, should incongruities recommend *Falstaff* to the favour of the Prince?—
Because the Prince is supposed to possess a high relish of humour and to have a
temper and a force about him, which, whatever was his pursuit, delighted in excess.
This, *Falstaff* is supposed perfectly to comprehend; and thereupon not only to
indulge himself in all kinds of incongruity, but to lend out his own superior wit and
humour against himself, and to heighten the ridicule by all the tricks and arts of
buffoonery for which his corpulence, his age, and situation, furnish such excellent
materials. This compleats the Dramatic character of *Falstaff,* and gives him that
appearance of perfect good-nature, pleasantry, mellowness, and hilarity of mind,
for which we admire and almost love him, tho' we feel certain reserves which
forbid our going that length; the true reason of which is, that there will be always
found a difference between mere appearances, and reality: Nor are we, nor can
we be, insensible that whenever the action of external influence upon him is in
whole or in part relaxed, the character restores itself proportionably to its more
unpleasing condition.

A character really possessing the qualities which are on the stage imputed to
Falstaff, would be best shewn by its own natural energy; the least compression

would disorder it, and make us feel for it all the pain of sympathy: It is the artificial condition of *Falstaff* which is the source of our delight; we enjoy his distresses, we *gird at him* ourselves, and urge the sport without the least alloy of compassion; and we give him, when the laugh is over, undeserved credit for the pleasure we enjoyed. If any one thinks that these observations are the effect of too much refinement, and that there was in truth more of chance in the case than of management or design, let him try his own luck;—perhaps he may draw out of the wheel of fortune a *Macbeth,* an *Othello,* a *Benedict,* or a *Falstaff.*

Such, I think, is the true character of this extraordinary buffoon; and from hence we may discern for what special purposes *Shakespeare* has given him talents and qualities, which were to be afterwards obscured, and perverted to ends opposite to their nature; it was clearly to furnish out a Stage buffoon of a peculiar sort; a kind of Game-bull which would stand the baiting thro' a hundred Plays, and produce equal sport, whether he is pinned down occasionally by *Hal* or *Poins,* or tosses such mongrils as *Bardolph,* or the Justices, sprawling in the air. There is in truth no such thing as totally demolishing *Falstaff;* he has so much of the invulnerable in his frame that no ridicule can destroy him; he is safe even in defeat, and seems to rise, like another *Antæus,* with recruited vigour from every fall; in this as in every other respect, unlike *Parolles* or *Bobadil:* They fall by the first shaft of ridicule, but *Falstaff* is a butt on which we may empty the whole quiver, whilst the substance of his character remains unimpaired. His ill habits, and the accidents of age and corpulence, are no part of his essential constitution; they come forward indeed on our eye, and solicit our notice, but they are second natures, not *first;* mere shadows, we pursue them in vain; *Falstaff* himself has a distinct and separate subsistence; he laughs at the chace, and when the sport is over, gathers them with unruffled feather under his wing: And hence it is that he is made to undergo not one detection only, but a series of detections; that he is not formed for one Play only, but was intended originally at least for two; and the author we are told, was doubtful if he should not extend him yet farther, and engage him in the wars with *France.* This he might well have done, for there is nothing perishable in the nature of *Falstaff.* He might have involved him, by the vicious part of his character, in new difficulties and unlucky situations, and have enabled him, by the better part, to have scrambled through, abiding and retorting the jests and laughter of every beholder.

But whatever we may be told concerning the intention of *Shakespeare* to extend this character farther, there is a manifest preparation near the end of the second part of Henry IV. for his disgrace: The disguise is taken off, and he begins openly to pander to the excesses of the Prince, intitling himself to the character afterwards given him of being *the tutor and the feeder of his riots. 'I will fetch off',* (says he) *'these Justices.—I will devise matter enough out of this* Shallow *to keep the prince in continual laughter the wearing out of six fashions.—If the young* dace *be a bait for the old* pike,' (speaking with reference of his own designs upon Shallow) *'I see no reason in the law of nature but I may snap at him.'*—This is showing himself abominably dissolute: The laborious arts of fraud, which he practices on *Shallow* to induce the loan of a thousand pound, create *disgust:* and the more, as we are sensible this money was never likely to be *paid back,* as we are told that *was,* of which the travellers had been robbed. It is true we feel no pain for *Shallow,* he being a very bad character, as would fully appear, if he were unfolded; but *Falstaff's* deliberation in fraud is not on that account more excusable.—The event of the old King's death draws him out almost into detestation.—'*Master* Robert Shallow, *chuse what office thou wilt in the land,—'tis thine.—I am fortune's steward.—Let us take any man's horses.—The laws of England are at my commandment.—Happy are they who have been my friends;— and woe to my* Lord Chief Justice.'—After this we ought not to complain if we see Poetic justice duly executed upon him, and that he is finally given up to shame and dishonour.

But it is remarkable that, during this process, we are not acquainted with the success of *Falstaff's* designs upon *Shallow* 'till the moment of his disgrace. '*If I had had time',* (says he to *Shallow,* as the King is approaching,) '*to have made new liveries, I would have bestowed the thousand pounds I borrowed of you';*—and the first word he utters after this period, is, '*Master* Shallow, *I owe you a thousand pounds':* We may from hence very reasonably presume, that *Shakespeare* meant to connect this fraud with the punishment of *Falstaff,* as a more avowed ground of censure and dishonour: Nor ought the consideration that this passage contains the most exquisite comic humour and propriety in another view, to diminish the truth of this observation.

But however just it might be to demolish *Falstaff* in this way, by opening to us his bad principles, it was by no means *convenient.* If we had been to have seen a single representation of him only, it might have been proper enough; but as he was to be shewn from night to night, and from age to age, the disgust arising from the *close,* would by degrees have spread itself over the whole character; reference would be had throughout to his bad principles, and he would have become less acceptable as he was more known: And yet it was necessary to bring him, like all other stage characters, to some conclusion. Every play must be wound up by some event, which may shut in the characters and the action. If some *hero* obtains a crown, or a mistress, involving therein the fortune of others, we are satisfied;—we do not desire to be afterwards admitted of his council, or his bed-chamber: Or if through jealousy, causeless or well founded, *another* kills a beloved wife, and himself after,—there is no more to be said;—they are dead, and there an end; Or if in the scenes of Comedy, parties are engaged, and plots formed, for the fur- thering or preventing the completion of that great article Cuckoldom, we expect to be satisfied in the point as far as the nature of so nice a case will permit, or at least to see such a manifest *disposition* as will leave us in no doubt of the event. By the bye, I cannot but think that the comic writers of the last age treated this matter as of more importance, and made more bustle about it, than the temper of the present times will well bear; and it is therefore to be hoped that the Dramatic authors of the present day, some of whom, to the best of my judgment, are deserving of great praise, will consider and treat this business, rather as a common and natural incident arising out of modern manners, than as worthy to be held forth as the great object and sole end of the Play.

But whatever be the question, or whatever the character, the curtain must not only be dropt before the eyes, but over the minds of the spectators, and nothing left for further examination and curiosity.—But how was this to be done in regard to *Falstaff?* He was not involved in the future of the Play; he was engaged in no action which, as to him, was to be compleated; he had reference to no system, he was attracted to no center; he passes thro' the Play as a lawless meteor, and we wish to know what course he is afterwards likely to take: He is detected and disgraced, it is true; but he lives by detection, and thrives on disgrace; and we are desirous to see him detected and disgraced again. The *Fleet* might be no bad scene of further amusement;—he carries *all* within him, *and what matter* where, *if he be still the same,* possessing the same force of mind, the same wit, and the same incongruity. This, *Shakespeare* was fully sensible of, and knew that this character could not be compleatly dismissed but by death. 'Our author, (says the Epilogue to the Second Part of Henry IV.) will continue the story with Sir *John* in it, and make you merry with fair *Catherine* of *France;* where, for any thing I know, *Falstaff* shall dye of a sweat, unless already he be killed with your hard opinions.' If it had been prudent in *Shakespeare* to have killed *Falstaff* with *hard opinion,* he had the means in his hand to effect it;—but dye, it seems, he must, in one form or another, and a *sweat* would have been no unsuitable catastrophe. However we have reason to be satisfied as it is;—his death was worthy of his birth and of his life: *'He was born',* he says, *'about three o'clock in the afternoon with a white head, and something a round belly.'* But if he came into the world in the evening with these marks of age, he departs out of it in the morning in all the follies and vanities of youth;—*'He was shaked'* (we are told) *'of a burning quotidian tertian;—the young King had run bad humours on the knight;—his heart was fracted and corroborate; and a' parted just between twelve and one, even at the turning of the tide, yielding the crow a pudding, and passing directly into* Arthur's bosom, *if ever man went into the bosom of* Arthur.'—So ended this singular buffoon; and with him ends an Essay, on which the reader is left to bestow what character he pleases: An Essay professing to treat of the Courage of *Falstaff,* but extending itself to his Whole character; to the arts and genius of his Poetic-Maker, SHAKESPEARE; and thro' him sometimes, with ambitious aim, even to the principles of human nature itself.

A. C. Bradley

THE REJECTION
OF FALSTAFF

Of the two persons principally concerned in the rejection of Falstaff, Henry, both as Prince and as King, has received, on the whole, full justice from readers and critics. Falstaff, on the other hand, has been in one respect the most unfortunate of Shakespeare's famous characters. All of them, in passing from the mind of their creator into other minds, suffer change; they tend to lose their harmony through the disproportionate attention bestowed on some one feature, or to lose their uniqueness by being conventionalised into types already familiar. But Falstaff was degraded by Shakespeare himself. The original character is to be found alive in the two parts of *Henry IV.,* dead in *Henry V.,* and nowhere else. But not very long after these plays were composed, Shakespeare wrote, and he afterwards revised, the very entertaining piece called *The Merry Wives of Windsor.* Perhaps his company wanted a new play on a sudden; or perhaps, as one would rather believe, the tradition may be true that Queen Elizabeth, delighted with the Falstaff scenes of *Henry IV.,* expressed a wish to see the hero of them again, and to see him in love. Now it was no more possible for Shakespeare to show his own Falstaff in love than to turn twice two into five. But he could write in haste—the tradition says, in a fortnight—a comedy or farce differing from all his other plays in this, that its scene is laid in English middle-class life, and that it is prosaic almost to the end. And among the characters he could introduce a disreputable fat old knight with attendants, and could call them Falstaff, Bardolph, Pistol, and Nym. And he could represent this knight assailing, for financial purposes, the virtue of two matrons, and in the event baffled, duped, treated like dirty linen, beaten, burnt, pricked, mocked, insulted, and, worst of all, repentant and didactic. It is horrible. It is almost enough to convince one that Shakespeare himself could sanction the parody of Ophelia in the *Two Noble Kinsmen.* But it no more touches the real Falstaff than Ophelia is degraded by that parody. To picture the real Falstaff befooled like the Falstaff of the *Merry Wives* is like imagining Iago the gull of Roderigo, or Becky Sharp the dupe of Amelia Osborne. Before he had been served the least of these tricks he would

From *Oxford Lectures on Poetry* (London: Macmillan, 1909), pp. 247–73. First published 1902.

have had his brains taken out and buttered, and have given them to a dog for a New Year's gift. I quote the words of the impostor, for after all Shakespeare made him and gave to him a few sentences worthy of Falstaff himself. But they are only a few—one side of a sheet of notepaper would contain them. And yet critics have solemnly debated at what period in his life Sir John endured the gibes of Master Ford, and whether we should put this comedy between the two parts of *Henry IV.,* or between the second of them and *Henry V.* And the Falstaff of the general reader, it is to be feared, is an impossible conglomerate of two distinct characters, while the Falstaff of the mere playgoer is certainly much more like the impostor than the true man.

The separation of these two has long ago been effected by criticism, and is insisted on in almost all competent estimates of the character of Falstaff. I do not propose to attempt a full account either of this character or of that of Prince Henry, but shall connect the remarks I have to make on them with a question which does not appear to have been satisfactorily discussed—the question of the rejection of Falstaff by the Prince on his accession to the throne. What do we feel, and what are we meant to feel, as we witness this rejection? And what does our feeling imply as to the characters of Falstaff and the new King?

I

Sir John, you remember, is in Gloucestershire, engaged in borrowing a thousand pounds from Justice Shallow; and here Pistol, riding helter-skelter from London, brings him the great news that the old King is as dead as nail in door, and that Harry the Fifth is the man. Sir John, in wild excitement, taking any man's horses, rushes to London; and he carries Shallow with him, for he longs to reward all his friends. We find him standing with his companions just outside Westminister Abbey, in the crowd that is waiting for the King to come out after his coronation. He himself is stained with travel, and has had no time to spend any of the thousand pounds in buying new liveries for his men. But what of that? This poor show only proves his earnestness of affection, his devotion, how he could not deliberate or remember or have patience to shift himself, but rode day and night, thought of nothing else but to see Henry, and put all affairs else in oblivion, as if there were nothing else to be done but to see him. And now he stands sweating with desire to see him, and repeating and repeating this one desire of his heart—'to see him.' The moment comes. There is a shout within the Abbey like the roaring of the sea, and a clangour of trumpets, and the doors open and the procession streams out.

FAL.: God save thy grace, King Hal! my royal Hal!
PIST.: The heavens thee guard and keep, most royal imp of fame!
FAL.: God save thee, my sweet boy!
KING: My Lord Chief Justice, speak to that vain man.
CH. JUST.: Have you your wits? Know you what 'tis you speak?
FAL.: My King! my Jove! I speak to thee, my heart!

KING: I know thee not, old man: fall to thy prayers;
How ill white hairs become a fool and jester!
I have long dream'd of such a kind of man,
So surfeit-swell'd, so old and so profane;
But being awaked I do despise my dream.
Make less thy body hence, and more thy grace;
Leave gormandizing; know the grave doth gape
For thee thrice wider than for other men.
Reply not to me with a fool-born jest:
Presume not that I am the thing I was;
For God doth know, so shall the world perceive,
That I have turn'd away my former self;
So will I those that kept me company.
When thou dost hear I am as I have been,
Approach me, and thou shalt be as thou wast,
The tutor and the feeder of my riots:
Till then, I banish thee, on pain of death,
As I have done the rest of my misleaders,
Not to come near our person by ten mile.
For competence of life I will allow you,
That lack of means enforce you not to evil:
And, as we hear you do reform yourselves,
We will, according to your strengths and qualities,
Give you advancement. Be it your charge, my lord,
To see perform'd the tenour of our word.
Set on.

The procession passes out of sight, but Falstaff and his friends remain. He shows no resentment. He comforts himself, or tries to comfort himself—first, with the thought that he has Shallow's thousand pounds, and then, more seriously, I believe, with another thought. The King, he sees, must look thus to the world; but he will be sent for in private when night comes, and will yet make the fortunes of his friends. But even as he speaks, the Chief Justice, accompanied by Prince John, returns, and gives the order to his officers:

Go, carry Sir John Falstaff to the Fleet;
Take all his company along with him.

Falstaff breaks out, 'My lord, my lord,' but he is cut short and hurried away; and after a few words between the Prince and the Chief Justice the scene closes, and with it the drama.

What are our feelings during this scene? They will depend on our feelings about Falstaff. If we have not keenly enjoyed the Falstaff scenes of the two plays, if we regard Sir John chiefly as an old reprobate, not only a sensualist, a liar, and a coward, but a cruel and dangerous ruffian, I suppose we enjoy his discomfiture and consider that the King has behaved magnificently. But if we *have* keenly enjoyed the Falstaff scenes, if we have enjoyed them as Shakespeare surely meant them to be enjoyed, and if, accordingly, Falstaff is not to us solely or even chiefly a reprobate and ruffian, we feel, I think, during the King's speech, a good deal of pain and some resentment; and when, without any further offence on Sir John's part, the Chief Justice returns and sends him to prison, we stare in astonishment. These, I believe, are, in greater or less degree, the feelings of most of those who really enjoy the Falstaff scenes (as many readers do not). Nor are these feelings diminished when we remember the end of the whole story, as we find it in *Henry V.,* where we learn that Falstaff quickly died, and, according to the testimony of persons not very sentimental, died of a broken heart.[1] Suppose this merely to mean that he sank under the shame of his public disgrace, and it is pitiful enough: but the words of Mrs. Quickly, 'The king has killed his heart'; of Nym, 'The king hath run bad humours on the knight; that's the even of it'; of Pistol,

> Nym, thou hast spoke the right,
> His heart is fracted and corroborate,

assuredly point to something more than wounded pride; they point to wounded affection, and remind us of Falstaff's own answer to Prince Hal's question, 'Sirrah, do I owe you a thousand pound?' 'A thousand pound, Hal? a million: thy love is worth a million: thou owest me thy love.'

Now why did Shakespeare end his drama with a scene which, though undoubtedly striking, leaves an impression so unpleasant? I will venture to put aside without discussion the idea that he meant us throughout the two plays to regard Falstaff with disgust or indignation, so that we naturally feel nothing but pleasure at his fall; for this idea implies that kind of inability to understand Shakespeare with which it is idle to argue. And there is another and a much more ingenious suggestion which must equally be rejected as impossible. According to it, Falstaff, having listened to the King's speech, did not seriously hope to be sent for by him in private; he fully realised the situation at once, and was only making game of Shallow; and in his immediate turn upon Shallow when the King goes out, 'Master Shallow, I owe you a thousand pound,' we are meant to see his humorous superiority to any rebuff, so that we end the play with the delightful feeling that, while Henry has done the right thing, Falstaff, in his outward overthrow, has still proved himself inwardly invincible. This suggestion comes from a critic who understands Falstaff, and in the suggestion itself shows that he understands him.[2] But it provides no solution, because it wholly ignores, and could not account for, that which follows the short conversation with Shallow. Falstaff's dismissal to the Fleet, and his subsequent death, prove beyond doubt that his rejection was meant by Shakespeare to be taken as a catastrophe which not even his humour could enable him to surmount.

Moreover, these interpretations, even if otherwise admissible, would still leave our problem only partly solved. For what troubles us is not only the disappointment of Falstaff, it is the conduct of Henry. It was inevitable that on his accession he should separate himself from Sir John, and we wish nothing else. It is satisfactory that Sir John should have a competence, with the hope of promotion in the highly improbable case of his reforming himself. And if Henry could not trust himself within ten miles of so fascinating a companion, by all means let him be banished that distance: we do not complain. These arrangements would not have prevented a satisfactory ending: the King could have communicated his decision, and Falstaff could have accepted it, in a private interview rich in humour and merely touched with pathos. But Shakespeare has so contrived matters that Henry could not send a private warning to Falstaff even if he wished to, and in their public meeting Falstaff is made to behave in so infatuated and outrageous a manner that great sternness on the King's part was unavoidable. And the curious thing is that Shakespeare did not stop here. If this had been all we should have felt pain for Falstaff, but not, perhaps, resentment against Henry. But two things we do resent. Why, when this painful incident seems to be over, should the Chief Justice return and send Falstaff to prison? Can this possibly be meant for an act of private vengeance on the part of the Chief Justice, unknown to the King? No; for in that case Shakespeare would have shown at once that the King disapproved and cancelled it. It must have been the King's own act. This is one thing we resent; the other is the King's sermon. He had a right to turn away his former self, and his old companions with it, but he had no right to talk all of a sudden like a clergyman; and surely it was both ungenerous and insincere to speak of them as his 'misleaders,' as though in the days of Eastcheap and Gadshill he had been a weak and silly lad. We have seen his former self, and we know that it was nothing of the kind. He had shown himself, for all his follies, a very strong and independent young man, deliberately amusing himself among men over whom he had just as much ascendency as he chose to exert. Nay, he amused himself not only among them, but at their expense. In his first soliloquy— and first soliloquies are usually significant—he declares that he associates with them in order that, when at some future time he shows his true character, he may be the more wondered at for his previous aberrations. You may think he deceives himself here; you may believe that he frequented Sir John's company out of delight in it and not merely with this cold-blooded design; but at any rate he *thought* the design was his one motive. And, that being so, two results follow. He ought in honour long ago to have given Sir John clearly to understand that they must say good-bye on the day of his accession. And, having neglected to do this, he ought not to have lectured him as his misleader. It was not only ungenerous, it was dishonest. It looks disagreeably like an attempt to buy the praise of the respectable at the cost of honour and truth. And it succeeded. Henry *always* succeeded.

You will see what I am suggesting, for the moment, as a solution of our problem. I am suggesting that our fault lies not in our resentment at Henry's conduct, but in our surprise at it; that if we had read his character truly in the light that Shakespeare gave us, we should have been prepared for a display both of hardness and of policy at this point in his career. And although this suggestion does not suffice to solve the problem before us, I am convinced that in itself it is true. Nor is it rendered at all improbable by the fact that Shakespeare has made Henry, on the whole, a fine and very attractive character, and that here he makes no one express any disapprobation of the treatment of Falstaff. For in similar cases Shakespeare is constantly misunderstood. His readers expect him to mark in some distinct way his approval or disapproval of that which he represents; and hence where *they* disapprove and *he* says nothing, they fancy that he does *not* disapprove, and they blame his indifference, like Dr. Johnson, or at the least are puzzled. But the truth is that he shows the fact and leaves the judgment to them. And again, when he makes us like a character we expect the character to have no faults that are not expressly pointed out, and when other faults appear we either ignore them or try to explain them away. This is one of our methods of conventionalising Shakespeare. We want the world's population to be neatly divided into sheep and goats, and we want an angel by us to say, 'Look, that is a goat and this is a sheep,' and we try to turn Shakespeare into this angel. His impartiality makes us uncomfortable: we cannot bear to see him, like the sun, lighting up everything and judging nothing. And this is perhaps especially the case in his historical plays, where we are always trying to turn him into a partisan. He shows us that Richard II. was unworthy to be king, and we at once conclude that he thought Bolingbroke's usurpation justified; whereas he shows merely, what under the conditions was bound to exist, an inextricable tangle of right and unright. Or, Bolingbroke being evidently wronged, we suppose Bolingbroke's statements to be true, and are quite surprised when, after attaining his end through them, he mentions casually on his death-bed that they were lies. Shakespeare makes us admire Hotspur heartily; and accordingly, when we see Hotspur discussing with others how large his particular slice of his mother-country is to be, we either fail to recognize the monstrosity of the proceeding, or, recognising it, we complain that Shakespeare is inconsistent. Prince John breaks a tottering rebellion by practising a detestable fraud on the rebels. We are against the rebels, and have heard high praise of Prince John, but we cannot help seeing that his fraud is detestable; so we say indignantly to Shakespeare, 'Why, you told us he was a sheep'; whereas, in fact, if we had used our eyes we should have known beforehand that he was the brave, determined, loyal, cold-blooded, pitiless, unscrupulous son of a usurper whose throne was in danger.

To come, then, to Henry. Both as prince and as king he is deservedly a favourite, and particularly so with English readers, being, as he is, perhaps the most distinctively English of all Shakespeare's men. In *Henry V.* he is treated as a national hero. In this play he has lost much of the wit which in him seems to have depended on contact with Falstaff, but he has also laid aide the most serious faults of his youth. He inspires in a high degree fear, enthusiasm, and affection; thanks to his beautiful modesty he has the charm which is lacking to another mighty warrior, Coriolanus; his youthful escapades have given him an understanding of simple folk, and sympathy with them; he is the author of the saying, 'There is some soul of goodness in things evil'; and he is much more obviously religious than most of Shakespeare's heroes. Having these and other fine qualities, and being without certain dangerous tendencies which mark the tragic heroes, he is, perhaps, the most *efficient* character drawn by Shakespeare, unless Ulysses, in *Troilus and Cressida,* is his equal. And so he has been described as Shakespeare's ideal man of action; nay, it has even been declared that here for once Shakespeare plainly disclosed his own ethical creed, and showed us his ideal, not simply of a man of action, but of a man.

But Henry is neither of these. The poet who drew Hamlet and Othello can never have thought that even the ideal man of action would lack that light upon the brow which at once transfigures them and marks their doom. It is as easy to believe that, because the lunatic, the lover, and the poet are not far apart, Shakespeare would have chosen never to have loved and sung. Even poor Timon, the most inefficient of the tragic heroes, has something in him that Henry never shows. Nor is it merely that his nature is limited: if we follow Shakespeare and look closely at Henry, we shall discover with the many fine traits a few less pleasing. Henry IV. describes him as the noble image of his own youth; and, for all his superiority to his father, he is still his father's son, the son of the man whom Hotspur called a 'vile politician.' Henry's religion, for example, is genuine, it is rooted in his modesty; but it is also superstitious—an attempt to buy off supernatural vengeance for Richard's blood; and it is also in part political, like his father's projected crusade. Just as he went to war chiefly because, as his father told him, it was the way to keep factious nobles quiet and unite the nation, so when he adjures the Archbishop to satisfy him as to his right to the French throne, he knows very well that the Archbishop *wants* the war, because it will defer and perhaps prevent what he considers the spoliation of the Church. This same strain of policy is what Shakespeare marks in the first soliloquy in *Henry IV.*, where the prince describes his riotous life as a mere scheme to win him glory later. It implies that readiness to use other people as means to his own ends which is a conspicuous feature in his father; and it reminds us of his father's plan of keeping himself out of the people's sight while Richard was making himself cheap by his incessant public appearances. And if I am not mistaken there is a further likeness. Henry is kindly and pleasant to every one as Prince, to every one deserving as King; and he is so not merely out of policy: but there is no sign in him of a strong affection for any one, such an affection as we recognise at a glance in Hamlet and Horatio, Brutus and Cassius, and many more. We do not find this in *Henry V.*, not even in the noble address to Lord Scroop, and in *Henry IV.* we find, I think, a liking for Falstaff and Poins, but no more: there is no more than a liking, for instance, in his soliloquy over the supposed corpse of his fat friend, and he never speaks of Falstaff to Poins with any affection. The truth is, that the members of the family of Henry IV. have love for one another, but they cannot spare love for any one outside their family, which stands firmly united, defending its royal position against attack and instinctively isolating itself from outside influence.

Thus I would suggest that Henry's conduct in his rejection of Falstaff is in perfect keeping with his character on its unpleasant side as well as on its finer; and that, so far as Henry is concerned, we ought not to feel surprise at it. And on this view we may even explain the strange incident of the Chief Justice being sent back to order Falstaff to prison (for there is no sign of any such uncertainty in the text as might suggest an interpolation by the players). Remembering his father's words about Henry, 'Being incensed, he's flint,' and remembering in *Henry V.* his ruth-lessness about killing the prisoners when he is incensed, we may imagine that, after he had left Falstaff and was no longer influenced by the face of his old companion, he gave way to anger at the indecent familiarity which had provoked a compromising scene on the most ceremonial of occasions and in the presence alike of court and crowd, and that he sent the Chief Justice back to take vengeance. And this is consistent with the fact that in the next play we find Falstaff shortly afterwards not only freed from prison, but unmolested in his old haunt in Eastcheap, well within ten miles of Henry's person. His anger had soon passed, and he knew that the requisite effect had been produced both on Falstaff and on the world.

But all this, however true, will not solve our problem. It seems, on the contrary, to increase its difficulty. For the natural conclusion is that Shakespeare *intended* us to feel resentment against Henry. And yet that cannot be, for it implies that he meant the play to end disagreeably; and no one who understands Shakespeare at all will consider that supposition for a moment credible. No; he must have meant the play to end pleasantly, although he made Henry's action consistent. And hence it follows that he must have intended our sympathy with Falstaff to be so far weakened when the rejection-scene arrives that his discomfiture should be satisfactory to us; that we should enjoy this sudden reverse of enormous hopes (a thing always ludicrous if sympathy is absent); that we should approve the moral judgment that falls on him; and so should pass lightly over that disclosure of unpleasant traits in the King's character which Shakespeare was too true an artist to suppress. Thus our pain and resentment, if we feel them, are wrong, in the sense that they do not answer to the dramatist's intention. But it does not follow that they are wrong in a further sense. They may be right, because the dramatist has missed what he aimed at. And this, though the dramatist was Shakespeare, is what I would suggest. In the Falstaff scenes he overshot his mark. He created so extraordinary a being, and fixed him so firmly on his intellectual throne, that when he sought to dethrone him he could not. The moment comes when we are to look at Falstaff in a serious light, and the comic hero is to figure as a baffled schemer; but we cannot make the required change, either in our attitude or in our sympathies. We wish Henry a glorious reign and much joy of his crew of hypocritical politicians, lay and clerical; but our hearts go with Falstaff to the Fleet, or, if necessary, to Arthur's bosom or wheresomever he is.[3]

In the remainder of the lecture I will try to make this view clear. And to that end we must go back to the Falstaff of the body of the two plays, the immortal Falstaff, a character almost purely humorous, and therefore no subject for moral judgments I can but draw an outline, and in describing one aspect of this character must be content to hold another in reserve.

II

Up to a certain point Falstaff is ludicrous in the same way as many other figures, his distinction lying, so far, chiefly in the mere abundance of ludicrous traits. *Why* we should laugh at a man with a huge belly and corresponding appetites; at the inconveniences he suffers on a hot day, or in playing the footpad, or when he falls down and there are no levers at hand to lift him up again; at the incongruity of his unwieldy bulk and the nimbleness of his spirit, the infirmities of his age and his youthful lightness of heart; at the enormity of his lies and wiles, and the suddenness of their exposure and frustration; at the contrast between his reputation and his real character, seen most absurdly when, at the mere mention of his name, a redoubted rebel surrenders to him—*why*, I say, we should laugh at these and many such things, this is no place to inquire; but unquestionably we do. Here we have them poured out in endless profusion and with that air of careless ease which is so fascinating in Shakespeare; and with the enjoyment of them I believe many readers stop. But while they are quite essential to the character, there is in it much more. For these things by themselves do not explain why, beside laughing at Falstaff, we are made happy by him and laugh *with* him. He is not, like Parolles, a mere *object* of mirth.

The main reason why he makes us so happy and puts us so entirely at our ease is that he himself is happy and entirely at his ease. 'Happy' is too weak a word; he is in bliss, and we share his glory. Enjoyment—no fitful pleasure crossing a dull life, nor any vacant convulsive mirth—but a rich deep-toned chuckling enjoyment circulates continually through all his being. If you ask *what* he enjoys, no doubt the answer is, in the first place, eating and drinking, taking his ease at his inn, and the company of other merry souls. Compared with these things, what we count the graver interests of life are nothing to him. But then, while we are under his spell, it is impossible to consider these graver interests; gravity is to us, as to him, inferior to gravy; and what he does enjoy he enjoys with such a luscious and good-humoured zest that we sympathise and he makes us happy. And if any one objected, we should answer with Sir Toby Belch, 'Dost thou think, because thou art virtuous, there shall be no more cakes and ale?'

But this, again, is far from all. Falstaff's ease and enjoyment are not simply those of the happy man of appetite;[4] they are those of the humorist, and the humorist of genius. Instead of being comic to you and serious to himself, he is more ludicrous to himself than to you; and he makes himself out more ludicrous than he is, in order that he and others may laugh. Prince Hal never made such sport of Falstaff's person as he himself did. It is *he* who says that his skin hangs about him like an old lady's loose gown, and that he walks before his page like a sow that hath o'erwhelmed all her litter but one. And he jests at himself when he is alone just as much as when others are by. It is the same with his appetites. The direct enjoyment they bring him is scarcely so great as the enjoyment of laughing at this enjoyment; and for all his addiction to sack you never see him for an instant with a brain dulled by it, or a temper turned solemn, silly, quarrelsome, or pious. The virtue it instils into him, of filling his brain with nimble, fiery, and delectable shapes—this, and his humorous attitude towards it, free him, in a manner, from slavery to it; and it is this freedom, and no secret longing for better things (those who attribute such a longing to him are far astray), that makes his enjoyment contagious and prevents our sympathy with it from being disturbed.

The bliss of freedom gained in humour is the essence of Falstaff. His humour is not directed only or chiefly against obvious absurdities; he is the enemy of everything that would interfere with his ease, and therefore of anything serious, and especially of everything respectable and moral. For these things impose limits and obligations, and make us the subjects of old father antic the law, and the categorical imperative, and our station and its duties, and conscience, and reputation, and other people's opinions, and all sorts of nuisances. I say he is therefore their enemy; but I do him wrong; to say that he is their enemy implies that he regards them as serious and recognises their power, when in truth he refuses to recognise them at all. They are to him absurd; and to reduce a thing *ad absurdum* is to reduce it to nothing and to walk about free and rejoicing. This is what Falstaff does with all the would-be serious things of life, sometimes only by his words, sometimes by his actions too. He will make truth appear absurd by solemn statements, which he utters with perfect gravity and which he expects nobody to believe; and honour, by demonstrating that it cannot set a leg, and that neither the living nor the dead can possess it; and law, by evading all the attacks of its highest representative and almost forcing him to laugh at his own defeat; and patriotism, by filling his pockets with the bribes offered by competent soldiers who want to escape service, while he takes in their stead the halt and maimed and the gaol-birds; and duty, by showing how he labours in his vocation—of thieving; and courage, alike by mocking at his own capture of Colvile and gravely claiming to have killed Hotspur; and war, by offering the Prince his bottle of sack when he is asked for a sword; and religion, by amusing himself with remorse at odd times when he has nothing else to do; and the fear of death, by maintaining perfectly untouched, in the face of imminent peril and even while he *feels* the fear of death, the very same power of dissolving it in persiflage that he shows when he sits at ease in his inn. These are the wonderful achievements which he performs, not with the sourness of a cynic, but with the gaiety of a boy. And, therefore, we praise him, we laud him, for he offends none but the virtuous, and denies that life is real or life is earnest, and delivers us from the oppression of such nightmares, and lifts us into the atmosphere of perfect freedom.

No one in the play understands Falstaff fully, any more than Hamlet was understood by the persons round him. They are both men of genius. Mrs. Quickly and Bardolph are his slaves, but they know not why. 'Well, fare thee well,' says the hostess whom he has pillaged and forgiven; 'I have known thee these twenty-nine years, come peas-cod time, but an honester and truer-hearted man—well, fare thee well.' Poins and the Prince delight in him; they get him into corners for the pleasure of seeing him escape in ways they cannot imagine; but they often take him much too seriously. Poins, for instance, rarely sees, the Prince does not always see, and moralising critics never see, that when Falstaff speaks ill of a companion behind his back, or writes to the Prince that Poins spreads it abroad that the Prince is to marry his sister, he knows quite well that what he says will be repeated, or rather, perhaps, is absolutely indifferent whether it be repeated or not, being certain that it can only give him an opportunity for humour. It is the same with his lying, and almost the same with his cowardice, the two main vices laid to his charge even by sympathisers. Falstaff is neither a liar nor a coward in the usual sense, like the typical cowardly boaster of comedy. He tells his lies either for their own humour, or on purpose to get himself into a difficulty. He rarely expects to be believed, perhaps never. He abandons a statement or contradicts it the moment it is made. There is scarcely more intent in his lying than in the humorous exaggerations which he pours out in soliloquy just as much as when others are by. Poins and the Prince understand this in part. You see them waiting eagerly to convict him, not that they may really put him to shame, but in order to enjoy the greater lie that will swallow up the less. But their sense of humour lags behind his. Even the Prince seems to accept as half-serious that remorse of his which passes so suddenly into glee at the idea of taking a purse, and his request to his friend to bestride him if he should see him down in the battle. Bestride Falstaff! 'Hence! Wilt thou lift up Olympus?'

Again, the attack of the Prince and Poins on Falstaff and the other thieves on Gadshill is contrived, we know, with a view to the incomprehensible lies it will induce him to tell. But when, more than rising to the occasion, he turns two men in buckram into four, and then seven, and then nine, and then eleven, almost in a breath, I believe they partly misunderstand his intention, and too many of his critics misunderstand it altogether. Shakespeare was not writing a mere farce. It is pre-posterous to suppose that a man of Falstaff's intelligence would utter these gross, palpable, open lies with the serious intention to deceive, or forget that, if it was too dark for him to see his own hand, he could hardly see that the three misbegotten knaves were wearing Kendal green. No doubt, if he *had* been believed, he would have been hugely tickled at it, but he no more expected to be believed than when he claimed to have killed Hotspur. Yet he is supposed to be serious even then. Such interpretations would destroy the poet's whole conception; and of those who adopt them one might ask this out of some twenty similar questions:—When Falstaff, in the men in buckram scene, begins by calling twice at short intervals for sack, and then a little later calls for more and says, 'I am a rogue if I drunk to-day,' and the Prince answers, 'O villain, thy lips are scarce wiped since thou drunk'st last,' do they think that *that* lie was meant to deceive? And if not, why do they take it for granted that the others were? I suppose they consider that Falstaff was in earnest when, wanting to get twenty-two yards of satin on trust from Master Dombledon the silk-mercer, he offered Bardolph as security; or when he said to the Chief Justice about Mrs. Quickly, who accused him of breaking his promise to marry her, 'My lord, this is a poor mad soul, and she says up and down the town that her eldest son is like you'; or when he explained his enormous bulk by exclaiming, 'A plague of sighing and grief! It blows a man up like a bladder'; or when he accounted for his voice being cracked by declaring that he had 'lost it with singing of anthems'; or even when he sold his soul on Good-Friday to the devil for a cup of Madeira and a cold capon's leg. Falstaff's lies about Hotspur and the men in buckram do not essentially differ from these statements. There is nothing serious in any of them except the refusal to take anything seriously.

This is also the explanation of Falstaff's cowardice, a subject on which I should say nothing if Maurice Morgann's essay, now more than a century old, were better known. That Falstaff sometimes behaves in what we should generally call a cowardly way is certain; but that does not show that he was a coward; and if the word means a person who feels painful fear in the presence of danger, and yields to that fear in spite of his better feelings and convictions, then assuredly Falstaff was no coward. The stock bully and boaster of comedy is one, but not Falstaff. It is perfectly clear in the first place that, though he had unfortunately a reputation for stabbing and caring not what mischief he did if his weapon were out, he had not a reputation for cowardice. Shallow remembered him five-and-fifty years ago breaking Scogan's head at the court-gate when he was a crack not thus high; and Shallow knew him later a good back-swordsman. Then we lose sight of him till about twenty years after, when his association with Bardolph began; and that association implies that by the time he was thirty-five or forty he had sunk into the mode of life we witness in the plays. Yet, even as we see him there, he remains a person of consideration in the army. Twelve captains hurry about London searching for him. He is present at the Council of War in the King's tent at Shrewsbury, where the only other persons are the King, the two princes, a nobleman and Sir Walter Blunt. The messenger who brings the false report of the battle to Northumberland mentions, as one of the important incidents, the death of Sir John Falstaff. Colvile, expressly described as a famous rebel, surrenders to him as soon as he hears his name. And if his own wish that his name were not so terrible to the enemy, and his own boast of his European reputation, are not evidence of the first rank, they must not be entirely ignored in presence of these other facts. What do these facts mean? Does Shakespeare put them all in with no purpose at all, or in defiance of his own intentions? It is not credible.

And when, in the second place, we look at Falstaff's actions, what do we find? He boldly confronted Colvile, he was quite ready to fight with him, however pleased that Colvile, like a kind fellow, gave himself away. When he saw Henry and Hotspur fighting, Falstaff, instead of making off in a panic, stayed to take his chance if Hotspur should be the victor. He *led* his hundred and fifty ragamuffins where they were peppered, he did not *send* them. To draw upon Pistol and force him downstairs and wound him in the shoulder was no great feat, perhaps, but the stock coward would have shrunk from it. When the Sheriff came to the inn to arrest him for an offence whose penalty was death, Falstaff, who was hidden behind the arras, did not stand there quaking for fear, he immediately fell asleep and snored. When he stood in the battle reflecting on what would happen if the weight of his paunch should be increased by that of a bullet, he cannot have been in a tremor of craven fear. He *never* shows such fear; and surely the man who, in danger of his life, and with no one by to hear him, meditates thus: 'I like not such grinning honour as Sir Walter hath. Give me life: which if I can save, so; if not, honour comes unlooked-for, and there's an end,' is not what we commonly call a coward.

'Well,' it will be answered, 'but he ran away on Gadshill; and when Douglas attacked him he fell down and shammed dead.' Yes, I am thankful to say, he did. For of course he did not want to be dead. He wanted to live and be merry. And as he had reduced the idea of honour *ad absurdum,* had scarcely any self-respect, and only a respect for reputation as a means of life, naturally he avoided death when he could do so without a ruinous loss of reputation, and (observe) with the satisfaction of playing a colossal practical joke. For *that* after all was his first object. If his one thought had been to avoid death he would not have faced Douglas at all, but would have run away as fast as his legs could carry him; and unless Douglas had been one of those exceptional Scotchmen who have no sense of humour, he would never have thought of pursuing so ridiculous an object as Falstaff running. So that, as Mr. Swinburne remarks, Poins is right when he thus distinguishes Falstaff from his companions in robbery: 'For two of them, I know them to be as true-bred cowards as ever turned back; and for the third, if he fight longer than he sees reason, I'll forswear arms.' And the event justifies this distinction. For it is exactly thus that, according to the original stage-direction, Falstaff behaves when Henry and Poins attack him and the others. The rest run away at once; Falstaff, here as afterwards with Douglas, fights for a blow or two, but, finding himself deserted and out-matched, runs away also. Of course. He saw no reason to say. *Any* man who had risen superior to all serious motives would have run away. But it does not follow that he would run from mere fear, or be, in the ordinary sense, a coward.[5]

III

The main source, then, of our sympathetic delight in Falstaff is his humorous superiority to everything serious, and the freedom of soul enjoyed in it. But, of course, this is not the whole of his character. Shakespeare knew well enough that perfect freedom is not to be gained in this manner; we are ourselves aware of it even while we are sympathising with Falstaff; and as soon as we regard him seriously it becomes obvious. His freedom is limited in two main ways. For one thing he cannot rid himself entirely of respect for all that he professes to ridicule. He shows a certain pride in his rank: unlike the Prince, he is haughty to the drawers, who call him a proud Jack. He is not really quite indifferent to reputation. When the Chief Justice bids him pay his debt to Mrs. Quickly for his reputation's sake, I think he feels a twinge, though to be sure he proceeds to pay her by borrowing from her. He is also stung by any thoroughly serious imputation on his courage, and winces at the recollection of his running away on Gadshill; he knows that his behaviour there certainly looked cowardly, and perhaps he remembers that he would not have behaved so once. It is, further, very significant that, for all his dissolute talk, he has never yet allowed the Prince and Poins to *see* him as they saw him afterwards with Doll Tearsheet; not, of course, that he has any moral shame in the matter, but he knows that in such a situation he, in his old age, must appear contemptible—not a humorist but a mere object of mirth. And, finally, he has affection in him—affection, I think, for Poins and Bardolph, and certainly for the Prince; and that is a thing which he cannot jest out of existence. Hence, as the effect of his rejection shows, he is not really invulnerable. And then, in the second place, since he is in the flesh, his godlike freedom has consequences and conditions; consequences, for there is something painfully wrong with his great toe; conditions, for he cannot eat and drink for ever without money, and his purse suffers from consumption, a disease for which he can find no remedy.[6] As the Chief Justice tells him, his means are very slender and his waste great; and his answer, 'I would it were otherwise; I would my means were greater and my waist slenderer,' though worth much money, brings none in. And so he is driven to evil deeds; not only to cheating his tailor like a gentleman, but to fleecing Justice Shallow, and to highway robbery, and to cruel depredations on the poor woman whose affection he has secured. All this is perfectly consistent with the other side of his character, but by itself it makes an ugly picture.

Yes, it makes an ugly picture when you look at it seriously. But then, surely, so long as the humorous atmosphere is preserved and the humorous attitude maintained, you do not look at it so. You no more regard Falstaff's misdeeds morally than you do the much more atrocious misdeeds of Punch or Reynard the Fox. You do not exactly ignore them but you attend only to their comic aspect. This is the very spirit of comedy, and certainly of Shakespeare's comic world, which is one of make-believe, not merely as his tragic world is, but in a further sense—a world in which gross improbabilities are accepted with a smile, and many things are welcomed as merely laughable which, regarded gravely, would excite anger and disgust. The intervention of a serious spirit breaks up such a world, and would destroy our pleasure in Falstaff's company. Accordingly through the greater part of these dramas Shakespeare carefully confines this spirit to the scenes of war and policy, and dismisses it entirely in the humorous parts. Hence, if *Henry IV.* had been a comedy like *Twelfth Night,* I am sure that he would not more have ended it with the painful disgrace of Falstaff than he ended *Twelfth Night* by disgracing Sir Toby Belch.[7]

But *Henry IV.* was to be in the main a historical play, and its chief hero Prince Henry. In the course of it his greater and finer qualities were to be gradually revealed, and it was to end with beautiful scenes of reconciliation and affection between his father and him, and a final emergence of the wild Prince as a just, wise, stern, and glorious King. Hence, no doubt, it seemed to Shakespeare that Falstaff at last must be disgraced and must therefore appear no longer as the invincible humorist, but as an object of ridicule and even of aversion. And probably also his poet's insight showed him that Henry, as he conceived him, *would* behave harshly to Falstaff in order to impress the world, especially when his mind had been wrought to a high pitch by the scene with his dying father and the impression of his own solemn consecration to great duties.

This conception was a natural and a fine one; and if the execution was not an entire success, it is yet full of interest. Shakespeare's purpose being to work a gradual change in our feelings towards Falstaff, and to tinge the humorous atmosphere more and more deeply with seriousness, we see him carrying out his purpose in the Second Part of *Henry IV.* Here he separates the Prince from Falstaff as much as he can, thus withdrawing him from Falstaff's influence, and weakening in our minds the connection between the two. In the First Part we constantly see them together; in the Second (it is a remarkable fact) only once before the rejection. Further, in the scenes where Henry appears apart from Falstaff, we watch him growing more and more grave, and awakening more and more poetic interest; while Falstaff, though his humour scarcely flags to the end, exhibits more and more of his seamy side. This is nowhere turned to the full light in Part I.; but in Part II. we see him as the heartless destroyer of Mrs. Quickly, as a ruffian seriously defying the Chief Justice because his position as an officer on service gives him power to do wrong, as the pike preparing to snap up the poor old dace Shallow, and (this is the one scene where Henry and he meet) as the worn-out lecher, not laughing at his servitude to the flesh but sunk in it. Finally, immediately before the rejection, the world where he is king is exposed in all its sordid criminality when we find Mrs. Quickly and Doll arrested for being concerned in the death of one man, if not more, beaten to death by their bullies; and the dangerousness of Falstaff is emphasised in his last words as he hurries from Shallow's house to London, words at first touched with humour but at bottom only too seriously meant: 'Let us take any man's horses; the laws of England are at my commandment. Happy are they which have been my friends, and woe unto my Lord Chief Justice.' His dismissal to the Fleet by the Chief Justice is the dramatic vengeance for that threat.

Yet all these excellent devices fail. They cause us momentary embarrassment at times when repellent traits in Falstaff's character are disclosed; but they fail to change our attitude of humour into one of seriousness, and our sympathy into repulsion. And they were bound to fail, because Shakespeare shrank from adding to them the one device which would have ensured success. If, as the Second Part of *Henry IV.* advanced, he had clouded over Falstaff's humour so heavily that the man of genius turned into the Falstaff of the *Merry Wives,* we should have witnessed his rejection without a pang. This Shakespeare was too much of an artist to do—though even in this way he did something—and without this device he could not succeed. As I said, in the creation of Falstaff he overreached himself. He was caught up on the wind of his own genius, and carried so far that he could not descend to earth at the selected spot. It is not a misfortune that happens to many authors, nor is it one we can regret, for it costs us but a trifling inconvenience in one scene, while we owe to it perhaps the greatest comic character in literature. For it is in this character, and not in the judgment he brings upon Falstaff's head, that Shakespeare asserts his supremacy. To show that Falstaff's freedom of soul was in part illusory, and that the realities of life refused to be conjured away by his humour—this was what we might expect from Shakespeare's unfailing sanity, but it was surely no achievement beyond the power of lesser men. The achievement was Falstaff himself, and the conception of that freedom of soul, a freedom illusory only in part, and attainable only by a mind which had received from Shakespeare's own the inexplicable touch of infinity which he bestowed on Hamlet and Macbeth and Cleopatra, but denied to Henry the Fifth.

NOTES

[1] See on this and other points Swinburne, *A Study of Shakespeare,* p. 106ff.

[2] Rötscher, *Shakespeare in seinen höchsten Charaktergebilden,* 1864.

[3] That from the beginning Shakespeare intended Henry's accession to be Falstaff's catastrophe is clear

from the fact that, when the two characters first appear, Falstaff is made to betray at once the hopes with which he looks forward to Henry's reign. See the First Part of *Henry IV.*, Act I., Scene ii.

[4] Cf. Hazlitt, *Characters of Shakespear's Plays.*

[5] It is to be regretted, however, that in carrying his guts away so nimbly he 'roared for mercy'; for I fear we have no ground for rejecting Henry's statement to that effect, and I do not see my way to adopt the suggestion (I forget whose it is) that Falstaff spoke the truth when he swore that he knew Henry and Poins as well as he that made them.

[6] Panurge too was 'naturally subject to a kind of disease which at that time they called lack of money'; it was a 'flux in his purse' (Rabelais, Book II., chapters xvi., xvii.).

[7] I seem to remember that, according to Gervinus, Shakespeare did disgrace Sir Toby—by marrying him to Maria!

Harold C. Goddard

HENRY IV

VI

Who at this late date can hope to say a fresh word about Falstaff? Long since, his admirers and detractors have drained language dry in their efforts to characterize him, to give expression to their fascination or detestation. Glutton, drunkard, coward, liar, lecher, boaster, cheat, thief, rogue, ruffian, villain are a few of the terms that have been used to describe a man whom others find the very incarnation of charm, one of the liberators of the human spirit, the greatest comic figure in the history of literature. "A besotted and disgusting old wretch," Bernard Shaw calls him. And isn't he?—this man who held up unprotected travelers for pastime, betrayed innocence in the person of his page, cheated a trusting and hard-working hostess, borrowed a thousand pounds from an old friend with no intention of repaying it, abused his commission by taking cash in lieu of military service, and insinuated his way into the graces of the heir apparent with an eye to later favor. And yet after three centuries there the old sinner sits, more invulnerable and full of smiles than ever, his sagging paunch shaking like a jelly, dodging or receiving full on, unperturbed, the missiles his enemies hurl at him. Which is he? A colossus of sack, sensuality, and sweat—or a wit and humorist so great that he can be compared only with his creator, a figure, to use one of Shakespeare's own great phrases, livelier than life? One might think there were two Falstaffs.

The trouble with the "besotted and disgusting old wretch" theory is that Shakespeare has given us that old wretch exactly, and he is another man: the Falstaff of *The Merry Wives of Windsor*. The disparagers of Falstaff generally make him out a mixture, in varying proportions, of this other Falstaff, Sir Toby Belch, and Parolles, each of whom was an incalculably inferior person. But to assert that Falstaff is another man is not saying that he does not have many or even all of the vices of the "old wretch" for whom his defamers mistake him. Salt is not sodium, but that

---

From *The Meaning of Shakespeare* (Chicago: University of Chicago Press, 1951), pp. 175–90.

is not saying that sodium is not a component of salt. The truth is that there *are* two Falstaffs, just as there are two Henrys, the Immortal Falstaff and the Immoral Falstaff, and the dissension about the man comes from a failure to recognize that fact. That the two could inhabit one body would not be believed if Shakespeare had not proved that they could. That may be one reason why he made it so huge.

Curiously, there is no more convincing testimony to this double nature of the man than that offered by those who are most persistent in pointing out his depravity. In the very process of committing the old sinner to perdition they reveal that they have been unable to resist his seductiveness. Professor Stoll, for instance, dedicates twenty-six sections of a long and learned essay to the annihilation of the Falstaff that his congenital lovers love. And then he begins his twenty-seventh and last section with the words: "And yet people like Falstaff"! And before his first paragraph is done, all his previous labor is obliterated as we find him asserting that Falstaff is "supremely poetic" (even his most ardent admirers would hardly venture that "supremely") and that "his is in many ways the most marvelous prose ever penned." (It is, but how did the old sot, we wonder, ever acquire it?) Before his next paragraph is over, Stoll has called Falstaff "the very spirit of comradeship," "the king of companions," and "the prince of good fellows." "We, too, after all, like Prince Hal and Mrs. Quickly," he goes on, "take to a man because of his charm, if it be big enough, not because of his virtue; and as for Falstaff, we are bewitched with the rogue's company." (A Falstaff idolater could scarcely ask for more than that.) "Under the spell of his presence and speech," Stoll concludes, we should forget, as she does, the wrong he has done Mrs. Quickly, "did we not stop to think."

"Stop to think"! One may determine the orbit of the moon, or make an atomic bomb, by stopping to think, but when since the beginning of time did one man ever get at the secret of another by means of the intellect? It is all right to stop to think after we have taken a character to our hearts, but to do so before we have is fatal. Dr. Johnson stopped to think about Falstaff and as a result he decided that "he has nothing in him that can be esteemed." A child would be ashamed of such a judgment. But a child would never be guilty of it. "As for *Henry IV*," wrote one of the most imaginatively gifted young women I have ever known, "I love it. And I must have an utterly vulgar nature, for I simply adore Falstaff. He is perfectly delightful—not a fault in his nature, and the Prince is a DEVIL to reject him." That young woman evidently did not "stop to think." When she does, she will moderate that "not a fault in his nature," for that is the function of thinking—to hold our imagination within bounds and cut down its excrescences. Meanwhile, Falstaff has captured her, and she has captured Falstaff, for, as Blake said, enthusiastic admiration is the first principle of knowledge, and the last. Those who think about Falstaff before they fall in love with him may say some just things about him but they will never enter into his secret. "Would I were with him, wheresome'er he is, either in heaven or in hell!" Those words of poor Bardolph on hearing the account of Falstaff's death remain the highest tribute he ever did or ever could receive. In their stark sincerity they are worthy (irreverent as the suggestion will seem to some) to be put beside Dante's sublime incarnation of the same idea in the Paolo and Francesca incident in *The*

Inferno, or even beside the words addressed to the thief who repented on the cross.

The scholars have attempted to explain Falstaff by tracing his origins. He has been found, variously, to have developed from the Devil of the miracle plays, the Vice of the morality plays, the boasting soldier of Plautine comedy, and so on. Now roots, up to a certain point, are interesting, but it takes the sun to make them grow and to illuminate the flower. And I think in this case we can find both roots and sun without going outside Shakespeare. If so, it is one of the most striking confirmations to be found of the embryological nature of his development.

If I were seeking the embryo of Falstaff in Shakespeare's imagination, I should consider the claims of Bottom—of Bottom and another character in *A Midsummer-Night's Dream.* "What!" it will be said, "the dull realistic Bottom and the lively witty Falstaff? They are nearer opposites." But embryos, it must be remembered, seldom resemble what they are destined to develop into. Bottom, like the physical Falstaff at least, is compact of the heaviness, the materiality, the reality of earth; and the ass's head that Puck bestows on him is abundantly deserved not only in special reference to his brains but in its general implication of animality. But instead of letting himself be humiliated by it, Bottom sings, and Titania, Queen of the Fairies, her eyes anointed by the magic flower, awakening, mistakes him for an angel, and taking him in her arms, lulls him to sleep. The obvious meaning of the incident of course is that love is blind. Look at the asinine thing an infatuated woman will fall in love with! But whoever stops there, though he may have gotten the fun, has missed the beauty. The moment when Bottom emerges from his dream, as we pointed out when discussing *A Midsummer-Night's Dream,* is Shakespeare at one of his pinnacles. By a stroke of genius he turns a purely farcical incident into nothing less than a parable of the Awakening of Imagination within Gross Matter. It is the poet's way of saying that even within the head of this foolish plebeian weaver a divine light can be kindled. Bottom is conscious of transcendent things when he comes to himself. A creation has taken place within him. He struggles, in vain, to express it, and, in his very failure, succeeds:

> God's my life! . . . I have had a most rare vision. I have had a dream, past the wit of man to say what dream it was. Man is but an ass, if he go about to expound this dream. Methought I was—there is no man can tell what. Methought I was,—and methought I had,—but man is but a patch'd fool, if he will offer to say what methought I had. The eye of man hath not heard, the ear of man hath not seen, man's hand is not able to taste, his tongue to conceive, nor his heart to report, what my dream was. I will get Peter Quince to write a ballad of this dream. It shall be called "Bottom's Dream," because it hath no bottom.

The dreamer may still be Bottom. But the dream itself is Puck. For one moment the two are one. Ass or angel? Perhaps Titania was not so deluded after all.

Do not misunderstand me. I am not suggesting that Shakespeare ever consciously connected Puck and Bottom with Falstaff in his own mind. But having achieved this inconceivable integration of the two, how easily his genius would be tempted to repeat the miracle on a grander scale: to create a perfect mountain of flesh and show how the same wonder could occur within it, not momentarily, but, humanly speaking, perpetually. That at any rate is what Falstaff is: Imagination conquering matter, spirit subduing flesh. Bottom was a weaver—a weaver of threads. "I would I were a weaver," Falstaff once exclaimed. He was a weaver—a weaver of spells. Here, if ever, is the embryology of the imagination. "Man is but a patch'd fool, if he will offer to say. . . ." Who cannot catch the very accent of Falstaff in that?

> I'll put a girdle round about the earth
> In forty minutes.

It might have been said of Falstaff's wit. His Bottom-like body is continually being dragged down, but his Puck-like spirit can hide in a thimble or pass through a keyhole as nimbly as any fairy's. What wonder that this contradictory being—as deminatured as a satyr or a mermaid—who is forever repeating within himself the original miracle of creation, has taken on the proportions of a mythological figure. He seems at times more like a god than a man. His very solidity is solar, his rotundity cosmic. To estimate the refining power we must know the grossness of what is to be refined. To be astounded by what lifts we must know the weight of what is to be lifted. Falstaff is levitation overcoming gravitation. At his wittiest and most aerial, he is Ariel tossing the terrestrial globe in the air as if it were a ball. And yet—as we must never forget—he is also that fat old sinner fast asleep and snoring behind the arras. The sins, in fact, are the very things that make the miracle astonishing, as the chains and ropes do a Houdini's escape.

To grasp Falstaff thus *sub specie aeternitatis* we must see him, as Titania did Bottom, with our imagination, not with our senses. And that is why we shall never see Falstaff on the stage. On the stage there the monster of flesh stands—made, we know, mainly of pillows—with all his sheer material bulk and greasy beefiness, a palpable candidate for perdition. It takes rare acting to rescue him from being physically repulsive. And as for the miracle—it just refuses to happen in a theater. It would take a child to melt this too too solid flesh into spirit. It would take Falstaff himself to act Falstaff. But in a book! On the stage of our imagination! That is another matter. There the miracle can occur—and does for thousands of readers. Falstaff is a touchstone to tell whether the juice of the magic flower has been squeezed into our eyes. If it has not, we will see only his animality. To the vulgar, Falstaff will be forever just vulgar.

The problem of Falstaff himself cannot be separated from the problem of the fascination he exercises over us. Critics have long since put their fingers on the negative side of that secret. Half his charm resides in the fact that he is what we long to be and are not: *free.* Hence our delight in projecting on him our frustrated longing for emancipation. It is right here that those who do not like Falstaff score a cheap victory over those who do. The latter, say the former, are repressed or sedentary souls who go on a vicarious spree in the presence of one who commits all the sins they would like to commit but do not dare to. Like some of Falstaff's own hypotheses, the idea has an air of plausibility. But it involves a pitifully superficial view of Falstaff—as if his essence lay in his love of sack! No! it is for liberation from what all men want to be rid of, not just the bloodless few, that Falstaff stands: liberation from the tyranny of things as they are. Falstaff is immortal because he is a symbol of the supremacy of imagination over fact. He forecasts man's final victory over Fate itself. Facts stand in our way. Facts melt before Falstaff like ice before a summer sun—dissolve in the *aqua regia* of his resourcefulness and wit. He realizes the age-old dream of all men: to awaken in the morning and to know that no master, no employer, no bodily need or sense of duty calls, no fear or obstacle stands in the way—only a fresh beckoning day that is wholly ours.

But we have all awakened that way on rare occasions without becoming Falstaffs. Some men often do. An untrammeled day is not enough; we must have something to fill it with—besides lying in bed. Freedom is only the negative side of Falstaff. Possessing it, he perpetually does something creative with it. It is not enough for him to be the sworn enemy of facts. Any lazy man or fool is that. He is the sworn enemy of the factual spirit itself, of whatever is dull, inert, banal. Facts merely exist—and so do most men. Falstaff lives. And where he is, life becomes bright, active, enthralling.

Who has not been a member of some listless group on whom time has been hanging heavy when in the twinkling of an eye a newcomer has altered the face of everything as utterly as the sun, breaking through clouds, transforms the surface of a gray lake? Boredom is banished. Gaiety is restored. The most apathetic member of the company is laughing and alert and will shortly be contributing his share to the flow of good spirits. What has done it? At bottom, of course, the mysterious fluid of an infectious personality. But so far as it can be analyzed, some tall tale or personal adventure wherein a grain of fact has been worked up with a pound of fiction, some impudent assumption about the host or absurd charge against some-body present rendered plausible by a precarious resemblance to the truth. Always *something made out of nothing*, with power, when added to the facts, to get the better of them. Never an unadulterated lie, but always some monstrous per-version, some scandalous interpretation, of what actually happened. An invention, yes, but an invention attached to reality by a thread of truth—the slenderer the better, so long as it does not break. What is Falstaff but an aggrandized, univer-salized, individualized version of this familiar phenomenon? He makes life again worth living.

And so, whether we approach Falstaff from the mythological or the psycho-logical angle, we reach the same goal.

But alas! We have been neglecting the other Falstaff, the old sot. Unluckily—or perhaps luckily—there is another side to the story. Having fallen in love with Falstaff, we may now "stop to think" about him without compunction. And on examining more closely this symbol of man's supremacy over nature we perceive that he is not invulnerable. He has his Achilles heel. I do not refer to his love of Hal. That is his Achilles heel in another and lovelier sense. I refer to a tiny fact, two tiny facts, that he forgets and that we would like to: the fact that his imagination is stimulated by immense potations of sack and that his victories are purchased, if necessary, at the price of an utter disregard for the rights of others. We do not remember this until we stop to think. And we do not want to stop to think. We want to identify ourselves with the Immortal Falstaff. Yet there the Immoral Falstaff is all the while. And he must be reckoned with. Shakespeare was too much of a realist to leave him out.

The Greeks incarnated in their god Dionysus the paradox of wine, its combined power to inspire and degrade. *The Bacchae* of Euripides is the profoundest treatment of this theme in Hellenic if not in any literature. "No one can hate drunkenness more than I do," says Samuel Butler, "but I am confident the human intellect owes its superiority over that of the lower animals in great measure to the stimulus which alcohol has given to imagination—imagination being little else than another name for illusion."[1] "The sway of alcohol over mankind," says William James, "is unquestionably due to its power to stimulate the mystical faculties of human nature [the imagination, that is, in its quintessence], usually crushed to earth by the cold facts and dry criticisms of the sober hour. Sobriety diminishes, discriminates, and says no; drunkenness expands, unites, and says yes. It is in fact the great exciter of the *Yes* function in man ... it is part of the deeper mystery and tragedy of life that whiffs and gleams of something that we immediately recognize as excellent should be vouchsafed to so many of us only in the fleeting earlier phases of what in its totality is so degrading a poisoning."

James's contrast between the earlier and the later phases of alcoholic intoxication inevitably suggests the degeneration that Falstaff undergoes in the second part of *Henry IV*. That degeneration is an actual one, though several recent critics have tended to exaggerate it. Dover Wilson thinks that Shakespeare is deliberately trying to make us fall out of love with Falstaff so that we may accept with good grace his rejection by the new king. If so, for many readers he did not succeed very well. (Of that in its place.)

It is significant that we never see Falstaff drunk. His wit still scintillates practically unabated throughout the second part of the play, though some critics seem set on not admitting it. He is in top form, for instance, in his interview with the Chief Justice, and, to pick a single example from many, the reply he gives to John of Lancaster's reproach,

When everything is ended, then you come,

is one of his pinnacles: "Do you think me a swallow, an arrow, or a bullet?" No, the degeneration of Falstaff is not so much in his wit or even in his imagination as in his moral sensibility. The company he keeps grows more continuously low, and his treatment of Shallow and of his recruits shows an increasing hardness of heart. Shakespeare inserts too many little realistic touches to let us take these scenes as pure farce, and while no one in his senses would want to turn this aspect of the play into a temperance tract it seems at times like an almost scientifically faithful account of the effect of an excess of alcohol on the moral nature. In view of what Shakespeare was at this time on the verge of saying about drunkenness in *Hamlet* and of what he was to say about it later in *Othello, Antony and Cleopatra,* and *The Tempest,* it is certain that he was profoundly interested in the subject; and it is not far-fetched to suppose that he had in the back of his mind in portraying the "degeneration" of Falstaff the nemesis that awaits the artificially stimulated mind. If so, the fat knight is Shakespeare's contribution, in a different key, to the same problem that is treated in *The Bacchae,* and his conclusions are close to those at which Euripides arrives.

VII

And then there is *The Merry Wives of Windsor.* (Here appears to be the right place for a brief interlude on that play.) Criticism has been much concerned over the connection, if any, between the Falstaff of *The Merry Wives* and the Falstaff of *Henry IV*—with something like a consensus that with the exception of a few dying sparks of the original one this is another man. Yet one link between the two Falstaffs cannot be denied: with respect to wit and resourcefulness they are exact opposites. The Falstaff we admire is an incarnation of readiness; this one of help-lessness. Nothing is too much for the former. Anything is too much for the latter. They are, respectively, presence and absence of mind. Such an utter antithesis is itself a connection. Shakespeare must have meant something by it.

Nearly everyone is acquainted with the tradition that *The Merry Wives of Windsor* was written in a fortnight at the command of Queen Elizabeth, who wished to see the fat man in love. Shakespeare does appear to have "tossed off" this sparkling farce-comedy, his one play of purely contemporary life and of almost pure prose, and along with *The Comedy of Errors,* his most inconsequential and merely theatrical one. Several hypotheses, or some combination of them, may account for the Falstaff of this play.

Poets, as distinct from poets laureate, do not like commissions. It would be quite like Shakespeare, ordered by the Queen to write another play about Falstaff, to have his playful revenge by writing one about another man entirely, under the same name. That was precisely the sort of thing that Chaucer did when com-manded by another Queen to write a *Legend of Good Women.* It is fun to make a fool of royalty. Then, too, the conditions under which the play was written, if the tradition is true, practically compelled it to keep close to farce. And farce is the very atmosphere in which parody thrives. This Falstaff is a kind of parody of the other one. But the closer Shakespeare gets to farce, fancy, or nonsense, as he proves over and over, the more certain he is to have some serious underintention. On that principle, what better place than *The Merry Wives of Windsor* in which to insert an oblique comment on the Falstaff of *Henry IV?* Be that as it may, the Falstaff of this play is, as we said, an almost perfect picture, in exaggerated form and in a farcical key, of the Immoral Falstaff of the other plays, the old wretch of Bernard Shaw. Only the light tone of the piece keeps him from being "besotted and disgusting" also. Critics have seriously tried to determine at what spot chronologically this play should be inserted in the Henry series. Such an attempt betrays a curious ignorance of the ways of the imagination. But, after all due discount for the farce and fooling, the Falstaff of *The Merry Wives* looks like pretty good natural history of the latter end of an "old soak." From him it is a relief to get back, after our interlude, to the Immortal Falstaff, who, however entangled with the Immoral Falstaff, as the soul is with the body, breathes another and more transcendental air.

VIII

Is there any activity of man that involves the same factors that we find present in this Falstaff: complete freedom, an all-consuming zest for life, an utter subjugation of facts to imagination, and an entire absence of moral responsibility? Obviously there is. That activity is play.

Except for that little item of moral responsibility, "play" expresses as nearly as one word can the highest conception of life we are capable of forming: life for its own sake, life as it looks in the morning to a boy with

> no more behind
> But such a day to-morrow as to-day,
> And to be boy eternal,

life for the fun of it, as against life for what you can get out of it—or whom you can knock out of it. "Play" says what the word "peace" tries to say and doesn't. "Play" brings down to the level of everyone's understanding what "imagination" conveys to more sophisticated minds. For the element of imagination is indispensable to true play. Play is not sport. The confusion of the two is a major tragedy of our time. A crowd of fifteen-year-old schoolboys "playing" football on a back lot are indulging in sport. They are rarely playing. The one who is playing is the child of five, all alone, pretending that a dirty rag doll is the rich mother of a dozen infants—invisible to the naked eye. Even boys playing war, if they are harmonious and happy, are conducting an experiment in peace. Play is the erection of an illusion into a reality. It is not an escape from life. It is the realization of life in something like its fulness. What it *is* an escape from is the boredom and friction of existence. Like poetry, to which it is the prelude, it stands for a converting or winning-over of facts on a basis of friendship, the dissolving of them in a spirit of love, in contrast with science (at least the science of our day), which, somewhat illogically, stands first for a recognition of the absolute autonomy of facts and then for their impressment and subjection to human demands by a kind of military conquest.

Now Falstaff goes through life playing. He coins everything he encounters into play, often even into a play. He would rather have the joke on himself and make the imaginative most of it than to have it on the other fellow and let the fun stop there. Whenever he seems to be taken in because he does not realize the situation, it is safer to assume that he does realize it but keeps quiet because the imaginative possibilities are greater in that case.

Watching him, we who in dead earnest have been attending to business or doing what we are pleased to call our duty suddenly realize what we have been missing. "The object of a man's life," says Robert Henri, "should be to play as a little child plays." If that is so we have missed the object of life, while Falstaff has attained it, or at least not missed it completely, as we have. It is his glory that, like Peter Pan, he never grew up, and that glory is the greater because he is an old man. As his immense size and weight were utilized by Shakespeare as a foil for the lightness of his spirit, so his age is used to stress its youthfulness. "You that are old," he says to the Chief Justice, who has been berating him for misleading the Prince, "consider not the capacities of us that are young." The Chief Justice replies that Falstaff is in every part "blasted with antiquity," his belly increasing in size, his voice broken, "and will you yet call yourself young? Fie, fie, fie, Sir John!" Falstaff retorts that as for his belly, he was born with a round one; as for his voice, he has lost it hollaing and singing of anthems; and as for his age, he is old only in judgment and understanding. Though the Lord Chief Justice has all the facts on his side, Falstaff has the victory. There has seldom been a more delicious interview.

As this scene suggests, the right way to take the Falstaff whom we love is to take him as a child. Mrs. Quickly did that in her immortal account of his death: he went away, she said, "an it had been any christom child." To call him a liar and let it go at that is like being the hardheaded father of a poetic little son who punishes him for falsehood when he has only been relating genuine imaginative experiences —as Blake's father thrashed him for saying he had seen angels in a tree. And to call him a coward and let it go at *that* is being no profounder.

But if it is the glory of the Immortal Falstaff that he remained a child, it is the shame of the Immoral Falstaff that he never became a man—for it is a child's duty to become a man no less than it is a man's duty to become a child. Falstaff detoured manhood instead of passing through it into a higher childhood. He is like the character in *The Pilgrim's Progress* who tried to steal into Paradise by climbing over the wall near its entrance instead of passing through the wicket gate and undergoing the trials that it is the lot of man to endure. He wanted the victory without paying the price. He wanted to be an individual regardless of the social consequences, to persist in the prerogatives of youth without undertaking the responsibilities of maturity. But if his virtues are those of a child rather than those of a man, that does not prevent him from being immensely superior to those in these plays who possess the virtues of neither man nor child, or from giving us gleams of a life beyond good and evil.

Dover Wilson[2] would have us take *Henry IV* as a morality play wherein a madcap prince grows up into an ideal king. Falstaff is the devil who tempts the Prince to Riot. Hotspur and especially the Lord Chief Justice are the good angels representing Chivalry and Justice or the Rule of Law. It is a struggle between Vanity and Government for the possession of the Royal Prodigal.

The scene is superbly simple and as moral as a Sunday-school lesson. But it calmly leaves the Immortal Falstaff quite out of account! If Falstaff were indeed just the immoral creature that in part he admittedly is, Wilson's parable would be more plausible, though even then the words he picks to characterize Falstaff are singularly unfortunate. "Vanity" by derivation means emptiness or absence of substance, and "riot" quarrelsomeness. Imagine calling even the Immoral Falstaff empty or lacking in substance—or quarrelsome! He had his vices but they were not these. For either vanity or riot there is not a single good word to be said. To equate Falstaff with them is to assert that not a single good word can be said for him—a preposterous proposition. Wit, humor, laughter, good-fellowship, insatiable zest for life: are these vanity or does Falstaff *not* embody them? That is the dilemma in which Mr. Wilson puts himself. And as for the Lord Chief Justice, he is indeed an admirable man; a more incorruptible one in high position is not to be found in Shakespeare. But if the poet had intended to assign him any such crucial role as Mr. Wilson thinks, he certainly would have presented him more fully and would have hesitated to let Falstaff make him look so foolish. For the Chief Justice's sense of justice was better developed than his sense of humor. And even justice is not all.

Henry IV does have a certain resemblance to a morality play. The two, however, between whom the younger Henry stands and who are in a sense contending for the possession of his soul are not Falstaff and the Chief Justice, but Falstaff and the King. It is between Falstaff and the Father—to use that word in its generic sense—that Henry finds himself.

Now in the abstract this is indeed Youth between Revelry and Responsibility. But the abstract has nothing to do with it. Where Henry really stands is between this particular companion, Falstaff, and this particular father and king, Henry IV. Of the two, which was the better man?

Concede the utmost—that is, take Falstaff at his worst. He was a drunkard, a glutton, a profligate, a thief, even a liar if you insist, but withal a fundamentally honest man. He had two sides like a coin, but he was not a counterfeit. And Henry? He was a king, a man of "honour," of brains and ability, of good intentions, but withal, a "vile politician" and respectable hypocrite. He *was* a counterfeit. Which, if it comes to the choice, is the better influence on a young man? Shakespeare, for one, gives no evidence of having an iota of doubt.

But if even Falstaff at his worst comes off better than Henry, how about Falstaff at his best? In that case, what we have is Youth standing between Imagination and Authority, between Freedom and Force, between Play and War. My insistence that Falstaff is a double man, and that the abstract has nothing to do with it, will acquit me of implying that this is the whole of the story. But it is a highly suggestive part of it.

The opposite of war is not "peace" in the debased sense in which we are in the habit of using the latter word. Peace ought to mean far more, but what is has to come to mean on our lips is just the absence of war. The opposite of war is creative activity, play in its loftier implications. All through these dramas the finer Falstaff symbolizes the opposite of force. When anything military enters his presence, it instantly looks ridiculous and begins to shrink. Many methods have been proposed for getting rid of war. Falstaff's is one of the simplest: laugh it out of existence. For war is almost as foolish as it is criminal. "Laugh it out of existence"?

If only we could! Which is the equivalent of saying: if only more of us were like Falstaff! These plays should be required reading in all military academies. Even the "cannon-fodder" scenes of Falstaff with his recruits have their serious implications and anticipate our present convictions on the uneugenic nature of war.

How far did Shakespeare sympathize with Falstaff's attitude in this matter? No one is entitled to say. But much further, I am inclined to think, than he would have had his audience suspect or than the world since his time has been willing to admit. For consider the conditions under which Falstaff finds himself:

Henry has dethroned and murdered the rightful king of England. The Percys have helped him to obtain the crown, but a mutual sense of guilt engenders distrust between the two parties, and the Percys decide to dethrone the dethroner. Falstaff is summoned to take part in his defense. "Life is given but once." Why should Falstaff risk his one life on earth, which he is enjoying as not one man in a hundred million does, to support or to oppose the cause of either of two equally selfish and equally damnable seekers after power and glory? What good would the sacrifice of his life accomplish comparable to the boon that he confers daily and hourly on the world, to say nothing of himself, by merely being? This is no case of tyranny on one side and democracy on the other, with the liberty or slavery of a world at stake. This is a strictly dynastic quarrel. When two gangs of gunmen begin shooting it out on the streets of a great city, the discreet citizen will step behind a post or into a doorway. The analogy may not be an exact one, but it enables us to understand Falstaff's point of view. And there is plenty of Shakespearean warrant for it.

See the coast clear'd, and then we will depart,

says the Major of London when caught, in *I Henry VI,* between similar brawling factions,

Good God! these nobles should such stomachs bear;
I myself fight not once in forty year.

And Mercutio's "A plague o' both your houses!" comes to mind. Shakespeare meant more by that phrase than the dying man who coined it could have comprehended.

"But how about Falstaff's honor?" it will be asked. "Thou owest God a death," says the Prince to him before the battle of Shrewsbury. " 'Tis not due yet," Falstaff answers as Hal goes out,

I would be loath to pay him before his day. What need I be so forward with him that calls not on me? Well, 'tis no matter; honour pricks me on. Yea, but how if honour prick me off when I came on? how then? Can honour set to a leg? No. Or an arm? No. Or take away the grief of a wound? No. Honour hath no skill in surgery, then? No. What is honour? A word. What is in that word honour? What is that honour? Air; a trim reckoning! Who hath it? He that died o' Wednesday. Doth he feel it? No. Doth he hear it? No. 'Tis insensible, then? Yea, to the dead. But will it not live with the living? No. Why? Detraction will not suffer it. Therefore I'll none of it. Honour is a mere scutcheon: and so ends my catechism.

"You must be honorable to talk of honor," says a character in *A Raw Youth,* "or, if not, all you say is a lie." The word "honor" as that sentence of Dostoevsky's shows, is still an honorable word. It can still mean, and could in Shakespeare's day, the integrity of the soul before God. The Chief Justice had honor in that sense. But "honour" in its decayed feudal sense of glory, fame, even reputation, as page after page of these Chronicle Plays records, had outlived its usefulness and the time had come to expose its hollowness. The soul, lifted up, declared Saint Teresa (who died in 1582), sees in the word "honor" "nothing more than an immense lie of which the world remains a victim. . . . She laughs when she sees grave persons, persons of orison, caring for points of honor for which she now feels profoundest contempt. . . . With what friendship we would all treat each other if our interest in honor and in money could but disappear from the earth! For my own part, I feel as if it would be a remedy for all our ills."

Saint Teresa and Sir John Falstaff! an odd pair to find in agreement—about honor if not about money. In the saint's case no ambiguity is attached to the doctrine that honor is a lie. In the sinner's, there remains something equivocal and double-edged. Here, if ever, the two Falstaffs meet. The grosser Falstaff is himself a parasite and a dishonorable man, and coming from him the speech is the creed of Commodity and the height of irony. But that does not prevent the man who loved Hal and babbled of green fields at his death from revealing in the same words, as clearly as Saint Teresa, that life was given for something greater than glory or than the gain that can be gotten out of it.

"Give me life," cries Falstaff on the field of Shrewsbury. "Die all, die merrily," cries Hotspur. That is the gist of it. The Prince killed Hotspur in the battle, and Falstaff, with one of his most inspired lies, claimed the deed as his own. But Falstaff's lies, scrutinized, often turn out to be truth in disguise. So here. Falstaff, not Prince Henry, did kill Hotspur. He ended the outworn conception of honor for which Hotspur stood. The Prince killed his body, but Falstaff killed his soul—or rather what passed for his soul.

The dying Hotspur himself sees the truth. The verdict of his final breath is that life is "time's fool" and he himself dust. And the Prince, gazing down at his dead victim, sees it too, if only for a moment.

Ill-weav'd ambition, how much art thou shrunk!
When that this body did contain a spirit,
A kingdom for it was too small a bound,

he exclaims, and, turning, he catches sight of another body from which life has also apparently departed:

What, old acquaintance! could not all this flesh
Keep in a little life? Poor Jack, farewell!
I could have better spar'd a better man.

But nobody was ever more mistaken on this subject of life and flesh than was Henry on this occasion, as the shamming Falstaff proves a moment later, when the Prince goes out, by rising from the dead. " 'Sblood," he cries,

> 'twas time to counterfeit, or that hot termagant Scot had paid me scot and lot too. Counterfeit? I lie, I am no counterfeit. To die is to be a counterfeit; for he is but the counterfeit of a man who hath not the life of a man; but to counterfeit dying, when a man thereby liveth, is to be no counterfeit, but the true and perfect image of life indeed. The better part of valour is discretion.

> I fear thou art another counterfeit,

Douglas had cried, coming on Henry IV on the field of Shrewsbury,

> Another king! they grow like Hydra's heads.
> I am the Douglas, fatal to all those
> That wear those colours on them. What art thou,
> That counterfeit'st the person of a king?

The literal reference of course is to the knights, disguised to represent the King, that Henry had sent into the battle to divert the enemy from his own person. "The better part of valour is discretion." This, and that repeated word "counterfeit," is Shakespeare's sign that he intends the contrast, and the deeper unconscious meaning of Douglas'

>   What art thou,
> That counterfeit'st the person of a king?

(a king, notice, not the king) is just one more of the poet's judgments upon Henry. For all his "discretion," the Douglas would have killed this counterfeit king who tries to save his skin by the death of others if the Prince had not come to his rescue in the nick of time.

But that was earlier in the battle. At the point we had reached the Prince comes back with his brother John and discovers the "dead" Falstaff staggering along with the dead Hotspur on his back—a symbolic picture if there ever was one.

> Did you not tell me this fat man was dead?

cries Lancaster.

> I did; I saw him dead,
> Breathless and bleeding on the ground,

replies Henry. He has underrated the vitality of the Imagination, and even now thinks he sees a ghost:

>   Art thou alive?
> Or is it fantasy that plays upon our eyesight?
> I prithee, speak; we will not trust our eyes
> Without our ears. Thou art not what thou seem'st.

"No: that's certain," retorts Falstaff, "I am not a double man." And to prove it, he throws down the body of Hotspur he is carrying. But beyond this obvious meaning, who can doubt that Falstaff, in the phrase "double man," is also having a thrust at the dual role of the man he is addressing, or that Shakespeare, in letting Falstaff deny his own doubleness, is thereby calling our attention to it? At the very least the expression proves that the world did not have to wait for Dostoevsky before it heard of the double man.

Truth has made it necessary to say some harsh things about Prince Henry; so it is a pleasure to recognize the character of his conduct on the field of Shrewsbury: his valor in his encounter with Hotspur, his courage and loyalty in rescuing his father from Douglas, and his generosity in letting Falstaff take credit for Hotspur's death. Dover Wilson makes much of this last point—too much, I think, for the good of his own case—declaring that it proves the Prince thought nothing of renown, of "the outward show of honour in the eyes of men, so long as he has proved himself worthy of its inner substance in his own." But if he was as self-effacing as all that, why did he cry at the moment he met Hotspur?—

> all the budding honours on thy crest
> I'll crop, to make a garland for my head.

Those words flatly contradict the "grace" he does Falstaff in surrendering to him so easily the greatest honor of his life. The paradox arises, I think, from the presence of those conflicting personalities, Hal and the Prince. Touched momentarily at the sight of what he believes to be his old companion dead at his feet, the fast-disappearing Hal returns and survives long enough after the surprise and joy of finding him still alive to accept Falstaff's lie for truth. But we wonder how much longer. Wilson's assumption that the Prince would or could have kept up the fiction permanently is refuted by the fact that Morton had observed the death of Hotspur at Henry's hands and reports the event correctly:

> these mine eyes saw him in bloody state,
> Rendering faint quittance, wearied and outbreath'd,
> To Harry Monmouth; whose swift wrath beat down
> The never-daunted Percy to the earth,
> From whence with life he never more sprung up.

Everything, from the famous first soliloquy on, proves that the Prince not only craved renown but craved it in its most theatrical form.

NOTES

[1] It is usually presumptuous to disagree with Samuel Butler's use of words. But if he had substituted "mind" for "intellect" in the foregoing quotation I think he would have been nearer the mark. And only the unwary reader will think that by "illusion" Butler means the same thing as delusion or lie.
[2] Following Professor R. A. Law.

Peter J. Seng

SONGS, TIME, AND THE REJECTION OF FALSTAFF

I

Any inquiry into the functions of the songs in Shakespeare's plays should be based on some consideration of what songs and music meant to Shakespeare and his contemporaries. Three points need to be kept in mind. First of all, Renaissance Englishmen knew a great deal more about music—especially its technical and social aspects—than do most people today. That Shakespeare's England was 'a nest of singing birds' has been pointed out by scholars with the wearisome regularity that only such a crystalline phrase can acquire. The famous metaphor is intended not only to connote the deep interest that music held for Elizabethan Englishmen, but also their strong impulse to lyric poetry at a time when those arts were not so separated as they are today. The songs in Shakespeare's England ranged from the madrigals, canzonets, and airs of the upper classes to the carols, cozier's catches, and street-songs of the lower orders of society. The astonishing volume of poetry produced in that era was swelled not only by courtly sonnets but also by broadside ballads. Consequently it seems fair to extend the famous metaphor a little by saying that while those singing birds included among them many nightingales and larks, they also included a goodly number of choughs, rooks, and daws.

A second point, also something of a truism, is that Shakespeare and his contemporaries thought about music in some ways that are considerably different from the ways it is thought about at the present time. For them music had real powers: it could exert a civilizing influence on rude men, turning 'savage eyes . . . to a modest gaze'. They felt that music could induce sleep, charm away madness, and cure all manner of physical and spiritual ills; it could abet right thinking and right doing and, if it were music of the right sort, could put man into harmony with the world around him and with the sweet music of the spheres. They believed, finally,

From *Shakespeare Survey* 15 (1962): 31–40.

that the kind of music a man sang or enjoyed might well be a valid index of his inner psychological being.

A third point, less well-known perhaps, needs only to be mentioned to become obvious. Because of the habit of music in all ranks of Shakespeare's society, the performances of songs in his plays must have seemed far more natural and organic to the spectators in his audiences than renditions of song in the modern theatre seem to us who are, by and large, a non-singing people. We accept songs in a musical comedy today as a theatrical convention, whereas an actor on Shakespeare's stage who broke into song was very likely regarded as doing exactly what was to be expected under the circumstances. An Elizabethan lover could and was expected to serenade his lady; old cronies together in a tavern were expected to troll catches over their pots of ale. Even the 'spinsters and the knitters in the sun, And the free maids that weave their thread with bones' were accustomed to lighten their labours with song. Songs in Shakespeare's plays could be as natural and 'realistic' as the action or the dialogue.

All of these points are relevant to the songs—fragments of song, really—that occur in *The Second Part of King Henry the Fourth*. The snatches of ballads, carols, and drinking songs in that play reflect the lower spectrum of musical life in Shakespeare's England; they arise organically out of their dramatic situations and are realistic in terms of actual life; but those bits of song chiefly function in the play as ironic commentaries on the characters, episodes, and themes in *2 Henry IV*.

In structure that play consists of a serious and a comic plot. The serious plot has to do with the King's attempts to put down the various rebellions against his rule; the comic plot is concerned with the intrigues of Falstaff and his companions. Between these two plots moves Prince Hal who, like a hero in an allegory, must on the one hand disengage himself from 'that reverend vice, that grey iniquity' Falstaff, and on the other 'redeem the time' and establish himself as a qualified and legitimate heir to the throne. Into this double plot, as I see it, are woven three themes or *leitmotifs* having to do with Justice, Disease, and Time. The serious plot makes a number of comments on the theme of Justice: it keeps in remembrance Henry's usurpation of the throne, his feelings of guilt over Richard's death; it details a new, a Machiavellian, kind of justice in John of Lancaster's treacherous offer of amnesty to the rebels, and a warmer, more human justice in Hal's reconciliation with the Lord Chief Justice of England. This same theme in the comic plot is woven into Falstaff's encounters with the Lord Chief Justice, with the abuses to which Falstaff puts the King's power of impressment, and into all his dealings with those suffragan Justices, Shallow and Silence. What Falstaff must learn is that the laws of England are *not* at his commandment, and that he is to have no voice of influence toward disorder and injustice in the court of Henry V.

The theme of Disease is carried over into *2 Henry IV* from *Richard II*. As the dying John of Gaunt had pointed out in the earlier play, England was already ill and so was her king; and throughout both parts of *Henry IV* political intrigue and rebellion in England are referred to as a disease afflicting the country, a sickness that can only be cured by the letting of blood. This theme is further echoed in the fact that in Part Two the King becomes fatally ill and his old opponent Northumberland 'lies crafty-sick' (Induction, II. 36–7). In the comic plot it is Falstaff who is diseased; he is literally and figuratively the infected member who must be cut away before order and health can be restored to Hal's moral universe.

The third motif woven into both plots has to do with Time, particularly time past put into sharp contrast with time present. This contrast provides an *ambiance* for both parts of *Henry IV,* but it presses most strongly on the second part. In the serious plot the past is represented by the frequent references to events and persons in *Richard II,* and by the pervasive sense of revolutionary sweep that is experienced in taking the three plays in order. First there is the melancholy Richard whose forlorn cry marks him as the last of England's medieval kings:

> Not all the water in the rough rude sea
> Can wash the balm off from an anointed king;
> The breath of worldly men cannot depose
> The deputy elected by the Lord.   (III, ii, 54–7)

Then there is 'that vile politician, Bolingbroke', who knew better, and who by shrewd policy, including a fundamentally insincere promise of penance in the Holy Land, manages to establish his own dynasty on the throne. Finally, there is the newly crowned Henry V who rejects Falstaff, reunites himself with his brothers, takes the Chief Justice as a second father, and turns his eyes toward France. Henry IV's transitional role was to thrust a medieval and chivalric England firmly into the past, and to establish on the throne a patriotic, nationalistic, and Renaissance English king. On the comic level of the play an 'Old England' has passed away as well: Nell Quickly and Doll Tearsheet are haled off by the beadles, Eastcheap roguery is no longer to be countenanced, and Falstaff, Shallow, and Silence reminisce in a Gloucestershire orchard about events that never were and a past that cannot be recaptured.

II

It is here, perhaps, well to deal with first matters first; and what has occupied more critics for more time than anything else in *2 Henry IV* has been the rejection of Falstaff at the end of the play. Some critics, indeed, have been so concerned with this problem that they have neglected other responsible moral issues with which the play is concerned: it has sometimes seemed as if they would give up virtuous standards before they would forgo cakes and ale. Whatever the reason, there has been an evident sentimental strain in Falstaffian criticism ever sense Morgann's *Essay on the Dramatic Character of Sir John Falstaff* in 1777. Long before Morgann it was possible for Rowe to describe Falstaff as 'a lewd old Fellow . . . a Thief, Lying, Cowardly, Vainglorious, and in short every way Vicious'.[1] In 1765 Samuel Johnson pointed out that Falstaff 'has never uttered one sentiment of generosity, and with all his powers of exciting mirth, has nothing in him that can be esteemed'.[2] Both are severe critics by modern standards, yet coming before Morgann they were allowed their say. But since Morgann's *Essay* most critics have chiefly been concerned with exonerating their hero from every least breath of censure while crying up Hal as a censorious prig who blasts the old knight with a frigid, 'I know thee not, old man'. Among the few important modern critics who have *not* gone along with Morgann's sentimental estimate of Falstaff's character are J. Dover Wilson and E. E. Stoll;[3] but sixteen closely printed pages in the New Variorum Edition of the play[4] record the attempts of a majority of critics to justify Falstaff in one way or another.

There is no pleasure in opposing such an array of defenders nor in electing one's self a devil's advocate to calumniate the old knight's character; but those commentators who seek to canonize Sir John seem to be ignoring much evidence that tells against his alleged geniality and virtue. The most important piece of evidence seems to be Shakespeare's own dramatic intention.

In the highly amusing scene at the Boar's Head tavern in *1 Henry IV*, the playwright himself appears to raise the important dramatic problem he had to face in the *Henry IV* plays: what is to be done with Sir John Falstaff? In a burlesque dialogue Prince Hal imitates his father, the King, while Falstaff, playing the Prince, pleads his own cause:

> That he is old, the more the pity, his white hairs do witness it; but that he is, saving your reverence, a whoremaster, that I utterly deny. If sack and sugar be a fault, God help the wicked! if to be old and merry be a sin, then many an old host that I know is damned: if to be fat be to be hated, then Pharaoh's lean kine are to be loved. No, my good lord; banish Peto, banish Bardolph, banish Poins: but for sweet Jack Falstaff, kind Jack Falstaff, true Jack Falstaff . . . banish not him thy Harry's company . . . banish plump Jack, and banish all the world.
>
> (II, iv, 514–27)

It is precisely at this moment that the sheriff and his officers arrive to arrest the Gadshill robbers. In the confusion that attends upon their arrival we are apt to miss Hal's words, 'I do, I will'. Whether Hal speaks them in *propria persona* or not, these words may be taken to indicate that Shakespeare's mind was made up.[5] Yet how was he to banish plump Jack and not banish all the world?

He found his solution to this problem, I believe, in the deliberate degradation of the character of Falstaff in *2 Henry IV*. There is a striking difference between the characters of the knight in the two plays. In *1 Henry IV* Falstaff is a capon-and-sack knight, and such villainy as he possesses is always softened and humanized by his ebullient good humour—laughter, in this instance, covering a multitude of sins. In *2 Henry IV* Falstaff is still the buffoon, but the high comedy that once attended his every entrance has now taken a bitter turn. He is indeed the cause 'that wit is in other men'; as of old he inspires their wittiest sallies, but now he has also become the butt of their coarsest jokes. It is no longer merely his corpulence and preposterous impudence that provokes laughter; it is his diseases. The change in his character and the change in the tone of humour is signalled from Falstaff's very first entrance on the stage:

Enter FALSTAFF, *with his page, bearing his sword and buckler.*
FAL.: Sirrah, you giant, what says the doctor to my water?
PAGE: He said, sir, the water itself was a good healthy water; but, for the party
     that owed it, he might have moe diseases than he knew for. (I, ii, 1–6)

Thus begins the bitterer comedy of the sequel.

At the end of this scene a cruel light is thrown on the doctor's jest: Falstaff's
visits to the stews have evidently made him a victim of their diseases. As the old
knight says in a brief soliloquy:

A pox of this gout! or, a gout of this pox! for the one or the other plays the
rogue with my great toe. 'Tis no matter if I do halt; I have the wars for my
colour, and my pension shall seem the more reasonable. A good wit will make
use of anything: I will turn diseases to commodity.   (II. 272–8)

Falstaff's first entrance in the play is clearly echoed at his entrance in II, iv. He
has been partying at the Boar's Head with Mistress Quickly and with that 'pagan' of
the old sect Doll Tearsheet. Supper is over as the scene begins, and the ladies, Doll
somewhat indisposed, enter first. After a moment Falstaff follows them on to the
stage singing the opening lines of an old broadside ballad. 'When Arthur first in
court'—he sings; then he interrupts his song to mutter an order to a servant, 'Empty
the jordan'. Then he resumes his song again, 'And was a worthy king,' only to break
off his song once more as he turns to the women and addresses one of them, 'How
now, Doll?' An appropriate gloss on the whole passage is one critic's naturalistic
comment in Latin: *Raro mingit castus.*[6]

Shakespeare's audience, undoubtedly knowing the ballad, would have appreciated the ironies of this song. The lines Falstaff sings come from 'The Noble Acts
newly found, of *Arthur* of the Table Round. To the tune of flying Fame.' According
to Hales and Furnivall, Thomas Deloney was probably the author of the ballad, and
the ballad itself is 'nothing more than a rhymed version of certain chapters in
Malory's "Most Ancient and Famous history of the Renowned Prince Arthur" '.[7]
Rollins has suggested that this ballad may have been the one entered in the Stationers' Registers in 1565/6 as 'a pleasaunte history of an adventurus knyghte of
kynges arthurs Couurte', and has definitely identified with it the ballad entered by
Edward Aldee, 8 June 1603, 'The noble Actes nowe newly found of Arthure of the
round table'.[8]

There is little or no question about the popularity of this ballad in
Shakespeare's day and hence its familiarity to his audiences. It was frequently
quoted in the drama of the time, imitated, many times reprinted, and parodied
even as late as 1656 in a pre-Restoration song-book. The name of the ballad even
became, finally, the title to the tune to which it was sung, replacing the old tune-
name, 'Flying Fame'.[9] It is possible, indeed, that this ballad helped to make its tune
popular. Surviving copies of this broadside are to be found in the Pepys, Wood,
Lord Crawford, Roxburghe, and Bagford ballad collections; there is a fragmentary
version of it in the Percy Folio MS., and a reprinted version in Deloney's *Garland*

of Good-Will, 1631.[10] The tune for the ballad has been transcribed by Chappell.[11]

The general character of the song Falstaff begins to sing is sufficiently indicated by its first few stanzas:[12]

> When *Arthur* first in Court began,
>   and was approued King:
> By force of Armes great Victories won,
>   and conquest home did bring:
>
> Then into *Brittaine* straight he came,
>   where fiftie good and able
> Knights then repaired vnto him
>   which were of the Round-table.
>
> And many Justes and Turnaments,
>   before him there were brest:
> Wherein both Knights did then excell,
>   and far surmount the rest:
>
> But one Sir *Lancelot du Lake,*
>   who was approoued well:
> He in his sight and deeds of Armes
>   all other did excell.

Even with only so much of the ballad in mind we can discern Shakespeare's purpose in putting this song on Falstaff's lips. As a jolting broadside ballad it is a good index to the old knight's taste in verse and music; beyond this, the substance of the song is wholly inappropriate to Sir John, for it celebrates the antique world of romance and chivalry, a world of knights and ladies far more honourable than Falstaff and his dinner companions. Falstaff, in whom desire has outlived the performance, as Poins says, (II, iv. 283–4) is no Lancelot; nor, if one further ironic reverberation of this song may be permitted, is the politician-king Bolingbroke a King Arthur. The kind of chivalry the song is about is a kind that died in England with John of Gaunt, Richard, and Hotspur.

Not only is the substance of the song totally inappropriate to Falstaff, but it is also set in shocking contrast to the interpolated order to the servant: 'Empty the jordan.' The command echoes Falstaff's earlier concern with his 'diseases'. Lest the audience should miss the connection, Shakespeare has the knight allude to his infection a few lines further on:[13]

> You make fat rascals, Mistress Doll.
> DOLL: I make them! gluttony and diseases make them; I make them not.
> FAL.: If the cook help to make the gluttony, you help to make the diseases, Doll: we catch of you, Doll, we catch of you; grant that, my poor virtue, grant that.
> DOLL: Yea, joy, our chains and our jewels.
> FAL.: 'Your brooches, pearls, and ouches:' for to serve bravely is to come halting off, you know: to come off the breach with his pike bent bravely,

and to surgery bravely; to venture upon the charged chambers bravely,—
DOLL: Hang yourself, you muddy conger, hang yourself!   (II. 45–57)

In fact when Falstaff says of Doll 'she's in hell already and burns poor souls' (II.
365–6) he may be making the ungentlemanly suggestion that she is the source of
his affliction.

If all of this seems like a cruel conclusion to what was once so much high
comedy, that is only because we are more sentimental about Falstaff than Shakespeare and his contemporaries were, and because our taste in humour is less broad
than theirs. In 2 Henry IV an old epoch had to make way for a new; Shakespeare had
to banish Jack Falstaff, so he degraded him first and thereby avoided banishing the
whole world. Finally, it should be noted that Falstaff is not the only person in the
Boar's Head set who is degraded and banished; he is merely the first. In Henry V
Bardolph and Nym are hanged for thievery, Pistol deserts the army to become a
bawd, Nell Quickly dies of 'malady of France', and Doll Tearsheet becomes 'a lazar
kite of Cressid's kind'.

III

Even as he had degraded the character of Falstaff in 2 Henry IV, Shakespeare
also made him a victim of Time. He degraded the knight to make the rejection
palatable; he subjected him to Time to make it inevitable. The leitmotif of time
irrecoverably past is sounded with Falstaff's first appearance in the play. With his
accustomed impudence he pleads youth as an extenuation of his follies:

You that are old consider not the capacities of us that are young; you do
measure the heat of our livers with the bitterness of your galls: and we that
are in the vaward of our youth, I must confess, are wags too.

(I, ii, 195–200)

But the true facts are revealed in the Chief Justice's reproof which sounds like a
literary 'Character of an Old Man':

Do you set down your name in the scroll of youth, that are written down old
with all the characters of age? Have you not a moist eye? a dry hand? a yellow
cheek? a white beard? a decreasing leg? an increasing belly? is not your voice
broken? your wind short? your chin double? your wit single? and every part
about you blasted with antiquity?   (II. 201–8)

And to this portrait can be added Sir John's salient vice—a vice of old men—
avarice. He has practised upon Mistress Quickly 'both in purse and in person' and
perhaps upon Doll Tearsheet, too.[14] He has used the King's power of impressment
to line his own pockets, and his call on Shallow enables him to swindle that Justice
of a thousand pounds.

It is the Gloucestershire episodes of the play that give the fullest colour and
development to the Time motif in 2 Henry IV. Time past is summed up in the

reminiscences of Falstaff, Shallow, and Silence about days in the dim past when Jack Falstaff was a boy and a page to Thomas Mowbray, and John of Gaunt laid wagers on the skill in archery of one of Silence's friends.[15] They talk, too, about wild days and wilder nights at Clement's Inn. 'We have heard the chimes at midnight', says Falstaff; but then a little later, 'Lord, how subject we old men are to this vice of lying!' (III, ii, 229, 325–6). They not only live in the past but they delude themselves about it. Then in a final Gloucestershire scene which exactly parallels the after-dinner scene in Eastcheap, the three old men sit in Shallow's orchard after supper and delude themselves about the present as well. Thinking Falstaff is a person of influence at Court, Shallow curries favour with him; hearing of the King's death, Falstaff brags of his importance:

> Master Robert Shallow, choose what office thou wilt in the land, 'tis thine. Pistol, I will double-charge thee with dignities.... Master Shallow, my Lord Shallow,—be what thou wilt; I am fortune's steward.... Let us take any man's horses; the laws of England are at my commandment.   (V, iii, 129–44)

The scene is punctuated with six little snatches of song by Silence, songs prompted by the postprandial conversations of Shallow and Falstaff. These songs serve to underline the ironic disparity between past and present, youth and age, and between the expectations of Falstaff and his companions and the fulfilment that awaits those expectations on a street in London.

Silence's first two songs are Shrovetide carols, once used to celebrate the three days of feasting and revelry that preceded the onset of Lent. Silence, too, has evidently heard 'the chimes at midnight', and probably many a carol as well in the long years of his life. 'I have been merry twice and once ere now (V, iii, 42)', he tells Falstaff. Senile and drunken at the board he probably feels that any party is a feast, and any feast a time for Shrovetide carols. 'We shall', he sings,

> Do nothing but eat, and make good cheer,
> And praise God for the merry year;
> When flesh is cheap and females dear,
> And lusty lads roam here and there
> So merrily,
> And ever among so merrily.

With Shallow's hospitable admonition to his guests, 'Be merry, be merry', Silence breaks into song again:

> Be merry, be merry, my wife has all;
> For women are shrews, both short and tall:
> 'Tis merry in hall when beards wag all,
> And welcome merry Shrove-tide.
> Be merry, be merry.

The songs are more appropriate than he knows. They celebrate a present feasting and revelry before a long lean Lent which is to come when King Henry V rejects

Falstaff and his friends. The first song, hailing the glut of meat in the Lenten markets and regretting the scarcity of (suddenly Lenten-penitential) females, is probably further intended to remind an audience of Shallow's earlier boasts about his youthful amours in days long past:

> I was once of Clement's Inn, where, I think they will talk of mad Shallow yet.
>
> SIL.: You were called 'lusty Shallow' then, cousin. . . .
>
> SHAL.: I was called any thing; and I would have done any thing indeed too, and roundly too. There was I, and little John Doit of Staffordshire, and black George Barnes, and Francis Pickbone, and Will Squele, a Cotswold man; you had not four such swinge-bucklers in all the inns o'court again: and I may say to you, we knew where the bona-robas were and had the best of them all at commandment.   (III, ii, 15–26)

The second song is a little more advanced in time; it eschews female company for a recreational night away from shrewish wives, a night of drinking with other greybeards. Neither the original tunes nor the sources of these fragmentary carols are known.

All the bona robas of earlier days are toasted in two of Silence's next three songs. The servant Davy has only to offer 'A cup of wine, sir?' and the old man starts to sing again:

> A cup of wine that's brisk and fine,
> And drink unto the leman mine;
> And a merry heart lives long-a.

Falstaff pledges a health to Silence who immediately responds:

> Fill the cup, and let it come;
> I'll pledge you a mile to the bottom

And again:

> Do me right,
> And dub me knight:
> Samingo.

Behind the first and third songs may lie a drinking custom of young gallants in Shakespeare's time. The custom was first pointed out by Malone and then by Douce.[16] Illustrating the first song Douce cited Thomas Young's *Englands Bane: or, The Description of Drunkenesse* (1617), sigs. B3–B3ᵛ:

> Their father the Diuell will suffer no dissentions amongst them, vntill they have executed his wil in the deepest degree of drinking, and made their sacrifice vnto him, & most commonly that is done vpon their knees being bare. The prophanenes whereof is most lamentable and destestable, being duely considered by a Christian, to thinke that that member of the body which is appointed for the seruice of God, is too often abused with the adoration of a Harlot, or a base Drunkard, as I my selfe haue seen (and to my griefe of

conscience) may now say haue in presence, yea and amongst others been an actor in the businesse, when vpon our knees, after healthes to many priuate Punkes, a Health haue beene drunke to all the Whoores in the world.

Young's account, to be sure, is tinged with Puritanical horror at such boisterous doings; but it is supported by Malone's note on the third song:

It was the custom of the good fellows of Shakespeare's days to drink a very large draught of wine, and sometimes a less palatable potation, on *their knees*, to the health of their mistress. He who performed this exploit was dubb'd a *knight* for the evening.

Malone does not give source for his information about this custom, but he cites *A Yorkshire Tragedy* (1608), sigs. A3–A3ᵛ:

SAM.: Why then follow me, Ile teach you the finest humor to be drunk in, I learnd it at London last week.

AM.: I faith lets heare it, lets heare it.

SAM.: The bravest humor, twold do a man good to bee drunck in't, they call it knighting in London, when they drink vpon their knees.

AM.: Faith that's excellent.

[SAM.:] Come follow me, Ile giue you all the degrees ont in order.

And there are numerous other allusions to the song and the custom in the drama of Shakespeare's time.[17] Neither the sources nor music for the first two songs is known, but the original words and melody of the third song have survived in a number of manuscript copies.[18] The functions of the three songs are clear. What might be appropriate songs to lusty young London gallants provide an incongruous background for the old men sitting about Shallow's orchard. In this scene, ironically, their meretricious remembrance of things past is put into sharp contrast with the realities of desire that has outlived the performance; and they drink, and revel, and make plans for a future that has already been made vain.

The songs in *2 Henry IV* end exactly as they had begun, with a fragment of a ballad that refers to the ancient days of the past.[19] In his typically ranting fashion Pistol rushes in to announce that Prince Hal has succeeded to the throne: 'I speak of Africa and golden joys'. To which Falstaff replies in kind:

O base Assyrian knight, what is thy news?
Let King Cophetua know the truth thereof.   (V, iii, 105–6)

The antique reference is enough to set Silence off again with a line which is probably from the ballad 'Robin Hood and the Pinder of Wakefield'. This song like the first one sung by Falstaff in the play evokes a world of the past, a world concerned with a kind of honour and *gentilesse* that the fat old knight and his cronies in Eastcheap and Gloucestershire are far from sharing.

Aside from the specific functions mentioned above, the songs in *2 Henry IV* serve other purposes as well. As sung by Falstaff and the drunken Silence they are in themselves comic. They establish an atmosphere of rowdiness, dissolute conduct, and irresponsibility which reaches its apogee in Falstaff's cry, 'The laws of England are at my commandment'. They heighten the comic climax of the play and aggravate the downfall of Falstaff when he is rejected by King Henry V. Finally they set the new order in sharp contrast to the old. All that remains of an old world at the end of *2 Henry IV* is an aged Sir John Falstaff and his withered old companions. The world of Richard, Hotspur, and of Falstaff's youth has passed away just as surely as has the romantic world of Arthur, Lancelot, and Robin Hood. In a sense it was not Hal who rejected Falstaff at all; it was Time.

NOTES

[1] In his edition of 1709; quoted in *A New Variorum Edition of Shakespeare: The Second Part of Henry the Fourth,* ed. Matthias A. Shaaber (Philadelphia, 1940), p. 584.

[2] The same.

[3] See, especially, chapter I of Wilson's *The Fortunes of Falstaff* (Cambridge, 1943), and Stoll's 'Falstaff' in his *Shakespeare Studies* (New York, 1927).

[4] Pp. 584–99.

[5] Harold C. Goddard, *The Meaning of Shakespeare* (Chicago, 1951), pp. 206–7, calls attention to the fact that this play episode is in a sense a 'rehearsal' of the banishment to come.

[6] Henry Halford Vaughan, *New Readings and New Renderings of Shakespeare's Tragedies* (2 vols. 1878–81), I, 494.

[7] *Bishop Percy's Folio Manuscript. Ballads and Romances* (3 vols. 1867–8), I, 84.

[8] 'An Analytical Index to the Ballad-Entries (1557–1709) in the Registers of the Company of Stationers of London', Studies in Philology, XXI (1924), nos. 2107, 1951, and 2915.

[9] Quotations, imitations, and parodies are to be found in Marston's *The Malcontent* (1604), sig. D1ᵛ, Beaumont and Fletcher's *The Little French Lawyer* (1647) (*Works,* ed. Waller and Glover, 1906, III, 399), Heywood's *The Rape of Lucrece* (1608), sig. C1ᵛ, Richard Johnson's *The Golden Garland of Princely Delight* (1620), sig. B3, *Choyce Drollery: Songs & Sonnets* (1656), p. 70, and in *The Golden Garland of Princely Delight* [1690], sig. B4. In his unpublished Harvard doctoral dissertation, 'English Broadside Ballad Tunes (1550–1700)' [1936], I, 17, Roy Lamson Jr. pointed out that the tune ranks as no. 17 in a list of the twenty-eight most frequently used broadside ballad tunes.

[10] Since Deloney died in 1600 this ballad, if written by him, antedates the posthumous *Garland* (1631) by a considerable number of years. Copy for the *Garland* version of the ballad was undoubtedly a much earlier broadside issue.

[11] *Popular Music of the Olden Time* (2 vols. 1855), I, 199, 272. Two distinct melodies went by the name 'Flying Fame', and Chappell transcribes both.

[12] These opening stanzas are from a broadside copy, c. 1620–30, in the Houghton Library, Harvard, a copy described in *The Harvard Library Bulletin,* X (1956), 130–4.

[13] The whole passage is a highly articulated *double entendre.* Literally it refers to the pikeman who charges in battle against the breaches and heavy guns, is wounded, and put into the hands of surgeons for treatment. The underlying meaning refers to sexual encounter and the need to undergo treatment for venereal infection. For specific interpretation see the notes, pp. 168–70, of the *Variorum Edition,* and Eric Partridge, *Shakespeare's Bawdy* (1955). As repellent as it may seem to Falstaff's modern friends to find their hero diseased in this noxious way, the fact seems clear from his own words: 'A man can no more separate age and covetousness than'a can part young limbs and lechery: but the gout galls the one, and the pox pinches the other: *and so both degrees prevent my curses'* (I, ii, 256–60). It would be gratifying to perform a general asepsis on the old knight's moral character. *De mortuis nil nisi bonum.* But it is impossible to give a clean bill of health to a man who continually infects himself.

[14] See II, i, 25–41, 124–8, and II, iv, 36ff.

[15] The most poignant and realistic scenes in the play deal with such reminiscences. See III, ii and V, iii.

[16] Malone in his edition of the play, 1790, and Douce in *Illustrations of Shakespeare and of Ancient Manners* (1839), p. 293.

[17] See Jonson's *Epicoene* (1609) (*Works,* ed. Herford and Simpson (1937), V, 226), Lodge's and

Greene's *A Looking Glasse for London and England* (1594) (*Plays and Poems*, ed. Collins (1905), I, 189), Chapman's *All Fools* (1605) (*Plays and Poems*, ed. Parrott (1914), II, 156), Massinger's *The Great Duke of Florence* (1627) (ed. Stockholm (1933), p. 59), Randolph's *The Drinking Academy* (edited from manuscript by Tannenbaum and Rollins (1930), p. 8), Marston's *Antonio and Mellida* (1602), sig. H4, and Nashe's *Summer's Last Will and Testament* (1600), ed. McKerrow (1958), III, 264.

[18] Frederick W. Sternfeld, 'Lasso's Music for Shakespeare's "Samingo" ', *Shakespeare Quarterly*, IX (1958), 106–16, includes a transcription of the treble setting of Lasso's music for the song, and an account of other instances of the music. See, also, John P. Cutts, 'The Original Music of a Song in *2 Henry IV*', *Shakespeare Quarterly*, VII, (1956), 385–92.

[19] The source is probably 'Robin Hood and the Jolly Pinder of Wakefield', broadside copies of which are preserved in the Bagford, Pepys, Crawford, Roxburghe, and Wood ballad collections. Falstaff also refers to this ballad in *The Merry Wives of Windsor*, I, i, 177. Curiously enough in the Pepys copy this ballad is printed together with the ballad from which Falstaff's own fragment of song earlier in the play is derived.

Harold E. Toliver

FALSTAFF, THE PRINCE, AND THE HISTORY PLAY

I

A rational eighteenth-century man of letters such as Maurice Morgann would undoubtedly bristle a little at our abandon in destroying his premises. He would have difficulty recognizing our portraits of Henry IV, for example, whom, in his simplicity, he had thought to be a rather impressive king despite a certain weakness at first for another man's crown. And he would be even more mystified by Henry V as Machiavellian strongman and confused war-maker. Ignorant of Frazer and Freud, he would not think to look for the key to the complexity and interest of Falstaff, the "whoreson, obscene, greasy tallow-catch", in ritualistic and magical analogues;[1] he would probably want to ask whether critics ought to be getting into such things in the first place, and if so, how the a-rational elements of motivation, imagery, and symbolic action, if they exist, can be made intelligible. For when we consider these elements, the discussion of "character" in the sense of certain definite traits appears extremely limited; questions such as whether or not Falstaff is a coward are not important in themselves, and the facts were never really facts anyway. And concepts of form naturally grow more uncertain as response to character shifts. Hence, the question of what *kind* the history play belongs to can no longer be answered in strictly Aristotelian terms.[2] Once over the initial shock, however, the traditional rationalist might discover certain fruitful interactions between his approach to the history play and modern approaches. In the matter of the relative place of comic and heroic figures in the history play, for example, the neoclassicist's sense of "decorum"—of a form following certain laws of plot, character, and language—might be made to engage more profoundly the raw stuff of the human psyche and its institutions and rituals imitated in the form. And in return, we might have to admit that while it may not be necessary for all purposes to read history plays under the auspices of a category, we gain from being aware that they

From *Shakespeare Quarterly* 16, No. 1 (Winter 1965): 63–80.

are not simply studies in isolated problems of motivation, or fragments of primitive ritual. They do indeed have "form", as some kings have "character". Approaching the history play through either perspective by itself is likely to leave us unsatisfied, as though we had gone hunting kudu and flushed jerboa.

For the history play at its best attempts to do more than evoke purely chauvinistic emotion through heroic pageantry and spectacle, as it was once assumed; and it is not totally incapable of containing its Saturnalian kings of misrule and its Oedipal overtones in a form that transcends and orders them. Shakespeare, at least, appears to have sought in the history play a fresh artistic form capable of integrating providential order, pragmatic political concerns, and timeless human impulses.[3] One of the primary effects of that integration is an adjustment between inner and outer worlds, both in the hero and, since the history play is more nationalistic and "rhetorical" than other dramatic forms, through the hero in the audience, didactically. In ethical matters, the adjustment is between the inner conscience and the amoral demands of political life; in economic motives, between personal and collective "property"; and in broadly social and religious matters, between the old Adam who rushes impulsively to Eastcheap and the redeemed Adam who takes his fixed place in the ranks or at Whitehall.

These adjustments involve the audience in a communal "rhythm" through a language generally more openly incantational than the language of Shakespearian tragedy and ritualistic in a different sense. For more than one kind of ritual and one kind of magic is involved in dramatic action. In a broad sense, "ritual" means any closely patterned visual ceremony or rhythmic language that engages the emotions of its participants and fuses them into a harmonious community. Both spectacle and rhythm work by raising like emotions throughout an audience and providing a common symbolic or "pulsing" medium for their transmission. Some rituals depend upon primitive forms of magic, and Falstaff, as J. I. M. Stewart, C. L. Barber, and Philip Williams believe, reflects certain fragments of them. But others become assimilated into sophisticated art and are consciously manipulated as one of its dimensions. In less primitive forms, they work not only through contact with highly charged currents from the subconscious, which criticism, as Morgann conceived of it, is ill-equipped to deal with, but also through a complex assortment of powers released by formal art. In the rejection scene, for example, the ritual of the new king depends upon the total of thematic, imagistic, and formal pressures brought to bear by the whole play or series of plays—and their social and political context. If tragic ritual reconciles the audience to a higher destiny of some sort, perhaps to the power of the gods or to a world of suffering beyond the protagonist's control, the ritual of the history play aims somewhat lower, at adjustment to political life—which may be thought to reveal destiny also, but destiny at least *filtered through* a social medium.

Social and political context is thus especially important in the history play, which in England developed under special historical conditions that caused it to rise and decline rapidly as literary types go. Though other dramatists experimented with it, Shakespeare (with the possible exception of the anonymous author of

Woodstock) was the only one to see its full potential as a separate form. In his variation, it appealed strongly to an audience prepared to see it in a certain way, or in Mr. Barber's term, to "participate" in its special kind of ritualized nationalistic emotion. Like English tragedy, it arose partly out of the old morality and mystery plays; but unto these it grafted chronicle accounts of past events, folk-lore, native myth, and a new spirit of nationalism, all of which it shaped into moral patterns designed to bring out the providential guidance, the "meaning", of history. Since an audience removed from the original context cannot "participate" in historical ritual with the same intensity as an Elizabethan royalist who believed in the king's divine prerogatives, the historical context and content create problems that are less obtrusive in other dramatic forms, if present at all. But despite its inherent short-comings, the history play at its best (in the series of plays from *Richard II* to *Henry V*) achieves an essentially new structure and dramatic rhythm, both peculiar to itself and effective.

Some aspects of that structure are borrowed from comedy and tragedy, and here again the neoclassicist, if put to the test, might be quick to see some aspects of the blend that others would overlook. Aristotle's concept of *anagnorisis* and *catharsis* would seem relevant, for example, in describing Falstaff's role as tragic victim—only one role among several, needless to say, but involved and crucial.[4] In one aspect the "plot" of *2 Henry IV* can be taken as a *mixed variation* of comic and tragic action, culminating in a sacrificial act with the new king acting as personal vicegerent for destiny. The effectiveness of the rejection speech as incantation depends upon our seeing the accumulated evidence as to the way of a world that Falstaff has affronted and does not fit, a world *requiring* a certain political order that cannot tolerate Falstaff as Chief Justice. The evidences of tragic form are clear enough before that, once we set aside the oversimplified notion that a figure must be either comic or tragic and not both. The implications of Falstaff's childlike self-love and hedonism from the beginning of *I Henry IV* compose, in Francis Fergusson's Jamesian analogy, one of a set of "mirrors" reflecting the central action, the search for an effective adjustment between the inner self and the collective social organism. Since the aim of this action is ultimately to "redeem time" (and thus to redeem the times),[5] both in the sense of justifying "history" and in reconciling the audience to its historical role, Falstaff is best seen as a rebel against history, as guilty of *hubris* as he is of Saturnalian misrule.

The Falstaffian mirror, of course, is not entirely separable from the others. In Part One, the opening scenes reflect various inner-outer disturbances for which partial and ineffective cures are proposed. Bolingbroke's opening speech, for ex-ample, suggests a relatively easy, pragmatic cure for the illness of the state, which he describes in his own terms, a cure demanding only that the right people get the point quickly enough:

> So shaken as we are, so wan with care,
> Find we a time for frighted Peace to pant
> And breathe short-winded accents of new broils

To be commenc'd in strands afar remote.
No more the thirsty entrance of this soil
Shall daub her lips with her own children's blood;
No more shall trenching war channel her fields,
Nor bruise her flowerets with the armed hoofs
Of hostile paces. Those opposed eyes,
Which, like the meteors of a troubled heaven,
All of one nature, of one substance bred,
Did lately meet in the intestine shock
And furious close of civil butchery,
Shall now, in mutural well-beseeming ranks,
March all one way and be no more oppos'd
Against acquaintance, kindred, and allies.   (I. i. 1–16)

Since the sickness lies solely in civil insurrection, the cure is to be a simple resto-
ration of national unity, or rather the appearance of unity. Henry stresses the one
nature, one substance of the constituents, the unnaturalness of civil "butchery", and
the attractiveness of a united body. His rhetoric attempts to embody and make
attractive the rigorous, ceremonial order for which he asks. But the diagnosis is
shallow and the appeal, as we eventually learn, partly bogus in that the proposal to
engage in a holy war is strategic rather than religious. He hopes simply to call "Fall
in!" and see the chaotic crisscrossing of insurrection and "intestine shock" transformed into "well-beseeming ranks", all marching one way.

In thinking about the Prince's "riot and dishonour" and his alliance with Falstaff,
Henry reveals almost accidentally that the disturbance runs deeper. He lapses into
the kind of wishful dream that characterizes Richard II:

O that it could be prov'd
That some night-tripping fairy had exchang'd
In cradle-clothes our children where they lay,
And call'd mine Percy, his Plantagenet!   (I. i. 86–89)

That he is mistaken about the Prince is perhaps less important than the indication
that the rhetoric of politic calculation is not sufficient to draw the community, or
even the king, together, as Falstaff easily demonstrates. His wish for a different son
appears more and more ironic as we realize that his own "tender conscience"
needs a different image to put on display. But he is not simply trying to avert civil
chaos through an appearance of public order; he wants also to *be* something
different from himself, the follower of "indirect crook'd ways" to an undeserved
crown; and he would like his son, who is really very much his, to be his justification.
Obviously, if the Prince turns out to be another Richard, the crooked path will only
lead back to the same morass; his public ceremonies will turn out to have been
private orgies, held in full view of a commonwealth he thinks should not see too
much of a king.

The Hotspur mirror reveals an impulsive drive for self-glorification undermin-

ing the community without twinges of conscience. Hotspur in a sense bribes the
moral sense by making a religion of chivalric virtues; he discovers or manufactures
opponents such as the perfumed "popinjay", Henry, and the Prince, against whom
he can legally exercise those virtues. He thinks of heroism as a leaping upward to
the pale-faced moon and a plunging downward where fathom line could never
reach to pluck up maiden-honor, both places suggesting dream fulfillment; but his
"vision" is more dynamic than rational. His is an aggressive, individual dream, like
those of romance knights, that would make history primarily a chronicle of individual heroic events, incapable of uniting a community except as a collection of
followers. (Even so, Hotspur is no further from an adjustment of self and society
than John of Lancaster, who has little understanding of personal, subversive tendencies. His strategem at the Forest of Gaultree is justified insofar as Authority
needs desperately to keep control, but it cannot, of course, lead to permanent
psychic or communal well-being: he submerges the inner self in the machinations of
politics, though it reappears now and then, a little strangled, on the surface.)

Falstaff reflects all of these deficiencies, but in a more dangerous form because
he has an effective mechanism to handle them. Rather than curing sickness, he
explodes tension in laughter, which reconciles us to incongruities without eliminat-
ing them. Whereas Hal aims at a comprehensive integration of aggressive and
self-transcending tendencies (to borrow Arthur Koestler's terms[6]), Falstaff adjusts
to the former—as long as he can—through comic strategies, and grows fat on
pretensions to the latter that he sees all around him. The "tragedy" he ultimately
faces makes such a static adjustment impossible and forces the audience to abandon
it, to reach upward toward some sort of extra-personal fulfillment. To prevent our
substituting resentment for political insight, Shakespeare makes the "tragedy" implicit throughout in the very nature of the humor. In Falstaff's first appearance in
I Henry IV, for example, though the Prince and Falstaff play lightly with the subject
of sickness, the disease goes too deep for purely comic adjustment or purgation. If
hours were indeed "cups of sack, and minutes capons, and clocks the tongues of
bawds, and dials the signs of leaping-houses, and the blessed sun himself a fair hot
wench in flame-coloured taffeta" (I. ii. 7), time would be unredeemable. (The sun
image is soon connected to providential order, an objectively stable and redeem-
able time, and the "epiphany" of the new king.) To "go by the moon" as Falstaff
proposes, is to lose one's will and become as changeable as the sea; it leads to an
ebb as low as the foot of the ladder and a flow as high "as the ridge of the gallows"
(I. ii. 42), not so high as Hotspur plans to leap, but high enough.

The mock interview is perhaps a clearer example in that the tragic undertones
that prepare the audience to transcend the sea-moon sickness and accept the
duties of *Respublica* are more central to the dramatic *agon.* The scene demonstrates the insufficiency of the comic mode in handling the disturbances of the
"times". Whereas comic rebels are ordinarily animated mannerisms of some kind,
or collections of them, which the dramatist can set in place without destroying,
when Falstaff's "meanings collapse" in absurdity, something besides mannerism and
"make-believe" is lost.[7] The make-believe and the mannerisms are part of a Fal-

staffian ceremony of self-creation that Hal is invited to join at the end of the scene (he has only to concede that his corporeal friend is more or less permanent). In his failure "to make his body and furnishings mean sovereignty" and thus finally to mean "all the world", as Mr. Barber aptly puts it, and in his inability to redeem time through a private ritual divorced from political and religious duties, Falstaff himself is destroyed, first symbolically in mock rejection and finally, of course, in actual "history". The Prince's answer cuts through the comic façade like a precise surgical instrument. If "each repetition of 'sweet Jack Falstaff, kind Jack Falstaff' aggrandizes an identity which the serial clauses caress and cherish" (Barber, p. 182), even though caressing with some irony, the entire structure comes down at the Prince's sharp pronouncement, "I do, I will." As a kind of official proclamation, his answer expresses not a timeless dream but a present impulse to reject comic ritual and to seek some other adjustment. Though brief, it has its own rhythm and force; neither self-aggrandizement nor its protective irony can stand against it.

The sacrificial theme is already explicit at this point and already rhetorically effective in that we must begin to choose one commitment in preference to the other, or at least to find some other way to accommodate both. The Prince plans to confront history—which overwhelms a tragic hero and scarcely involves a comic hero at all—by transcending the self. And insofar as he takes the audience with him, he makes it share his distrust of the ironic ritual of self, as through Hotspur it learns to distrust the dream of personal heroism and through John of Lancaster the suffocation of individual honor in the common will.

The Prince's control over impulses of the minute comes primarily through his capacity to see history as a continuous succession of events linking present to past and future. As he learns to control "time", Falstaff more and more loses himself in the present. Living in a timeless, fleeting moment precludes fulfilling future promise, profanes "the precious time", and cuts off the past as a useful, educative force. For to Falstaff, youth is not a time of growth leading continuously to fulfillment; it is adventure, a slim waist, and bells at midnight, seen through a haze of nostalgia (even though that nostalgia can be realistically exploited in others). The present is a rush of officers at the door, interrupting the private life and dragging one off to Shrewsbury. Or it is an attempt to conceal past actions like the performance at Gadshill by recreating them, with changes, in the present—in a sense "mythologizing" them to accommodate self-respect. And the future will be uncertain because if time is essentially a flow of sack, "minutes capons, and clocks the tongues of bawds", absence will be oblivion: "It grows late", Falstaff laments to Doll; "we'll to bed. Thou't forget me when I am gone" (II. iv. 299, Part Two). The Prince, on the other hand, in the process of validating the future king's future community, expiates a past curse in the processes of time, experience, and growth. When he gets the best of Falstaff, it is only by connecting past and future as one continuum. Ironically, to do so in the rejection scene, he must make himself appear discontinuous:

Presume not that I *am* the thing I *was;*
For God doth know, so shall the world perceive,

That I have turn'd away my former self;
So will I those that kept me company.
When thou dost hear I *am* as I *have been,*
Approach me, and thou *shalt be* as thou *wast* . . .   (V. v. 60, Part Two)

Falstaff must be made to think he has changed whether he has or not. But Falstaff's blessings would be lost anyway in the essential discontinuity of his own life, in time's always increasing curse: "Thou whoreson little tidy Bartholemew boar-pig", Doll says affectionately, "when wilt thou leave fighting o' days and foining o' nights, and begin to patch up thine old body for heaven?" Falstaff will never be ready for the Totentanz: "Peace, good Doll! do not speak like a death's-head. Do not bid me remember mine end." Which is to say that he attempts to separate present existence from historical continuity, while the Prince submits existence to the controls of honor, duty, public ceremony—in short, social and political tradition.

It is necessity for controls of this kind that makes the sacrifice of Falstaff inevitable. With this in mind, we might think of the history play as a dramatic demonstration of how to counter the disintegrative and antisocial impulses of self through a sense of continuous historical "transcendence". Such transcendence does not necessarily involve freedom from time and the demands of ego—Hal accepts past guilt and future duties, and is personally ambitious—but with some qualifications, as we shall see later, it puts such demands in a meaningful historical framework that liberates hero and audience from any particular demand: a moment in history is less overpowering when connected in sequence with what has passed and what is to come.

Some of the limitations of the function of Falstaff's "tragedy" in the series are implicit in this stress on continuity and tradition. The province of the history play is not the inner world or the world of fable but a historical world like the one outside the theater, engrossed in politics and asking that taxes be paid. Its hero never quite escapes into legend or touches the deepest layers of our sympathy. It is concerned with the redemptive virtues, or lack of them, and leaves unexplored the more absorbing depths of individual motivation that ordinarily occupy tragedy. For this reason, Falstaff's "tragic" slavery to time, like his comic absurdity, is perhaps best interpreted as simply a failure in historical vision, a failure in adjustment to "history". The history play, through its hero or exposure of non-heroes, shows the audience how to make the adjustment.

II

Not until his public denunciation of Falstaff does the Prince become the manifest center of community tradition. Before the redemptive process reaches that completion, he must undergo several trials—against Hotspur and the sick king as well as against Falstaff—all of which force him to rise above himself as an apparent rioter-in-time and become someone the world can "perceive", who is without discrepancy between inner self and outer act. As he helps defeat the rebels, he takes over their powers in the manner of a morality-play hero and consigns to the grave their unredeemable qualities—the hidden conspiracies, inner guilt, and aggressive egoism—which cause discontinuity in both personal life and public tradition. At each step he thus becomes more clearly the purified and evident "continuator" who will assume the inherited crown and weld, after his epiphany, an unbroken chain of order from God to man, past to future. (Quelling political rebellion, of course, is but one of the purgative acts.[8]) In the deaths of both Hotspur and the king, the transfer and purgation which make that chain possible are explicit:

> PRINCE: . . . And all the budding honours on thy crest
> I'll crop, to make a garland for my head. (V. iv. 71)

> KING: . . . God knows, my son
> By what by-paths and indirect crook'd ways
> I met this crown; . . .
> To thee it shall descend with better quiet,
> Better opinion, better confirmation;
> For all the soil of the achievement goes
> With me into the earth. (IV. v. 184 ff., Part Two)

> KING [HENRY V]: My father is gone wild into his grave
> For in his tomb lie my affections;
> And with his spirit sadly I survive,
> To mock the expectation of the world,
> To frustrate prophecies, and to raze out
> Rotten opinion, who hath writ me down
> After my seeming. (V. ii. 123, Part Two)

The discontinuity between son and father can be resolved completely only when the son becomes father and casts off his childhood, or sublimates its Oedipal impulses, or whatever, on behalf of the "fatherland". Feelings toward the state as a kind of super-parent—the "womb of kings" and the fatherland all in one—are much less ambivalent than those toward the king-father. Hence, as the "soil" of the king's achievement is buried, the Prince's own "offending" qualities are purged. As Canterbury recalls in *Henry V,*

> Consideration like an angel came
> And whipp'd th' offending Adam out of him,
> Leaving his body as a paradise
> T' envelop and contain celestial spirits. (I. i. 28)

Canterbury is less than critical of the Prince's strategy, but "consideration's" final banishment of prodigality is clearly to be taken as a purification, the full effects of which are revealed only in *Henry V.* Time and death, which defeat Falstaff, sanctify the lineal descent, wash the blood from the inherited crown, and establish the Prince as vicegerent of cosmic stability.

The rebellious spirit dies differently in each case, but the same general process holds true: in each *agon* the Prince gains tighter control of the "intestine shocks" that disturb both the individual and the nation. In the psychomachian battle of Shrewsbury, Shakespeare brings together the main rebels of Part One and has the Prince collect his honors. The insurrectionists appear misled and willfully blind. Douglas, for example, attacks various false images of the king and supposes Falstaff to be dead. (The Prince is misled in a different way: his address to the "dead" friend is a stylized and symbolic rejection rather than a comic mistake that discredits him.) From these acts, we surmise that Douglas does not have his finger on either the national or the individual pulse. Though in both cases he admittedly has reason for confusion, he cannot tell a true king or a live man. The persistent reappearance of the "kings" suggests that the rightful government is omnipresent and a bit mystifying to the outsider. Despite his huffing and puffing, the House of Lancaster refuses to come down and Falstaff, thinking reluctantly of reforming, springs back up again. Rebellion can do nothing but fly headlong "upon the foot of fear". As the entire fabric of self-seeking masquerading as public interest and moral indignation collapses, history appears to have justified the "crook'd ways" and reformed the rioters.

Once we grant the peculiar way the folk hero has of expelling antitypes and absorbing their strength, we are less likely to dispute the Prince's capacity at Shrewsbury to assume Hotspur's chivalric prowess or, in Part Two, his right to acquire his father's political acuteness. That Henry V likewise absorbs something of Falstaff is more difficult to demonstrate; I think, however, that in a sense the new king has learned from Falstaff. To be sure, the Prince's avowed pretexts for plucking the "base strings" would not indicate a profound educational process; and when he thinks Falstaff dead, his grief is significantly qualified by the disenchanting remark, "O, I should have a heavy miss of thee / If I were much in love with vanity!" which substitutes a contrary-to-fact conditional for regret. (If the lines are spoken as a kind of ritual disclaimer, some of the personal quality disappears; and since Falstaff is not dead, an encomium would be out of place and perhaps suggest that Hal's "I do, I will" was not seriously intended after all.) As a final, apparently gratuitous, insult he threatens to have Falstaff "embowell'd" to suit him for lying beside "noble Percy", which may seem to de-Falstaff what is left (though Falstaff is listening, of course, which makes that threat, too, a mixture of comic and tragic foreboding).

But if the strategy of the history play is to convince the audience that nothing is lost in the state's relentless pursuit of its Manifest Destiny, even sacrifices must pay dividends. Falstaff's vitality must not be entirely lost. It is less easily transferred than Percy's chivalry and the sick king's power, but like these it must be made continuous if it is to survive; its "body" must be made less, its "grace" more. In a sense, then, it is left for *Henry V* to demonstrate the validity of the sacrifices required during the course of the Henry IV plays and *Richard II*, which first began shattering dream worlds in the interest of efficient government: the slaying of individual impulses and anarchistic dreams is justified only if public action makes self-fulfillment possible in some other way. Henry V as a public figure thus becomes very central to the series of plays. The audience must have a protagonist of some dimension, both human and "public", to make the center of its circle. The shell of tradition without inner life is no more binding than the verbal observance of love that Lear forces upon his daughters.

Shakespeare has no trouble, of course, making Henry V transcend Hotspur, Henry IV, and himself as truant Prince. Though he has been a comparatively passive and shifting figure at Gadshill and Eastcheap, merely the chief knight at Shrewsbury, and an outsider at the Forest of Gaultree, in *Henry V* he becomes the center and wholesale manipulator of the action. Beyond that, on a few occasions his coolness of judgment and his hot quest for honor are animated by a comparatively high degree of vitality and humanity. I suspect that Shakespeare meant to suggest *vestigia Falstaffi* in places other than the dialogue of Pistol and the Hostess, which is designed to lay to rest whatever miscellaneous emotions might still be getting in the way. The shrewdness, expediency, and courage which Henry has taken from his father and Hotspur are significantly altered in the composite character of the new king, not by what Falstaff has taught him directly, but by what Falstaff represents. Irony and humor, of course, have been suppressed because, as we have seen, these lead to a static adjustment of aggressive tendencies rather than to reform and heroic action. The jest of the tennis balls Henry turns into a provocation for war, or pretends to; the practical joke he sets in motion on the eve of battle he drains of humor the next day, when the king must appear king. But some of the vitality of Eastcheap and Gadshill remains. Henry unites realistic pragmatism, ability to accommodate personal impulses quickly to difficult situations, and the bearing of a man-among-men. In doing so he rises above the average patrician and the inflexible professional hero.

Whatever he might have learned from Eastcheap, Henry seems clearly meant to illustrate the highest potentials of the active life. Even his coldbloodedness can work two ways: it may be an operation of pure, disinterested intelligence taking calculated risks, or it may embrace alternatives and choose the right one out of a comprehensive moral perspective, impossible without some degree of humanity. Spiritual energy is clearly part of his impelling force—though this does not mean that he cannot be shrewd at the same time. In handling the treachery of Cambridge, Grey and Scroop, to choose a representative example, he is compassionate as well as crafty. Meeting calculation with calculation, he brings the three conspirators to an unavoidable moral recognition and finally to contrition. Though the transformation may seem unbelievable in psychological terms, the idea of shifting the burden of execution to the conspirators themselves is scarcely reprehensible in itself. In the context of the play, they are responsible for their inner values in the same way that soldiers are for their souls upon entering battle: Henry insists that maintaining fine distinctions between what belongs to the community and what is one's own is necessary to the health of both individual and state. Considering the "kingdom's safety" he believes to be the king's first duty; to act more mercifully, as again in the execution of Bardolph, would be soft-hearted cruelty (III. vi. 115). *Given the conspiracy to begin with,* repentance is the highest good salvageable.

Henry thus finds personal fulfillment in the "office" rather than in self-definition. The "affection" which Bradley finds in short supply in him, he reserves for this "happy few, [this] band of brothers"—with himself at the head, of course. But Shakespeare, in the Henry plays at least, does not imply that being public in this way requires sacrificing the "citadel of absolute truth, the inner self."[9] Although it is not difficult to diminish the king by measuring him against later tragic protagonists, he is not without virtues. Seen strictly from the standpoint of adjustment to polity, he compares favorably with other Shakespearian heroes: beside him, Coriolanus is an ego-maniac, Caesar an impostor, Antony unscrupulous (in one play) and weak (in the other), and Brutus confused; even Hamlet, as a Prince, appears unbalanced, deprived by the sickness of his world of shaping the state to his inherent magnanimity. After the tragic hero has departed with the sickness and strength of his egoism upon him, Shakespeare ordinarily has a public figure such as Malcolm or Fortinbras reassemble the scattered energies of the community and give it coherence and historical duration. Personal isolation and the shattering of communal bonds he shows to be consequences of seeing too intently the "citadel of absolute truth". Henry is not so destructive or so interesting as that, but his limitations do not necessarily indicate that "Falstaff wins after all."

What they do indicate is not easy to determine, but if we were to ignore them we would tend to make an historic epic of some sort out of an historic drama. It may be that Shakespeare is realistic about the king simply to show the irrelevance of personal flaws in the fully absorbing center of community emotion. The intensity of the myth can be measured by the amount of reality it supports without collapsing, which in Shakespeare can be a good deal. In Henry's case, the myth is reinforced by the authorial chorus and by imagistic patterns and echoes from scripture suggesting an analogy between divine and temporal order. The mirror of Christian kings *in his way* is the mirror of the Christian King: the action of redeeming time imitates the Redemption; the epiphany of the new king imitates the Epiphany; the hierarchal structure of the kingdom imitates cosmic structure. Henry's imitation remains imperfect because the history play, unlike mystery or morality plays, remains essentially indeterminate. But despite these limitations, Henry as folk hero fuses a diversity of individual impulses into a unified, social organism that is more than the sum of uses one segment makes of another.

The pre-battle speech (IV. iii. 18) reveals something of how the fusion is accomplished. (Since it is long and familiar, I shall not quote it.) We know from the nighttime dialogues that the king does not ignore the dangers he has put his subjects in, but neither does he allow responsibility to paralyze him. The hard-headed plainness, the blunt wit, and the colloquial idiom of the wooing scene are evident before he reaches the drawing room. We know, too, how far democratic instincts have penetrated, without destroying, distinctions of rank and social level. The main point here is that his rhetoric, despite its hortative battlefield simplicity, catches all of this in its net. It uses but goes beyond the Hotspurian logic of chivalry and the policy involved in rousing the troops at a crucial moment. The repetition is less mechanical, less calculated than Bolingbroke's, which plays upon the emotions without emotion through an intellectual balance of clauses and a manufactured pattern of images and figures. Henry, like Falstaff in the mock-rejection scene, obviously enjoys words which name and glorify tangible objects close to the center of his self-interest; he savors the names which when sounded in the future will continue to weld into a brotherhood those who were initiated at Agincourt. The difference between his rhetoric of names and Falstaff's ritual is that the former creates a group myth, the latter sanctifies the person and personality of the speaker; one looks forward and the other magnifies the present. But both are adept at word-magic. They add communion to communication, in Allen Tate's phrase, and thus avoid a dehumanized rhetoric that reveals nothing of the inner self and leaves even vital community interests untouched.

Henry's speech is partly a wishful dream of heroism but is unquestionably alive and realistic. It is thus well suited to the form and purpose of the history play. Like the total action, it argues for the sacrifice of personal life in a communal act which will repay the men "with advantages"—provided, of course, that they believe in the king. It is a national version of finding selfhood by losing it, to be sealed by the ritual of bloodshed which makes all men equal, "gentling" those to whom the king has talked in the darkness and who in no tangible political or economic sense will ever be raised.

In the history play, the function of an "epic" speech such as this is to redeem those times that can imaginatively share in the myth: to shape the present so that men "in their flowing cups", "yearly on the vigil feast", will remember the myth. For such history, Shakespeare implies, is never remote to an audience held by the "muse of fire"; relived in the theater, it will make a nationalistic group once again a "band of brothers".[10] Henry is probably meant to be justified both in envying the peasant's "best advantages" and in doing everything in his power to secure his grasp on the crown, even though preventing civil turmoil entails a foreign war. To withdraw from responsibility is impossible, or at least risky, as Lear discovers; to assume it without reservation will violate some things, strengthen others. Pursuing a course inherently contaminating, Henry never quite loses equilibrium or allows public obligations to reduce inner life to mechanism.

III

The process of purified absorption undoubtedly has less tangible aspects also. Folk heroes acquire powers, as they mount horses, differently from public school boys:

> I saw young Harry with his beaver on,
> His cuisses on his thighs, gallantly arm'd,
> Rise from the ground like feathered Mercury,
> And vaulted with such ease into his seat
> As if an angel dropp'd down from the clouds
> To turn and wind a fiery Pegasus
> And witch the world with noble horsemanship.   (IV. i. 104ff., Part One)

(That a rider's control of his mount was a common figure for the soul's control of its body explains away some but not all of the witching skill.) Despite the suggestions of superhuman power in the king, however, Shakespeare's dramatic method in presenting him is at least as close to realism as to the technique of the morality and miracle plays. "Participation" in the communal emotion centered in the king results not only from the king's mythological stature and incantational rhetoric but also from a realistic examination of alternatives in various counter-actions or dialectical "plots" that close off other channels.

The attempt to turn "disease" to commodity is one of these counter-actions. Nearly everyone in the series from *Richard II* to *Henry V* at one time or another thinks of exploiting the weaknesses of the realm or of other parties in it, partly by conjuring the right spirits and partly by simple political trickery. In *2 Henry IV*, the rebels, having been "o'erset", venture again; the Archbishop of York "turns insurrection to religion" and attempts to capitalize upon "a bleeding land, / Gasping for life" (I. ii. 207); Northumberland lies, as Rumour says, "crafty sick" and awaiting a time to emerge and redeem his honor when the state seems weak enough to allow it. Falstaff is again the key figure, of course. If he comes on stage asking about time in Part One, in Part Two he appears inquiring about his ailing health and advanced age, both equally beyond fixing but not beyond "use". "A man can no more separate age and covetousness than 'a can part young limbs and lechery", he rationalizes; "the gout galls the one, and the pox pinches the other"; but a "good wit will make use of anything. I will turn diseases to commodity" (I. ii. 256, 277). His inability to do so is the source of both comedy and tragedy, as we have seen. Desire, outliving performance, becomes grotesque, like the clawing of poll by parrot, in the Prince's figure. The pressure of time is unbalancing, as a note of desperation comes into the Eastcheap follies. Hostess Quickly chants imperatively to Doll (who also turns disease to commodity): "O, run, Doll, run; run, good Doll. Come. (*She comes blubbered.*) Yea, will you come, Doll?" (II. iv. 420, Part Two).

The emphasis upon commodity is one side of Falstaff's partly real and partly mock gentleman-capitalist role, which complements his Puritanism. He is a "robber" both of "pilgrims going to Canterbury with rich offerings" and of "traders riding to London with fat purses" (I. ii. 140). As Gadshill observes, he goes with "burgomasters" who "pray continually to their saint, the commonwealth; or rather, not pray to her, but prey on her" (II. i. 87). His expenses, though hardly frugal, are itemized. Shakespeare apparently attaches this cluster of middle-class values to the aristocrat in order to purge them along with other things that "offend". After Falstaff's death, an increased acquisitiveness characterizes his old group, as it slips further and further toward the periphery of the legitimate community. Pistol *owns* Quickly and advises Nym to get papers on Doll as fast as possible (II. i. 77): "My Love," he commands the Hostess, "give me thy lips. / Look to my chattels and my moveables" (II. iii. 49). He plans to sell provisions to the army and thus acquire whatever profits war will afford (II. ii. 116). Falstaff had at least held upper and lower levels together; now that he is dead, Pistol says, "we must earn" (II. iii. 5), that is, both "grieve" and make a living.[11] And "earning" as they do leads to petty thievery, even to the gallows.

Shakespeare thus minimizes the kind of bourgeois communal power that economic bonds have in Heywood, Dekker, and other middle-class dramatists. But the spiritual bonds of the medieval community have also weakened, and any dramatist interested in more than individual profit motives must do something with the Goddess Utility on a social scale. Hence Henry, like the Bastard, is made aware of lost spiritual bonds and the power of commodity—a money-minded church plays easily into his hands—but he substitutes for them chivalric and heroic virtues, by and large, rather than middle-class virtues. Because the motives behind Falstaff's desire to turn disease to commodity are primarily egoistic and unheroic, he rejects them and turns to the old framework of higher virtues. (After the Histories, Shakespeare will place "chivalry" in a tragic environment and show it to be disintegrating. Someone like Edmund, who has violated the old hierarchies and grown possessive will usually give the death blow. Its potential weakness is already clear in *1 Henry IV* when Hotspur momentarily becomes acquisitive and makes the rebellion—supposedly on behalf of honor—look dangerously like a land grab.) The Henry plays explore the profit motive thoroughly, however, in return subjecting the heroic virtues to Falstaff's utilitarian wit. That honor and criticism of his "betters" should be Falstaff's steady diet is an indication that rank and the chivalric distinctions it is based on can now be threatened from below, as Richard II discovers, without flights of angels coming to their defense. A king who has taken the crown expediently must be especially aware of "what the people are saying": the new freedom to climb entails an increasing danger of falling. Public life on all levels, from Iago-like disputes over status and promotion to the politics of a Coriolanus, is a different and more complicated concern.

Falstaff, of course, with his easy movement among levels—from Eastcheap taverns to pre-battle councils—and his threat to make the Prince a career robber of the king's treasury, is a champion of anti-chivalric flexibility. If it takes a war to "gentle" the lowly, wit levels kings without stirring from the chair. In turning disease to commodity, he attacks more than the economic order, however; he also translates moral distinctions downward to purely physical phenomena, and in doing so indirectly affirms the relentless natural law to which he eventually falls. Commodity and naturalism are closely linked in him, as in Edmund. Though the links are made with more wit than cunning, beneath the humor the way is continually being prepared for the king's comment, "know the grave doth gape / For thee thrice wider than for other men", a caustic remark that only recapitulates what Falstaff himself has implied:

CH. JUST.: Well, the truth is, Sir John, you live in great infamy.

FAL.: He that buckles himself in my belt cannot live in less.

CH. JUST.: Your means are very slender, and your waste is great.

FAL.: I would it were otherwise; I would my means were greater, and my waist slenderer. (I. ii. 156, Part Two)

Through the puns Falstaff tries to convert moral disease to mere physical disproportion, which seems the lesser sin—until the Prince suggests that the wider the "grave" for those "surfeit-swell'd", the less the "grave". His last attempt to convert disease to commodity in working Justice Shallow for a thousand pounds carries him rushing into disaster; ironically, he goes to "cure" the young king, "sick" for him, by taking him for what he can.

In "observingly" distilling his experience, the Prince, too, turns disease to commodity, but differently. What he takes from the public till he repays, and what he takes from his antitypes would have been lost or misused anyway. Theoretically, there is nothing at fault with the strategy provided it is made subject to moral controls. Warwick describes it quite accurately when he remarks that

> The Prince but studies his companions
> Like a strange tongue, wherein, to gain the language,
> 'Tis needful that the most immodest word
> Be look'd upon and learn'd; . . .
>   So, like gross terms,
> The Prince will in the perfectness of time
> Cast off his followers; and their memory
> Shall as a pattern or a measure live,
> By which his Grace must mete the lives of others,
> Turning past evils to advantages.   (IV. iv. 67ff., Part Two)

Thus even Falstaff serves the kingdom "in the perfectness of time"—that is, in the perfection of time redeemed by the new king—because past evils, or evil of any kind, can be turned to advantage by the scrupulously unscrupulous. Thus Henry V can play upon the acquisitive instinct without being corrupted by it. His kind of expediency rejects, but with open eyes, the ways which many realists in the audience knew of "getting ahead".

IV

We can now return to the rejection scene, which brings together many of the aspects of the history play we have observed, and see it from what I think is a slightly different perspective from either "character" or "ritualistic" criticism. If equilibrium between self and society is indeed achieved in it, we should expect to find Falstaff's "death" appearing inevitable; it should serve to unite the community in the theater, as in the play, by ridding it of the egocentrism that has crystallized around Falstaff and his ways of confronting time, seeking commodity, curing disease, and so forth. The rejection scene is the first time, of course, that Falstaff is aware that a tutor and feeder of riots is unwelcome in court. His recognition is thus nicely timed to coincide with and contribute to the final manifestation of the king and the *anagnorisis* of the audience. His defensive masks are stripped off and he is suddenly faced with the blatant fact of public life. His heart, Pistol says, is "fracted and corroborate", which is partly humorous and partly pathetic; it is "killed by the King".

The slayer-king speaks not only as an ex-truant but also as the exemplar of psychological order. Falstaff's appeal, "My king! my Jove! I speak to thee, my heart!"

recognizes that the "head" of the temporal order functions on at least three levels simultaneously, as king, Jove, and heart of his subjects; he speaks with the rhetoric of elevated majesty, personal teacher, and last judge.[12] It is significant that the first time we are fully convinced of the unity of Hal's impulses and the wholeness of his character, he is playing his most complex role: he cannot *be* himself until he is king. The disjunction in his former life as a rioter under bond to promise is healed by making the promise reality and by consigning the rest to unreal dream. The discrepancy between present and past appearance has never "really" existed, however, for he *is* the thing he *was,* even if not the thing Falstaff and the kingdom took him to be. His educational process has added to his essential character but not disturbed its underlying continuity.

But the chief dramatic point would seem to be that Shakespeare refuses to negotiate the loss of Falstaff, as Bradley wishes he had (p. 253). The language is harsh because *under the circumstances* it could not have been dramatically effective otherwise: the realities of time and disease which the play has made important must be confronted without evasion, conservatism being more deeply ingrained in the play than Falstaff. Thus, though comedy could not expel "such a kind of man" with a clear conscience, history must contrive to get along without him. If we expect a purely tragic "resolution", however, we shall not be quite prepared for what we receive. Falstaff is too human to be dealt with like Malvolio but not of high enough stature for pure tragedy. The rejection scene lacks the kind of language that could transform the unpleasant "fact" to cathartic poetry, nor does it attempt to do so entirely. The community must be made a charmed circle through another kind of rhetoric, part public speech and part confession, flexible, direct, and capable of embracing reality freed from the "long dream".

Difficulties besides that of the language are involved also. The history play must be plotted so as to satisfy our sense of form as though it had beginning, middle, and end, and yet must somehow be left open. Its subject matter leads to plays in a series rather than to single, self-contained works, and even the series cannot be decisively ended. In the tragical histories, Shakespeare emphasizes the new reign, or England's possibilities if it "to itself do rest but true", or the new unity between "the white rose and the red". In the rejection scene, he divides attention about equally between the promising community surrounding the new king and the "catastrophe" of personal life.[13] The result is a kind of *concordia discors;* to borrow Canterbury's words, heaven divides

> The state of man in divers functions,
> Setting endeavour in continual motion;
> To which is fixed, as an aim or butt,
> Obedience.   (*Henry V,* I. ii. 185ff.)

But even such formulas as this are not completely "fixed"; they must be tested continually against the circumstances of history. (For this reason I have used the word "adjustment" rather than "reconcilement" or "resolution".) Rather than concluding things once and for all, the history play ends at a plateau or brief breathing space from which the state looks backward with relief but forward with appre-hension. Even the glories of Henry V, as the audience knew, were to wither in the continued curse of Henry VI and Richard III. (Despite the apparently romantic-comedy ending of *Henry V,* Shakespeare goes out of the way to recall the future.) And it is doubtful that Elizabethans felt collectively and spontaneously that some-how Elizabeth had fixed mutability once and for all.

The best that *2 Henry IV* can do is make its auditors participants in a historical ceremony which frees them from the gormandizing dream without robbing them of their individual wills. It demands "obedience" but not an absolute regimentation of "diverse functions" and endeavors set "in continual motion". Shakespeare will have his squire of the night's body—and thus the dark, protected center of self-interest—and not have him either, if he can transubstantiate part of him; and failing that, he would not likely suffer so much from the incongruity of loving and hating the same man as modern readers might, who are that much further from gothic ambivalences: who have never experienced the weird illogic of the moralities, which award the official palm to Order and make us remember Riot. He would probably not hesitate, in other words, to choose Order, with whatever ritual can be put in it, over an instinctive anarchy insufficiently protected from the world by comic strategies. And when we consider that such "magic" as Henry performs in redeeming time—and thus as Shakespeare performs in redeeming history—is effective without demanding that we accept simply on faith the night-tripping "elfin guardians",[14] we can perhaps avoid adding new levels to the schizophrenic feeling for Falstaff. It is not a question of either swallowing duty, sweetly covered with ritual, or rebelling on behalf of all that Falstaff stands for—and feeling dissatisfied in either case: the community which the history play imitates has its own legitimate life.

As to the form of that imitation, we can perhaps let Morgann have the last word after all; for in his role as pre-romantic critic, he leaves room both for the categories into which we put dramatic types and for the unique, organic form by which a given play "takes in" its audience, sometimes in defiance of normal expec-tations and tendencies to favor certain elements. He has Aristotle (surprisingly) rebuke such critics-by-generic-rule as Thomas Rymer who expect the old catego-ries to hold true for all times: "True poesy is *magic*", Aristotle admonishes, "not *nature*; an effect from causes hidden or unknown. To the magician I prescribed no laws; his law and his power are one; his power is his law." Shakespeare, seeing something even in a king who remains alive at the end of the play, made new laws of genre to accommodate him.

NOTES

[1] See C. L. Barber's essay, "Saturnalia in the Henriad", which is printed in *Shakespeare: Modern Essays in Criticism,* ed. Leonard F. Dean (New York, 1957), pp. 169–191, and in *Shakespeare's Festive Comedy.* Cf. J. I. M. Stewart, *Character and Motive in Shakespeare* (Bristol, 1949), p. 127; Northrop Frye, "The Argument of Comedy", *English Institute Essays* (1949), p. 71; and Philip Williams, "The Birth and Death of Falstaff Reconsidered", *SQ,* VIII (1957), 359–365.
[2] The most complete attempts to arrive at a working concept of the history play *sui generis* are Irving

Ribner's "The Tudor History Play: An Essay in Definition", *PMLA*, LXIX (1954), 591–609 and *The English History Play in the Age of Shakespeare* (Princeton University Press, 1957), pp. 1–32; H. B. Charlton's *Shakespeare: Politics and Politicians*, The English Association Pamphlet no. 72 (1929), pp. 7, 11, 13; Una Ellis-Fermor, *The Frontiers of Drama* (London, 1945), pp. 5–14, 34–55; Felix Schelling, *The English Chronicle Play* (New York, 1902); G. K. Hunter, "Shakespeare's Politics and the Rejection of Falstaff", *Critical Quarterly*, I (1959), 229–236. See also Coleridge's *Literary Remains*, H. N. Coleridge, ed. (London, 1836), VI, 160ff.; A. C. Bradley, *Oxford Lectures on Poetry* (London, 1909), pp. 247–275; John Palmer, *Political Characters of Shakespeare* (London, 1945), pp. 184ff.; W. H. Auden, "The Fallen City: Some Reflections on Shakespeare's *Henry IV*", *Encounter*, XIII, no. 5 (1959), 25; and, of course, Maurice Morgann, *An Essay on the Dramatic Character of Sir John Falstaff*, first published in 1777. Northrop Frye's *Anatomy of Criticism* is stimulating as usual, especially the following remarks: "The History merges so gradually into tragedy that we often cannot be sure when communion has turned into catharsis", and "The central theme of Elizabethan history is the unifying of the nation and the binding of the audience into the myth as the inheritors of that unity, set over against the disasters of civil war and weak leadership" (pp. 283–284). Finally, A. P. Rossiter's brief book *English Drama from Early Times to the Elizabethans* (London, 1950) illuminates the "mungrell" forms brilliantly, from an inclusive perspective.

[3] Shakespeare's experimentation with the form is clear from the varieties he tried and from devices such as Rumour's induction to *2 Henry IV* (which suggests the uncertainty of historical events as experienced and yet offers the broader vision of the chronicler who sees everything with accuracy) and the chorus in *Henry V*, which moves the play toward dramatized epic.

[4] This role has been mentioned occasionally but has not been extensively explored. See D. A. Traversi, *An Approach to Shakespeare* (New York, 1956), p. 32, and *Shakespeare from* Richard II *to* Henry V (Stanford University Press, 1957), pp. 77ff; Stewart, pp. 127ff.; Auden, p. 25; Williams, p. 363.

[5] Cf. J. A. Bryant, Jr., "Prince Hal and the Ephesians", *Sewanee Review*, LXVII (1959), 204–219; Benjamin T. Spencer, "*2 Henry IV* and the Theme of Time", *University of Toronto Quarterly*, XIII (1944), 394–399; Paul A. Jorgensen, "'Redeeming Time' in Shakespeare's *Henry IV*", *Tennessee Studies in Literature*, V (1960), 101–109.

[6] *Insight and Outlook* (New York, 1949), pp. 57ff.

[7] Barber, p. 189.

[8] Hugh Dickinson oversimplifies the redemptive process, I think, in pinning it entirely on the defeat of Percy. See "The Reformation of Prince Hal", *Shakespeare Quarterly*, XII (1961), 33–46.

[9] Ellis-Fermor, p. 54.

[10] The levels of awareness in an audience thus told that it would re-enact what it was in fact re-enacting must have been complex. One of the functions of the Chorus, which provides an unusually elaborate mediation between playwright, audience, and play, is to sharpen awareness of the play as play. The Olivier film version carries the point even further. At the conclusion, "Henry" is suddenly revealed as the actor-who-has-been-king: the "performance" is over and the myth shrinks back into present reality. And since the film begins from a perspective outside the Globe and circles in upon the action, there is a further movement from the Shakespearian to the modern theater. The Elizabethan golden age has been part of the myth; and so the modern audience, finding itself outside both the community of the old king and the world of 1599, must make a double "adjustment". The film becomes not so much an apology for *Respublica* as distant history in two layers.

[11] The economic aspect of Pistol's "earning" are reinforced by his speech a few lines later:

> Look to my chattels and my movables.
> Let senses rule; the word is "Pitch and Pay".
> Trust none;
> For oaths are straws, men's faiths are wafercakes,
> And hold-fast is the only dog, my duck. . . .
> Let us to France; like horse-leeches, my boys,
> To suck, to suck, the very blood to suck!   (II. iii. 50)

Rather than ritualizing theft as Falstaff had in his role as Saturnalian king, Pistol turns from ritual—the elegy for Falstaff—to economic "blood-sucking". (The pun on "earn" is the pivot.) And whereas Falstaff's game had attracted and educated the young Prince, the serious business of Pistol and his group cannot hold the "boy", who finally seeks out "some better service" (III. ii. 54). The counter-action has lost its dialectical, Saturnalian function.

[12] See Harold Jenkins, *The Structural Problem in Shakespeare's* Henry the Fourth (London, 1956), p. 14.

[13] Public duty and private impulse are not "represented" in Hal and Falstaff as in an allegory, of course. If the Prince absorbs some of Falstaff, Falstaff in turn picks up a Lancastrian political device or two. He is well aware of the figure he and his companions will cut when arraigned before the emerging king, for example. Even their tattered clothes he will turn to advantage, appearing "to stand stained with travel and sweating with desire to see him; thinking of nothing else, putting all affairs else in oblivion, as if there were nothing else to be done but to see him" (V. v. 24). We know that the "as if" is justified and that even with Falstaff friendship and patronage go hand in hand: "woe to my Lord Chief Justice" and "Blessed are they that have been my friends."

[14] Cf. A. P. Rossiter's statement in *Woodstock: A Moral History* (London, 1946), "magic is part of the Tudor world, not least where Monarchy is touched" (p. 12).

Willard Farnham
FALSTAFF AND
THE GROTESQUE

Falstaff and the Monstrous

I

Before Falstaff the Shakespearean grotesque gives promise of producing some-thing like him, but when he appears he is startling in his generous fulfilment of the promise. It is a question whether Shakespeare himself is not startled by what he has conjured up in him, and whether he does not as a result hurry him to his death in *Henry V,* as he gives him only a briefly reported presence off-stage for its accom-plishment.

In the two parts of *Henry IV* the presumptuous low within the post-classical grotesque tradition goes for the first time so far beyond being extraneous to the high that it takes a firm stand within the borders of the high and for a time holds a place there. It even has hopes that are not groundless of winning high place there. As Falstaff sets himself to be an apostle of the low and nevertheless indulges such hopes, he trades upon impudence, but by no means upon that alone. He has wit, both for saying and for doing, and this is not the wit of the underling or the boor. Shakespeare has taken pains to put into his background of upbringing the means for him to be in many ways acceptable to the high. It is not for nothing that Justice Shallow speaks of him as having been in boyhood a page to Thomas Mowbray, Duke of Norfolk. Nor is it for nothing that Falstaff has in some way, however devious it might have proved to be if Shakespeare had put it into the picture, gained a knighthood. He is, of course, not to be taken as owing his knighthood solely to Sir John Oldcastle as his prototype. Shakespeare was well able to reject what he did not fancy when working from a source. In short, Falstaff is presented as having had

---

From *The Shakespearean Grotesque: Its Genesis and Transformations* (Oxford: Clarendon Press, 1971), pp. 47–60, 69–70, 88–96.

what are called early advantages and as being in that way no merely rude interloper in the realm of the mundane high. More than that, he offers to those of this realm the benefits of his wit. In doing so he can be thought to offer only amusement, and yet his is the wit of a special understanding which is well worthy of attention from the high. If the benefits Falstaff offers can be received and appreciated by the high only in the person of a truant prince, there is nevertheless profit in them for the high—and of course profit for the offerer, though it falls far short of his expectations. After Falstaff the low of the Shakespearean grotesque has a more thorough success in joining itself with the high, but the Falstaffian low must be given full credit for the success it has.

In bringing the Falstaffian low to this success Shakespeare takes the grotesque well beyond anything that seems to have been conceived for it in comment of his age. One may think of a remark upon the grotesque made by Montaigne. It is to be granted that Montaigne stands at some remove from developments in England that lead to the appearance of the Shakespearean grotesque on the stage. Nevertheless, it is curious that a man of Montaigne's late-Renaissance quality, writing over 400 years after St. Bernard of Clairvaux, should view the grotesque in a way much like the way we have found taken by St. Bernard. Montaigne too sees grotesque art only as monstrosity that has a strange and irrational appeal and has no relation to non-grotesque art. He calls his essays grotesque because, as he says by way of modesty, they are like fantastic painted figures shaped in casual fashion. They are to be thought of as deserving a place only outside the realm of right form. In the words of Florio's 1603 translation of *The Essayes,* Montaigne says at the beginning of his Chapter XXVII, 'Of Friendship':

> Considering the proceeding of a Painters worke I have; a desire hath possessed me to imitate him: Hee maketh choise of the most convenient place and middle of every wall, there to place a picture, laboured with all his skill and sufficiencie; and all voyde places about-it, he filleth-up with antike Boscage or Crotesko works; which are fantastical pictures, having no grace, but in the varietie and strangenes of them. And what are these my compositions in truth, other than antique workes, and monstrous bodies, patched and huddled-up together of divers members, without any certaine or well ordered figure, having neither order, dependencie, or proportion, but casual and framed by chaunce?

> *Desinit in piscem mulier formosa supernè.*

> A woman faire for parts superior,
> Endes in a fish for parts inferior.

What is perhaps most surprising here is that Montaigne is not moved to say anything about a diverting play of imagination as having at least some part in the fashioning of 'monstrous bodies' in grotesque design as he knows it. He appears not to recognize as present something that by his account we should find there. Yet he is assuredly a man not without appreciation of the imagination in various forms. It seems hardly sufficient to say in explanation that he comments as he does simply because he reveres the classicism of Horace, whose line upon a representation of the mermaid quoted by him from the beginning of the *Ars Poetica* was written not that any play of fancy might be found in the imagined monstrous form it describes but merely that the form might be condemned for its lack of unity and simplicity.

Though low comedy in Elizabethan drama receives some contemporary English recognition for its diverting effect when it is interjected into decorous matter, there is in that recognition, as it now appears, a curiously limited range of view. The English genius that achieves Falstaff and the lesser figures of his kind seems, fortunately for posterity, to give itself the more fully to creating them in that it has only a rudimentary urge to deal with them in criticism. Very significantly, for example, it does not begin the debate which has discovered in Falstaff a part of his monstrous grotesqueness that makes him both a coward and not a coward. The longer this debate continues the more one is surprised that, as Arthur C. Sprague says at the beginning of a shrewd review of its arguments, 'for about a hundred and eighty years after Sir John Falstaff for the first time ran roaring from Gadshill, the fact of his cowardice was taken for granted'.[1]

II

Falstaff is a 'monstrous body' in the tradition of grotesque animal and man-animal figures that Montaigne draws upon to characterize the form of his essays. At the same time he is part of something that may today be called, in Joycean terms, the 'fun-animal world', a world where man's animal 'comicity' can join with 'cosmicity'.[2]

What is done by imagery in the formation of Falstaff gives him monstrosity that ranges from the very simple to the very unsimple. At its simplest his monstrosity is made almost purely one of distortion. He is hugely fat, as we are not allowed to forget. Imagery that has to do merely with the fat Falstaff makes him almost completely simple in the narrow range of response it evokes for him. It may make him mildly unappealing, as he is, for example, in the guise of a 'woolsack', or a 'tun of man'. Or it may make him something thoroughly repellent, like a 'swol'n parcel of dropsies', a 'gross watery pumpion', or a 'stuff'd cloakbag of guts'.[3] What it does not make him is anything that truly takes hold of our sympathies.

In a way that often accords with his having a great burden of flesh Falstaff has within him an excessive amount of the animal. Imagery having to do with the animal Falstaff, sometimes in relation to the fat Falstaff and sometimes not, can make an additional presentation of unattractiveness.[4] Repulsively it shows him as animal material fit for the butcher's handling. He is a rolled-up ball of tallow, a 'whoreson obscene greasy tallow-catch', ready to be sent by the butcher to the candle-maker. He is more than that; he is a 'whoreson candle-mine', a candle-maker's reservoir of tallow. Or he simply answers to the name of Tallow. In another aspect he is a 'damn'd brawn', a fat pig ready for slaughter, and in still another (as Falstaff himself is made to suggest wryly in *The Merry Wives of Windsor*) he is no better than butcher's discard, a 'barrow of butcher's offal'. If his essentially beastly quality is to be given expression, he is a 'bolting hutch of beastliness', a receptacle for sifted and Simon-Pure beastly substance.

But the Falstaff of beastly substance is not entirely unable to get from the hands of the butcher into those of the cook and to be dressed as food. When he does, he can be not merely no longer repulsive but attractive in an extraordinary way. As food he can take on the special aura of attractiveness that is possessed by meat served on a festival occasion, and can even do so immediately after he has been found by the Prince to have the gross unattractiveness of a 'stuff'd cloakbag of guts'. The Prince in his next breath makes him into a 'roasted Manningtree ox with the pudding in his belly' (*I Henry IV*, II. iv. 496). Since the 'pudding' here is a filling of meat, herbs, and other tasty edibles put into the animal's body cavity before roasting, there is reason enough to think of Shakespeare as allowing his imagination to leap from a picture of unattractiveness to one of attractiveness merely because belly-stuffing plays a part in each. But his arrival at the second picture through a 'chance' association with the first does not make the second less valid. Instead it gives it a special validity. The effect of the ox made savoury by stuffing is so much opposed to that of the cloakbag made unsavoury by stuffing that Shakespeare cannot have failed to recognize at once what he had done in making one of these images follow the other. He must have recognized and yet accepted. And his acceptance is proved to have been utterly right by what he does to Falstaff in general as he takes him well beyond the simplicities of being the fat man.

For Falstaff comes more and more to show that he has savouriness and unsavouriness strangely joined to help make him complexly monstrous. A savouriness to match that of the roasted Manningtree ox is found in Falstaff by Doll Tearsheet. She calls him a 'whoreson little tidy Bartholomew boar-pig' when he has just crossed swords with the obstreperous Pistol, driven him off, and returned to taking his ease at his inn with her and the Hostess (*2 Henry IV*, II. iv. 250–1). There is little to choose between roast pig as it was served traditionally at the fair held at Smithfield on St. Bartholomew's day and roast ox as it was served traditionally at the fair in Manningtree. Each is meat fit for a feast. But Doll is not made by Shakespeare to arrive in the same way as the Prince at a view of Falstaff as having so much as this to be said for him. She is made to come to it wholeheartedly and the Prince to come to it very much otherwise. Falstaff the Bartholomew boar-pig has just proved himself to his doxy as being, in her words, a 'whoreson little valiant villain', and is fully to her taste. Falstaff the Manningtree ox, however, has just been unmercifully made game of by the Prince for running away at Gadshill in a fashion that could only, by everyone in the tavern company except Falstaff, be taken as showing downright cowardice.

When a spectator of the two parts of *Henry IV* comes to Doll's commendation of Falstaff for defending her from the insults of Pistol, and doing so in no unknightly fashion, he may perhaps not agree with her that Falstaff is 'as valorous as Hector of Troy, worth five of Agamemnon'. Nevertheless, he may think that she has some reason to praise him. Falstaff carries off his bout with Pistol steadfastly and not without danger to his life. The encounter is not bloodless. We hear afterward that he has 'hurt' Pistol 'i' th' shoulder'. There has been shrewd thrusting by Pistol at Falstaff's precious belly, and this has been effectively parried. The spectator may at this point conclude that the balance has been tipped in favour of Falstaff's not being a coward. It may cross his mind that Falstaff at Gadshill can in truth have known the Prince all the while, just as has said he knew him, and that there he ran away magnanimously instead of ignominiously, pretending fright in order to save the heir to the throne from endangering his life in the encounter. As for Falstaff's playing dead to save his life on the battlefield at Shrewsbury, one may easily come to think of this in retrospect as showing Falstaff's skill as a professional soldier in following the doctrine that all is fair in love and war.

But if the viewer of Falstaff's combat with Pistol does have thoughts like these, he is due to have them threatened and perhaps to find his judgement left completely at a stand. What happens next is Falstaff's picturing to Doll of the Prince as a shallow youngster fit only to be a pantler and of Poins as a baboon, Falstaff all the while not knowing that these two stand behind him disguised as drawers. When the disguised two reveal themselves, Falstaff, presuming on what he has achieved in the way of place among the high, says to the Prince: 'I am a gentleman; thou art a drawer.' The Prince answers with a challenge that forces the avowed gentleman to engage or basely avoid: 'Very true, sir; and I come to draw you out by the ears.' Falstaff basely avoids. Sad to say, he fawns like any dog that crawls to his master intimating worthlessness after being caught in dereliction. He answers the Prince: 'Thou whoreson mad compound of majesty, by this light flesh and corrupt blood, thou art welcome.' At this point Doll turns upon the knight who has fought and shed blood for her and disdains him utterly: 'How, you fat fool? I scorn you.' The viewer may well, for the moment at least, find himself entirely in agreement with her. He may see the suddenly abject Falstaff as a cowardly fat fool, even when he claims once more, as he has claimed at Gadshill, to have been protecting the Prince from harm. Falstaff's pretence this time, that he has only been saving the Prince from being admired by one of 'the wicked' who might seduce him, has nothing to be said for it except that it is amusingly preposterous. Since Gadshill the pretender has been falling off in cleverness, as he has been falling off in other ways that help to prepare for his final banishment.

It is partly as a dog currying favour in the domain of a higher order, sometimes shrewdly and engagingly, sometimes abjectly and revoltingly, that Falstaff must be seen when account is taken of the animality Shakespeare has given him. Marked preparation is made for the scene with Doll in which he becomes an offending dog that the Prince is ready to draw out 'by the ears' and punish. It comes in the scene where the Prince and Poins make their plan to wait upon him disguised as drawers and where the Prince, upon receiving a letter from him, offers the comment: 'I do allow this wen to be as familiar with me as my dog; and he holds his place, for look you how he writes' (*2 Henry IV*, II. ii. 115–17).

But when it is a matter of finding the dog in man, Falstaff can find in the Prince a wayward dog even before the Prince finds in him a too familiar dog. After the Lord Chief Justice has accused him of having misled the Prince, he is ready with the retort that the Prince is his dog and has misled *him*. The implication is that the Prince is held on a leash by Falstaff and has failed his master, who is dependent on him for guidance in the dark. This reversal of places between high and low is a triumphant achievement of presumption in the tradition of grotesque animality. Another achievement in the same tradition is that in which Falstaff, after being a bullcalf running and roaring for fear at Gadshill, imaged thus by the Prince, becomes a lion acting nobly there, imaged thus by himself. He becomes the king of beasts prevented by instinct from harming a true prince. Here there is admirable effrontery but of a lower grade. It merely joins Falstaff with the Prince in the ranks of human and animal royalty instead of pulling the Prince down from human royalty to animal subserviency and making Falstaff his human master.

III

Falstaff is complexly monstrous in the variety of his animality, but he is more intricately and at the same time more essentially monstrous in what he is as man and animal in one figure. The joining of the two in him has relationship to that figuration of doubleness in the mermaid which Montaigne takes to have an essentially grotesque quality, or to the figuration of doubleness in the centaur, equally favoured in the grotesque tradition of the Middle Ages and the Renaissance. But in Falstaff the beast and the non-beast are not joined with so violent an opposition to each other or so sharp a line of demarcation between them as to make a centaur form of the kind that Shakespeare brings the mad Lear to find in women:

> Down from the waist they are Centaurs,
> Though women all above.
> But to the girdle do the gods inherit,
> Beneath is all the fiend's.   (IV. vi. 126–9)

A figure of doubleness that may well be taken to exhibit an aspect of Falstaff is one put forward by his own wit but not for application to himself. He calls the Hostess an otter and, when the Prince succumbs to curiosity and demands his reason, says: 'Why, she's neither fish nor flesh; a man knows not where to have her' (*I Henry IV*, III. iii. 144–5). The Hostess inevitably falls into the trap and protests that any man knows where to have her. Falstaff is a human being as much as the otter is a land creature and he is a brutish being as much as the otter is a water creature. The joining of man and beast in him, like the joining of creatures in the otter, is so much by way of interpenetration that it is not always easy to know where to have him. And of course he does not protest that he can be had.

For instance, Falstaff has all the animal desire that Lear attributes to centaur womanhood, but in him the beast is not by any means all beneath the girdle. It penetrates so far into what is above the girdle that it helps to make him the sensual man, the natural man *par excellence,* and yet it leaves generous space within him for a something more than natural. This other something affords him a lively understanding of his own grotesqueness as man and beast together, and of its relation to a general human grotesqueness with reaches of high and low even greater than his own. In *The Merry Wives of Windsor* he fails in many ways to come up to his best as revealed in earlier plays, but in a demonstration of that kind of understanding near the end of *The Merry Wives* there is no such failure. As he waits for the meeting with Mistress Ford and Mistress Page in Windsor Forest, disguised as Herne the Hunter with stag horns on his head, he offers a pagan prayer: 'Now, the hot-blooded gods assist me! Remember, Jove, thou wast a bull for thy Europa; love set on thy horns. O powerful love, that in some respects makes a beast a man; in some other, a man a beast! You were also, Jupiter, a swan for the love of Leda. O omnipotent love! how near the god drew to the complexion of a goose!' (V. v. 2–9). As he goes on to pray for 'a cool rut-time' and then welcomes Mistress Ford as 'My doe with the black scut', he is only another version of 'the town bull' among 'the parish heifers' which the Prince has made of him in relation to Doll Tearsheet and her kind. But he has just proved to have vision that is denied to stag or bull. The irony is that, though he is given vision to see love as making beast into man, the last thing anyone would expect him to be granted under any circumstances is a transforming love of which such vision could make him worthy. It seems to be commonly assumed that when the command was received from Queen Elizabeth to show Falstaff in love, if indeed there was that command, all Shakespeare could possibly show of Falstaff while keeping any artistic integrity was something like what he did show in *The Merry Wives.*

There is much truly that Shakespeare has not granted to Falstaff, but yet in what must be recognized as making him man there is that endowment of the very first order, his wit. He honours it duly and cherishes it as sacred. He looks up to it as Hamlet looks up to reason. For Hamlet it is reason that sets man most truly above the beast. For Falstaff it is wit, though he does not soliloquize philosophically on the subject. When Doll Tearsheet questions him about the association of the Prince with Poins, while these two are eavesdropping in disguise, she makes a suggestion: 'They say Poins has a good wit.' Falstaff replies by reducing Poins to presumptuous animal lowness: 'He a good wit? hang him, baboon!' (*2 Henry IV,* II. iv. 261). For Hamlet reason is that which looks before and after and reaches toward the understanding of all that has been or will be. For him wit is one of the ways of understanding provided by reason. For Falstaff wit is that which looks at all within the immediate foreground and reaches toward the understanding of a present situation. For him wit is reason itself. Because it is, he does not speak of the faculty of reason by name in any such way as Hamlet does. But Hamlet no less than Falstaff takes infinite delight in the play of wit.

Falstaff has been given a much more restricted human understanding than Hamlet's, but that which he has deserves his own high opinion of it, though this is saying much. It benefits by being narrowly channelled. When Falstaff has the need to act, he is not at all embarrassed by a wealth of conflicting perceptions such as

Hamlet's and he has no hampering doubt that he can prevail. His faith is always in what he calls 'my admirable dexterity of wit' and in the principle that 'a good wit will make use of anything'. By wit which creates action as much as by that which creates idea and expression he comes to the achievement of authentic *tours de force* and is masterful at bringing them about until Fortune first reduces favour to him and finally becomes his foe.

Behind Falstaff is a line of notable Shakespearean clowns. To say how much he rises above what they offer is to grant him all that he claims about his wit as being both a virtue in himself and a cause of that virtue in others. After him there are again notable Shakespearean clowns, and they too do not come up to his level of witty knowingness. But a Shakespearean grotesque figure that after him at times rises even higher than he does is the fool, who is related to the clown and occasionally gets the name of clown but comes more and more to be distinguished from him.

In Falstaff, a participator in civil war as the companion of a prince, clownage has travelled far beyond that of the rustic simpleton who can stumble amusingly across the stage of a conflict among the great. It has left well behind what the early Shakespearean clown is in *Titus Andronicus*. A rustic in this play is persuaded by Titus to deliver a 'supplication' to the Emperor and, because he is ignorant of the conflict between Titus and the Emperor, gets himself hanged (IV. iii and iv). From a world lying on the margin of that in which there is a struggle for power he is swept suddenly to the centre of the struggle and as suddenly swept aside. He is granted a certain amount of grotesque genius in what he says, though he is wholly without any proud Falstaffian understanding that he has it. The mad Titus thinks him a carrier of letters from heaven concerning appeals made by Titus for justice against the Emperor. Titus asks, 'What says Jupiter?' The clown's answer, if one considers the fate that is all too soon to have him hanged, seems to be given to him by an inspiring power that mocks his innocent foolishness and makes him foreshadow unwittingly his own downfall: 'Who? the gibbet-maker? He says that he has taken them down again, for the man must not be hanged until the next week.' The word-twisting that makes 'Jupiter' into 'gibbet-maker' is not to be thought of as produced by wilful mistaking in the way that word-play often is with more sophisticated Shakespearean clowns. When the name 'Jupiter' is repeated to him, the clown is completely the honest simpleton as he says: 'Alas, sir, I know not Jupiter. I never drank with him in all my life.' Possibly, as has been suggested, there is an implication that he hears the name 'Jupiter' at first as 'gibbeter'.[5] If so, the mocking power that inspires him provides a neater piece of wordplay than the bumbling clown can reproduce.

One never feels that Fate plays cat and mouse with Falstaff in this way. In his knowingness he is simply not made to invite such treatment. Fate does finally turn against him, but only after it has many times befriended him and after he has often dared it outrageously to prove that what Bardolph calls the 'monstrous devices' of his wit are not equal to getting him out of any tight place whatever.

Nor does one ever feel that Falstaff's wit shown in repartee is in any way fortuitous. He is always the summoner and the master of it. When the Lord Chief Justice lectures him, he is at his masterful best in reply after reply. The Lord Chief Justice is not without ability to turn a phrase himself when he says: 'There is not a white hair on your face but should have his effect of gravity' (*2 Henry IV*, I. ii. 182–3). But Falstaff has ability to transform neatly the Justice's neatly turned phrase and thus with an imaginative economy of words to present an aspect of his case. Each of those white hairs, he answers, should have 'his effect of gravy, gravy, gravy'. The Justice has happiness in taking the side of man the more-than-animal, of man the stander on his dignity. But Falstaff has delight in taking the side of man the food- and sex-desirous animal. He takes that side with all the force of wit given to him as a man that is actually a good bit more than animal. The implication is not that he wants to be no more than an animal. It is that he wants to be and joyously is, an animal well endowed with man's mental cleverness, a witty animal, a monstrous animal.

Falstaff's play on the words 'gravity' and 'gravy' is thus different indeed from the play on 'Jupiter' and 'gibbet-maker' that in *Titus Andronicus* is given to the clown but is not made truly to belong to the clown. It is also very different from any ignorant or pretendedly ignorant word-play such as that in the typical malapropism.

Falstaff himself is always above committing malapropisms, but in the tavern world that he dominates they are, as one might expect, not lacking. It is strange that they come into that world late, for there is no reason why they should not come early, since they play a well developed part in the Shakespearean grotesque before the appearance of Falstaff. The Hostess is not at all a Mrs. Malaprop in *1 Henry IV*, but in *2 Henry IV* she becomes one of the best of the kind. It is plain that Shakespeare found the unknowingness of the Hostess to be something that demanded cultivation from him as it came on to prove itself.

The grotesqueness of the Hostess, being of a more primitive order than Falstaff's, has from the beginning an inevitable potentiality as a foil for Falstaff's. Her naïvety falls into the trap of his artfulness. When he tantalizingly calls her a 'thing', she presses him to say 'what thing, what thing', and he answers, 'Why, a thing to thank God on.' As his foil she is exactly the thing to be thankful for that he says she is, and of course she proves it by retorting, 'I am no thing to thank God on . . . and, setting thy knighthood aside, thou art a knave to call me so' (*1 Henry IV*, III. iii. 131–7). Falstaff's calling her an otter, which immediately follows this exchange, even draws the Prince into his trap of wit, in a manner that has just been spoken of. The truth is that both the Hostess and Falstaff are things to thank God on, though thanks are due more for Falstaff's existence than for hers.

Such lack of knowingness as is thus developed early in the Hostess invites naturally enough the later giving to her of a string of malapropisms. They begin at her first appearance in *2 Henry IV*, at the opening of the second act, when she has Falstaff arrested by the sheriff's officers Fang and Snare. There is much to be said for her making of 'homicidal' into 'honeysuckle' and 'homicide' into 'honeyseed' in the epithets 'honeysuckle villain' and 'honeyseed rogue' which she applies to Falstaff and Bardolph when they start the fray with the officers. In *The Merry Wives of Windsor* she has undergone great change in setting and some change in quality, just as Falstaff has. She is no longer Mistress of the Boar's Head in Eastcheap but servant to Doctor Caius. Yet she still has the name of Mistress Quickly, and still lends irony to it by being not so quick-witted as she would have to be to avoid malapropisms and keep from being made game of by Falstaff. Along with her name and her large lack of knowingness she brings over from *2 Henry IV* the pet exclamation 'what the good-yere!' (or 'what the goodier!'), apparently meaning about the same as 'what the devil!' As she produces her malapropisms in *The Merry Wives* Falstaff can find opportunity to benefit from her naïvety no less than he has benefited earlier. He does so notably when she defends Mistress Ford after he has been thrown into the Thames from the buck-basket. She makes the excuse that the servants of Mistress Ford misunderstood what she directed them to do: 'She does so take on with her men! They mistook their erection.' It is for Falstaff to say, inevitably: 'So did I mine, to build upon a foolish woman's promise' (III. v. 40–3).

Falstaff and the Codes of High Endeavour

I

As the low is joined with the high in Falstaff himself, so his tavern world of low endeavour, where thieves and master-thieves are made, is joined with a political world of high endeavour where nobles and kings are made. The union is recurrently shown in the two parts of *Henry IV* to be one in which inner correspondences link the two worlds. But that the world of high endeavour is thus put before us in a satirical spirit as being really no different from the world of Falstaff and his fellows is not a conclusion that seems justified by Shakespeare's dramatization. This higher world seems to be no more made the butt of satire by being subtly joined to the Falstaffian world than the Falstaff of finished wit is made so by being joined to the Falstaff of gross animality through involved ties of common interest.

The typical 'better man', whom the reforming Prince has come to think 'dearer' than the 'fat deer' that he finds supposedly dead on the battlefield, is judged by the Prince's higher world to be of special worth in so far as he lives by a code of honour. Whatever antipathy this code may at times arouse today, Shakespeare clearly gives it a large measure of support, dramatically and poetically, as a valid expression of high endeavour. He does so despite errors of commission and omission that are to be charged against those whom he presents as trying to live by it.

Yet when Shakespeare provides a code of dishonour for Falstaff and makes him a devoted follower of it, his hand is again in large measure an accepting and supporting one. It is so generous with its support that the appeal of Falstaff to human sympathy becomes the demanding thing we know. Moreover, to use Joycean terms that I have referred to at the beginning of the foregoing chapter, the 'comicity' of Falstaff becomes undeniably a part of the 'cosmicity' of the drama of history. ⟨...⟩

IV

Falstaff is not the complete image of anti-honour that he makes himself out to be in the well-known soliloquy where he says of honour, 'I'll none of it' (*1 Henry IV*, V. i. 128–39). He confirms his monstrosity of doubleness by the way he supports honour as well as rejects it.

Valour is represented as the first demand made upon men by honour, and Falstaff can be found demanding valour with all the very considerable eloquence Shakespeare has given him. He does so in his soliloquy on the virtue of sherris-sack (*2 Henry IV*, IV. iii. 92–135). Here we have a prose paean not merely to sack but also to the men that sack can bring into being. These are not 'demure' and 'sober-blooded' boys who beget wenches when they marry and who 'are generally fools and cowards'. They are in every way men, outstanding in both their sophisticated and their natural faculties. They allow sack to fill their brains with 'nimble, fiery, and delectable shapes' which their tongues can make into 'excellent wit'. More heroically, they allow sack to make their bodies into puissant small kingdoms that rouse themselves valiantly for warfare. Sack works thus on a man: 'It illumineth the face, which, as a beacon, gives warning to all the rest of this little kingdom, man, to arm; and then the vital commoners and inland petty spirits muster me all to their captain, the heart; who, great and puff'd up with this retinue, doth any deed of courage.'

No follower of the religion of honour could object to the poetic ardour that Falstaff brings to this praise of courage in combat. Even Hotspur (that self-declared Philistine who hates 'mincing poetry') might well appreciate it. For Hotspur is moved by Shakespeare to show comparable ardour when he vows himself ready to leap to the moon or dive to the bottom of the deep in his quest for honour.

It may be thought that Falstaff is of course an old fraud who does not really mean what he says when he engages in praise of valour and that by contrast Hotspur very naïvely means just what he says in praise of it. Likewise it may be thought that when Falstaff in his more famous soliloquy rejects honour as no more than an airy word and scorns the death-defying valour it demands from a combatant, he is obviously a sensible realist and means just what he says. To think thus is to think that where Shakespeare has presented doubleness in Falstaff we are challenged to discover in which part of him lies the Simon-Pure Falstaff. That way peril lies. Whenever one finds Falstaff to be double one must beware of diminishing his grotesqueness—and losing him—by discarding something of him. Falstaff can be a trap for his dramatic associates in the two parts of *Henry IV*, and for us too he can be a trap. It is not only by tempting us to make a neat yes or no decision on whether he is a coward that he can trap us.

Support that Falstaff as a praiser of sack gives to valour is grotesque to the full in the Falstaffian manner, and hence it both joins with and opposes such non-grotesque support as Hotspur and the reformed Prince. The toper's valour eulogized by Falstaff is not to be counted as high courage, but nevertheless in the soliloquy on sack Shakespeare has taken pains to win acceptance for Falstaff as a true admirer of valour according to his lights. He has given us ground to believe without any question whatever that Falstaff means wholeheartedly what he says when he begins by praising sack for helping the mind of man (his own surely included) to create delectable shapes imaginatively and excellent wit verbally. And it is plain that he would lead us on from our acceptance of wholeheartedness in Falstaff here at the outset of his sack-praising to an acceptance of honest feeling in him at its climax when the sack that has been made the cause of valour generally in mankind is more particularly made its cause in the 'very hot and valiant' reformed Prince. At that point Shakespeare goes so far as to touch our hearts for Falstaff's benefit by making praise of the valiant Prince, whom Falstaff regards himself as having nurtured, lead to a revelation in Falstaff of the instincts of a grotesque father: 'If I had a thousand sons, the first humane principle I would teach them should be to forswear thin potations and addict themselves to sack.' It follows that the very modern suggestion can be made, as it is made by J. I. M. Stewart, that in ascending to the kingship the Prince 'kills Falstaff instead of killing the king, his father', since in a sense 'Falstaff *is* his father; certainly is a "father-substitute" in the psychologist's word'.[6]

Though Falstaff the generous drinker of sack makes no claim to possession of a fierce courage, Falstaff the animal-man offers an image of himself as a predator. He does so with a strangely becoming modesty. As he plans what he is to do to Justice Shallow he is in his own eyes not a beast of prey such as a lion, or a bird of prey such as a hawk. He is not a rapacious creature high enough in nature's scheme to be counted noble by the nobly combative among the non-grotesque. With grotesque aptness he is a fish of prey, and his victim is a foolish fishling: 'If the young dace be a bait for the old pike, I see no reason in the law of nature but I may snap at him' (*2 Henry IV*, III. ii. 356–8).

In connection with the grotesque support Falstaff gives to the combative honour that makes warfare a major pursuit it is revealing to look at the form he takes as not an ordinary Vice but one for whom war is his element. For he follows the wars in a manner that was developed within a part of the Vice tradition that Shakespeare shows he knew. When Falstaff prepares for acting the part of the Prince's father in the mock interview scene and says he will do it 'in King Cambyses' vein' (*I Henry IV*, II. iv. 427), there is no reason to doubt that Shakespeare has in mind Thomas Preston's *Cambises* (entered in 1569 and printed without date). Through Falstaff Shakespeare is having sport with an old pretentiousness of dramatic high style in that play. But in making Falstaff allude thus to *Cambises* he does more than point back to passages of attempted high seriousness in that play alone.[7] Among other plays to which he may be said to draw attention is a morality I have mentioned in my first chapter as being very similar in cast to *Cambises* and of the same early Elizabethan period. This is John Pickering's *Horestes* (printed in 1567).

It not only has passages of high style 'in King Cambyses' vein' but like *Cambises* has a Vice that takes the form of a soldier of fortune.

Cambises and *Horestes,* as I have said, are examples of what may be called the morality-tragedy. They look forward to forms of tragedy and chronicle-history drama established on the later Elizabethan stage.[8] The first play dramatizes a Renaissance account of the reign of Cambyses, King of Persia, and the second a medieval version of the Orestes saga, and each puts into its classical setting a Vice who brings about or rejoices in subversion of virtue among the high but welcomes opportunities to turn his attentions to the low. This Vice goes to war because the hero goes to war and also because he enjoys strife in any form, among the low as well as among the high. The hero goes to war because he desires to 'proceed in virtuous life' according to the code of combative honour, as Cambises is urged to do at the beginning of his reign by a councillor who might, in good morality fashion, have been named Wisdom. For Cambises the pursuit of honour is the conquering of Egypt and for Horestes it is the taking of revenge for his father's murder.

The Vice in each play has doublenesses that resemble to a certain extent the much subtler ones in Falstaff. In *Cambises* his name, aptly enough, is Ambidexter and he says he has it because he 'plays with both hands'. As he elaborates his meaning and demonstrates his ability, it develops that he has many kinds of ambidexterity. For example he can be double by deceitfully seeming what he is not or even by doing good as well as evil. In *Horestes* the Vice is not so variously double. He deceives, of course, and practises an old trick of his kind by taking at will a virtuous name to cover his vicious quality. To deceive his low companions he calls himself Patience. To deceive Horestes he puts himself on the side of honour by saying that his name is Courage and that he has come as a messenger from the gods to announce that Horestes must take revenge for his father's murder. At the end of the play he changes his name to Revenge to mark the success he has had, but he bewails the fact that he is now rejected and must go begging because Horestes no longer needs Revenge. There seems to be confusion as to whether the taking of revenge is here a sin for Horestes that is nurtured by the Vice or is a true deed of honour for Horestes brought about deviously by the Vice to provide for himself the pleasure of seeing strife and bloodshed produced by the execution of justice. Pickering's quality as a dramatist in general does not invite the thought that he tries subtly to show the very concept of revenge for honour as having aspects of both good and evil.

A doubleness given to Preston's Vice and Pickering's that resembles with great particularity a doubleness in Falstaff is that which displays on one side a fascination with combat and an urge to enter into it, even with some daring, and on the other side a fascination with staying alive and an urge to keep escape routes from combat always open. Ambidexter and Patience-Courage-Revenge are almost as ambidextrous as Falstaff in ability either to accept or reject a fight. Each can justify rejection of a fight with a wise saw, just as Falstaff can. Says Ambidexter, laughing at himself after avoiding a fight:

It is wisdome (quoth I) by the masse, to save one.[9]

Says Patience-Courage-Revenge, after swallowing what he takes to be a slight upon his honour made when a country clown has misheard his name of Patience as Past Shame:

Good slepinge in a hole skynne, ould foulkes do saye.[10]

And says Falstaff, who is just as obviously past shame as he rises up from feigning death after being bested in his fight with Douglas: 'The better part of valour is discretion; in the which better part I have saved my life' (*1 Henry IV*, V. iv. 118–19).

V

Falstaff makes his contribution to the theme of conscience in the two parts of *Henry IV* by declaring and proving that he does not have any conscience. He has no prickings within to bother him when he goes against established codes of action. When the Prince prepares to hear the complaint of the Sheriff after the Gadshill robbery and says, 'Now, my masters, for a true face and a good conscience', Falstaff replies matter-of-factly, 'Both which I have had; but their date is out, and therefore I'll hide me.' It is an animal-like lack of both good and bad conscience that can allow him to fall asleep behind the arras and be found, 'snorting like a horse' when the Sheriff is gone. This monstrous lack of something proper to man's more-than-animal state outdoes a monstrous lack of man's proper staff of life in Falstaff's diet that is revealed by papers rifled from his pockets while he is asleep. Upon what is charged to him there as part of a supper the Prince makes the comment: 'O monstrous! but one halfpennyworth of bread to this intolerable deal of sack!' (*1 Henry IV*, II. iv. 589–90.)

It may at first appear that in *The Merry Wives of Windsor* Falstaff is at last given a conscience. Certainly in the final scene of that play he comes to feel shame that he has not known before and fails for the first time to rise triumphantly above disgrace. But this shame of his proves upon examination to be different indeed from shame over wrongdoing. It is shame over a lack of cleverness in perceiving and doing. The lack is one that he has never thought himself capable of, any more than we have thought him capable of it after following him through *Henry IV*. He is completely 'dejected' because he has been 'made an ass' and because he has 'liv'd to stand at the taunt' of a Welsh parson, 'one that makes fritters of English'. When he wonders whether he has laid his brain 'in the sun, and dried it', and concludes that degradation he has come to experience 'is enough to be the decay of lust and late-walking through the realm', he must be taken to mean that what he is called upon to do is not to repent and follow virtue but to regain his knowingness and thus counter any further threat to his untrammelled way of life.

The consciencelessness of Falstaff thus preserves itself even while he is in many ways transformed in *The Merry Wives*. It is elementally strong. The animal man in Falstaff is domesticated, but it insisted upon living according to codes of its own.

Falstaff is less bound to humanity around him than is the dog that has a master, though the Prince does compare his familiarity with a dog's. Along with the animal man in him there is also the Vice to give an aspect of inevitability to his conscience-lessness. These two of the Falstaffian components lend strength to each other.

The morality Vice from whom Falstaff inherits, who is both a Vice that follows the hero in war, as in *Cambises* and *Horestes,* and a Vice with whom the hero goes roistering in taverns, as in some other plays, can be so much at one with the animal nature in man that he merges with it. For the Vice of the morality play, as seems to be plain, is an unregenerate quality in mankind, striving to undo humanity from within instead of being a diabolic force working upon it from without, though of course he can consort with devils. If the Vice is called Sensuality, as, for example, in Henry Medwall's *Nature* (written at the end of the fifteenth century), he can be recognized as having a just claim upon man because he is a natural part of him. But he is a dangerous lower part and must be ruled by a higher part, that is, by Reason, who has his place in man because man is 'halfe angelyke'. In *Nature* even Nature herself gives to Man a warning against being too much the creature of nature:

> I wot well sensualyte / ys to the naturall
> And graunted to the / in thy furst creacyon
> But not wythstandying / yt ought to be ouerall
> Subdued to reason / and vnder hys tuycyon.[11]

Inevitably Man in this play falls before temptation, leaves Reason, and lets Sensuality introduce him to Falstaffian delinquency in the tavern before he gives due heed to the angelic within him.

But, compared with Ambidexter in *Cambises* and Patience-Courage-Revenge in *Horestes,* this Sensuality in *Nature* reveals a lack of verve in his creator. One should be charitable to Medwall and remember that he wrote *Nature* more than half a century before the other two plays were written and that in the intervening time there was a rising tide of dramatic and other development within the Renaissance from which the authors of these later plays benefited. A great difference between Sensuality and the Vices in *Cambises* and *Horestes* is that he is weighed down with responsibility, first for arguing his rights in man and then for making man exclusively his own, while they are unburdened and have a vivacity of some appeal both as speakers and doers. They have an elfin quality. They are Puckish. They do man harm or benefit him indifferently and according to whim, and thus they take the natural in man into a relationship with essences of nature such as are traditionally represented by the realm of faerie. Ambidexter particularly is given an elfin cast as he attends upon both the doing of good and the doing of evil and as he takes mischievous pleasure in their mixture within the worldly scheme of things.

Ironically the grossly fat Falstaff also has a side that is elfin. It is a side without which he could not have the strong appeal he does have. He makes the most of it, so much so that he becomes more ingratiating than an Ambidexter and more engaging than a Puck. One thing he reveals which always works favourably upon our feelings is a natural amiability. He is utterly conscienceless but not intrinsically cruel. He preys upon the Hostess or Justice Shallow, not because he delights in causing them pain, but because he delights in getting from them what cries out to be transferred to himself. Moreover, in a way most striking he lacks anything at all of the deep-set mischievous quality of an Ambidexter or a Puck. He does not foment cat-and-dog fights among persons around him. And it redounds greatly to his credit that though he is cruelly tricked by the Prince, first as he trustingly engages with him in highway robbery and later as he takes an evening's ease with Doll Tearsheet, yet he never descends to playing practical jokes, in the way of retaliation or otherwise. He does not even play them on a person so defenceless as the drawer Francis, whom the Prince victimizes with no compunction at all.

At the end of *The Merry Wives of Windsor* the elfin Falstaff suffers the climactic indignity of being offered up for judgement to a troop of provincials in fairy disguises. But in *Henry V* the sending of him after death to 'Arthur's bosom'— to some grotesque Elysium in Avalon where his 'fracted and corroborate' heart can undergo faerie healing—is a malapropistic inspiration on the part of the Hostess that gives him his due.

NOTES

[1] 'Gadshill Revisited', *Shakespeare Quarterly*, IV (1953), p. 125.

[2] The terms are to be found with Joycean application in Jacques Mercanton, 'The Hours of James Joyce, Part II', trans. Lloyd C. Parks, *Kenyon Review*, XXV (1963), p. 96.

[3] My quotations from Shakespeare are as a rule from the text of G. L. Kittredge.

[4] For a view of animal metaphor in the presentation of Falstaff as adding to his comicality by disparaging him see Audrey Yoder, *Animal Imagery in Shakespeare's Character Portrayal*, New York, 1947, pp. 45ff.

[5] Helge Kökeritz, *Shakespeare's Pronunciation*, New Haven, 1953, p. 118.

[6] *Character and Motive in Shakespeare*, London, 1949, p. 138.

[7] For indications that *Cambises* was a 'stock joke' and was made to stand for a stylistic trend see an appendix contributed by J. C. Maxwell to the Arden Shakespeare *1 Henry IV*, ed. A. R. Humphreys, London, 1960, pp. 199–200.

[8] The contribution of these morality-tragedies to the shaping of Elizabethan tragedy I have discussed at some length in *The Medieval Heritage of Elizabethan Tragedy*, Berkeley, 1936, pp. 258ff.

[9] *Cambises*, ed. John S. Farmer, Tudor Facsimile Reprints, London, 1910, sig. B4.

[10] *Horestes*, ed. Daniel Seltzer, Malone Society Reprints, Oxford, 1962, l. 117.

[11] *Nature*, ed. Alois Brandl, *Quellen des weltlichen Dramas in England vor Shakespeare*, Strassburg, 1898, pp. 75–158, ll. 162–5.

Michael Platt

FALSTAFF IN THE VALLEY OF THE SHADOW OF DEATH

Jack Falstaff is barely present in *Henry V*. We do not see him, we only hear about him; we only hear about him in two brief reports; and the most revealing is provided by a very imperfect reporter. Aside from it, few persons recall him, and they stand low in place, degree, and form. The highest person to recall him, Captain Fluellen, disapproves of him. Most important, the chief speaker in the play, the man who dominates all its great actions, King Henry himself, never refers to Falstaff.[1]

And why should he? After all, when Henry became king, he put aside Falstaff with other wayward things. Whether Falstaff was the misleader of Henry's youth, as many thought, or merely a base, contagious cloud that the cunning Hal used as camouflage, new King Henry would have been required by the ceremony that clothes a monarch to banish Falstaff, however much the vital, witty fun Falstaff *is* would be missed on the lonely throne. Since Henry banished Falstaff at the end of the last play, there is no need to do it again in this one.

From his near absence from *Henry V* and from the utter absence of Henry, once his best companion, from his deathbed, we might, then, well conclude that Falstaff has little to do with King Henry V, his glorious victory at Agincourt, and the subsequent royal marriage that brings an imperial peace to the Kingdoms of England and France.

Such a conclusion would be wholly satisfying, if it were not for the fact that both Henry's absence from Falstaff's death and Falstaff's 'absence' from the play are conspicuous. Knowing of our fondness for Falstaff, the Epilogue of *2 Henry IV* promised us a continuation of "the story" with "Sir John in it."[2] However, *Henry V* gives us less of Falstaff than we expected, and the little it does give is disappointing. Falstaff barely appears and then only as he is disappearing utterly. We love the living Falstaff, we get him dying. Even then, we would have liked to have been with him as he lay dying; instead we only hear of his death later. Hearing of it too late, we may well feel a vicarious guilt for not having been there. Really, we wanted to see Falstaff alive, in the flesh, on stage, and, deep down, we wished he would have lived

From *Interpretation* 8, No. 1 (January 1979): 5–29. Revised by the author 1990.

forever. There is just enough of Falstaff in life to make us sad, and just enough of him in the play to make us disappointed. The one imitates the other and compounds it. The absence of Falstaff is very conspicuous.

The same is true of Henry's absence from Falstaff's deathbed, for the censures of those who are present make Henry's absence conspicuous (2.1.84 and 117–22; 2.3.40). To this day, Henry is still reproached by some who hoped he would comfort Falstaff dying. And in truth, he is reproached, or at least criticized, by something in all of us. Censuring a friend because *he* remained the same seems unfriendly, breaking with him because he did not change might be perfidious, and denying that you ever were friends is sanctimonious. It would have been easy for Henry to have appeared at Falstaff's deathbed, for Shakespeare to have shown him affected by the news of it, or for Shakespeare to have presented that death on stage. We expect something like this and we were virtually promised it at the end of the last play. As the King may have 'killed Falstaff's heart,' so Shakespeare may have saddened ours.

Why did Shakespeare rouse these our hopes and then dash them? The scene of Falstaff dying, right in front of us, perhaps with Henry there and both reconciled, would have been a great one. It would have been immediately moving and long remembered.[3] It might have equalled Falstaff's story of the multiplying men in buckram, his explanation of the true discretion in his apparent cowardice at Gad's Hill, or his playing of King and Prince with Hal. Falstaff facing death might have rivaled Falstaff facing honor, Falstaff on sack, or Falstaff on recruiting. He who authored the death of Little Nell would not have passed up the death of big Falstaff. And Shakespeare could have done it even better. Yet Shakespeare chose not to. We must wonder, then, what important reason he had to not write this great scene, but instead the great scene that he did.

It is true that not all surfaces have a depth beneath them. Those, however, that are marked by conspicuous absences hint that they do, and by so doing incite some to search in that depth.

I. A Tale Told by a Woman

The death of Falstaff is hard to understand. For one thing, it is entrusted to report rather than immediate presentation. Shakespeare has also endangered the scene he does present by entrusting it to the scatter-brained Hostess Quickly. The gift of speech to such a woman is risky. Her elisions, ellipses, shifts of direction, sighs, and frequent errors make us think of a small boat in a big storm. Still, giving the death of Falstaff to Hostess Quickly is less risky than it first seems. A clever person might deceive us. Her more palpable mistakes must put us on guard, remind us of the difference between hearsay and eyewitness, and set us to learning what really happened to Falstaff.

To encourage such inquiry, Shakespeare has Falstaff's pageboy present at his death and has him correct the Hostess (2.3.29). Being a woman and a sensual one as well, Hostess Quickly denies or diminishes that part of Falstaff's last speeches which dealt with women. According to the Boy, Falstaff warned against women as well as sack, calling women devils incarnate. Herself distracted, Mistress Quickly would distract others by taking "incarnation" as carnation, a color (2.3.30–31). But the Boy will not be diverted into a red or carnation herring discussion of Falstaff's favorite or his unfavorite colors:

> 'A said once the devil would have him about women.   (2.3.32)

Witness Quickly begins to give ground:

> 'A did in some sort, indeed, handle women;   (2.3.33)

Having conceded something, and given away more than she meant in the double-sensed "handling women," Mistress Quickly tries to slip away with:

> but then he was rheumatic, and talked of the Whore of Babylon.
> (2.3.33–35)

Previous to this exchange, the Hostess has been unable to report all those portions of Falstaff's end that made reference to the Bible (e.g., "Arthur's bosom," of which more in a moment). Now, when it suits her, she is able to come out with the Whore of Babylon. It would seem that her previous mistakes do not reveal an ignorance of the Bible, but the opposite. Precisely because she has just seen a sinner dying in terror, knows she is a sinner, and knows her Bible with the fear it calls for is she so given to such mistakes. Yet there is more method in her mistakes than it seems or she would confess. Her evasions are half chosen, half passionate.

It is not surprising that it is the Boy, a steadier witness, who reports something else she omits:

> Do you not remember 'a saw a flea stick upon Bardolph's nose, and 'a said it
> was a black soul burning in hell.   (2.3.36–37)

Recalling the witty old Falstaff, we are tempted to think that Falstaff retained his wit in the face of the afterlife, that he was being sportive with both the terrors of hell and Bardolph's complexion. We would like to think so. There seemed to be a perpetual gaiety about Falstaff, casting out fear whenever he appeared. The memory of this gaiety makes Bardolph, the butt of many of his jokes, want to be with him whether he is in heaven or hell (2.3.7–8); for Bardolph the jests of Falstaff cast out even the fear of hell. Yet Bardolph has reason to know otherwise. Falstaff looked at Bardolph, but he did not see Bardolph, he saw souls burning in hell.

Was Falstaff deluded? We are only permitted to say 'yes' if we can prove that there is no such thing as hell. Can we? Probably not, for that would take a complete account of the whole. Or if we can show Shakespeare thinks there is no hell and shows it. Does he? If so, then where and how? From the fact that Shakespeare never shows us hell in his works, and never heaven, we cannot conclude he does not believe in them; it may only be that he thinks their representation not possible for or proper to his art. Not even Christ, in the Gospels, shows much about them, far less than Dante. Certainly the vast majority of his characters believe in hell and heaven. And some even have good rational grounds to. Hamlet, the most doubting of all Shakespeare's characters has, for example, very good reason to. Although the Ghost of Old Hamlet raises many rational doubts, the story he tells of his own murder is supported by Claudius' rising at its re-presentation in the Murder of Gonzago, rendered probable by the fact of his subsequent confession, and then proved true, for us the audience, by the substance of that confession, which we hear. Perhaps, then, the rest of the Ghost's story is true. Perhaps there is a Lethe's wharf, things that would freeze our young blood, harrow our souls, and a time when we will be doomed to fast in fires, till our foul crimes done in our days of nature are burnt and purged away.

One conclusion we are surely permitted by Shakespeare in *Henry V;* as death approached, the fear of hell certainly cast out all Falstaff's gaiety. That Falstaff did not make a witty end is apparent from the Hostess' report. It is introduced to contradict the possibility, mentioned in Bardolph's wish (2.3.7–8), that Falstaff is right now in hell. It is a frightening thought, and so she begins:

> Nay sure, he's not in hell! He's in Arthur's bosom, if ever man went to Arthur's bosom. 'A made a finer end, and went away an it had been any christom child. 'A parted ev'n just between twelve and one, ev'n at the turning o' th' tide. For after I saw him fumble with the sheets, and play with flowers, and smile upon his finger's end, I knew there was but one way; for his nose was as sharp as a pen, and 'a babbled of green fields. 'How now, Sir John?' quoth I. 'What, man? be o' good cheer.' So 'a cried out 'God, God, God!' three or four times. Now I, to comfort him, bid him 'a should not think of God; I hoped there was no need to trouble himself with any such thoughts yet. So 'a bade me lay more clothes on his feet. I put my hand into the bed and felt them, and they were as cold as any stone. Then I felt to his knees, and so upward and upward, and all was as cold as any stone.   (2.3.9–24)

Here truth must emerge in spite of its reporter. The first of her many errors is the phrase, "Arthur's bosom"; she means to say "Abraham's bosom," where members of the chosen nation dying are gathered. The phrase appears in the New Testament, especially in connection with the parable of Lazarus and the rich man, one of Falstaff's 'favorites,' not incidentally because it gives the believer such incontrovertible evidence of the Lord's judgment, of heaven, and of hell (Luke 16:19–31). Mistress Quickly is so eager to assure others, and thus reassure herself, that Falstaff is in heaven, she does not notice her malaprop metamorphosis of a Hebrew patriarch into an English prince. This kind of error cues us for a larger one that follows.

The Hostess reports that Falstaff's nose was as sharp as a pen, which was regarded as a sign of rapidly approaching death. Then the unamended text of the Folio, which most editors regard as superior to the 1600 quarto and its progeny,[4] reads:

> For his nose was a sharp as a pen, and *a table of green fields.*
>
>   (2.3.15–16)

The phrase I have italicized has given rise to the most famous emendation in all Shakespeare, one which has seemed both needed and satisfying. Unsatisfied with the text as it is, Lewis Theobald suggested that it must have read "and 'a babbled of green fields."[5] It seems to me that this emendation is unnecessary.[6] The unemended text, "a table of green fields," is obscure, but only because the defects of the Hostess were bound to make it so. The ears of the Hostess, if not the Hostess, heard Falstaff trying to recite the Twenty-third Psalm.[7] Despite her, yet through her, we can hear the dying Falstaff, in the shadow of death, considering his life, in the light or in the darkness of what awaits him, try and try to drink the comfort of the familiar psalm of King David:

> The Lord is my shepherd; I shall not want.
> He maketh me to lie down in green pastures:
> He leadeth me beside the still waters. He restoreth my soul:
> He leadeth me in the paths of righteousness for his name's sake.
> Yea, though I walk through the valley of the shadow of death,
> I will fear no evil: for thou art with me;
> Thy rod and thy staff they comfort me.
>
> Thou preparest a table before me in the presence of mine enemies:
> Thou anointest my head with oil; my cup runneth over.
> Surely goodness and mercy shall follow me all the days of my life:
> And I will dwell in the house of the Lord for ever.[8]

Perhaps the feverish Falstaff was able to recite only snatches, perhaps he broke off in despair, or perhaps he carried it through, but in any case the Hostess was so afraid of the scene before her that her mind refused to recognize the psalm. As upset as the fretful porpentine, the Hostess has converted the "green pastures" of the psalm to "green fields" and, dimly hearing the line about "thou preparest a table before me in the presence of mine enemies," she has put the table before the "green pastures." The result, "a table of green fields," is a kind of kenning of the whole psalm, a kenning not from a poet, but from a pathetically frightened woman. That there is something frightening in "a table of green fields" for the Hostess is indicated by her very next words: " 'How now, Sir John?' quoth I. 'What, man? be o' good cheer.' " Falstaff said something about a table and green fields, and the Hostess saw nothing cheerful in those words.

The actress who takes the part of the frightened Hostess must steer skillfully down the slalom of these lines. She must let the truth in the report come through and, at the same time, the fright that confuses the reporter and flaws her report. Thus, after remarking that his nose was as sharp as a pen, she might draw a long breath. From this, the audience must realize that Falstaff was coming to his end. Then the actress must utter the words "a table of green fields" so that the audience realizes she is impersonating Falstaff, and the actress must confirm the audience in this understanding by returning to the Hostess's own voice, asking, "How now, Sir John?" with a fluster and a tremble. One way or the other, the audience must in their mind's eye see Falstaff, his nose pen-sharp, death approaching, and reciting or mumbling snatches of the psalm. It is a difficult passage, and it is understandable if the actress is tempted to resort to Theobald's emendation. Falstaff was babbling of green fields, the Hostess was babbling to him, and she is still babbling about him. Both would like to keep death and judgment at a distance.

What happened next is hard to know precisely. Either Falstaff replied to the Hostess's wish that he be of good cheer with the words, "God, God, God," or, entirely oblivious of her wish or even her presence, he simply screamed, "God, God, God." No other part of the account of Falstaff's death suggests that he was much interested in speaking with those around him, so one is inclined to think that he was oblivious of the Hostess; he knew he had nothing to be cheerful about. The same reasons incline one to believe that his words, "God, God, God," are a plea rather than a curse. Either way, the terror comes through. If anything, it is magnified by the efforts of the Hostess to be cheerful. If Falstaff finished the Twenty-third Psalm, he did not taste the comfort it vouchsafes. In his death there is nothing of still waters, of fearing no evil, of the cup running over, of green pastures, or of a table prepared in the presence of one's enemies. Falstaff knew himself to be in the valley of the shadow of Death, and it filled him with dread.[9] By filling him with dread it fills Mistress Quickly, too. It is as difficult for plump Jack, one sensualist, one lover of sack and women, to face the terrors of eternal punishment as it is for another sensualist, Mistress Quickly, to report them.

Shakespeare shows us not only the winds from heaven, but the poplars shivering on earth. More exactly, we know of those winds only from observing these poplars. Shakespeare's indirect mode of presentation seems to imitate death itself, for death most makes us feel the absence of a person as conspicuous.

Yet if Shakespeare imitates death, he does not spare us the greater terror of damnation. The Epilogue of *2 Henry IV* promised us a continuation of "the story" with "Sir John in it," and jested that he might die "of a sweat." And of a sweat, or a plague, is exactly what Falstaff does die of. The various details of his death, his fever, his thirst, his pointed nose, his hallucinations, his fumbling with the sheets, the creeping coldness, and the by turns vexed, excited, despairing state of his mind all suggest that Falstaff died of the plague.[10] Although they did not understand its efficient cause, our Elizabethan forefathers and foremothers were well acquainted with the plague. They could recognize it. Many had seen it kill someone before their eyes. During Shakespeare's life it swept through England often, and during his career it several times interrupted the theater season.

The death of Falstaff is one of the very few deaths in all Shakespeare that we would speak of as natural; it is a notable exception to the rule that most deaths in Shakespeare are violent, by the hand of another human being. We would speak of it as a "natural death," but the Elizabethans, being Christians, would not, at least not unqualifiedly. Being Christians, they would understand death as having an ultimate supernatural cause. Death entered human life as a consequence of man's original sin in Eden. For that sin man was not only cast out of the Garden, but destined to die as well. Death is the wages of sin (Romans 5.12; I Corinthians 15.21–22).

Moreover, the plague, with its unpredictable orbit and wide yet pall-mall swathe, was understood by them to be especially supernatural. "Our sinnes are the chiefe and the true cause of the plague," says Beza and a hundred others.[11] The punishment being special, the sins must be special, and the providence as well. Whatever the efficient causality of the plague, its providential agency might well be God. In the plague, then, its victims felt the finger of an angry God. To die of the plague was not only to die, but very likely to be damned soon after, unless one could turn things around before the end. That is why Mistress Quickly is so anxious to say, " 'A made a finer end, and went away and it had been any christom child." No wonder then that Falstaff cries out to God, and no wonder "a plague" is the favorite oath of this God-fearing Christian.

Mistress Quickly's report of Falstaff's death ends in a strange way. Despite her flaws, the Hostess is capable of great accuracy, or rather, a great accuracy can shine through her. A gesture she makes goes right to the center of Falstaff. She says she put her hand into Falstaff's bed and found his feet as cold as any stone. Then she felt to his knees "and so upward and upward, and all was as cold as any stone." The heat she sought had fled. Her report ends on the word "stone," and it ends with her hand somewhere above Falstaff's knee seeking heat, the son of life. In making this gesture and iterating the word "stone" the Hostess trips over Shakespeare's bawdy. "Stone" is a word for testicle.[12] We cannot help but imagine her feeling Falstaff amorously, trying to rouse him, tickle his catastrophe. Since we are not supposed to laugh in the presence of those gripped by fear or oppressed by misery, we suppress this irreverent fancy. If we share the fear gripping Falstaff, some of our own fear may escape in such a laugh.

In that laugh a perplexity peeps through as well as is hidden. How could any thing so warm, stirring, and happy as life disappear? What intricate knot ties the very spring of life to the death that ends it? Thinking of death, we may wonder why we live at all. Thinking of life, we wonder why we die. What is death? A door with nothing on the other side? Or something? Something turbulent and terrible, or something serene and joyful? The wheel of these great perplexities turns through all Shakespeare. Again and again, he has us meet these questions and various answers to them. Claudio would not like to lose this warm, sensible motion and fears to go he knows not where; Hamlet dreads something after life, something that would freeze his young blood; and old Lear fears there is nothing, nothing, nothing. Others feel confident there must be a still felicity beyond our mortal motions, or a happiness compensatory for our misery. Who knows? Certainly we would like to, and certainly Shakespeare knows we would like to. Much in life as he knew it, life as it is, depends on it.

By writing the death of Falstaff as he did, Shakespeare makes us feel the perplexity of that question and especially the terrors of damnation. That he could take us further into such painful mysteries is shown by *Hamlet* and *Lear*, but the death of Falstaff is, as he promised at the end of *2 Henry IV*, in "the story" of *Henry V*. It is *in* the story of the most glorious English King, the story that has the most to teach about political life in the country and regime most native to Shakespeare. While the death of Falstaff looks out to death itself, then, it is to be understood in the context of the England of *Henry V*.

The death of Falstaff is one of four scenes in *Henry V* to show us men preparing to die. The first of these (2.3) immediately precedes Falstaff's death; in it we see several traitors prepare for death penitently, quickly, composedly, almost easily. So far as we can judge the souls of others, they die well. Henry is conspicuous in this scene; it is he who unmasks them, sentences them, hears their prayers, and assists them to death. The third of the four scenes to show us men preparing for death (4.1) comes long after Falstaff's death; in it we see the men of Henry's English army, on the eve of Agincourt, preparing for death. Here, too, Henry is conspicuous, even when hidden; with his majesty cloaked, he is able to assist his soldiers in their preparation for death. Shortly after, he makes his own preparation, unassisted. This is the fourth scene in which we witness men preparing for death.

Henry is, then, conspicuously present in three of these four scenes, and conspicuously absent from one, the second, the death of Falstaff. This scene shows us the problem of death, pure and simple; the others show us the problem of death as understood and encountered by the prince or political man.

Preparation for death is the core of Henry's political religion. The battle of Agincourt must be fought by men much like Falstaff, men whose bravery is hardly fearless, men who may have a weakness for sack, for late sleep, for women, who, unable to correct these "weaknesses," live in mortal terror of a God who may punish them with eternal damnation. The wish that fitfully recurs to Englishmen the night before Agincourt, the wish to enjoy the night of a private man, is none other than the wish to live the life of Falstaff. The tavern is a long way from Agincourt. If their wishes (4.3.16–67; 4.1 passim; cf. 2.3.10) point to Falstaff, so do their terrors. The same terrors that scatter Falstaff's gaiety and wit are the ones Williams speaks of:

> But if the cause be not good, the king himself hath a heavy reckoning to make . . . I am afeard there are few die well that die in a battle; for how can they charitably dispose of anything when blood is their argument? Now, if these men do not die well, it will be a black matter for the king that led them to it; who to disobey were against all proportion of subjection.
>
> (4.1.127–38)

In his reply, Henry neither repulses nor deflects the thrust of Williams's questions, which point soldier and king alike toward a judging God. Instead, Henry incorporates them so as to win all the more the obedience of the Christian soldier. "Every subject's duty is the king's, but every subject's soul is his own," is the burden of his answering parables (4.1.167–68). However, since obedience can be unspirited and unspirited troops often lose, Henry aims for more. As a Christian, he knows that the better prepared his men are for death and judgment, the more likely they are to fight well and to prevail. And, so well prepared by him, they do prevail, over the numerous, Christian, but entirely unprepared French host.

In making, in his reply, these terrors of damnation an instrument of political religion and an engine of military valor, Henry shows that he has learned from the death of Falstaff. Even though he was not present at that death, received no report of it, and never speaks of it, he has learned from it. How can this be?

First, one must ask whether it is really true that Henry never speaks of Falstaff's death. He seems to speak of it when he teaches Williams, and even puts it in the very center of his teaching:

> Therefore should every soldier in the wars do as every sick man in his bed–wash every mote out of his conscience; and dying so, death, is to him advantage; (4.1.168–70)

In other words, every soldier should imitate the only vivid example of a sick man in his bed in the play. Every soldier should imitate Falstaff. It can only be that Henry knows of Falstaff's death because Henry always knew of his death. Indeed, this is so. Long ago Henry remarked to Falstaff, "Thou owest God a death" (*1 Henry IV*, 5.1.126). Again, his final words to Falstaff began, "I know thee not, old man. Fall to thy prayers" (*2 Henry IV*, 5.5.48). Henry did not need to be present at the death of Falstaff in order to know it, he knew Falstaff and hence he knew what his death was most probably to be like. Nor did Henry need to get a report of that death, for he not only knew Falstaff, but knew himself.

The tale of Falstaff dying is told by a woman, it is about a man, and it is understood by the prince. It is clear how the death of Falstaff is in Henry V, as Shakespeare promised at the end of *2 Henry IV*.

Nothing more need be said about the death of Falstaff in *Henry V* were it not for the fact that Shakespeare also backs it with a tempting depth. It is not only that through it Shakespeare makes us confront the painful mystery of death and whatever lies after it, but that by allusion he reminds us of three of the most remarkable, poignant, and enigmatic deaths in the long history of the West. The tale of Falstaff dying was fashioned by Shakespeare, it is about man, and it signifies something.

II. Falstaff and Socrates

The gesture of the Hostess, moving her hand up Falstaff's body, is unusual and even peculiar, but it is not unique.

Consider the death of Socrates as reported by Plato in his dialogue, the *Phaedo*.[13] After Socrates took the hemlock, everyone present broke into passionate weeping, everyone except Socrates, who said:

> Why, that was my main reason for sending away the women, to prevent this sort of disturbance, because I am told that one should make one's end in a tranquil frame of mind. Calm yourselves and try to be brave. (117e)

The reporter, Phaedo, continues his narrative:

> This made us feel ashamed, and we controlled our tears. Socrates walked about, and presently, saying that his legs were heavy, lay down on his back— that was what the man recommended. The man—he was the same one who

had administered the poison—kept his hand upon Socrates, and after a little while examined his feet and legs, then pinched his foot hard and asked if he felt it. Socrates said no. Then he did the same to his legs, and moving gradually upward in this way, let us see that he was getting cold and numb. Presently he felt him again and said that when it reached the heart Socrates would be gone.

The coldness was spreading about as far as his waist [groin] when Socrates uncovered his face, for he had covered it up, and said—they were his last words—Crito, we ought to offer a cock to Asclepius. See to it, and don't forget.

No, it shall be done, said Crito. Are you sure that there is nothing else?

Socrates made no reply to this question, but after a little while he stirred, and when the man uncovered him, his eyes were fixed. When Crito saw this, he closed the mouth and eyes.

Such, Echecrates, was the end of our comrade, who was, we may fairly say, of all those whom we knew in our time, the bravest [best] and also the wisest [most prudent] and most upright [most just].[14]   (117e–18a)

If the gesture of moving one's hand up a dying man's body were a common feature of famous death scenes, say, if it appeared in the reports of the deaths of Achilleus, Archimedes, Caesar, Christ, Njal, Thomas Aquinas, or Werther, then we could dismiss this resemblance as an accident, but since no other death scene known to us save these two, of Falstaff and of Socrates, contains this gesture, it is hard to believe that Shakespeare did not intend this resemblance and, therefore, intend some of his audience to recognize it.

That Shakespeare wishes us to investigate this comparison is suggested by the hints he has dropped long before the death of Falstaff. While impersonating his father, Prince Hal himself called Falstaff "That villainous abominable misleader of youth" (1 Henry IV, 2.4.439) . . . the very charge often made against Socrates,[15] and one of the two formal charges brought against him by Meletus, Anytus, and Lycon.[16] Like Socrates, Falstaff is accused of making the worse appear the better reason.[17] Falstaff is always asking Socratic questions, of the type: What is a thing? With them he, like Socrates, examines things and disturbs people. With his question, What is honor?, Falstaff calls into question the life of the gentleman.[18] With his deeds and speeches and laughter, he seems to ask, What is courage? the very question which arises when Socrates meets with the distinguished generals Laches and Nicias in the Laches. Like Socrates, Falstaff serves in his country's armies and, like Socrates, he serves on foot rather than on horse.[19] Falstaff says he is witty and the cause of wit in other men (2 Henry IV, 1.2.6); the friends of Socrates think that he is wise and the cause of wisdom in themselves. Falstaff drinks much, and so can Socrates.[20] Neither Falstaff nor Socrates is beautiful, yet both exercise an extraordinary attraction upon other men.[21] Together with their deaths, all these resemblances show that Shakespeare likens Falstaff to Socrates.

If, as it seems, Shakespeare intends us to investigate the resemblance between Falstaff and Socrates, still, he has not made it easy. What Shakespeare thought of Socrates would seem to be unavailable to us. Outside his plays he says nothing of Socrates, and in them he never portrays him. He only alludes or gestures towards Socrates. So we are compelled to study the relation of Falstaff and Socrates without distinguishing Shakespeare's Socrates and the real Socrates. The real Socrates! That it is not easy to understand the real Socrates would seem to be evident from the labors of minds greater than ours: Xenophon, Aristophanes, Plato, Diogenes Laertius, Cicero, Montaigne, Hegel, Kierkegaard, Nietzsche, and Strauss.

Nevertheless, a beginning seems possible. Since Shakespeare makes his most explicit and decisive allusion to Socrates in the course of the report of Falstaff's death,[22] perhaps he means us to begin with the last minutes. We have before us those minutes and the last minutes of Socrates. Beginning here means beginning near death. Already we may have discovered something important. Socrates speaks of the philosophic life as one of constant preparation for death. According to this Socratic remark, the life of Falstaff cannot be philosophic. But according to a favorite author of Shakespeare, philosophy is not preparation for death; it is un-philosophic to pay death such constant attention. Young Montaigne thought philosophy was studying to die; old Montaigne, become a philosopher, thought unreflective peasants die as well as students. What do we think? By bringing in Socrates, Shakespeare means each of us to think about death, about the afterlife, about the fear of both, and about what view it is best for us to take toward these things.[23]

Both deaths are reported deaths, and in both the reporter is decidedly inferior to the person who dies. All Socratic dialogues take place between Socrates and his inferiors, or between the young Socrates, the Socrates who was not yet Socrates, and his superiors; there is no Socratic dialogue between the mature Socrates and Plato, young or mature. The dialogue we might most want to overhear, entitled *The Philosopher,* is not represented at all in the Platonic dialogues. Still, it is mildly surprising to find that Plato is not present at the death of Socrates. It can only be that he does not need to be present, that he would learn nothing new from being present, and that he already knows about that death. Just as the most intelligent pupil of Socrates, Plato, does not witness his death, and as the most princely companion of Socrates, Alcibiades, was also absent, so the most intelligent, princely companion of Falstaff is absent from his death. Indeed, as we have seen, Henry did not need to be present at the death of Falstaff in order to learn what can be learned from that death.

According to the jailor, Socrates dies when the poison reaches his *heart;* by contrast, Falstaff seems to die when coldness reaches his *organs of generation.* What does this mean? What difference between the two is indicated by the difference between heart and genitals? Perhaps the answer lies this way. The most obvious difference between the two deaths is the terror of Falstaff and the equanimity of Socrates. Faced with death, Falstaff cries out; Socrates simply discourses as he has always done. Falstaff's terror rests upon a certain kind of opinion or knowledge, available only through revelation, which punishes excessive appetite, especially sexual appetite.[24] Socrates' courage rests upon a knowing ignorance that ranks and tames all the appetites. According to Socrates, we do not know what follows life;[25] those who fear it suppose too much; here, too, our best wisdom is a kind of ignorance. The difference between Falstaff and Socrates reminds one of the difference between ancient philosophy and Christian religion.

This difference between the heart and the genitals corresponds to the different place of women and womanish things in the two reports. The death of Falstaff is reported by a woman and, despite her obfuscation, we learn that Falstaff warned those at his deathbed about women. The death of Socrates is reported by a man and only men are present at that death, for Socrates had taken the precaution to exclude all women from his cell, including his wife. Nevertheless, most of the men cried anyway. Weeping is more of womanish than a mannish thing. Nevertheless, the difference between men and women proves not so great as the difference between philosophers and nonphilosophers. Socrates did not weep; he did not cry out; he did not wail or gnash his teeth.[26] According to Socrates, too great attachment to life is a womanish thing. Though alive and married, Socrates seems not very attached to either life or wife. Though Falstaff was a bachelor, we cannot say the same of him. Once he pursued women, now he warns against them in womanish fear.

Ancient metaphysics understands truth, or the ideas, as male rather than female: unchanging, self-sufficient, beautiful, enduring, hard, steadfast, intelligent; and the ancient philosopher understands himself as an image of this truth. It is a modern metaphysican who suspects that truth might be a woman, divers, wily, undulating, veiled, perhaps beautiful, perhaps ugly, but in any case alluring, and it is the founder of modern political philosophy who tells us that the god presiding over human things is Fortuna and a woman.[27] However, *Henry V* is neither ancient nor modern; at Agincourt Henry prays to a Providential Deity who can intervene in human affairs to work His just will. This is not Chance, whom you can hope to master, nor Truth as a Woman, whom you can hope will love you in return; this is God, the Supreme Statesman of the World, God the Sagacious, whom you can only strive to be in accord with and hope to please. This first principle is male but mysterious.

The dying Falstaff cries out; the living Falstaff was wont to laugh. He laughed much and was cause of much laughter in other men. Living, he reminds us of the laughing atomist, Democritus, dying of the weeping oraclist, Heraclitus. The greatest laugh Falstaff provided began with the cowardice or love of life he exhibited at Gad's Hill, but it culminated with his witty acquittal from the charge of cowardice (*1 Henry IV,* 2.4.253). If we turn to Socrates, we find that he never wept or cried out, and that he laughed only a few times. The *Phaedo* is filled with the long arguments with which Socrates tried to soothe and charm his death-fearing interlocutors (77e–78a); how little these men are able to take these arguments seriously, how little they are soothed, is suggested by two remarks of theirs which make Socrates laugh gently. The second of these occurs at the end of the discussion (*Phaedo,* 115c–e; cf. 84d). Though Crito has heard all Socrates has said, still he asks: "How shall we bury *you?*" To which Socrates replies, "Any way you like, that is, if you can catch me and I don't slip through your fingers." The narrative continues:

He laughed gently as he spoke, and turning to us went on: I can't persuade Crito that I am this Socrates here who is talking to you now and marshalling all the arguments; he thinks that I am the one whom he will see presently lying dead; and he asks how he is to bury me! As for my long and elaborate explanation that when I have drunk the poison I shall remain with you no longer, but depart to a state of heavenly happiness, this attempt to console both you and myself seems to be wasted on him.[28]

Socrates laughs at Crito; though gentle, his laughter is at the expense of those who cling to life. According to Socrates, it is not philosophic to weep; philosophers may laugh, but not weep. According to Socrates, then, the laughter of Falstaff approaches philosophy, but his crying out "God" three or four times retreats from it.

Thomas More, who knew something about Socratic philosophy and was wont to jest, was also a Christian saint. Awaiting execution in the Tower, he wrote the *Dialogue of Comfort against Tribulation,* and in it he says:

And for to prove that this life is no laughing tyme but rather the tyme of wepyng, we fynd that our saviour hym selfe wept twise or thrise, but never fynd we that he laughed so much as onse, I will not swere that he never did but at the lest wise he left us no samples of it.[29]

More has in mind the passage, in John (11.35), where Christ weeps over the death of Lazarus, whom he subsequently revives, and the passage in Luke (19.41), where Christ weeps over the future destruction of Jerusalem. Perhaps the "thrice" More mentions was no weeping but His cry from the cross.

Although one might observe that with both Socrates and Christ, there was a remarkable equanimity in the face of calumny, judicial injustice, and death, there is, nonetheless, this great difference. Socrates would never cry over the death of another human being, not even Plato; this we partly know from the fact that Plato himself seems not only not to have wept over Socrates, but was not even there at his death. Likewise, we cannot imagine Socrates weeping over the destruction of any city, even the Athens that had allowed him to philosophize for so long. Human things are not that important. Socrates sleeps the night before his death, Christ stays up the whole night alone; Socrates laughs, for the first time in his life, about his trial,[30] Christ suffers His; Socrates speaks at his trial, Christ barely so. We may describe the differences in terms of comedy and tragedy. For Socrates comedy is superior to tragedy, for Christ, who never laughs, tragedy is superior to comedy.[31]

Exactly the opposite is true of Socrates. Socrates never weeps, but laughs twice or thrice. The living Falstaff bears some resemblance to Socrates; dying, he resembles Christ. The living Henry V resembles both; he laughs with Falstaff, prays for his men, and cries over the death of York.

III. Modern Falstaff and His Genealogy

If Falstaff is in most ways the antithesis of Socrates and classical political philosophy, he is not the antithesis of all antiquity. In their quarrel with the ancients, the moderns found allies among the ancients themselves. Modern mathematical physics found an ally in Epicurean physics; the founder of modern political philosophy, Machiavelli, found an ally in the half of Xenophon devoted to Cyrus (and not the half devoted to Socrates); the covert disciples of Machiavelli found an ally in Tacitus. But in the pages of Plautus and Terence modern men discovered themselves; true, they also discovered themselves in the letters of Cicero and were thrilled with the tales of Plutarch, but the taste for Cicero and the admiration for Plutarch belong to the first blush of modernity. Who now reads Plutarch the way Montaigne read him, with admiration, or the way Rousseau still did, with the thrill of virtue burning in his heart? Modernity prefers Plautus to Plutarch. From the vantage point of the French Revolution and the proclamation of the equal rights of man, Hegel discerned the important achievements of reason to owe more to slaves than to masters.[32] Hegel gave reasons for what the taste of modernity had long ago chosen. In the slaves and braggart warriors of Plautus and Terence, modernity saw itself; probably the most favored tag of the early humanists of Europe comes from Terence: *homo sum: humani nil a me alienum puto*.[33] Montaigne had it carved on one of the rafters of his chateau tower. One hears it repeated today wherever there are humanists.[34] We understand the genealogy of modernity better when we come to know that these words proceed from the mouth of a gentleman who objects to another gentleman who has undertaken menial labor and is being beaten as if he were a slave. According to the speaker, laboring is for slaves. The Ancients were not humanists.

Since Falstaff was, from the beginning, the favorite character in Shakespeare,[35] it is safe to say that audiences have always preferred Falstaff to Caesar. It is a good illustration of modern taste. It also accords with a choice of Plautus over Plutarch, for as Plutarch stands behind Shakespeare's Caesar, the multitude of slaves and braggart warriors in Plautus stand behind Falstaff. The character types Plautus left dispersed, the tricky slave and the braggart warrior, Shakespeare succeeded in combining, and thereby won the taste of modernity. The combination could have resulted in a tricky warrior, an Odysseus, but instead we have a bragging slave. A bragging slave, unlike a bragging warrior, purposes his own discovery; in the discovery of his bragging, he hopes to laugh honor to death. The life of honor is the life of the master. As a slave, Falstaff is not like the tricky slave in Plautus; he does not beat his masters to the spoils. Instead he conquers the class of masters, gentlemen, knights, and nobles, in principle. His bragging and his trickery are merely instrumental to his slavishness. (Lest this seem an insulting inaccuracy, we must remember that the life of a house slave was not unlike that of a modern bourgeois; both have to work for a living and prefer to leave honor to others.) But if he is fundamentally a slave, he is unlike any slave in Plautus because he is a philosophic slave. Montaigne and others professed to discover philosophy in the mouths of Plautine slaves; with Falstaff one does not need to profess.

A very great ancient prince to whom Henry is frequently compared[36] was not only educated by a philosopher, but stood in a direct studious line to Socrates. Alexander was the pupil of the pupil of the pupil of Socrates. While a very great ancient prince looked through Aristotle to Socrates, a modern prince will look to the likes of Falstaff. Modern politics begins low, with things as they are deemed to be, with Falstaff; ancient politics never lost sight of the high, of justice, of wisdom, of Socrates. Ancient cities seem to have existed for the sake of virtue, as theaters in which it could shine; modern countries seem to exist for the sake of pleasure and liberty, for the sake of what Hobbes called self-preservation and what Locke called comfortable self-preservation. But Falstaff is not yet bourgeois man, for he still fears the afterlife as much as he fears violent death or natural death. Between ancient and modern morals, there stands Christianity. Falstaff dies a Christian, in terror of the afterlife. The most powerful passion in him is not thirst for the sweetness of life or enjoyment of the mere sentiment of existence,[37] but terror of supernatural punishment. Though this terror is not powerful enough to make Falstaff or his kind moderate, it does make him immoderate in fear. While Christianity attacked the ancient love of honor as a "splendid vice," Falstaff attacks it as a "word." The Christian attack on honor is ascetic and lean; Falstaff's is luxurious and fat. Though the life of Falstaff is very far from that of Pascal, it is not as far as it might be. Falstaff cannot throw off Christian terrors; the result is big appetites and big fears; to hide from one's fears, one drinks and wenches and jests; but sack and women and jests fill one with dread—so one drinks and wenches and jests. Whenever the wit of Falstaff scores through Biblical allusion, it exposes Biblical fear. He seems to be a combination of bourgeois pleasures and Christian terrors. His pleasures are never thoughtless, carefree, serene. Falstaff is no Barnardine.

The modern Christian principality that Henry is building must not only include the likes of Falstaff but will build the regime on them. Some clerics there will be, such as Canterbury and Ely, but with restricted scope, and some clerics still cloistered, such as Henry has set to expiate his father's crime, but some nobles there will be, such as York and Westmoreland, but in the new polity Henry is fashioning, most citizens will be farmers, tradesmen, and merchants. The souls of such citizens will combine desire for comfortable self-preservation, ambition for gain, and fear of damnation. Some separate arrangement of public prosperity and private morality, of commerce and piety, such as Locke and others argued for, and Tocqueville saw in the American democracy, will be the likely consequence of the regime's departure from the agitation of honor, the honoring of contemplation, and the encouragement of heroic virtue. Such regimes will, like Falstaff, tend to prefer peace to war and, like Falstaff, much exaggerate their infrequent military enterprises. The military virtues that war requires and rewards, the daring of a Hotspur, the courage of an Exeter, the fortitude of a Grant, will be regarded as instrumental to the good, not something shining in themselves. In war, the regime will put its faith in the captains and sergeants, such as Fluellen, recruited from the citizens, as much as in the nobles bred to it. In such a regime, the prince's art of rule will more often be to balance fear against fear, appetite against appetite, than to set reason to rule directly over all by teaching the soul the way up to virtues.

Strip Falstaff of his wit and his zest for pleasure and you have Ivan Ilych. And an admiration for Socrates and a clear eye to Falstaff's genial, divers, shifty, essaying mind and you have Michel de Montaigne.

IV. Dissembling, Entertaining, and Thinking

However, we do Falstaff wrong if we see only the low things in him. If he is modern man, he is also modern man writ witty. We love Falstaff for his wit and for making us wittier. Even if we are heroic, we are still human. If we love God, does that mean we should not fear Him? Falstaff is us, we him, and his wit helps us to see it. His wit, like Socrates', can liberate us from many of the profitable servitudes of the world. Much honor is vain, much ambition empty, much wealth unhappy. By examining these idols from the point of view of pleasure, Falstaff disenchants us, and in so doing he promotes a very high pleasure. For friendship some release from vexation and respite from necessity is needed, and each jest of Falstaff provides some. During his life, though not his last days, Falstaff's wit separated men briefly and ever so slightly from a most powerful force in their lives, opinion. In this respect, Falstaff is not inferior to Socrates. Falstaff sees through things, he disenchants. Unlike Socrates, he does not seem able to replace the enchantments he destroys with something better, either with a new and more beneficial enchantment[38] or with a glimpse of truly enchanting things. While the modern prince enjoys a disenchanting friend like Falstaff, he also desires a probing friend like Williams. What was united in Socrates seems dispersed into Falstaff and Williams, with this omission, that neither has the power to enchant with both noble stories and the enchanting things themselves, as Socrates does. For that, the modern prince would have to turn to Shakespeare himself.

Both Falstaff and Socrates are dissemblers. Falstaff pretends to be more than he is, especially to be more brave than he is, while Socrates pretends to be less. Falstaff is a braggart; there is no name for its opposite, and so we can only say that Socrates is ironic. To understand the irony of Socrates, we must free ourselves from the modern confusion of irony with human insult, impersonal fate, or divine affliction, however belatedly revealed. The irony of Socrates is seldom sarcasm. Only the boastful feel pain because of him, and then never because he vilifies them. If his interlocutors feel ignorant, it is because of the evident collapse of their arguments; if they feel shame, it is because of the evident emptiness of their personal claims. From them and from the other inferiors, Socrates hides his thoughts; should his interlocutors perceive their excellence and thus his, he would no longer be protected and their self-education would no longer be encouraged.[39] The ironic manner of Socrates is a superficial sign of a deep reflection upon both writing and human nature.[40] For the majority of listeners, the nonphilosophers, the speeches of Socrates are meant to be taken at face value, but for a very few listeners the irony of those speeches is intended to be perceived. The dissembling of Socrates, then, is meant to divide his audience, but so only the few know who they and the many are.

It would seem then that his dissembling is very different from that of the boaster who surely will not wish his boasts to be seen by any one for the hollow things they are. If this is so, then we must hesitate to call Falstaff a genuine boaster or an ordinary boaster, for it would seem that he wishes to have his pretenses and boasts uncovered. A man who wants a reputation and who boasts to get it does not wish anyone to see the discrepancy between his deeds and his words; should that discrepancy be discovered he will hide his face, lower his head, put his tail between his departing legs, or lash out sullenly. When Falstaff is unmasked after Gad's Hill, he never grows ashamed or sullen. He has nothing in him of the red-faced animal; to him 'honor' is a word; he is shameless. Hence, he cannot be a braggart, for the braggart loves honor. How is it that he seems to be a braggart? He is an entertainer, and to entertain men he takes the part of the braggart. Thus it is that his bragging and pretending are always meant in the end to give men the pleasure of discovery. If, after Gad's Hill, Falstaff began by saying that he was set upon by fourteen men in buckram, we might think him a genuine boaster and liar; that he in fact changes the number of assailants with each new sentence tells us that he is perfectly aware of the transparency of his tale; it is hard to doubt that a man of his wit did not know what pleasure he was giving and did not purpose that pleasure. Someone who wished his lie about men in buckram to be believed would have chosen one number and stuck to it. Study his other boasts and deceptions and you will see that he always cooperates with those who wish to unmask and expose him. Here is his real deception. He would not wish these men to know that he wishes to be unmasked. Deeper than his wish to be thought brave is his wish to entertain.

The entertainer is both a master and a slave. The entertainer has only to drop a word to make a spontaneous convulsion grip his listeners. The mastery present in making people laugh is more easily apparent in the phenomenon of tickling. Children and those who care for them enjoy tickling. Among them one hears the expression, "tickle you to death." Children struggle to be the one doing the tickling. Awkward uncles fall back upon their one trick; a few tickles will break the ice, a few more will put someone "in stitches." Anyone who has been held down and tickled for a long while knows what it is to be helpless, what it is to be ready to say "uncle." The man who can make others laugh, at a greater distance, with words rather than bony fingers, remains, despite the change of means, an uncle or master. There is something spontaneous in laughter, like sneezing or other bodily reflexes. To be able to make that happen in another person is a kind of mastery. But if the entertainer like Falstaff is a master, he is also a slave. The occupation of making others laugh is absorbing. Everyone knows a crude example of this; everyone has met a man who cannot stop cracking jokes, who finally makes jokes about how bad his jokes are, how he is not getting a rise tonight, how he will soon be taken off the air. For the man who is really witty, who succeeds with his jests, it is even harder to break the habit than for a dull-witted fellow. Yet each is slavish; the one in a crude, the other in a sad manner. Both need an audience in order to continue their way of life. The case of the man with real wit is the sadder of the two because his great gifts are wasted; he drowns the solitude necessary for mental endeavor, which his wit ought to be able to endure, in perpetual jests. In this way he is likely to blunt his gifts; if he wishes to be always making men laugh, he must keep within the bounds of what *they* think laughable.[41] In this way he also becomes the servant or slave of their opinions. Himself a slave, he enslaves others, and all the more because of his great gifts.[42]

The element of mastery in making men laugh brings the entertainer close to the ruler; it brings Falstaff close to Henry. Seeing his effect upon others, the entertainer will come to enjoy it; soon he will seek to increase it, bringing more and more men under his humorous sovereignty, attaching more and more retainers with the silken strings of his jests. The place where he drinks will become *his* tavern, himself an attraction, drawings others there. Still, as much as any king, he will lack liberty. He will not easily surrender or abdicate the center of attention he now occupies. (Was there ever a jester who wished to share the same stage with another?) To cling to his warm tavern throne, he may not care how much he now causes men to laugh at *him* as he once caused them to laugh at his wit. He will more and more play to the ruder majority of his audience.[43] When a man entertains an audience, it is hard to tell the ruler from the ruled. When an Elizabeth asks for "more Falstaff," is she exercising rule or Falstaff? And what of Shakespeare?

Shakespeare has Falstaff say something true about himself when he has him remark that he is not only witty in himself, but the cause of wit in other men (*2 Henry IV,* 1.2.6). This moment of self-knowledge is rare for Falstaff. Falstaff always knows that he is the cause of wit in other men, and he forgets he is witty in himself. He is deaf to the call of wit in his own ear. It is a dreadful thing to fear, and the wit of Falstaff cannot protect him from the afterlife. He was too much the cause of wit and laughter in other men and not enough witty in himself. He spent lavishly of his lavish gifts. For what? To entertain men, to entertain the prince. If Falstaff is a part of Shakespeare, as he surely is, then he is also a warning. It is not truly witty to be *always* the cause of wit in other men. It is very hard to be true to oneself or true to other men. To be true to both is harder still.

Falstaff has many of the Socratic charms that allow one to divorce men from their prejudices and opinions, but he cannot replace them with anything but the pleasures of the body, and thus also the pains. Against the terrors of the afterlife, he is not impious enough, as Machiavelli would say, or honest fearing enough as Pascal would say. Socrates has a demon who occasionally warns him not to do things; this demon did not warn Socrates not to give his apology to the Athenian jury, that is: it did not warn him not to die. Falstaff has his devils. They are always with him though they are invisible to us. When we first meet Falstaff, we say, "Here is a happy man and he will make me happy too." Our own pursuit of a certain happiness causes us to ignore the devils hovering about him. But when we look back over his speeches from the vantage of his last hours, we see that the devils were always there; yes, he was always talking about Lazarus and the rich man burning in hell (*2 Henry IV,* 1.2.33; cf. 2.4.217–18; *1 Henry IV,* 3.3.29ff.; 4.2.24). The jokes he used to make about Bardolph's nose (*2 Henry IV,* 2.4.247, 310; *1 Henry IV,* 3.3.24ff.) covered a terror that is only revealed at his death when he sees a soul burning in hell on Bardolph's nose (2.3.36–37). Falstaff in the valley of the shadow of the afterlife is not a new man in a new place. His jests always pointed there.

One of the few things in ordinary life which points to truth is laughter; there, right out in the open, are all the fears, dreads, tensions, and questions[44] which point to and call for a quest for truth. However, the very nearness of laughter to the quest for truth is its utility for common life. Truth is silenced as well as glimpsed in laughter. A laugh opens a path to truth suddenly; soon it is closed by the very same laugh. The long laughs of the perpetually laughing are tombstones of thought. Even more than Falstaff, Shakespeare has been the cause of wit in other men. He has noticed that when men laugh they do not think. He has laughed about this and he has thought about it. He has thought about those who like to make other men laugh and suspects that, though they could not make others laugh without great wit, they too like to laugh at their own jokes, and they too do not think when they laugh. It would seem that according to Shakespeare it is not at all easy to laugh and think at the same time.

V. Falstaff and David

If the death of Falstaff is designed to recall the death of Socrates, it is also designed to recall the death of King David. Again, Mistress Quickly points the way, with her mistake of Arthur for Abraham, with the fact that Falstaff was trying to recite the Twenty-third Psalm, which not even she could suppress, and literally with her woman's hand malaproply seeking to find out if his stones still give heat. Let us examine how these three combine to point toward King David.

The Twenty-third Psalm, which Falstaff tried to recite, bears the superscription, "A Psalm of David." Orthodox opinion attributes the composition of the majority of the Psalms to David and the rest perhaps to his redaction. Nor is this foolish. David was renowned as a harpist (I Samuel 16–18); the lament of David over Abner is worthy (II Samuel 3.33ff.); and the lament of David over Saul and Jonathan is splendid:

> The beauty of Israel is slain upon thy high places:
> how are the mighty fallen!
> Tell it not in Gath, publish it not in the streets of Askelon:
> (II Samuel 2.19–20)

So too, the song attributed to David in II Samuel 22 appears as Psalm Eighteen. Finally, just before David speaks his last words he is called "the sweet psalmist of Israel" (II Samuel 23.1). David was beautiful, loved beauty (in Bath-sheba, in Absalom), and was the cause of much beauty for others, such as his psalms, whose beauty can cast out even the fear of death, as we see especially in the Twenty-third of them.

It is natural, then, when we hear Falstaff trying to recite this very psalm to think of David and, since Falstaff is dying and is trying to draw serenity from this psalm,

to wonder what kind of death David, the author of it, had. Of the old and ailing King
David in his bed, we read:

> Now king David was old and stricken in years;
> and they covered him with clothes, but he gat no heat.
> Wherefore his servants said unto him,
> Let there be sought for my lord the king a young virgin:
> and let her stand before the king, and let her cherish him,
> and let her lie in thy bosom, that my lord the king may get heat.
> So they sought for a fair damsel throughout all the coasts of Israel,
> And found Abishag a Shunammite, and brought her to the king.
> And the damsel *was* very fair, and cherished the king,
> and ministered to him:
> but the king knew her not.   (I Kings, 1.1–4)

The test of whether David is nearer death than life is whether his loins put forth heat.
Though the maiden Abishag cherished him and ministered to him, no doubt passing
her hand upward and upward above the knee, or at any rate arriving there from
whatever cherishing direction, David gat no heat. This quick-or-dead test is virtually
the same as the one Mistress Quickly seemed, in her malaprop-bawdy way, to ad-
minister to the dying Falstaff. There, too, his stones gat no heat and the man was dead.

What are we to make of these resemblances? What is the connection between King David and Falstaff? Of David, we know almost more than any other
figure in the Bible. Not until the Gospels will we learn as much of one man, his
childhood, his youth, his eventful life, and his death. Like Falstaff, David is very
winning; his beauty, his music, and his martial prowess all find favor with princes, just
as Falstaff's wit finds favor with Prince Hal. However, the winsome ways of David
find favor not only with heir apparent princes such as Jonathan, but with reigning
ones, such as Saul and Achish. Moreover, together with his dancing and his piety,
these winsome ways find favor with God, so much that David himself becomes a
prince. If Falstaff reminds in some ways of David, David reminds in more comprehensive ways of King Henry.

Both rise from slight reputations to great glory, leave private pursuits and gain
princely office, single handedly defeat far more experienced warriors, such as
Goliath and Hotspur, earn signal victories against inveterate enemies, and unite their
countries. Both receive God's frequent blessing and, despite their lapses, seem to
enjoy His abiding favor. The first and most astonishing victory of King David was his
victory over Goliath and the Philistines; the victories of Henry V first over Hotspur
and later over the French are no less surprising. We see the five smooth stones in
the one case and we suspect the longbows in the other; nevertheless, both remain
remarkable, perhaps mysterious. *Non nobis, Te deum.*

On the way to these princely achievements, both princes do as Machiavelli
says they should ;[45] they constantly practice the art of war. During war a prince may
do terrible things. In the course of his war, Henry finds himself saying that a king
does not "purpose" the damnation of his men when he undertakes it. This reminds

us of the example of Uriah the Hittite, who King David placed in the forefront of the hottest battle so that he might be slain (II Samuel 11). David is a perfect and most Biblical example of a king who "purposed" the death of one of his faithful soldiers, who employed war and the bowmen of besieged Rabbah as his "beadle."[46] Henry could have placed Williams, whom he disputes with in the night, in the forefront of the battle next morning, as David did Uriah. Henry does not do it, but still he must bear part of the burden of the man's possible damnation.

Other stray things may connect David and Henry. What are we to think of the name of the Welsh saint, St. Davy, whose victory in battle is celebrated by the wearing of leeks, and who was named for David, especially in connection with Mistress Quickly's substitution of Arthur for Abraham?[47] Is Henry a kind of David? And a sort of saint? Might the report of Falstaff's attempted recitation of the Twenty-third Psalm be meant to remind us that it is King Henry who has just, in the previous scene, been delivered in the presence of his enemies? When we "hear" Falstaff reciting the Twenty-third Psalm, are we meant to think of how King Henry has his army sing psalms after the victory at Agincourt, and that these psalms remind the pious listener of the Exodus of the Chosen from Egypt across the bed of the Red Sea?[48] Nor is the miraculously preserved and miraculously triumphant army of Henry V without its new psalms. Along with the *"Non nobis, Te Deum"* that they sing on the battlefield, they will in later celebrations repeat Henry's "We happy few" speech. The public speeches of King Henry fulfill the same purpose that the many public psalms of David fulfilled for his nation.[49]

All these resemblances, exact and general, tend to remind us that according to the Hebrews the Messiah will be a political man, more like King David than disappointing 'King' Christ. Under David the nation of Israel prospers, and under his son, Solomon, the Temple is established. For the Hebrews of that ancient time, "Judaism" was a political religion in a political state; it was not what was later called Judaism, either scribes and pharisees, or Rabbis and commentators, let alone Jewish studies. The God of Abraham gave His chosen a particular land, the God of Moses gave them the Torah, and He later granted them the monarchy they requested and the monarchs they deserved, David prominent among them, as Henry is among the English monarchs.

Shakespeare's great rival, Machiavelli, sharpened the contrast, between the armed prince and the unarmed prophet when, in his *Prince,* he explicitly names Moses among the five greatest princes, criticizes Savonarola, and when he says this about David:

> I wish also to recall to memory a figure of the Old Testament, made for this point. When David offered himself to Saul to fight Goliath, the Philistine challenger, Saul in order to give him courage armed him with his own arms, which as soon as David had them on, he rejected saying that he could not be of as good worth with them as by himself, and that he therefore wished to find the enemy with his sling and with his knife. In fine, the arms of others either fall off your back, weigh you down, or constrict you.[50]

That the prince just called exemplary for the same prudence is Hiero of Syracuse and that at the end of Chapter VI, Machiavelli tags this same Hiero onto the list of the greatest princes, indicates that David is, for Machiavelli, very exemplary indeed. In brief we may say that David is, for Machiavelli, the Old Testament antitype of the most unarmed prophet in the New, Christ.

Is Shakespeare insinuating something like the same lesson? Is Henry simply not man enough to institute new modes and orders? Not prince enough to practice modern virtù, introduce a new and civil religion, and restore ancient civic virtue? Failing to do these things, failing to extinguish the fear of invisible states in his citizens, is Henry then constrained to do as best he can. David would begin with the "fear of the Lord"; Henry is constrained to begin with the fear of hell.[51] Does Shakespeare mean to say that unless the modern prince can efface this signal difference, by extinguishing the fear of hell from his own heart as well as his subjects', modern principalities will be unable to resemble the ancient Hebrew principality? Certainly Henry omits to kill off the old blood, but although Machiavelli would certainly censure him for not having Mortimer killed, it is hard to say that Shakespeare does.

It is very hard to know precisely how far Shakespeare means his reader to follow out his allusions and hints. He leaves it up to the reader, in order to both to test and to please him, but he does not, I think, leave us without some guidance. Perhaps then we can gain some of the precision we seek if we remind ourself of a few conspicuous things. David and Falstaff resemble each other. Both lead way-ward lives; both enjoy pleasures, of women for example, and both provide plea-sure for others; and for the sake of their pleasures, both sacrifice soldiers in their command. Finally, the deaths of both are marked by the same sensual test of their vitality. These conspicuous resemblances between Falstaff and David bring to light one great difference in their deaths. Falstaff dies a Christian death, in terror of Damnation, while David dies quietly without a cry, or an oath, or a tear. He does not try to recite his own Twenty-third Psalm, he does not warn against sack, and he does not regard the fair Shunammite damsel as a devil incarnate. While Falstaff fears terrible punishments for his venereal sins, David is not ashamed of the broadness with which he cast his seed, his treatment of Michal, his adulterous union with Bath-sheba, or his murder of her husband, his captain, Uriah the Hittite.

One understands how the Hebrew prince's view of life and death differs from both the Christian Falstaff's and also the philosopher Socrates', if one recalls how David bore the death of the child, the first fruit of his union with Bath-sheba. Although the Lord gives them this child, and will later give them Solomon and others, He takes this child away.

> And Nathan departed unto his house.
> And the Lord struck the child
>   that Uriah's wife bare unto David,
>   and it was very sick.
> David therefore besought God for the child;

and David fasted, and went in, and lay all night upon the earth.
And the elders of his house arose, and went to him, to raise him up
    from the earth: but he would not,
    neither did he eat bread with them.
And it came to pass on the seventh day, that the child died.
And the servants of David feared to tell him
    that the child was dead:
for they said, Behold, while the child was yet alive,
    we spake unto him, and he would not hearken unto our voice:
how will he then vex himself, if we tell him that the child is dead?
But when David saw that his servants whispered,
David perceived that the child was dead:
therefore David said unto his servants, Is the child dead?
And they said, He is dead.
Then David arose from the earth, and washed,
    and anointed himself, and changed his apparel,
    and he came into the house of the Lord, and worshipped:
then he came to his own house; and when he required,
    they set bread before him, and he did eat.
Then said his servants unto him,
What thing is this that thou hast done?
    thou didst fast and weep for the child, while it was alive;
    but when the child was dead, thou didst rise and eat bread.
And he said, While the child was yet alive, I fasted and wept:
    for I said, Who can tell whether God will be gracious to me,
    that the child may live?
But now he is dead, wherefore should I fast?
    can I bring him back again?
I shall go to him, but he shall not return to me.   (II Samuel 12.15–23)

David is neither a philosopher nor a Christian. Unlike Socrates, David weeps for the sick child and, unlike Socrates, he comforts the mother; and unlike the Christian Falstaff, David does not brood upon his sins. With the death of the child God has punished him; he accepts it; he worships God, he eats bread, he resumes life. David is great of soul, but in the Hebrew, not the Hellene sense, so well described by Aristotle in his *Ethics* IV. No vain desecration of Hector's body because "I wasted Patroklus."[52] No fighting your better, surely losing, and having wife and child enslaved because of what the women of Troy might say if you did not fight.[53] David knows of glories greater than honor, of skills no gentleman would cultivate (music), gaiety none would practice (dancing), of sufferings greater than death, and of contentment greater than victory. Thus David both weeps over the child and is sure he will meet him again: "I shall go to him, but he shall not return to me."

It is an interesting question whether we suffer more for the death of those we love or for ourselves. It ranks a soul. Great David suffers more for the death of another than his own. At the death of his son Absalom, David suffers again; indeed, this time he suffers too greatly; while he gives himself over wholly to grief, he neglects the realm. Then he did not say, "I shall go to him, but he shall not return to me." Yet David's suffering for others, even in excess, can only be contrasted with the complete absence of suffering at his own death. Of it we hear only this:

> So David slept with his fathers, and was buried
> in the city of David.   (I Kings 2.10)

David sleeps with his fathers. To employ a phrase, coined by Christ, mauled by the Hostess Quickly, and plucked from Falstaff's favorite parable, David sleeps "in the bosom of Abraham" (Luke 16.19–16.31; cf. *2 Henry IV*, 4.4.61).

David's death is almost typical of the Hebrew Bible. Except for mentioning that he has a city, it is not different from the death of Abraham:

> And these are the days of the years of Abraham's life
> which he lived, an hundred threescore and fifteen years.
> Then Abraham gave up the ghost, and died in good old age,
> an old man, and full of years; and was gathered to his people.
>   (Genesis 25.7–8)

Nor are these deaths very different from the death of Moses:

> And Moses *was* a hundred and twenty years old when he died;
> his eye was not dim, nor his natural force abated. (Deuteronomy 34.7)

The calmness of these deaths is remarkable, and the disposition of the psalmist in the Twenty-third Psalm is something more. The graceful, steadfast gladness David manifests in it is even more impressive than the Spartans at Thermopylae combing their beautiful hair. That is why people, Falstaff included, try to say this psalm over: "If only I can say it right this time, I will enjoy the serenely ready state of soul its author enjoyed when he wrote it and which is still in the words, if I can say them with my whole soul this time."

These deaths, of Moses, of Abraham, and of the David may well seem not only remarkable and admirable, but unattainable. What are we to conclude then? That in the twin pillars of the West, in Jerusalem and in Athens, in David and in Socrates, we find examples of good deaths, but not since then? And that the reason is the death of Christ. This would be the contention and the blasphemy of a super-Machiavellian, such as Nietzsche, but is it Shakespeare's?

VI. Christ and Falstaff

We come then to the question of Christianity.

Falstaff dies trying to say the Twenty-third Psalm, but not only did David not try to say it as he died, the Psalm itself did not mean, in his Hebrew, what it means in Falstaff's English. The original Hebrew psalm has nothing, or little, to do with the dread of something after life. The phrase "valley of the shadow of death" is very beautiful to Christian ears, but it does not translate the Hebrew; a more correct translation for the Hebrew would be "deep gloom"; the Hebrew words refer to deep ravines which cut the sheep pastures of the East and on whose sides lurk the enemies of the flock. Similarly, the phrase translated "for ever" in the final line of the Psalm could more truly be rendered "for length of days."[54] Falstaff is afraid he will go to hell, but the Hebrew scriptures know of no hell, which often terrifies the Christian, only of a *sheol*. And David himself says happily of the now dead child, "I will go to him."

More important, Falstaff not only dies a Christian death, rather than a Hebrew or Davidic one, but dies a death that is the very image of Christ's. If he fears the judging Father, he also resembles the dying Son. His cry of, "God, God, God," three or four times, cannot but remind us of "Our Saviour's" death as it is reported in the four canonical accounts left to us, especially Matthew's. There too Our Saviour avails himself of a psalm, at once reciting it and crying out through it; *"Eloi, Eloi, lama sabachthani?"* Falstaff's death is in the image of His death. Neither is wholly contented; there in the Gospel too, a man cries out, is ministered to by some who stand nearby (but also mocked), yet He pays ultimate attention to God only, crying finally "My God, my God, why hast thou forsaken me?" In both cases we do not expect these cries, in the one case because the man has always been witty, in the other because He has always been divine, as well as witty.

David is a great prince, a great man, and great in God's eyes. He seems to combine the virtues of a lover, a statesman, and a priest. Although he commits great crimes, must struggle with towering passions, and loves beauty too much, he is always great. He enjoys more vigorously than Falstaff, he dies more peacefully than Socrates, and he rules more successfully than Henry V. Although God does not let him build the Temple, he does let his son. By contrast, Henry's son, brought up by priests, loses not only everything his father gained, but what his father's father gained. Is David then the measure of everything in the world of Henry V? And is he the Trojan horse by which Shakespeare would breach the walls of Christendom and let in armed Greeks?

VII. Falstaff and Henry

By giving the death of Falstaff the depth he has, Shakespeare makes us feel the perplexity of death itself all the more than we may usually do. If Socrates did not quite understand it, if wayward David suffered it peacefully, and if Christ undergoing it felt forsaken by His own Father, then it is no wonder that Falstaff cries as he does. Probably we will, too. To adapt Pascal, about death we know too little to be dogmatists and too much to be skeptics. That Shakespeare could take us further into such painful mysteries we know from *Hamlet* and *Lear,* but the death of Falstaff is, as Shakespeare promised in *2 Henry IV,* in "the story" of Henry V. It is in the play in which he celebrates and examines the greatest English prince. While the death of Falstaff looks out to death itself then, it is to be understood in confrontation with the death of Henry V.

The resemblance of the death of Falstaff to the death of Christ seems to pose a challenge to the reader. And that challenge is met by Shakespeare's man, Henry himself. Henry meets it by meeting Falstaff and by being present at his death.

So, although Henry was not present at the death of Falstaff that Mistress Quickly reports in *Henry V*, in truth, Henry was present at one death of Falstaff, and one is enough. At Shrewsbury, after he slew Hotspur, Henry found Falstaff dead, and spoke this candid farewell:

> What, old acquaintance? Could not all this flesh
> Keep in a little life? Poor Jack, farewell!
> I could have better spared a better man.
> O, I should have a heavy miss of thee
> If I were much in love with vanity.
> Death hath not struck so fat a deer to-day.
> Though many dearer, in this bloody fray.
> Embowelled will I see thee by-and-by;
> Till then in blood by noble Percy lie.   (*I Henry IV*, 5.4.101–9)

Did Henry really like Falstaff or was he always using him? This speech tells us. We must credit his first response; his "Poor Jack, farewell!" is genuine; he did like Falstaff: "I could have *better spared* a *better* man." He misses Falstaff, yet even his expression of affection includes the knowledge that Falstaff is not a better man: "I could have better spared a *better* man." Henry likes Falstaff, but he does not love him, for he cannot love vanity. For us Falstaff may be a *memento libendi;* for Henry he is in addition always a *memento mori.*

In truth, throughout this speech Henry treats the corpse of Falstaff just as he treated the man with wit, both critical and delighted. He pokes at the corpse, as he did at the man, with puns and word plays (flesh, heavy, dear/deer), almost as if he were trying to rekindle life with wit, or make a last test of whether Falstaff is dead. Even the most candid expression of affection for Falstaff he ever utters is a pun: "I could have better spared a better man." Henry V only weeps over those who serve the general good courageously (his father and the noble York); over the 'corpse' of Falstaff he keeps up the spark of wit that they shared.

What he says next even suggests he knows, or suspects, Falstaff is now alive and will, as soon as he leaves, be upright and chatty. His declaration that he will see Falstaff embowelled (meaning disemboweled)[55] is like poking his friend to see if he is faking, or to prove he is. In any case, his very mode of address is telling. "Thee" he says to this 'corpse,' not "this body" or some phrase distinguishing Falstaff from his body. Falstaff is not lost and lamented by Henry. If Falstaff is anywhere, he is in that body.

Falstaff is indeed stirred by the idea of having his flesh pot opened and removed. What he fears, his wit takes care of:

> Embowelled? If thou embowel me to-day, I'll give you leave to powder
> me and eat me too to-morrow. 'Sblood, 'twas time to counterfeit, or that hot

termagant Scot had paid me scot and lot too. Counterfeit? I lie; I am no counterfeit. To die is to be counterfeit, for he is but the counterfeit of a man who hath not the life of a man; but to counterfeit dying when a man thereby liveth, is to be no counterfeit, but the true and perfect image of life indeed. The better part of valor is discretion, in the which better part I have saved my life. Zounds, I am afraid of this gunpowder Percy, though he be dead. How if he should counterfeit too, and rise? By my faith, I am afraid he would prove the better counterfeit. Therefore I'll make him sure; yea, and I'll swear I killed him. Why may not he rise as well as I? Nothing confutes me but eyes, and nobody sees me. Therefore, sirrah [stabs him], with a new wound in your thigh, come you along with me.   (5.4.110–27)

Falstaff's wit makes his "rising up" into a parody of the Resurrection. Those who saw him "crucified" ("ecce signum") will return to find him astonishingly alive (5.4.129ff.). If he is to be disemboweled, then he gives them leave to make of his body a communion. However, the meaning of this resurrection and communion is hardly Christian. Ignoring God and Son entirely ("nobody sees me" 5.4.125), Falstaff justifies all counterfeiting in the name of life. Courage is not worth dying for, and neither is salvation. Honor cannot set a leg, and neither can God.[56] Counterfeiting is the better part of resurrection, and good sack the better part of communion. For Falstaff, there is no better good than what flesh enjoys.

Falstaff's successful counterfeiting poses subtly the question whether it tells us the true story of a greater counterfeiting and dispels its claim to have conquered death.[57] This Machiavellian blasphemy is, however, contradicted by the whole that contains it, especially by the prince who governs it. Eating too much and too little can spring from the same excess. The fatness of Falstaff is a symptom of excessive attention to death, which his witty counterfeiting cannot deliver him or us from, whereas Henry's can. Like Christ, Henry V is neither fat nor ascetic. He can enjoy food and go without it. And he does not despise others for needing daily bread.

In his "I know you all" soliloquy, Henry claims to be a redeemer of time. This might amount to the claim that the true Messiah is a prince. In Machiavelli it would be such a blasphemy, and in his pupil Spinoza, it would fit with the forecast that one day the Jews might regain their polity, if they shed their effeminacy. To the Moses of Christ, Henry does seem to play David, but he is ever a David who acknowledges Christ as his Captain and God as the disposer of Battles and Thrones.

It was then as absolutely necessary that Henry never forget Falstaff—that every man is a Falstaff, that even he has Falstaff in him—as that King Henry never mention Falstaff. Henry cannot be present at the death of Falstaff or express grief for him because he must rule Falstaffs. To rule such men well, he must never draw close to them. Commanding them and befriending them are incompatible. When Henry replaces Falstaff with Fluellen, as a sign of the change from Hal to Henry, he never befriends Fluellen the way he did Falstaff. The ceremony that rings a good king makes his whole life as solitary as if it were lived in a prison.[58] You can do men good or you can be their friends, but not both. The conspicuous absence of Falstaff from the first part of the play is a preparation for the realization of the solitude of the King in the second half. Ruling means being lonely. The better the ruler the lonelier. If the death of Falstaff recalls the death of Christ, the deliberate absence of Falstaff from the play serves to remind us of how much the office of the king resembles Christ's, both being filled with service to others, and how much the career does too, both being one of progressive solitude. Although men, including Falstaff, obey and honor and even love Henry, they do not understand him. That Christ was neither understood, loved, honored, or obeyed, shows why Henry and his Kingdom are only in the image of He and His. Christ dies not fearful, but in sorrow, knowing His gifts most beneficial to man, Himself calumniated, murdered, and rejected by man, and even perhaps abandoned by God. He who comes with the greatest gifts requires the greatest love not only to endure their greatest rejection, but not to lose them, and even augment them.

Henry's own death is neither reported nor presented in *Henry V*. We learn of it only *en passant* in the Epilogue, which focuses upon the bad fortune that overwhelmed the realm under Henry's infant son. However, judging from Henry's preparation on the eve of Agincourt, it was a death more like David's or Abraham's or Socrates' than wretched Falstaff's. Looking ahead to his Judge and back over his life, King Henry must have felt as confident as a mere man can. Yet there is just enough Christ present in the death of Falstaff to make us wonder how much there was in the death of Henry. Judging from his prayer to the God of Battles, Henry must hold both that there is no sin so base as cowardice and yet that fear of the God of Battles is the beginning of wisdom. Elsewhere we hear him declare that adversity urges us to "dress us fairly for our end" and hear others mourn him as "blessed of the King of Kings."[59]

To suggest then that since the advent of Christ good deaths have been hard to find would be a Machiavellian blasphemy.[60] The unrepresented death of Henry V is such a good death. There was no need to represent it. Or rather, it is represented. It consists in his whole life of the man. His whole life, from his youthful time with Falstaff, through Shrewsbury, to Agincourt, and beyond was a preparation for death. He was always prepared, and that is why, unlike most of the other histories, the title of the one devoted solely to him, is *The Life of King Henry V*. His life included, every day of it, the death that with other kings required an illuminating death scene and highlighting in the title. The death of Henry V is absent from Shakespeare's account because it is so evenly, steadily, and thoroughly conspicuous.

NOTES

[1] An earlier version of this essay appeared in *Interpretation* 8, No. 1 (January 1979): 5–29, now augmented appears with their permission here, and will appear, both fuller and properly fitted in its whole, in my *Shakespeare's Christian Prince* (University Press of America, 1991).

[2] True, this Epilogue also mentions Falstaff dying "of a sweat," but only in jest. All quotations from the text of Shakespeare's works and references to it, unless otherwise noted, are to the Penguin one-volume Shakespeare under the general editorship of Alfred Harbage, *William Shakespeare: The Complete Works* (Baltimore: Pelican Books, 1969).

[3] The speculation that Shakespeare could have made the death of Falstaff a great onstage scene comes

from Robert G. Hunter; for it, for the point about 'stone' below, and for the pleasure of first teaching Shakespeare with him I am grateful. His account of Falstaff was later published as "Shakespeare's Comic Sense as It Strikes Us Today: Falstaff and the Protestant Ethic," in *Shakespeare, Pattern of Excelling Nature,* ed. David Bevington and Jay L. Halio (University of Delaware Press, 1978), pp. 125–32; the absence of Falstaff's death from this account is as conspicuous as the author's withdrawal from Shakespeare studies is lamentable.

[4] See the Arden editor's "Introduction," section 10.

[5] *Shakespeare Restored; or, A Specimen of the Many Errors . . .* (1726; rpt. New York: Augustus Kelley, 1970), pp. 137–38.

[6] While the emendation of Theobald seems unnecessary, there is something right about it, for someone is babbling, be it Falstaff or the Hostess or both. However, Theobald's emendation has the demerit of erasing, "a table," and making the reference to the Twenty-third Psalm more obscure than the unemended text justifies. A review of the various solutions proposed to emend or construe this line is to be found in Ephim G. Fogel " 'A Table of Green Fields': A Defense of the Folio Reading," *Shakespeare Quarterly* 9 (1958): 485–92, who defends the Folio text by glossing the line as the very picture of greenness.

[7] The Penguin editor, Alfred Harbage, makes the same point in his marginal note. He puts the Hostess's mistake down to, "defective religious education." Although I understand what he means, I would put it down to just the opposite; fear of the Lord is "the beginning of wisdom" (Proverbs 9.10) and the reason why she makes just these mistakes.

[8] I have used the King James Version (1611). A check of the versions of this Psalm available to Shakespeare and familiar to his first audience does not alter the interpretation offered here.

[9] To grant that Falstaff does die a desperate death would be fatal to the view of Falstaff's character advanced by Roy Battenhouse ("Falstaff as Parodist and Perhaps Holy Fool," *PMLA* 90, No. 1 [January 1975]: 32–52.). To Battenhouse it is a good (i.e., contented) Christian death (p. 436), for it follows a good Christian life. For the life of Falstaff, Battenhouse offers this apology: his intentions were always charitable. It is part of charity to hide one's charitable intentions. Out of charity Falstaff chose the role of Fool and in that role often quoted scripture. His charitable purpose? To mock kings like Henry IV and to instruct princes like Hal. What crimes and cruelties, what vices and flaws you may find in him you must put down to mere show. When he spoke to his recruits as, "cannon fodder," it was only to make a comment on the times. When the Prince found that wine bill, it was not evidence of immoderation; Falstaff put it there on purpose. Falstaff was a reborn Christian and we can even suggest when he was reborn (p. 49). This apology is disturbing, for it asks us to accept as an excuse for a crime or a vice the plea, "I did it to mock others." From the evident truth that much of what Falstaff does and says does mock and instruct, it does not follow that he purposes all the instruction, nor that the instruction is always or even ever Christian; nor does it follow that he leads an exemplary Christian life. I believe the Falstaff would be amused by Battenhouse's ingenious apology, and that he might even hail Battenhouse as one of his imitative sons, but I cannot believe Falstaff would be amused while he was dying. Then he needed a real apology and in the face of God dared not defend his life with transparent evasions, however witty.

[10] That Falstaff died of the plague is argued, convincingly I believe, by A. A. Mendilow in, "Falstaff's Death of a Sweat," *Shakespeare Quarterly* 9 (1958): 479–83. Several points made here were the basis of my response to J. Leeds Barroll's lecture, "Shakespeare and the Black Death," at the Shakespeare in a Comparative Perspective Conference at Texas Tech (1979).

[11] Quoted from footnote 6 of Mendilow (ibid.). Only one investigator in Shakespeare's time whom I have heard of suggested that the plague, while it could not be accounted for by the four humors theory, also could not be regarded as supernatural, that it must have some natural cause, something like whatever makes mad dogs mad, but this man, Jean Fernel, made this suggestion cautiously, in a dialogue (pub. 1548); see Sir Charles Sherrington, *Man on His Nature,* second ed. (Garden City: Doubleday, 1955), Chapter One.

[12] Eric Partridge, *Shakespeare's Bawdy* (New York: E. P. Dutton, 1960), s.v. After Shakespeare, James Joyce is our greatest punster; imagine his Bloom streaming consciously: "Falstaff, fallen staff, staff of life, penis drooping, Falstaff he is dead, the Fall of that staff, Fall! Staff, Aaron's rod, magic member, man with a sturdy staff, knight with a lance, a Hotspur, Fall-lance, Falstaff, fall feudalism. Falstaff beer, fallen ad-man, fallen English major. Fall-staff, Shake-speare, trembling spear, shaking spear, threatening spear, shake off, shake hands, shake off slumber, shake the superflux, Shakespeare, quivering spear, spear of grass, all things as grass, reed, quivering reed, fear in a handful of grass, thinking reed, Shakespeare, Shakespeare, Shake-Globe, Shake-scene; Shake-speare, no Fall-staff. What's in a name? Bottomless, Bottomless dream."

[13] After I discovered this resemblance, I discovered that others had done so too (David Lowenthal, Boston College, and Laurence Berns, St. Johns College). It seems that the first scholar to report this discovery was John Robert Moore ("Shakespeare's *Henry V*," *Explicator* I [June 1943], item 61). See also *Explicator* 2, No. 3, item 19 (Dec. 1943); Katherine Koller's "Falstaff and the Art of Dying," *Modern Language Notes* 60 (1945): 383–86; Roger Lloyd's "Socrates and Falstaff," *Time and Tide* 39 (1958): 219–20; an appendix in Thomas McFarland's *Shakespeare's Pastoral Comedy* (Chapel Hill: University of North Carolina Press, 1972) subsumes the resemblance under "pastoral." How Shakespeare came to read this passage in the *Phaedo*, I do not know. A good Greek edition was available, and for those with less Greek, but more Latin, there were Latin translations. A French one was available after 1553. The reasons why one might want to find out all about that death are all over one of Shakespeare's favorite authors, Montaigne, and a specific reason is mentioned below in note 22.

[14] Quoted in the translation of Hugh Tredennick from *The Collected Dialogues of Plato*, ed. E. Hamilton and H. Cairns (Princeton: Princeton University Press, 1961), pp. 97–98. My emendations are in square brackets; many commentators think Socrates felt himself and that it was he who declared Socrates would be dead when the coldness reached his heart; the Greek permits this dispute.

[15] Aristophanes, *The Clouds;* Socrates refers to these early charges in the beginning of Plato's *Apology* 18a–e.

[16] One should compare the charges against Socrates in Plato's *Apology* (24b) with the account given in Diogenes Laertius' *Life of Socrates* (section 40). It is significant that while, for example, Falstaff is accused of being a "white bearded Satan," he is not, like Socrates, accused of impiety, of disbelieving the gods of the country and introducing new gods. That he is certainly a scoffer, however, I show in the final section of this essay.

[17] E.g., cf. *2 Henry IV*, 2.1.104ff. with *Apology* 18b.

[18] E.g., cf. *I Henry IV*, 5.1.133 and surrounding with the *Republic*, especially 619b, in the myth of Er, where it is reported that the soul of the gentleman chooses the worst and most tyrannical life despite his good habituation in his previous life. It should be noted that Falstaff never asks, What is pleasure?, the question Socrates asks on the very morning of his death. Falstaff could not have asked that question without changing his way of life.

[19] Cf. *I Henry IV*, 3.3.178 with *Symposium* 221; Montaigne contrasts the strained virtue of Cato with the natural virtue of Socrates: *"Car, en Caton, on void bien à clair que c'est une alleure tenuë bien loing au dessus des communes: aux braves exploits de sa vie, et en sa mort, on le sent tousjours monté sur ses grands chevaux. Cettuy-cy* [Socrates] *ralle à terre, et d'un pas mol et ordinaire traicte les plus utiles discours; et se conduict et à la mort et aux plus espineuses traverses que se puissent presenter au trein de la vie humaine."* (*Essais*, III, 12, end of second paragraph.)

[20] *Symposium* 220a.

[21] *Symposium* 215b and ff.

[22] From Shakespeare's single explicit reference to Socrates, we might only gather that he understands Socrates not as the founder of classical political philosophy or as the example of the philosophic life, but as henpecked husband par excellence (*Taming of the Shrew*, 1.2.69). The third connection between Shakespeare and Socrates is Hamlet's "To be or not to be ..." soliloquy; as D. G. James (*The Dream of Learning* [Oxford: Clarendon Press, 1951], pp. 56–62) has noticed, Hamlet's dilemma and much of his imagery derive from the *Apology* via Montaigne's "Of Physiognomy." About that dilemma we might say this: Socrates does not imagine a dream-filled sleep as one of the two possible states which follow death. Hamlet does. Hamlet has heard ghostly revelations; in the Ghost and the dread he inspires, Shakespeare seems to have portrayed Christianity and the problems it makes for princes, men, and growing philosophers. Where does the Ghost go on the divided line? Indeed, it is a mote to trouble the mind's eye. Meeting it makes Hamlet contemn all "your philosophy."

[23] My thoughts on these matters are to be found in my dialogue, "Looking at the Body," *Hastings Center Reports* 5, No. 2 (April 1975): 21–28.

[24] Consider the place of fornicatio simplex in Christian morality; the troubles of Claudio and Juliet in *Measure for Measure* could not be the theme of a Greek drama; the question of whether their sin should be treated as a crime would be unintelligible to those who regard it as a minor folly.

[25] *Apology* 29a.

[26] Friedrich Nietzsche, *Götzen-Dämmerung*, No. 1, "Das Problem des Sokrates": "Selbst Sokrates sagte, als er starbe: 'leben—das heisst lange krank sein: ich bin dem Heilande Asklepios einen Hahn schuldig.' Selbst Sokrates hatte es satt." Cf. *Fröhliche Wissenschaft*, No. 340 and No. 36.

[27] See Nietzsche, "Vorrede," *Jenseits von Gut und Böse;* Montaigne, *Essais* (I,1); and Machiavelli, *Prince*, Chapter XXV, final paragraph; and for further thoughts, see my dialogue, "Interpretation," in *Interpretation* 5, No. 1 (Autumn 1975): 109–30.

[28] Precisely the same distinction is known to the Gravedigger in Hamlet (5.1.120–29).

[29] For the original More, see Volume 12 of *The Complete Works of St. Thomas More, A Dialogue of Comfort* (New Haven: Yale University Press, 1976), Book I, Chapter 13, p. 42; for a modernized version, see the paperback edition, p. 44. I am grateful to Dr. Leo Strauss for the conversations in which he pointed out this passage and its connection to Socrates. See his *The City and Man* (Chicago: Rand McNally, 1964), p. 61.

[30] When a follower complains that he is being put to death unjustly, Socrates asks him whether he would prefer that it be justly, and smiles or chuckles; Xenophon, *Apology of Socrates* 28.

[31] See my "Tragical, Comical, Historical," in *The Existential Coordinates of the Human Condition: Poetic—Epic—Tragic, Analecta Husserliana*, Volume XVIII, ed. A.-T. Tymieniecka (Dordrecht: D. Reidel, 1984), pp. 379–99.

[32] *The Phenomenology of Mind*, Baillie translation (New York: Harper, 1967), pp. 229–40. Cf. Diderot, *Jacques le fataliste.*

[33] Terence, *Heauton Timorumenos* 77.

[34] From the point of view of humanism, Dostoevsky does a devilish thing when he has the Devil, who visits Ivan Karamazov, declare *"Satan sum et nihil humanum a me alienum puto."* Ivan had wanted to know how the Devil can have a rheumatism and the Devil explained, "Why not, if I sometimes assume a human form. When I do, I suffer the consequences." It would seem that Dostoevsky knew the immediate context of the line his Devil alters from Terence. No doubt his Devil knew the blasphemous resemblance between his declaration and the passion of Christ. I quote the David Magarshack translation of *The Brothers Karamazov* (Penguin Books), Vol. 2, p. 751. Five pages later the Devil quotes Descartes' *Je pense donc je suis* with approval.

[35] G. E. Bentley, *Shakespeare and Jonson: Their Reputations in the Seventeenth Century Compared* (Chicago: University of Chicago Press, 1945), pp. 119–29.

[36] It is Fluellen who makes most of the comparisons. Ronald S. Berman has taken Fluellen's hints as Shakespeare's in his article, "Shakespeare's Alexander: *Henry V*," *College English* 23, No. 7 (1961–62): 532–39.

[37] So well expressed by condemned Claudio when he speaks of losing "this sensible warm motion" (*Measure for Measure*, 3.1.120).

[38] Consider the laws; Falstaff is a mocker of the laws; like the God of Battles, he weakens the force of law in modern political regimes; however much Socrates liberates individuals from opinion (*doxa*), he does not seem to liberate them from the laws (*nomoi*); in the *Crito* he seems to teach the unconditional obedience to laws, even to laws unjustly executed.

[39] Leo Strauss, *The City and Man* (Chicago: University of Chicago Press, 1964), pp. 50–62, and Jacob Klein, *A Commentary on Plato's Meno* (Chapel Hill: North Carolina University Press, 1965), pp. 3–31.

[40] *Phaedrus* 274d–77a.

[41] If one wishes to know a man who, though wishing to make men laugh, did not intend to keep within the bounds of what men think laughable, one has only to turn to Nietzsche. More exactly, the wit of Nietzsche aims to metamorphose present man, all too human man, into a superman with laughter. One might also consider Socrates, who only laughed at the "wrong place," and laughed alone.

[42] On the way in which the entertainer is the valet of corrupt publics and a fifth wheel to good ones, see Rousseau's *Letter to M. D'Alembert on the Theatre*, trans. Allan Bloom (Ithaca: Cornell University Press, 1960), especially section IV.

[43] Though the entertainer is a far different thing from the lecturer, still one should consider the lecturer and his jokes. The joke at the beginning of the lecture sets not only the audience but the lecturer at ease. At the beginning, it takes away a bit of the solitude he has prepared in. In the course of the lecture, it may allow him to locate and judge his audience before he meets them in dialogue. This reminds us of a resemblance between Falstaff and Socrates, which we had neglected until now: neither takes money for the wit he causes in other men.

[44] Let the reader attend a banquet or smoker and, refraining from the stimulants offered and imbibed, study the jests, toasts, and speeches together with the laughter they evince and see if, at the end of the evening, he has not discovered what lies not far below these jests and toasts, and the several senses in which philosophy is needed.

[45] It was a republican regime in Florence, in which Machiavelli held office, that commissioned Michelangelo's David to stand in the Piazza della Signoria; Machiavelli seems to have this statue in mind in *Discourses*, I:11, end of the fourth paragraph, for the block of marble furnished by the city to Michelangelo was marred; see also what Machiavelli makes of David, employing the single Biblical quotation in the work, in *Discourses*, I.26, at the beginning (see Strauss, *Thoughts on Machiavelli*, s.v.). For a slightly different use of the figure of King David in conjunction with Machiavellian themes, see Marvell's poems

on Cromwell, which are well interpreted by J. A. Mazzeo in his *Renaissance and Seventeenth Century Studies* (New York: Columbia University Press, 1964), pp. 166–208.

[46] Nor is the comparison farfetched; cf. Thomas Hobbes, *Leviathan* (1651), Chapter XXI, towards the middle.

[47] Mistress Quickly's mistake of Arthur's bosom for Abraham's accords well with the spirit of Henry's political religion; Henry is much more like Arthur than Abraham. Like Henry, Arthur united the countries of the North (in a war against Rome); like Henry, he came from Wales (4.1.51), and like Henry, he failed to perpetuate his kingdom.

[48] Richmond Noble, *Shakespeare's Biblical Knowledge* (New York: Macmillan, 1935), p. 81.

[49] The speeches of Abraham Lincoln, who spoke publicly of political religion ("Speech to the Young Men's Lyceum"), would seem to occupy this place in the public mind of the United States of America.

[50] I quote *The Prince* in the very exact Leo Paul S. de Alvarez translation (1980; rpt. Cleveland: Waveland Press, 1989). N.B. the knife Machiavelli gratuitously gives David is meant to remind us of the knife Cesare Borgia 'gave' Captain Remirro de Orco. Trusting in himself and, as he says to Goliath, in the Lord, David would surely reject such 'arms of another' as Machiavelli recommends.

[51] Here is the place to mention the relation of Falstaff to Oldcastle. Oldcastle, we know, died a martyr. Up until *Henry V* the wit of Falstaff mocks the morality of those Christians who might die martyrs. If honor is a word not worth dying for, is not, "Christ," also a word? No wonder the living descendants of Oldcastle objected to Falstaff's earlier name. But in *Henry V* it turns out that the man who mocks the religion of the martyr does not disbelieve in the God Oldcastle died for. Like many a Christian martyr, he dies with, "God, God, God," on his trembling lips.

[52] *Iliad* 18.82: *ton apōlesa*.

[53] Hektor, *Iliad* 22.

[54] See *The Psalms*, Hebrew text and English translation with commentary by A. Cohen (London: Soncino Press, 1945), s.v. Here the Geneva translation, the one best known to Shakespeare and his audience, is more faithful; it has "a long season."

[55] All the commentators I have seen on this phrase, rare in Shakespeare, say the Prince means to honor Falstaff's corpse by embalming it, since disemboweling is the first step in that process. I wonder. It is also the second step, after hanging and before quartering, in the dishonoring treatment English law prescribes for traitors. (Dr. Johnson notes this in discussing Richmond's mention of "embowell'd" at 5.2.10 of *Richard III* in his edition.) If Henry does mean to so dishonor Falstaff, then his later rejection of Falstaff should be no surprise. One other truth should be mentioned here: In Foxe's *Book of Martyrs*, Oldcastle, for whom Falstaff was at first named, is hanged and then burned while hanging, which shows, says Foxe, that he was not given the execution of a traitor, burning alone being for heretics, and hanging, drawing (disemboweling), and quartering being for traitors. Shakespeare seems to have changed the rejected companion of Henry V from heretic/traitor, burned and hanged, to traitor only. His Henry would seem to be a man who laments the loss of a dear companion, but intends to use or abuse his corpse to make a show of his own transformation. He will honor Hotspur's corpse and dishonor Falstaff's, but not because he cares a whit for corpses, which are indifferently food for worms.

[56] "Can honor set a leg?" Falstaff asked in *1 Henry IV* (5.1). What Jefferson wrote on limited government, perhaps echoing Falstaff's question, brings out its consequence for faith: "The legitimate powers of government extend to such acts only as are injurious to others. But it does me no injury for my neighbor to say there are twenty gods, or no God. It neither picks my pocket nor breaks my leg." *Notes on Virginia*, Query XVII.

[57] The same subtle question is advanced for thought by Shakespeare in *Romeo and Juliet*, where the natural magic of Friar Laurence allows him to simulate the death of Juliet for about the same number of hours it would have taken to simulate Christ's.

[58] Consider how Conrad agrees, in "The Secret Sharer," where the immature Captain learns the secret of his sharer, that to save a ship a captain by natural right may have to kill, and the further secret that this knowledge must be kept secret, even by getting rid of the man who has shared it with you. If it is naturally right to kill at sea in a storm to save the ship, it is, nonetheless, naturally right for conventional right on shore to try and then hang the killer.

[59] *Henry V*, 4.1.10; *1 Henry VI*, 1.1.28.

[60] Consider *Hamlet*, 3.1.56–88, and *The Tempest*, 1.1.49. By never showing how the Prince should prepare for bed, Machiavelli shows how he should consider death. His Prince will ignore Christian teaching and, agreeing with Caesar and Montaigne, deed a sudden death better than a prepared one. In doing so, he would seem to ignore Socrates—and Shakespeare as well.

Leo Salingar

FALSTAFF AND THE
LIFE OF SHADOWS

THESEUS: The best in this kind are but shadows; and the worst are no worse,
    if imagination amend them.
HIPPOLYTA: It must be your imagination then, and not theirs.
                       —*A Midsummer Night's Dream*

What is it that makes us laugh about Falstaff? This is perhaps a naïve, unanswerable question. In his magisterial lecture on 'The Rejection of Falstaff', Bradley set a part of it, the query why we laugh *at* the fat knight, judiciously aside. Nevertheless, it is still tempting to assail the indefinable and, throwing caution to the winds, to try to sprinkle salt on the tail of that particularly large but paradoxically lively bird, even at the risk of losing, along with the caution, the salt. It is particularly tempting if we want to examine the general nature of comedy and—a related but distinct set of questions—the place Falstaff occupies in the two parts of *Henry IV*.

Some of the unavoidable niggles that beset this sort of inquiry are that we do not all, as readers, laugh at the same things or even twice at the same place; that we are much more prone to laugh in company than alone; and that, even in the theatre, our laughter depends to some extent on accidents of the occasion. Further, the impulse to laugh, when studying Shakespeare, is to some extent lumbered with the ponderous gear of annotations. And, more generally, a perfect, utopian theory of laughter would take care of the difference between the occasions when we laugh outright and the occasions when we merely feel an inclination to laugh. But the present essay—caution having been disregarded—cannot pause over such niceties (just as it will only be concerned with the canonical or *echt* Falstaff, as the two historical plays body him forth).

Perhaps the best starting-place is Bergson's theory of laughter, insufficient though it is. According to Bergson, then, we laugh when we perceive 'something mechanical encrusted on something living', the physical encroaching upon the sphere of mental freedom, a human being behaving like a physical object; at bottom, our laughter is prompted by *raideur* rather than *laideur*, by 'the unsprightly' rather than 'the unsightly'.[1] In comedy, it is directed against the personage who has sunk his individuality in the routines of a social or professional or temperamental type, who has forfeited his waking spontaneity to some automatism of behaviour resembling

From *Dramatic Form in Shakespeare and the Jacobeans* (Cambridge: Cambridge University Press, 1986), pp. 32–52. First published in *Shakespearean Comedy,* edited by Maurice Charney (New York: New York: New York Literary Forum, 1980), pp. 185–205.

absentmindedness. And, since mechanical thought or behaviour, though necessary within limits, is ultimately hostile to social evolution, or the *élan vital*, the underlying function of comedy is to marshal our collective and corrective laughter against such obstacles to freedom. This theory applies well to a great deal in Molière, and to Labiche, Bergson's second choice for purposes of illustration; equally, it could apply almost intact to the superbly intricate contraptions for laughter devised by Bergson's contemporary, Georges Feydeau.

However, Bergson's purview is limited by assumptions traditional with criticism, especially in France, such as the assumption that comedy and laughter are very nearly the same thing. Even within those limits, he pays no attention to those characters who make us laugh *with* them and not at them. And, as Albert Thibaudet noted in his study of Bergson, the philosopher's analysis of stage comedy, even in Molière, omits the indispensable factor of mobility: 'a comedy is a movement, I don't mean necessarily an action'.[2] For Thibaudet, this is a correlative to the subliminal movement we experience inwardly when responding to any work of art. However, by the same token, it is also an expression of Bergsonian *élan*. And perhaps one can carry this observation a step further and save the appearances for Bergson's theory of the comic by supposing that those stage characters who make us laugh intentionally, and not inadvertently, have become, at least for the time being, delegates for the author by anticipating some threatened incursion of the mechanical upon the vital and triumphantly reversing the flow. If so, they represent the upsurge of spontaneity over automatism, a process more fundamental to comedy than any enforcement of social correction. This line of reasoning may account also for those stimuli to laughter that other theorists have emphasized, though they are only marginal from Bergson's point of view, such as the laughter due to surprise or incongruity or to release from the breaking of a taboo. Although in cases like those our laughter may not have been prompted by 'something mechanical encrusted on something living', it could still be argued that the cause of it was the mental jolt of expecting to see a logical or a moral rule at work but finding instead that the mechanism of the rule had been overcome. This still has less to do with social solidarity than with the subconscious pleasure of release. But in the theatre there is surely also a further level of interplay on some such lines between the mechanical and the vital. Once the train of laughter has been set going, we seem to store up a reserve for extra additional laughter precisely in our alerted uncertainty as to when next and which way the cat is going to jump.

Falstaff is surely the grand example of such multiplicity, or deep duplicity, in the causes of laughter. 'The brain of this foolish-compounded clay, man', he can fairly claim, 'is not able to invent any thing that intends to laughter more than I invent or is invented on me: I am not only witty in myself, but the cause that wit is in other men' (*2 Henry IV*, I. ii. 7–10). When Bradley and like-minded critics gloss over the causes why others laugh *at* Falstaff, it must be because they seem so obvious— 'gross as a mountain'—and not because they are unfathomable. First, of course, his fatness, a classic instance of what Aristotle would call the ludicrous arising from a defect that is not destructive or what Bergson would call the physical encroaching upon the mental (since it is represented as a consequence of his chosen way of life). Then his drinking, his cowardice (or, if you prefer, his 'instinct' not to be heroic), his apparently compulsive lying. Poins and the Prince foresee very well what mechanisms they will spring in him when they plan their 'jest' at Gad's Hill. And Shakespeare has made him a perpetual comic butt, because, as Harry Levin has pointed out, he has staged him as a walking paradox, a Renaissance knight without a horse; 'uncolted' (I Henry IV, II, ii. 39) by the Prince, and commissioned with nothing better for the war than 'a charge of foot'.[3]

On the other hand, when Poins anticipates 'the incomprehensible' (the illimitable) 'lies that this same fat rogue will tell', he hints at just the opposite side of Falstaff, his inventiveness, his inexhaustible resilience, his predictable unpredictability. These have to do with the reasons why we laugh *with* him. He is always quick at changing an awkward subject. And his lies are foxy evasions, not empty fantasies like the boasts of Baron Munchausen or the daydreams of Walter Mitty. They match the positive resourcefulness of his wit, his ability to play with words and, beyond that, to disconnect and recombine the accepted rules of moral judgement. In thought as in act, he is the arch-opponent of regularity: 'Give you a reason on compulsion? if reasons were as plentiful as blackberries, I would give no man a reason upon compulsion, I.' We laugh, one may suggest, at sallies like this both because he is cornered and knows he is cornered and because he can nevertheless trump up something almost indistinguishable from a valid reply, unexpected and, in the fullest sense, diverting. We laugh because he is caught out, because just the same he has been too quick for us, and further (I believe) because we are not sure which of these thoughts is uppermost. This kind of uncertainty is fundamental in comic tradition.

Falstaff's puns form one of his ways of circumventing mechanisms of thought, by taking advantage of what are possibly no more than accidental associations of ideas in language. He can treat 'reasons' like 'blackberries', for instance because the word was pronounced *raisins*; thereby evading an awkward truth. Or he can pun spontaneously, from high spirits, as when, later in the same tavern scene, he enjoins his companions to 'clap to the doors! Watch tonight, pray to-morrow' (I Henry IV, II. iv. 276–7)—out of sheer relief on learning that the stolen money he thought he had been filched of could be used for his benefit after all. His Biblical 'Watch and pray' not merely pretends to sanctify their proposed drinking-bout (or *watch*), but also recalls his fellow-thieves to their predatory highway code, thus covertly reinstating his own manliness at the same time.[4]

He is similarly inventive in the vocabulary of aggression, protestation, belittlement and abuse. If the others will not credit his valour on Gad's Hill, he is 'a shotten herring' or 'a bunch of radish'. Hal, disbelieving him, becomes 'you starveling . . . you dried neat's tongue, you bull's pizzle, you stock-fish'. All this Carnival, or Billingsgate, raillery is, of course, part of the game that he shares with the Prince. In their first scene together, when Hal has disobligingly knocked down his attempts to find expressions for his alleged 'melancholy', Falstaff retorts, 'Thou hast the most unsa-

voury similes and art indeed the most comparative, rascalliest, sweet young prince.'
Set point to the 'fat-witted' knight; but it seems clear enough why the Prince should
enjoy his company.

The game they play calls for stylistic agility (for the copiousness in words the
Elizabethans admired and for skill in calculated breaches of literary decorum)
besides licensing a free-for-all of mock aggression. It was fashionable in the 1590s
and was related to the new literary conception of wit that was then emerging.
Nashe, for example, relishes what he calls the 'sport' of railing; after a two-page
effusion over a literary enemy, he characteristically adds,

> Redeo ad vos, mei auditores [back to you, listeners]: have I not an indifferent
> pretty vein in spur-galling an ass? If you knew how extemporal it were at this
> instant, and with what haste it is writ, you would say so. But I would not have
> you think that all this that is set down here is in good earnest, for then you go
> by St Giles the wrong way to Westminster; but only to show how for a need
> I could rail if I were thoroughly fired.[5]

Shakespeare's courtly wits, as in Love's Labour's Lost, indulge themselves in a similar
vein. But it is especially appropriate to a Bohemian or adventurer of the pen like
Nashe; indeed, it becomes Nashe's principal stock-in-trade, as he bawls his aca-
demically certified wares in the market-place. And it is peculiarly appropriate to
Falstaff's position as a gently-bred adventurer who compensates through language
for deficiencies in the more solid advantages due to his rank. In language, Falstaff is
a lord. He commands a ruffianly composure of speech, a leisured pace permitting
lightning thrusts, and a compendious range of tone including masterful coarseness.
It is the coarseness that Hotspur wants to hear from Lady Percy when she swears
(I Henry IV, III. i. 247–56). It distinguishes Falstaff completely from a mere 'swaggerer' of the day and ranter of playhouse tags like Pistol; style is his real, and his only
real, ground of equality with the Prince. Yet his speech is repeatedly ambiguous in
tone, corresponding to the indeterminateness of his social position. As William
Empson has put it, 'Falstaff is the first major joke by the English against their class
system; he is a picture of how badly you can behave, and still get away with it, if you
are a gentleman—a mere common rogue would not have been nearly so funny.'[6]

Whether his tone for the moment is aggressive or not, Falstaff habitually
asserts himself by defeating expectation. His very first appearance must have come
as a surprise to the Elizabethans; they could have anticipated a wild gallant or a
rumbustious clown to accompany Hal on to the stage, but not a corpulent, benevolent, apparently deliberative greyhead. On his opening words, noncommittal in
tone ('Now, Hal, what time of day is it, lad?'), the Prince pounces with the imputation that his proper qualities are gluttony and sloth, which are much what stage
tradition, if not historical legend, would attach to such a personage:

> Thou art so fat-witted with drinking of old sack, and unbuttoning thee after
> supper, and sleeping upon benches after noon, that thou hast forgotten to

demand that truly which thou wouldest truly know. What a devil hast thou to do with the time of the day?

But Falstaff at once shows that he has, on the contrary, a concern of sorts with the passage of time, by asking a series of questions about the future, in the course of which, far from admitting to sloth or gluttony, he fleetingly adopts the voices of manly 'resolution', 'melancholy' solicitation, and even sorrowful 'amendment of life' (I. ii. 102). He may resemble Glutton or Sloth—or alternatively, Riot—but in himself, his manner implies, he is not to be identified with any of them (any more than Jaques's melancholy is the scholar's or the musician's or the courtier's, 'but it is a melancholy of mine own, compounded of many simples, extracted from many objects').

And Falstaff's personality seems always in movement, going against the stream of opinion. He repeatedly advances the idea of his own worth, not simply by bragging when occasion favours, but by jocular assertion and, especially in his early scenes, by insinuating that the standards he could be criticised by, the yardsticks that society commonly applies to worthiness, are habitually misconceived or misplaced. He does not expect his assertions to be taken 'in good earnest' any more (or any less) than Nashe; and, at least before the battle scenes, he does not single out any one of society's values for direct criticism (which might seem to fix him in the vulnerable position of a malcontent or satirist). Instead, he works through parody and calculated irrelevance, or the dissociation of received ideas. His counter-attack on public values is mobile and indirect, as, in the opening dialogue, when he responds to the Prince's sarcasm by dignifying (or affecting to dignify?) his occupation as a thief:

> Indeed you come near me now, Hal, for we that take purses go by the moon and the seven stars, and not by Phoebus, he, 'that wand'ring knight so fair' [which disposes of Hal's question about 'the time of the day']. And I prithee, sweet wag, when thou art a king . . . let not us that are squires of the night's body be call'd thieves of the day's beauty. Let us be Diana's foresters, gentlemen of the shade, minions of the moon, and let men say we be men of good government, being govern'd, as the sea is, by our noble and chaste mistress the moon, under whose countenance we steal.

Hearing this, an Elizabethan audience must have been so sidetracked, or delighted, by the pell-mell parodies of euphuism, balladry, popular romance, and even of the worship of Cynthia, mistress of the sea, herself, that they could not muster any of their proper indignation at the naked proposal Falstaff is putting forward or at his hint that it is only fancy names, arbitrary titles, that distinguish the honest citizen from the thief (as Gadshill supportively observes a few scenes later, ' "homo" is a common name to all men' [II. i. 95]).

Whatever else Falstaff may be set to do in *Henry IV*, he has begun with the ancient comic operation of turning the world upside-down. And soon he returns to this even more insidiously. After the Prince has rebuffed him with reminders about the gallows and has teased him with the promise of a hangman's job, instead of the momentarily hoped-for office of a judge, Falstaff shifts his key to the Biblical:

> But, Hal, I prithee trouble me no more with vanity; I would to God thou and I knew where a commodity of good names were to be bought;

and, as if mounting the pulpit:

> An old lord of the Council rated me the other day in the street about you, sir, but I mark'd him not, and yet he talk'd very wisely, but I regarded him not, and yet he talk'd wisely, and in the street too.   (*I Henry IV*, I. ii. 81–7)

Part of Falstaff's ploy here is to pretend, in all generosity, that he has been receiving blame because of Hal and not the other way about. And in the midst of his sermonising he can suddenly swerve into a good, downright tavernly oath: 'I'll be damn'd for never a king's son is Christendom' (I. ii. 97). But as soon as Hal, taking his cue from this, taunts him with a reminder about taking purses, Falstaff reverts to his Biblical strain: 'Why, Hal, 'tis my vocation, Hal, 'tis no sin for a man to labour in his vocation' (I. ii. 104–5). Critics, noting Falstaff's very frequent allusions to the Bible (particularly the book of Proverbs and the parable of the Prodigal Son), are fond of explaining that he is ridiculing the language of Puritanism; but it was equally the language of the Book of Homilies and the established Church.[7] As far as parody goes, his subversiveness is comprehensive.

Yet he is not simply a stage jester any more than he is simply a rogue. None of the roles that critics or other characters on the stage attribute to him defines him adequately as a character or as a figure in the play. He is not, for instance, a Morality-play Vice, however he may be compared to such. Apart from anything else, it makes nonsense of his relations with Hal to think of him as a personification of the Prince's human proneness to sin, or to speak as if he ever tempts the Prince successfully in the course of the play or gains any ascendancy over his will. He is not a traditional braggart soldier, if only because he is far too intelligent. He is not exactly a Lord of Misrule; if he can be said to preside over revels in Eastcheap, it is more in our imagination than in the view of his company as a whole. Nor is he exactly a trickster, or ironic buffoon, in the line of classical comedy, in spite of his aptitude for turning the world upside-down. He neither pursues any ingenious intrigue in the manner of New Comedy (though he swindles Mistress Quickly and Shallow) nor consistently entertains any world-changing fantasy like a hero from Aristophanes. He is too deeply enmeshed in common reality to imagine that he can change the world, and he takes his adventures as they come. He is constantly improvising, assuming a role. In the extemporised play scene that marks the highest point of his concord with Hal, he revels in parodying an actor; but through all his assumed voices we can hear a voice of his own, coming out most clearly perhaps in soliloquies—of which he has more than any other speaker in the play. It seems no accident that he became, in his own name, a legendary figure, as quickly and as lastingly as Hamlet. We seem to be in the presence of a richly complex personality, with a reserve of self-awareness underneath all his clowning.

In Maurice Morgann's apologia for Falstaff, there is a striking footnote where Morgann outlines the principles that, in his view, require a critic of Shakespeare to explain the characters of Shakespeare's people 'from those parts of the composition which are *inferred* only, and not distinctly shewn', and 'to account for their conduct from the *whole* of character, from general principles, from latent motives, and from polities not avowed'.[8] The 'historic' or biographical method of interpretation that Morgann erected upon this insight has been thoroughly, perhaps too thoroughly, exploded. And in Falstaff's case, such apparently solid biographical facts as we are given—that as a boy he had been 'page to Thomas Mowbray, Duke of Norfolk' and had known John of Gaunt—are not disclosed until the second half of the second play (*2 Henry IV*, III, ii. 25–6, 324). Nevertheless, one can hardly deny that Morgann brought out something vital about the *impression* (to use his own term) that Shakespeare gives us about Falstaff and gives us from the outset. Only, Shakespeare's methods were not biographical in anything like the way that (for example) Ibsen's methods could be so described. One of the means that Shakespeare uses is to suggest through the dialogue that a particular role will fit Falstaff or that he will display a particular disposition of mind, and then almost at once to make the character belie it. As Falstaff speaks, we perceive that the characteristics we have been led to expect of him are incorrect or incomplete or shadowy approximations at best. It quickly turns out that Hal's first description of him as Sloth and Gluttony is no more than a caricature. When he has behaved like a braggart soldier, he can switch to the ironic buffoon. When he is patently and professedly acting ('as like one of these harlotry players as ever I see!', says the Hostess [*I Henry IV*, II. iv. 395–6]), it turns out that he is pleading his own cause. He is reputed to be misleading the Prince, but Falstaff himself says just the opposite, and in any case we never see him do it.

Watching or reading the play, of course, we do not sift such conflicting bits of evidence and work out a decisive verdict that would justify a jury in a court of law. There is nothing like the question whether Hal is really the irresponsible his father and the others suppose him to be, a question Shakespeare takes care to set at rest very soon. But with Falstaff, allegations and half-truths are allowed to remain at the back of our minds, without being clearly dispelled. We neither confirm nor reject them completely but are allowed and even prompted to imagine that they may be true, but only to limited facets of his character, or true to something in his unseen conduct off-stage. These half-defined approximations are like shadows in a picture that throw the figure into relief. To defeat our expectations, then, is part of Falstaff's comic tactics, and to keep us uncertain about the essential Falstaff is part of Shakespeare's strategy as a comic playwright. But further, Shakespeare has given Falstaff hints of an inner consciousness, at variance with his outward roles, that go some way towards justifying Morgann's search for 'latent motives' and 'policies not avowed'.

Critics have been reluctant to consider that Falstaff has anything like a conscience or any doubts about himself. Hazlitt praises his 'absolute self-possession' and 'self-complacency',[9] and Bradley insists that we laugh *with* Falstaff precisely because he is so 'happy and entirely at his ease' in 'his humorous superiority to everything serious, and the freedom of soul enjoyed in it'.[10] And in W. H. Auden's view, 'time does not exist' for Falstaff (but then Auden holds that the essential man belongs to *opera buffa,* and is out of place in *Henry IV).*[11] However, Falstaff (a 'proud Jack' to the tavern-drawers, according to Hal [*I Henry IV,* II. iv. 11]) is not remarkable for *bonhomie*; and he never expresses himself as cheerful or satisfied for long. On the contrary, his favourite terms of reference for his favourite subject, himself, imply, if they are taken in earnest, a sense of injury and regret for neglected valour, lost innocence, and either material or spiritual insecurity. His first speeches are questions about the future, which we are given no reason to think are totally flippant. If he can loudly contradict his years in the heat of the robbery scene ('What, ye knaves, young men must live' [II. ii. 90–1]), his next scene shows him affectedly brooding over them: 'There lives not three good men unhang'd in England, and one of them is far and grows old' (II. iv. 30–2). This cadence swerves, of course, into ludicrous self-mockery—'I would I were a weaver, I could sing psalms, or anything'—and this whole speech is a typical mock diatribe or mock complaint, in which Falstaff's claims of 'manhood' and self-righteousness are incongruous with one another and doubly incongruous in the light of his behaviour.

Still, these are his two most frequent themes, with particular emphasis on the theme of religion. 'Before I knew thee, Hal', he has affirmed, 'I knew nothing, and now am I, if a man should speak truly, little better than one of the wicked' (I. ii. 92–5). And later, with no one more appreciative than Bardolph to hear him:

> Well, I'll repent, and that suddenly, while I am in some liking ... And I have not forgotten what the inside of a church is made of, I am a peppercorn, a brewer's horse. The inside of a church! Company, villainous company, hath been the spoil of me.[12]

Naturally, each of these outbursts of elderly grumbling, sorrowful grievance, or rueful contrition on the part of 'Monsieur Remorse', as Poins calls him, strikes us as yet another of Falstaff's jokes. And whenever he alludes to repentance, he quickly veers away from it. Nevertheless, persistent jokes on the same topic tell us something about what weighs on a man's mind; it seems as if Falstaff were one of those fat men in whom a thin man is struggling to get out. Without probing into 'latent motives', Shakespeare has portrayed in him, not 'absolute self-possession', but the condition of mind of a man of intellectual power, wounded in his self-esteem and conscience, who cannot bring himself to do anything about it, but finds an escape from his self-image in joking. Far from expressing 'self-complacency' or complete 'freedom of soul', his 'humorous superiority to everything serious', if it exists, seems to be gained at the cost of self-mockery—which mocks the world as well, in order to redress the balance. But without the potential, camouflaged seriousness in his jokes (together with the background of seriousness in the political action in the play), many of them would lose their force and point.

To return to his first scene for an example:

> But, Hal, I prithee trouble me no more with vanity; I would to God thou
> and I knew where a commodity of good names were to be bought . . .
> (I. ii. 81–3)

The word *vanity*, which initiates Falstaff's diversion to Biblical parody, is not simply
a pretended rebuke to Hal's 'unsavoury similes' but also an oblique acknowledge-
ment of the seriousness running through their previous talk, particularly by way of
Hal's references to hanging. And the irony about 'good names' (loaded with the
word *commodity*, which usually has a smack of skulduggery about it in
Shakespeare)[13] would lose half its dramatic point if it were no more than a
capricious quip or satiric side-thrust against the established order. There is the
second irony that Falstaff is pretending to be in earnest, while hinting to the Prince,
without openly admitting, that on another level he is seriously engaged as well. That
the two ironies should work against one another both contributes to the continuity
of Falstaff's part in the play and adds to the store of laughter from uncertainty in
the minds of the audience.

By way of contrast, consider the tone Shakespeare was to give to an ironist
of a different stamp, Iago:

> Good name in man and woman, dear my lord,
> Is the immediate jewel of their souls.
> Who steals my purse steals trash; 'tis something, nothing . . .
> (*Othello*, III. iii. 155–7)

These are the sententious accents of hypocrisy. Iago is quite indifferent to the
maxim he is manipulating, and must be felt to be indifferent so that we can
concentrate on the effect of his words upon Othello; whereas Falstaff knows very
well that he is not really pulling the wool over the eyes of the Prince, but he is
personally, if covertly, involved in what he says.

Once or twice in *Part I* this concern shows more directly. When Falstaff has
to hide from the sheriff, Hal tells the others, 'Now, my masters, for a true face and
good conscience' (IV. iv. 501–2) while Falstaff exists with an aside—'Both which I
have had, but their date is out, and therefore I'll hide me.' And as he approaches
the battlefield, he is given his second soliloquy. Since he comes on here in the
contemporary guise of a fraudulent recruiting officer and since this is the first time
he has gained any profit in the course of the play, we should expect to find him in
a mood of malicious glee if he were simply a conventional stage rogue or Morality
Vice. But instead, he is unexpectedly 'ashamed':

> If I be not asham'd of my soldiers, I am a sous'd gurnet. I have misus'd the King's
> press damnably . . . No eye hath seen such scarecrows. I'll not march through
> Coventry with them, that's flat . . .   (IV. ii. 11–13, 38–9)

He shrugs off his mood almost at once:

> There's not a shirt and a half in all my company ... But that's all one, they'll find linen enough on every hedge.

We are very nearly back to the atmosphere of Eastcheap and Gad's Hill. All the same, the tone of genuine surprise, a novel tone in Falstaff's voice, shows that there has been a progression in his part. The war becomes a testing experience for Falstaff as, on a very different scale, it becomes a testing experience for Hal. It imparts a continuous movement to Falstaff's share in the play, from his early, half-comic protest to Hal—'I must give over this life, and I will give it over' (I. ii. 95–6)—to the slyly conditional resolution or prediction in his last soliloquy, which is also his closing speech:

> If I do grow great, I'll grow less, for I'll purge [*repent*] and leave sack, and live cleanly as a nobleman should do.   (V. iv. 163–5)

From the beginning to end in *Part I*, Falstaff is engaged with the passage of time, with concern about the future.

The theme of time is crucial to Shakespeare's presentation of what Edward Hall had described as 'The Unquiet Time of King Henry IV'. The guiding thought in the over plot of Part I is the thought of 'redeeming time', with implications at once religious,[14] financial, chivalric and political. In financial terms, it branches out by way of talk about ransom and theft, auditing, debt, and repayment, to return, as it were, to the main line of the action by way of Hal's determination to 'pay the debt I never promised, / ... Redeeming time when men think least I will' (I. ii. 209, 217). In the opening scene, though he does not use the word, Henry IV dwells on the thought of the Redeemer. Shakespeare has antedated his project to lead a crusade, treating it as Henry's intended means of absolving England from civil war and, by inference, absolving himself from his guilt as an usurper.[15] Hotspur, eager to 'redeem' 'drowned honour' (I. iii. 205), tells his father and uncle that 'yet time serves wherein you may redeem / Your banish'd honours' (I. iii. 180–1)—by changing allegiance for a second time in rebellion.[16] On his side, Hal promises to 'redeem' his reputation 'on Percy's head' and his father confirms that he has 'redeem'd ... lost opinion' in the battle (III. ii. 132, V. iv. 48). For the leading political actors, 'time serves', not to achieve honour, like knights-errant, but to redeem the honour they have already lost, or appear to have lost.

With his ignoble ambition to find out 'where a commodity of good names were to be bought' Falstaff is a parody of this political world. In Hal's company he is like a grotesque father-substitute, and he echoes the King in his grumbles over time mis-spent. His lawlessness and braggartism throw light on Hotspur. Above all, Falstaff is a man in a false position, just as the King, Hotspur, and Hal are all, in their different ways, men in false positions. But Falstaff, of course, has the saving grace of humour. He has an inclusive, if usually ironic, self-awareness that men like Henry IV and Hotspur cannot afford, though some of it seems to have rubbed off on to Hal. This is the obverse of his comic 'remorse'; not a 'superiority to everything serious' or simply an addiction to the pleasures of the flesh, but a warm belief in the immediacy and, in the end, authenticity, of his personal existence. 'Banish plump Jack, and banish all the world', he exclaims to Hal, as their improvised play-acting breaks down in a moment of truth; and then, as he prepares to hide from the sheriff, 'Dost thou hear, Hal? Never call a true piece of gold a counterfeit' (II. iv. 491–2). This cryptic admonition takes on fuller significance later, in the battle scenes. Falstaff's development there, in close proximity to the political actors, is far from one-sided. His cynical betrayal of his troop of 'ragamuffins' (V. iii. 36) matches Worcester's double dealing. His low-minded 'discretion' is pitched against Hotspur's high-minded but futile 'valour'. The conclusion to his famous 'catechism', that 'Honour is a mere scutcheon' (V. i. 140), cannot efface the resplendent heroism that Shakespearean gives the Prince, though it still leaves the purely chivalric motives in war and politics open to question.

But at the same time, as at the beginning of the play, the dramatist sets Falstaff in relation to the King, by his arrangement of the kaleidoscopic battle episodes. Taking hint from Holinshed's statement that at Shrewsbury there were several knights' apparelled in the king's suit and clothing' (but reducing the chronicler's emphasis on the King's 'high manhood'),[17] Shakespeare shows two episodes in which Douglas is engaged with the 'likeness' or the 'shadows' or the 'counterfeit' of the King. In the first (V. iii. 1–29) Douglas kills Sir Walter Blunt, as he says he has already killed Lord Stafford, believing him to be the King himself, until Hotspur undeceives him ('The King hath many marching in his coats'). In the second (V. iv. 25–38), meeting the King in person, he can hardly believe that Henry is not 'another counterfeit'. Hal drives Douglas off. Then, while Hal encounters Hotspur in resonantly epic style, in the action to which the whole course of the play has pointed, Douglas re-enters briefly and, in dumb show, apparently kills Falstaff.

But as soon as Falstaff has been left alone on the stage, he jumps up again, undercutting the lofty tones of the champions' verse in his savoury prose:

> 'Sblood, 'twas time to counterfeit, or that hot termagant Scot had paid me scot and lot too. Counterfeit? I lie, I am no counterfeit. To die is to be a counterfeit, for he is but the counterfeit of a man who hath not the life of a man; but to counterfeit dying, when a man thereby liveth, is to be no counterfeit, but the true and perfect image of life indeed ...   (V. iv. 113–19)

In this folk-play-style sham resurrection, and in his farcical sham killing of Hotspur immediately afterwards, Falstaff counteracts the high talk of politics and war. Courage in battle has been shown as a reality in the play, and the need for royal authority has been vindicated. But the political scenes have revealed expedience, double dealing, and even a kind of inward privation, not because Henry IV has been shown as a downright Machiavellian like Richard III, but because his rule has been established on false foundations and because the forward drives of conflicting political interests have generated their own ruthless momentum. Falstaff's counterfeiting here revives basic human impulses which the affairs of state would have thwarted or excluded.

*   *   *

At Shrewsbury, Henry has safeguarded his life by the employment of 'shad-ows'. In another sense also, Shakespeare has extensively used 'shadows' in both parts of the play to give life and imagined reality to the world in which Henry and Falstaff belong. History could be said to require that the action should shift across the country between north and south and that the main actors should refer to characters and events that are not shown on the stage. But in *Henry IV* Shake-speare has taken particular pains, more I think than in any other of his plays, to go beyond the strict requirements of dramatising history and conjure up the thought of England as a country and, even more strikingly, to conjure up images of indi-viduals off-stage, known to the speakers in the play though unrecorded by the chroniclers.

What is at stake in the Percys' rebellion is the territory of England—'this soil', as Henry calls it in his opening lines. Shakespeare imagines this, in its continuity and specific variety, as no other poet before him had done. In the first scene of *Part I*, for instance, we hear of 'stronds' and 'fields' and 'acres', of Herefordshire and Windsor, and all 'the variation of each soil / Betwixt that Holmedon and this seat of ours'. Later, in the scene between Hotspur, Mortimer and Glendower, a map is an essential property. And when Hotspur falls, Hal reflects that

> When that this body did contain a spirit,
> A kingdom for it was too small a bound,
> But now two paces of the vilest earth
> Is room enough. This earth that bears thee dead
> Bears not alive so stout a gentleman.   (V. iv. 89–93)

Meanwhile, we have heard, for instance, of 'Severn's sedgy bank' and of Berkeley Castle (the name Hotspur cannot remember [I. iii. 98, 242–9]), of Moorditch and the Wild of Kent and Falstaff's route through Coventry. And in *Part 2*, to say nothing of Falstaff's boasted acquaintance with 'all Europe' (II. ii. 134), we hear of Northumberland's 'worm-eaten hold of ragged stone' at Warkworth (Induction, 35), of Oxford and Stamford fair, and particularly of localities in or near London— Eastcheap, the St Alban's road, Clement's Inn, Mile-End Green, Turnbull Street, Windsor, the Jerusalem chamber, the Fleet. Both parts are busy with the images of messengers, especially horsemen, hurrying with instructions or news or rushing to or from a battlefield. And each virtually begins with a striking image of this sort, of Sir Walter Blunt 'new lighted' (*I Henry IV*, I. i. 63) after his long ride from Holme-don or of the unnamed gentleman met by Northumberland's servant, Travers, 'spurring hard' and 'almost forespent with speed' on his 'bloodied horse', who had paused only to ask the road to Chester and then 'seem'd in running to devour the way' (*2 Henry IV*, I. i. 36, 37, 38, 47) in his headlong flight from Shrewsbury. Amid all this evocation of England's place-names and roads and 'uneven ground' (*I Henry IV*, II. ii. 25) the earthy and earthbound figure of Falstaff seems solidly congenial; he 'lards the lean earth as he walks along' (II. ii. 109).

Even closer to the sense of animated reality in both parts of the play are the allusive sketches of non-historical characters whom we hear of though never see.

In *Part 1*, they range from the 'old lord of the Council' who (allegedly) had 'rated' Falstaff about Hal 'the other day in the street' (I. ii. 83–4) by way of Hotspur's acid sketch of the 'popingay' who had 'so pest'red' him after the fighting at Holmedon (the 'certain lord' whose 'chin new reap'd/Show'd like a stubble-land at harvest-home'—men and country are thought of together [I. iii. 33–5]), on to the 'mad fellow' by the wayside who had taunted Falstaff about his troop of 'totter'd prodigals', and to the prodigals' victim, 'the red-nose innkeeper of Daventry' (IV. ii. 36, 34, 46–7). These marginal, off-stage figures, shadowlike but with separate lives of their own, intensify our sense of varied life in the stage characters themselves. They supply precisely what Morgann would call 'those parts of the composition which are *inferred* only, and not distinctly shewn'.

They are even more numerous in *Part 2*, especially in direct or indirect contact with Falstaff. Falstaff's first dialogue opens with a sarcasm reported from his doctor and with the knight's abuse of that 'year-forsooth knave', his obdurate mercer, Master Dummelton (I. ii. 36). (It is striking how, in *Part 2*, off-stage characters, as well as minor actors on the stage, are now given expressive, caricatural names.)[18] Through Mistress Quickly's chatter, we hear of her 'gossip', 'goodwife Keech, the butcher's wife' (II. i. 93–4) and of 'Master Tisick, the debuty', who had admonished her while 'Master Dumbe, our minister' (II. iv. 85, 88) was standing by. And in Shallow's scenes, at least (on my count) sixteen off-stage characters are identified, mostly by the ageing justice himself—from the three invisible Silences he asks after, and the four 'swingebucklers' and old Double (the bowman beloved of John of Gaunt), recalled from his 'Inns a' Court' days (III. ii. 22), back to the 'arrant knave' William Visor of Woncote, whom nevertheless his servant Davy trusts he will 'countenance' in a lawsuit (V. i. 38). With the help of names like Keech (butcher's fat), Simon Stockfish, Jane Nightwork and Silence's champion fat man, 'goodman Puff of Barson' (V. iii. 89–90), as well as with drinking episodes and snatches of song, these Boar's Head and Cotswold scenes project a continuing, subdued impression as of a sort of scrimmage between representatives of Carnival and of Lent. From another point of view, it is a confused medley between everyday rascality and everyday law, complicating and enriching the historical theme of high justice, now central to the main plot. And with grimly sympathetic touches, sharp as engravings by Callot, these profusely inventive comic scenes bring home the rhythm of insignificant lives and insignificant deaths that shadow the high historical drama of war and statecraft. Moreover, they contribute something vital to the state of mind or quality of experience projected by *Part 2*, as a whole, especially by way of Justice Shallow, that marvellous late-comer to *Henry IV*, with his trivial comforts and his senile reminiscences.

The predominant experience conveyed by *Part 2*, it seems to me, is the experience of uncertainty. It is the uncertainty, suspense, indecision that Northumberland expresses when he says:

> 'Tis with my mind
> As with the tide swell'd up unto his height,
> That makes a still-stand, running neither way.   (II. iii. 62–4)

Shakespeare makes the historical action unexciting, by contrast with *Part 1*, showing the rebellion suppressed, well before the end, by cold-blooded stratagem, not by fighting. He reduces even the death of Northumberland in battle to an incidental anticlimax, stripping it of the animation of circumstantial report (IV. iv. 97–101). He treats the passage of history he is dealing with as an interim period, a period of waiting rather than doing, thus throwing new emphasis on the way the actors perceive themselves as 'time's subjects' (I. iii. 110), peering into the future, reconsidering the past. One of his innovations in both parts of *Henry IV*, concurrent with the use of so many off-stage personalities, is the way Shakespeare now makes his characters recall past events at length, and this is particularly noticeable and effective in *Part 2*. The historical speakers think back to the battle of Shrewsbury and its antecedents—even, while Henry is dying, to the time before Richard II, as the anxious princes recall omens and popular beliefs preceding the death of Edward III:

> The river hath thrice flowed, no ebb between,
> And the old folk (time's doting chronicles)
> Say it did so a little time before
> That our great-grandsire, Edward, sick'd and died.   (IV. iv. 125–8)

This speech echoes both Northumberland's image about the tide and the theme introduced in the prologue by Rumour, the theme of 'surmises' and 'conjectures', of 'Conjecture, expectation and surmise' (Induction, 16; I. iii. 23).

Throughout the play, remembrance of the past is set in tension against 'likelihoods and forms of hope' about the future (I. iii. 35) or else 'forms imaginary' of apprehension (IV. iv. 59), which run from the uncertainties agitating the rebel camp in the early scenes to the anxieties, even in victory, surrounding the deathbed of Henry IV. It is this form of mental tension, this general human experience, that Shakespeare is dramatising here (though it must have struck a specially contemporary chord at the moment when the play first appeared). About mid-way (in Act III, Scene i), there is a turning-point in the speeches rehearsing past events, when Henry has been questioning his whole troubled career and Warwick tries to explain that 'There is a history in all men's lives' (III. i. 80) linking past and future in intelligible sequence. Whereupon the King exclaims, 'Are these things then necessities? / Then let us meet them like necessities.' But even here, what emerges is the expression of a frame of mind, not any decision affecting the plot. It is the characters' attitude towards current realities that Shakespeare is concerned with. As in *Part 1*, they are conscious of the pressures of 'time'. But in *Part 2*, it is more especially 'the condition of these *times*' that preoccupies them—'The times are wild'... 'these costermongers' times'... 'the revolution of the times'—together with the signs they seem to hold about the 'times that you shall look upon' (IV.i. 99, I.i.9, I.ii.168–9, III.i.46, IV.iv.60).

'Old folk' dominate the stage in *Part 2*, whereas youth is either dead and gone with Hotspur or subject to fears about the future with Hal (whose glory gained at Shrewsbury is kept, for good dramatic reasons, out of sight).[19] As L. C. Knights has pointed out, *Part 2* dwells on 'age, disappointment and decay'.[20] But this elegiac mood is countered in the comic scenes by the enjoyment of immediate, if trivial, pleasures, such as Mistress Quickly's appreciation of goodwife Keech's 'good dish of prawns' (I.i.96) or Shallow's enjoyment of 'any pretty little tiny kickshaws' to be produced by 'William cook' (V.i.27–8) and his anticipation of eating 'a last year's pippin of [his] own graffing, with a dish of caraways, and so forth' (V.iii.2–3). On the other side, Hal is obliged to regret that his princely appetite can still 'remember the poor creature, small beer. But indeed', he adds, 'these humble considerations make me out of love with my greatness' (II.ii.10–12). Such 'humble considerations' are made to seem relatively timeless; particularly where, towards the climax for Falstaff, Shakespeare cuts from the scene of preparations for dinner at Shallow's house (Act V, Scene I) to the scene at London announcing Henry IV's death and showing Henry V's reconciliation with the Chief Justice, and then back to Shallow's house for the fruit (Act V, Scene iii)—as if, for the moment, the national crisis belonged not only to a different world but to a different order of time. Yet the distinction between the low world and the high is finely shaded. There is no more than a shaky grasp of reality in Mistress Quickly's muddled, rambling, suggestible mind, and in Shallow's gullible self-importance and his vanity about the past. Doll Tearsheet and Silence are complementary, if opposite, types. Altogether, since he is kept at a distance from the Prince, Falstaff's chosen company in *Part 2* is more easygoing, less sharp-witted, than his company in *Part 1*.

There are corresponding changes in Falstaff himself. In spite of the credit he has gained, with the help of Rumour, from Shrewsbury, he still depends ultimately on patronage from Hal. But he is thrown more upon his own resources, so that his capture of a prisoner of war seems like an accident; and the main line of his action, until the last moments of the play, is a spiralling progress from debt to debt. We see more of his social versatility than before, but we also hear more of his private reflection, as he sizes up himself and his world. He can inspire affection, at least the maudlin affection of Doll and Mrs. Quickly. He is given less to outbursts of 'remorse' than before and more to exploiting the world as he finds it: 'A good wit will make use of anything. I will turn diseases to commodity' (something he can sell, this time, not something he wants to buy [I.ii.247–8]). He will fleece Justice Shallow if he can, on the strength of their old acquaintance, in sardonic complicity with 'the law of nature' (III.ii.331). He is as evasive and resourceful as before, but less impulsive, more detached and calculating. We hear more of the mellow, observant, leisured cadences in his prose. He is more of a philosopher and more of a rogue.

A recurrent subject of wryly amused reflection with Falstaff, in connection with the Page and then Prince John and finally Shallow, is the inequality between the Fat and the Lean. What occupies his mind is not so much thoughts of his own age and sickness, which he will evade if he can, as the contrast between his sense of implantation in life and the unsteadiness of his fortunes. His antipathy to Prince John inspires his most elaborate set speech (IV.iii.86–125), his soliloquy of mock-humanistic encomium in praise of drink and of wine-inspired wit, 'apprehensive, quick, forgetive, full of nimble, fiery and delectable shapes'. This is his most defiant plea for laughter and his own style of life. But his meeting with Shallow has begun to elicit another style from Falstaff, more objectively humorous but also more contemplative, as he measures the squire's history against his own. 'Lord, Lord, how subject we old men are to this vice of lying!' is a spontaneous (if ironic) reflection, not a set speech. And his first, richly grotesque, soliloquy about Shallow and how 'This same starv'd justice hath done nothing but prate to me of the wildness of his youth' is also Falstaff's first excursion of any length into his own past (III.ii.304–52); but—'now has he land and beefs' (III.ii.327–8). His second soliloquy on the same topic (V.i.62–85) is more detached, with exactly balanced clauses of amused observation:

> If I were saw'd into quantities, I should make four dozen of such bearded hermits' staves as Master Shallow. It is a wonderful thing to see the semblable coherence of his men's spirits and his. They, by observing him, do bear themselves like foolish justices; he, by conversing with them, is turn'd into a justice-like servingman.... It is certain that either wise bearing or ignorant carriage is caught, as men take diseases, one of another, therefore let men take heed of their company ...

This has the ring of shrewd, almost homely, unforced practical wisdom, so much that the dramatic irony in the last sentence is almost submerged. This speech marks the high point of Falstaff's role as an unruffled humorous critic of mechanical behaviour in other men. He goes on to anticipate how he will make 'Prince Harry' laugh over Shallow, though with a rueful glance at the gap between jester and patron—'a fellow that never had the ache in his shoulders!' In his next scene (Act V, Scene iii), the news that Pistol (of all select companions) brings from court releases a mechanism in Falstaff himself, in the wild dream that 'the laws of England are at my commandement'.

It seems almost impossible for critics to agree about the rejection of Falstaff. Perhaps this shows a flaw in the writing of the play as a whole. Admittedly, there is a jarring note in Henry's rejection speech, though on the other hand the whole action ends on an unheroic note of subdued expectation, on the *diminuendo* of a half-line of verse. But perhaps also those who, like Bradley, deplore the dismissal of a comic spirit of freedom and those who, like Dover Wilson, justify the regal severity of Henry V, both minimise the comic side of Falstaff's downfall and his own share in bringing it about. A Falstaff temperate enough to approach the new king for favours privately or submissive enough to wait until sent for would be less funny than the Falstaff we see. A more amiable separation from Hal would be less in keeping with the character of Falstaff and less true to the logic of comedy, which does not require benevolence, still less indulgence, so much as what Shaw called disillusionment or, rather, a developed engagement between our sense of reality and fixed habits of human behaviour or else between realism and voluntary fantasy. But a realistic appraisal of the sustained business of government cannot be the province of comedy, as distinct from satire, at all.

The two Parts of *Henry IV* form an unprecedented study of statecraft and of the relations of statecraft to other sides of life. More than any other English plays,

I think, they suggest the continuousness of the life of a whole people, through space and time and the mixture of typical human qualities. As such they must include more than comedy. On the other hand, the inclusive vision they contain of the ways men and women of different sorts confront social reality gives perspective and more salience than entirely comic surroundings could provide to the uniquely comic figure of Falstaff.

NOTES

[1] Henri Bergson, *Laughter* (1900), English trans. in Wylie Sypher (ed.), *Comedy* (New York, 1956), pp. 79, 97.
[2] Albert Thibaudet, *Le Bergsonisme* (Paris, 1923), II, 93; compare pp. 59–60.
[3] See Harry Levin, 'Falstaff Uncolted' (1946), in *Shakespeare and the Revolution of the Times* (New York, 1976).
[4] See A. R. Humphreys (ed.), *1 Henry IV*, Arden edn (1960), p. 71 n.
[5] Thomas Nashe, *Pierce Penniless* (1592), in *Selected Works*, ed. Stanley Wells (1964), p. 55. Compare parallels with Nashe in John Dover Wilson (ed.), *1 Henry IV*, New Shakespeare (Cambridge, 1946), pp. 191–6.
[6] William Empson, 'Falstaff and Mr. Dover Wilson' (1953), in G. K. Hunter (ed.), *Shakespeare, Henry IV, Parts I and II: A Casebook* (1970), p. 145. (Referred to here as *Casebook*.)
[7] See Richmond Noble, *Shakespeare's Biblical Knowledge* (1935), pp. 169–81.
[8] Maurice Morgann, *An Essay on the Dramatic Character of Sir John Falstaff* (1777), in D. Nichol Smith (ed.), *Eighteenth Century Essays on Shakespeare*, 2nd edn (Oxford, 1963), p. 230.
[9] William Hazlitt, *Characters of Shakespeare's Plays*, in *Liber Amoris and Dramatic Criticism*, ed. Charles Morgan (1948), p. 309.
[10] A. C. Bradley, 'The Rejection of Falstaff' (1902), in *Oxford Lectures on Poetry*, 2nd edn (1909), pp. 261, 269.
[11] W. H. Auden, 'The Prince's Dog' (1959), in *Casebook*, p. 188.
[12] Compare *1 Henry IV*, I.ii.81–7, II.ii.10–20, II.iv.329–33, III.ii.164–8, and so on.
[13] Compare *King John*, II.i.561–98; *Measure for Measure*, IV.iii.5. (Perhaps Falstaff is thinking of Proverbs, xxii. 1 at this point; compare Noble, *Shakespeare's Biblical Knowledge*, p. 169.)
[14] See Paul A. Jorgensen, ' "Redeeming Time" in Shakespeare's *Henry IV*' (1960), in *Casebook*, pp. 231–42.
[15] See Holinshed, in Geoffrey Bullough (ed.), *Narrative and Dramatic Sources of Shakespeare*, IV (1962), 276.
[16] Compare the King's words about Mortimer at I.iii.85–6: 'Shall our coffers then/Be emptied to redeem a traitor home?'
[17] Holinshed, in Bullough, *Sources*, IV, 191.
[18] See A. R. Humphreys (ed.), *2 Henry IV*, Arden edn (1966), p. 20; Levin, 'Shakespeare's Nomenclature' (1963), in *Shakespeare and the Revolution of the Times*, pp. 70, 75.
[19] See Humphreys (ed.), *2 Henry IV*, introduction, p. xxvi.
[20] L. C. Knights, 'Time's Subjects: The Sonnets and *2 Henry IV*', in *Some Shakespearean Themes* (1959) (*Casebook*, p. 174).

Barbara Freedman

FALSTAFF'S PUNISHMENT

We can understand the nature and the history of the criticism on *The Merry Wives* as a series of attempts to come to terms with the disturbing response that the buffoon, and the punishment he requests, evokes. Critics are unanimous in their annoyance at Falstaff's buffoonery, in their disgust at his cruel punishment at Windsor Forest, and in their desire to look outside the text to explain away both these responses. The apocryphal accounts of the play's origin offer critics one solution. If, as John Dennis asserted in 1702, the play was written in fourteen days at the Queen's command—or if, as Nicholas Rowe reported, these demands were further qualified by the Queen's request that Shakespeare write a play which portrayed Falstaff in love—it becomes easy to blame critical dissatisfaction on external grounds: the play was hastily written, was probably highly derivative, and could not, given such constraints, adequately reflect Shakespeare's creative genius.[1]

A second, more popular critical response has been literally to disown the play's main character, Falstaff. Such critics direct our attention to the discrepancies between the more vital Falstaff of the history plays and the "old, cold, withered" buffoon before them, concluding that this is neither Shakespeare's Falstaff nor our own. A. C. Bradley's response is indicative of this critical trend:

> [Falstaff is] baffled, duped, treated like dirty linen, beaten, burnt, pricked, mocked, insulted, and, worst of all, repentant and didactic. It is horrible. It is almost enough to convince one that Shakespeare himself could sanction the parody of Ophelia in the *Two Noble Kinsmen*. But it no more touches the real Falstaff than Ophelia is degraded by that parody.[2]

A third means of avoiding the problem of Falstaff's buffoonery has been to moralize the issue. Either the community is to be blamed for unfair behavior, or Falstaff is to be blamed for his villainy in order for these critics to accept the play's action. Jeanne Addison Roberts' article, "Falstaff in Windsor Forest: Villain or Victim?" bluntly states the moralizers' dilemma: "Is Falstaff ... a social menace who

From *Shakespeare Studies* 14 (1981): 163–73.

brings on himself a well-deserved punishment? Or is he a nearly-innocent victim, entrapped by the scheming wives and used by society for its own rather devious ends?"[3] Roberts concludes that he is both and turns to historical parallels of scapegoating to explain the ambiguity of Falstaff's criminal status.

The view of Falstaff as scapegoat eludes the moralizers' dilemma in enabling us to see him as guilty and innocent at once, but it demands an identification with the wives, with their community, and with certain professed social aims that is problematic, if not impossible, given the way in which the play is written. The result is a fourth means of evading our response to the play: focusing on historical situations which inform the play's pattern of events but which fail to explain Shakespeare's use of them. While vestiges of a primitive scapegoat ritual certainly loom large in *The Merry Wives*,[4] the fact remains that the Falstaff of *The Merry Wives* is not a ritual scapegoat but a realistically drawn dramatic character with psychological validity. The wives who punish him are not "defenders of the social order" but offended women with minds and plans of their own—both of which they refuse to share with the other members of their community. Even when the entire community is involved in Falstaff's punishment, and that is only one action in a much larger sequence of events, the punishment is not a ritual scapegoating but a self-conscious and playful parody of that ritual. Furthermore, Falstaff's humiliation in Windsor Forest is neither necessary nor successful in "purging" the Windsor community. The crisis of a manipulative view of others and of reality which plagues Windsor society is only "mythically" solved by the symbol of Fenton and Anne Page's freely willed marriage at the play's end; a tragicomic awareness of our inability to control the outcome of events, and our inability to stop trying to control events, is tellingly underlined by the fact of that wedding as well.

On the surface, the play reads as a citizen comedy: Falstaff is a threat to the community, and his punishment at the hands of the Windsor wives is merry, moral, and survival-oriented. Yet if we consider our emotional response to the play or attempt to understand what desires the author may be fulfilling through creating and sharing its core fantasy, there is a second possible view of the action. We don't—or I don't—always feel as if the wives simply represent the interests of a sane society. And Shakespeare apparently didn't either, for he has these wives doubt their own intentions and then protest far too much: "What think you?" Mrs. Ford asks Mrs. Page, "May we, with the warrant of womanhood and the witness of a good conscience, pursue him [Falstaff] with any further revenge?" (IV. ii. 179–81).[5] Mrs. Page's reply is a confident one: "The spirit of wantonness is, sure, scared out of him. If the devil have him not in fee simple . . . he will never, I think . . . attempt us again" (IV. ii. 182–85). The wives then blithely forge ahead with a new plan to "still be the ministers" of Falstaff's punishment, rationalizing their action with such pithy couplets as "Against such lewdsters and their lechery,/Those that betray them do no treachery" (V. iii. 20–21). Their vindictive reaction to Falstaff's "love letter" is understandable the first time, but they feed his flattery and egg him on to future sexual transgressions most cruelly—and unnecessarily. Quite simply, the wives and their "sane community" do not provide ample motivation for this fantasy, and if we identify with them, we won't fully understand why Shakespeare was writing this play. Facts are facts. Shakespeare was interested, for some strange reason, in writing about clownish male sexual humiliation and punishment, in making us laugh at something essentially disturbing: an aggressive and yet guilty sense of sexuality. The play expresses an obvious pleasure in being caught, in being humiliated, in being punished for sexual transgressions. Perhaps if we consider the play as Falstaff's fantasy—a self-directed farce of repeated self-humiliations—we will be closer to the true spirit of the play.

Punishing Falstaff could have been a good deal more fun if *The Merry Wives* were written as traditional farce. Central to that genre is a pattern of sexual transgression and punishment for that transgression which is usually well disguised. Insofar as farce, by definition, derives humor from absurd plot aggression directed against flat characters, it characteristically enables us to enjoy aggression whose cause and effect is denied. In *The Merry Wives*, however, we have a self-conscious use of farce for didactic aims: a self-conscious punishment for sexuality which is disturbing as much as it is humorous. Surely Shakespeare knew he would be losing a few laughs by having us chant, along with the Windsor community.

> Fie on sinful fantasy!
> Fie on lust and luxury!
> Lust is but a bloody fire,
> Kindled with unchaste desire,
>
> . . . .
> Pinch him, fairies, mutually;
> Pinch him for his villainy;
> Pinch him, and burn him, and turn him about,
> Till candles and starlight and moonshine be out.   (V. v. 91–100)

Punishing Falstaff may be fun at first, but without the disguises of traditional farce, it becomes serious business. By the second and third times around, as critics have noted, it becomes downright humiliating.

To understand the highly self-conscious, punitive view of sexuality in *Merry Wives*, it is useful to examine the play in the larger context of the plays Shakespeare wrote around the same time. It is enlightening, for example, to see how the play anticipates, and gives comic expression to, the same sexual conflicts that characterize such tragedies as *Othello* and *King Lear*. Common to Shakespeare's plays of this period is a focus on an aging male protagonist facing, or attempting to evade, a decrease in mental and physical agility, and facing, or attempting to evade, accompanying fantasies of emasculation and humiliation by women. Since there are two Lears and two Othellos, that there are two Falstaffs should not, perhaps, be so confusing; a play about Falstaff in love is a play about male sexuality in middle age, which for Shakespeare seems to connote a definite falling off from what one was before, a sense of impending impotence of mind and body. Shakespeare emphasizes Falstaff's decline by choosing to depict the comic defeat of a character with an established reputation for vitality, and by forcing him to acknowledge, early on in the play, a disturbing shift in the state of affairs and a need to adjust accordingly: "Well, sirs, I am almost out at heels," he complains to his men, adding: "There is no remedy—I must cony-catch, I must shift" (l. iii. 28–31). Shakespeare focuses on the onset of intellectual inadequacy when he has Falstaff repeatedly forget and need to be reminded of times and dates after demonstrating remarkable mental agility in the play's opening scene. But the comedy's major concern is with a sense of sexual inadequacy, a loss of manliness; hence, the majority of its plots concern impotent old men trying to prove their masculinity through foolishly conceived duels and even more foolishly conceived sexual liaisons, none of which comes to fruition.

One defense against this crisis is narcissistic self-aggrandizement, achieved through a costly dependence on external proofs of one's grandeur; this is most evident in the heroics of an Othello or a King Lear. *The Merry Wives* also begins with old men foolishly parading their official titles in a pathetic attempt to restore their shattered self-esteem. Falstaff's overblown self-image and subsequent downfall merely anticipate, in comic fashion, the hubris and destruction of the tragic heroes who are to follow. Unlike Lear, Falstaff manages to retain his preposterously grandiose self-image despite numerous humiliations, yet he does so only to be set up for repeated comic pratfalls.

A second defense characteristic of this crisis is a premature adjustment to declining powers in the form of a regression to an infantile posture of dependency upon woman. Lear would draw from Cordelia an absolute declaration of love so that he might comfortably fulfill his plans "to set my rest / On her kind nursery" (l. i. 123–24); without Desdemona, Othello's occupation is gone. Falstaff mirrors Lear in his wholly unrealistic plans to make a living off disinterested Windsor wives: "They shall be my East and West Indies, and I will trade to them both" (l. iii. 64–66). Ford, like Othello and Lear, is plagued with unrealistic fantasies of possessiveness and fears of abandonment. In sum, *The Merry Wives* is a world of impotent old men wholly dependent upon asexual maternal figures for financial and emotional well-being—so much so that the primary action of the play is the devising of crafty plots whereby one can draw from these women one's sustenance.

As taking from woman in this play is imagined in terms of an infantile dependency on maternal figures, it is not surprising that sexuality is described in oral images. Eating seems to be the major preoccupation of Windsor society; everyone is always coming from or going to a dinner. And close analysis reveals that the Windsor characters' attitudes towards dining parallel their attitudes towards coupling in the play. Basically, there are two dominant attitudes towards eating and sexuality in *The Merry Wives*. The creed of comedy, and its ideal of sexuality, is the benevolent oral merger, based on trust in the other, and represented by Master Page. For Page, eating is sharing, being a Host is not losing oneself but finding oneself, creating harmony. Page speaks of "drink[ing] down all unkindness" (l.i.175) and of making amends at the table; eating, for him, is a creative, restorative process. Correspondingly, Page is patient, trustful, and giving in his relationships with others, most obviously with his wife. The opposing creed of farce, and its view of sexuality, is the destructive oral merger, based on a distrustful compulsion greedily to devour or prey upon others, and a fear of like retribution for that sin. For Falstaff, eating is stealing, a sign of transgression which brings on punishment, a devouring which leads to being devoured. His monstrous size is our first clue to his greedy intent. In this play we first meet him eating stolen deer at Page's house; he soon attempts to steal Page's "dear," his wife, as well. Yet her desire appears to Falstaff to be as destructive and devouring as his own. He tells us that "she did so course o'er my exteriors with such a greedy intention that the appetite of her eye did seem to scorch me up like a burning-glass" (I.iii.59–61). Falstaff's burning by the Windsor fairies at the play's conclusion records the triumph of this maternal devouring. His hungry preying is similar to Ford's jealous possessiveness. The stealing and posses-siveness are simply two sides of one coin, resulting from a sense of not having enough inside, and so being unable to give to others, and from a feeling that one must take in order to counteract what others take from one, in turn. Ford fears that everyone will steal from him, and yet so does Falstaff; they simply defend against that threat differently. In sum, if Page is the perfect host, Falstaff is the perfect parasite; their attitudes towards eating and sexuality correspond to these roles.

Hostile fantasies of hurting, preying upon, and devouring that which sustains one naturally call forth guilty fantasies of retribution. The parasitical Windsor males who would prey upon women are punished through sexual frustration, sexual humiliation, symbolic castration, and symbolic devouring. Quickly cruelly leads on Anne Page's suitors in the subplot, as the merry wives entice and frustrate Falstaff in the main plot. Anne's suitors are publicly humiliated by being led into abortive duels and, even worse, abortive marriages (being wed to "great lubberly boys"); Falstaff is humiliated by having his sexual desires and desirability mocked by the community. Falstaff's symbolic castration is discussed by Jeanne Roberts who notes that the community's aim, as described by Mrs. Page, is to "dis-horne the spirit" (IV. iv. 62); Roberts also points out that the dialogue concerning the horns strongly suggests that Falstaff's horns are removed from his head by the community immediately.[6] The symbolic devouring of Falstaff occurs in the greasy knight's public burning. The traditional association of fire with a destructive devouring is already made by the community, who notes that "lust is but a bloody fire" (V.v.93) and then burns Falstaff accordingly for it.

Yet farce provides a partial solution to this guilty attack on the self for de-structive sexuality—a particular, defensive mode of dealing with guilty self-punishment. Unlike Lear, who is the passive victim of his daughter's cruel attacks, Falstaff unmans and humiliates himself. He is not only foolish to begin with, thereby already collaborating in the Windsor women's plot to punish him, but he plays the fool repeatedly, thereby helping it along. Whereas the tragic mode of heroic challenge and attack is followed by a martyred submission to persecutory fantasies, the farcical mode moves from mock transgression and self-emasculation through punishment to laughing forgiveness: the pattern of the buffoon. Falstaff dismisses his own train before the wives deceptively win away his page; Falstaff allows himself to be fooled without an Iago, although the women do egg him on in his self-flattery. Falstaff willingly dons Mother Prat's clothes in an attempt to avoid punishment, whereas Lear agonizes over the woman's tears that threaten his masculine self-image. As if to avoid punishment for womanish dependency, for an aggressive taking from woman, Falstaff becomes foolish woman, emasculates himself, and asks for ridicule and humiliation. In a sense, Falstaff takes the option that Lear couldn't and willingly plays the fool. It is this active role in the pattern of transgression and punishment that keeps the play a comedy and enables us to understand it in terms of the tragic works that follow.

In an article on the psychodynamics of clowning, Richard Simons presents a case study of a typical buffoon. The man's obsessive clowning is analyzed as a complex mode of enacting the same transgressions and simultaneously defending against the same fears, as those typical of circus clowning, of farce in general, and of *The Merry Wives of Windsor* in particular. The patient, about fifty years of age, described himself as "old, balding, toothless, obese, hard of hearing, and impotent."[7] He enjoyed telling the other patients of the one time a doctor had considered placing him in a nursing home. He lived with his mother and sister and felt deeply ambivalent toward them, bound in dependency upon them and yet despising their control. From childhood on, he recounted, he had played the fool; he was the student clown who was always caught drawing ugly pictures of the teacher on the blackboard just as she walked in the room. The patient expressed displeasure about being mocked by the other patients but seemed to derive a great deal of secret pleasure from it. For he would continually place himself in situations where he would be caught attacking someone, ideally female authority figures, and would then give his peers due information and cause to join in his reprimand and yet simultaneously laugh at his foolishness.

Simons explains this patient's clowning as a means of enabling an acceptable release of aggression. First, joking provides a socially acceptable means of releasing hostility, a means of projecting one's fears and one's deficiencies onto others and then mocking them for it. Second, the clown is a fool, so his self-abasement takes the sting out of his attacks. Yet insofar as clowning depends upon "being caught," it is particularly safe, for it provides the clown with a means of escaping the anxiety, guilt, and self-punishment arising from his hostile thoughts and acts. In being found out and punished, the clown can disown and project the role of superego onto an audience whom he can in turn bribe through humor and self-abasement. The typical student clown, then, manages to vent hostility against the teacher, and the pleasure in getting caught is a means of acting out and disowning superego aggression; he can then bribe the superego through his humorous self-abasement before teachers and peers.

The defense mechanism of clowning may also be understood as an effective means of mastering oral anxieties. The oral tendency is to preserve an attachment to the introjected object at all costs, yet maintaining that relationship is problematic, given the conflicts which characterize the disturbed oral personality's primary relationship. The first accessible defense mechanism for maintaining a frustrating object relationship is the splitting of the maternal image into idealized and malevolent components. Yet insofar as the oral personality has characteristically failed to master primary ambivalence towards the object, it is unable to neutralize destructive feelings towards the self and the other which derive from the split maternal image. Ridden with guilt over destructive feelings towards both the object and the self, the subject seeks a means of controlling the attacks of its irrationally harsh superego. Seeking punishment is a means of controlling inner hostility; through manipulative harassment, an external, regulatory process for doling out aggression is set up. Finally, insofar as seeking punishment is also a means of seeking attention, it provides a means of maintaining a relationship, however unsatisfactory the quality of that relationship may be.

Clowning as a technique provides the professional and literary buffoons with the same defensive means of expressing aggression that it affords the amateur. While clownish hostility is invariably directed against authority figures, both male and female, it is interesting to note that the clown is traditionally a male figure and serves the function, in our society, of playing on fears of and hostility toward women. The clown's traditional garb is itself an attack on women, a hideous caricature of her made-up face, stiff hairdo, and flimsy clothing. Like the typical buffoon and comedian, Falstaff projects his own deficiencies onto others and then laughs at them for it; in this case, the Windsor elders are ridiculed for their impotence and parasitic behavior. But Falstaff seems especially concerned with attacking powerful maternal figures and then being discovered and humiliated by them. His dependence on and aggression toward women have been analyzed, but we may add that they are given expression through costume as well as through action. In a memorable scene between Falstaff and his alter ego, Master Ford, Falstaff dresses up as Mother Prat—by name a punitive maternal figure. Ford vents his anger at the old woman because of her fortune-telling, her alleged control over situations "beyond our element" about which "we know nothing" (IV.ii.154). Aggression against a punitive maternal figure is thus released by both men in this scene. But Falstaff's aggression toward women upon whom he is dependent and his curious desire to be punished for it are most obvious in his ridiculous plan of writing degrading love letters to a number of maternal figures in the community who are sure to see through him and make him suffer for his advances. The traditional clown and Falstaff set themselves up to be caught; being chased and beaten is the essence of farce action, and Falstaff's role is to be continually found out and humiliated for the same sin. In both cases, we can understand this degrading clowning as a means of safely transgressing against authority figures and then safely being punished for it, by innocently playing out and disowning punishment. Or, to return to the familiar classroom paradigm, Falstaff is the class clown, the merry wives are the teacher, and we are his peers who both punish and laugh at this foolish figure.

To place the play in a larger context, I pose the following conundrum: Why is this image of man, with his aggressive and yet guilty sense of sexuality, his focus on humiliation and abuse at the hands of woman, preoccupying Shakespeare between the writing of a *Twelfth Night* and a *Hamlet?* Or "why," as William Green asks us in his introduction to the Signet edition of the play, "when engrossed in writing romantic comedy . . . does [Shakespeare] suddenly backtrack to the farcical treatment of love that he successfully presented in *The Taming of the Shrew*"[8] The most prevalent philosophical concern in Shakespeare's plays of the time period is not with the potential, ever renewing accommodations and adjustments to life which comedy celebrates but with a tragic awareness of man's limitations. Throughout the plays is a disturbing sense of the impossibility of purposive language and action in a world of flux, created by man and sustained by his frail faith in himself and in others. This conflict is commonly expressed in the form of a triad. One term is an ideal world order, received from one's fathers, and often represented by them: a world that in each subsequent incarnation, is increasingly revealed to be less viable and less self-aware. This is the ideal world of a Friar Laurence, a Richard II, an old Hamlet; it is Hector's ideal of intrinsic value, Othello's dream, and Lear's fantasy. A recognition of its flaws is necessary but, ultimately, neither comforting nor useful; threatening to take its place is a world of chaos. As Ulysses reminds us,

> Take but degree away, untune that string,
> And hark what discord follows. Each thing meets
> In mere oppugnancy. . . .
> . . . .
> Then everything include itself in power,
> Power into will, will into appetite.
> And appetite, an universal wolf,
> So doubly seconded with will and power,
> Must make perforce an universal prey
> And last eat up himself.   (I. iii. 109–24)

This is our second term, the chaotic world which Bolingbroke opened up like a Pandora's box: a world peopled by Ajax and Pompey Bum, Falstaff and his crew, Goneril and Regan, and Othello's Anthropophagi who eat each other up. In between the ideal and the real, the private and the public, the past and the present, is a mediator attempting to join the two; after Hamlet, that mediator simply represents a makeshift, manmade order subject to constant attack from without and within, sustained only by human imagination, faith, and respect.

The problem of maintaining a makeshift, imaginative, communal order in the face of external attack and a loss of faith in a previous order is given comic expression in *The Merry Wives of Windsor*. Representing the old order in the form of its institutions of law and religion are the farcical Windsor elders. Threatening to replace them are the chaotic forces of power, will, and appetite, represented by the ridiculous buffoon Falstaff and his farcically swaggering crew. Shakespeare reenacts his tragic dilemma on the familiar testing ground of English soil, Windsor community—and on the familiar testing ground of English comedy as well. What sustains Windsor society is its commitment to the opposite of the manipulative, predatory, capitalistic behavior in which both parties engage—its commitment to a creed of communal trust, faith, and harmony, as represented by Master Page. The possibility of tragedy threatens, however, when Shakespeare rests an order, as he must, on imaginative grounds; trust implies mistrust, and every Page has its counterpart Ford in Shakespeare's works. Yet Ford is here linked with Falstaff; the miser becomes the thief's alterego, and through this identification, the threat that Ford presents can be safely overcome. After all, this is a comedy. What makes the play humorous is Shakespeare's portrayal of the Windsor elders in such a way that their impotence is comic rather than tragic, and his portrayal of the forces of chaos in terms of comic weaknesses as well. What makes the play comedy, rather than farce, is the addition of an alternative which has all the trappings of success, a mediating term with which we can identify and which will save the community.

This triad has its psychological coordinates as well, and these are well brought out in Shakespeare's post-1600 plays. For the old world, the sanctioned order now revealed as hollow, we have an old, narrowly defined, heroic masculine persona which is no longer viable or appropriate. For the new, predatory "order," we have an identity based on dependency on others (particularly women) in time: a tragic sense of being as subject to continual redefinition by untrustworthy mirrors. In the post-1600 plays, these two options are often presented in the characters of the omnipotent superhero and the emasculated cuckold. The ideal mean, a secure masculine sexual identity dependent upon the possibility of intimacy without self-destruction, a successful sense of being with and through others, is depicted in *The Merry Wives* in the confident relationship of the Pages.

In the tragedies, Shakespeare becomes fascinated with attacking and exposing the world of the fathers, and exploring and resolving this sense of relationship with woman as dependent and devouring. There is a growing identification with heroic transgression, on the one hand, and with an ultimately passive submission to these destructive powers, be they the forces of evil without or within, glorified in the form of heavenly ministers, on the other. The comedies equally deal with transgressions against fathers and mothers, but they provide a defensive means of dealing with the accompanying guilt—in this case, through a manipulative, humorous baiting of others into an attack which enables regulation of hostile feelings, and through humorous self-abasement which mitigates that attack. Simons notes, "Clowning is thus an adaptive effort on the part of the ego to deal with . . . castrative fears, a defense against and a partial punishment for incestuous and aggressive impulses, an abandonment of the oedipal struggle with regression to more infantile levels, and a communication to the therapist: 'Don't be frightened of me. I'm no rival. I'm only a clown—a fool—old and weak—fat—bald—impotent.' "[9] How does clowning alleviate the punishment accompanying the transgressions enacted in the tragedies of the time period? "If," as Simons argues, "he [the clown] can actively play at these fears, perhaps they will not come true. If he can confess and expose them to ridicule, perhaps no further punishment will be exacted. If he can get his friends to laugh at them, perhaps they are not so terrifying as they seem."[10] In *The Merry*

Wives of Windsor, Shakespeare's friends agree to laugh with him once more, and to stall off the terrors that are to come.

NOTES

[1] Representative of this critical stance is Mark Van Doren's conclusion that this is a play for which Shakespeare felt little, written "with great talent but without love" (*Shakespeare* [New York: Henry Holt, 1939], p. 137).

[2] A. C. Bradley, *Oxford Lectures on Poetry* (London: Macmillan, 1959), p. 248.

[3] Jeanne Addison Roberts, "Falstaff in Windsor Forest: Villain or Victim?" *Shakespeare Quarterly,* 26 (1975), 9.

[4] As J. A. Bryant, Jr., has convincingly demonstrated, there are significant parallels between Falstaff's humiliations and elements of the scapegoat ritual of "Carrying Out Death" as described by Sir James Frazer in *The Golden Bough;* see his "Falstaff and the Renewal of Windsor," *PMLA,* 89 (1974), 296–301. More specifically, as Jeanne Addison Roberts has discovered, this "Carrying Out Death" is associated throughout *The Merry Wives* with traditional Halloween festivities, in turn associated by Frazer with the Celtic festival of the new year which marked the beginning of winter. See her *Shakespeare's English Comedy:* The Merry Wives of Windsor *in Context* (Lincoln: Univ. of Nebraska Press, 1979), pp. 78–83, as well as "*The Merry Wives of Windsor* as a Hallowe'en Play," *Shakespeare Survey,* 25 (1972), 107–12.

[5] All quotations from Shakespeare are from *William Shakespeare: The Complete Works,* ed. Alfred Harbage (Baltimore: Penguin, 1969), otherwise known as *The Pelican Shakespeare.*

[6] Jeanne Roberts, *Shakespeare's English Comedy,* p. 77.

[7] Richard C. Simons, "The Clown as a Father Figure," *The Psychoanalytic Review,* 52 (1965), 75–91; see p. 80.

[8] William Green, "Introduction to *The Merry Wives of Windsor,*" *The Signet Classic Shakespeare* (New York: New American Library, 1963), p. xxv.

[9] Simons, p. 84.

[10] Simons, p. 84.

C. L. Barber and
Richard P. Wheeler

FROM MIXED HISTORY
TO HEROIC DRAMA:
THE *HENRIAD*

The two parts of *Henry IV* open out onto what seems to be the whole of English society, with a splendid development of Shakespeare's range, both in subjects and in the complexity of attitudes toward experience poised against one another. In *Shakespeare's Festive Comedy* I emphasized the way this richness, which the criticism of the last fifty years has variously recognized, is organized by the polarity of holiday and everyday in Shakespeare's culture.[1] "Mingling kings and clowns" in the native theatrical tradition Sidney deplored, the two plays are organized so that *Part One* balances Misrule against Rule, with Falstaff, as Holiday, asking to be Everyday; then *Part Two,* by a kind of Trial of Carnival, leads to the sacrifice of Falstaff, who is made to carry off bad luck and sin as the Prince makes atonement with his strong but guilty father. In my view, the dramatist resorts to magical action instead of dramatizing it, in inviting us to accept the ritual expulsion of Falstaff as scapegoat for the social and political ills of England. By setting the Sonnets against these plays, I think we can see how the expulsion of Falstaff, and with it the inhibition of Falstaffian ironies, is part of an effort to use the drama to establish a new relationship to manhood.

Old Offenses and Affections New

Sonnet 146, "Poor soul, the center of my sinful earth," can serve as an entrance into a dramatic rhythm that uses the rejection of Falstaff to try to close over the ironic perspective on heroic action the two parts of *Henry IV* have opened up. After noting in chapter 6 that many regard this poem as a "Christian palinode" that resolves the conflicts engendered by the poet's search for fulfillment in human objects of love, we argued that this sonnet cannot be fully satisfying because it simplifies so drastically the complex sensibility engaged in the affirmations of human love. If we look at Sonnet 146 in relation to the Henry IV plays, we can see it as an effort by the poet to turn away from his former self, as Hal turns away from Falstaff:

From *The Whole Journey: Shakespeare's Power of Development* (Berkeley: University of California Press, 1986), pp. 198–217.

I know thee not, old man, fall to thy prayers.
How ill white hairs becomes a fool and jester!
I have long dreamt of such a kind of man,
So surfeit-swell'd, so old, and so profane;
But being awak'd, I do despise my dream.
Make less thy body (hence) and more thy grace,
Leave gormandizing, know the grave doth gape
For thee thrice wider than for other men.
Reply not to me with a fool-born jest,
Presume not that I am the thing I was,
For God doth know, so shall the world perceive,
That I have turn'd away my former self;
So will I those that kept me company.   (*2H4* V.v.47–59)

Here the newly crowned Henry V is "the soul of state" (*Troilus and Cressida* III.iii.202), and Falstaff is synoptic for its corrupted body: "Then, soul, live thou upon thy servant's loss" (Sonnet 146) is the order of the day. Hal is doing what he advises Falstaff to do, and what the poet urges on himself in the sonnet: "Buy terms divine in selling hours of dross." "Make less thy body (hence) and more thy grace" recalls the poet's repudiation of his own body in the sonnet: "let that pine to aggravate thy store." As Henry V's heroic-Christian resolve replaces the passive-Christian resolution of the sonnet, the grave that gapes for "gormandizing" Falstaff displaces the death to which the poet turns with religious resignation:

Within be fed, without be rich no more.
    So shalt thou feed on death, that feeds on men,
    And death once dead, there's no more dying then.

Behind the generalizing sonnets one can often hear echoes of other poems whose attitudes are in considerable tension with the sort of simplifying finality we get in Sonnet 146 ⟨. . .⟩. Just so, Henry's dismissive severity can recall Falstaff's characteristically ironic self-justifications, centered on the very surfeit-swelled excess now banished:

Dost thou hear, Hal? Thou knowest in the state of innocency Adam fell, and what should poor Jack Falstaff do in the days of villainy? Thou seest I have more flesh than another man, and therefore more frailty.

                                                          (*1H4* III.iii.164–68)

The repudiation of Falstaff, however, is serious business. Shakespeare *is* exploring the soul of state and the exigencies of political action. In the last act of *2 Henry IV* and in *Henry V* he is dramatizing the way a leader can become an organizing presence for a society by meeting needs cognate to those the poet has typically sought to fulfill, not in such Christian resignation as we find in Sonnet 146, but in the presence of the young man. In *Henry V* the Chorus gives explicit expression to the satisfaction the heroic presence of the young king provides:

... every wretch, pining and pale before,
Beholding him, plucks comfort from his looks.
A largess universal, like the sun,
His liberal eye doth give to every one,
Thawing cold fear, that mean and gentle all
Behold, as may unworthiness define,
A little touch of Harry in the night.   (IV. Cho. 41–47)

Here the Chorus uses the same sort of imagery to describe the King's countenance, in the night before Agincourt, that the Sonnets use about the largess of the young man's countenance. On the social, historical side, the Chorus is describing the process Freud deals with in *Group Psychology and the Analysis of the Ego,* by which a charismatic leader can enter into the psychic economy of followers in a way comparable to what happens in falling in love.[2] The play *Henry V* both generalizes about this and localizes it in persons (Fluellen, for instance, as he puts his Welsh individuality in the devoted service of "your Majesty's manhood" [IV. viii. 33–34]), while wrestling with what it involves in the person of the King.

Henry V also invites the audience to take its hero king in the same way that his society takes him. Just how far it goes in this direction, whether it is ironic about this, and if so, how, are questions that are perennially in dispute among good critics. In its incompletely controlled tone, *Henry V* is remarkably like such absolutely phrased but finally precarious sonnets as 146, or 116—"Let me not to the marriage of true minds"—and, I think, for the same reason: the poet is using the work to meet *part* of his need as if it met the whole of it, with part of his need and sensibility kept out. But the drama provides a crucial resource that the Sonnets do not; it allows the dramatist to throw the stress, not on the need that seeks realization in a young man who cannot be brought into the utterance directed to him, but on the realization of that need in the character who meets it in a dramatic action.

The religiousness of Sonnet 146, as was emphasized earlier, has no object of worship; the poem does not turn to God or Christ in place of the young man or mistress, as Donne, for example, turns from his dead wife to Christ. At the close of *2 Henry IV,* however, there *is* such an object, along with the prudential revulsion to piety of the sonnet; the object is Henry V, even as the dramatist rejects the part of the poet that has been in Falstaff. Although the scene of the rejection is a reprise of many similar gestures in the Sonnets, where the poet makes nothing of himself to make the beloved everything, it is taking place on the main line of Shakespeare's dramatic development, and with dramatic finality—for the moment at least. Because in the dramatic form Shakespeare can hypostatize what the Sonnets seek to hold together, it is possible to leave the Falstaff sensibility behind and still take as object a young man—in whom full manhood and authority are to be envisaged as being achieved. The sonneteer's role in realizing the life of the friend is taken over by the dramatist as dramatist. As in the Sonnets the all-or-nothing investment is not in a religious incarnation or transcendence but in a beloved friend, so here in *Henry V* Shakespeare invests in a secular hero king.

As we move from Falstaff's many-sided relationship with Hal to the celebration of Henry V's heroic virtues, the shift in dramatic perspective is akin to what we find in the Sonnets if we move from the action in poems that address Shakespeare's infidelity to the friend to the eloquent affirmation of unqualified love in Sonnet 116. I have already considered difficulties about the tone of the affirmation in this sonnet, "Let me not to the marriage of true minds," following Carol Neely in her analysis of the way certain of the sonnets attempt to stand back from the "motion in corruption" of the sequence and the way this attempt breaks down.[3] When viewed from the perspective of sonnets that explicitly bring out other, more disruptive dimensions of the love for the friend, the unqualified affirmation of love in Sonnet 116 becomes precarious. The tension between the affirmation of this sonnet and the poems around it is similar to the tensions *inside* neighboring sonnets, between their hopeful finales and the stressful acknowledgments with which they begin.

We have considered the self-knowledge such poems convey, in chapter 6. Here it is the locked-in tension of these sonnets that contrasts with the similar but different things we get with Falstaff and his way of knowing and affirming himself in relation to Hal. Falstaff certainly fits in many ways the poet's self-description in Sonnet 110, written after an interval of separation:

> Alas 'tis true, I have gone here and there,
> And made myself a motley to the view,
> Gored mine own thoughts, sold cheap what is most dear,
> Made old offences of affections new.
> Most true it is, that I have looked on truth
> Askance and strangely . . .

But instead of suffering regrets about having "sold cheap what is most dear," with the strain this puts on the poet's effort to repudiate his past self and proclaim renewal, Falstaff rejoices in selling dear what, with his powers, comes cheap:

> I will devise matter enough out of this Shallow to keep Prince Harry in continual laughter the wearing out of six fashions . . . O, it is much that a lie with a slight oath and a jest with a sad brow will do with a fellow that never had the ache in his shoulders! (*2H4* V.i.78–84)

In this instance, the self-congratulatory enthusiasm belongs to Falstaff riding for a fall in *Part Two*. We can participate fully in Falstaff's gall as he relishes future prospects for opportunistic intimacy. We can also see, as he cannot, the movement of a dramatic action that is fast putting such wishful prospects, and the Prince, out of Falstaff's range, however great the imaginative powers through which he seeks to exploit them. But with Sonnet 110—which moves in an opposite direction to this action, from self-depletion and separation to wishful renewal through the friend's love—it is hard to settle what the tone is; as often with the Sonnets, the poet is using the poetry for special pleading that is not framed by anything comparable to the controlled interplay of perspectives the drama can provide.

Like Sonnet 110, Sonnet 109 ("O never say that I was false of heart") broods over absences that have "seemed my flame to qualify." Pairing these poems as "nimble apologia," Stephen Booth sees *comic* reference to perversion in 109:

> Never believe, though in my nature reigned
> All frailties that beseige all kinds of blood,
> That it could so preposterously be stained
> To leave for nothing all thy sum of good.

Of the travel simile by which Shakespeare understands his return to his soul lodged in his beloved's breast—"That is my home of love; if I have ranged/Like him that travels I return again"—Booth comments: "Shakespeare's purpose is presumably to display a Falstaff-like gall in solemnly making a logical-sounding equation between two non-comparable things: the journeys of a traveler and the promiscuous sexual liaisons of an unfaithful lover."[4] But surely the tone of this poem is ardently conflictual: it pleads, partly by the poet's acknowledging polymorphous temptation, for reconciliation that would accept the actual complexity of the poet's nature. Sonnets 109 and 110 are as moving in their way as Sonnet 116 is in its way. But there is no freedom for Falstaff-like gall in the relationship to the young man as these poems present it—the all-or-nothing bond precludes it: "For nothing this wide universe I call,/Save thou, my rose; in it thou art my all" (Sonnet 109). Hence, surely, part of the joy in creating Falstaff.

Where "Let me not to the marriage of true minds" works to submerge disruptive possibilities within a sweeping affirmation of love, Falstaff's incantatory denials of his disabling age, whoring, drunkenness, gluttony, obesity, and cowardice become an outrageous affirmation of himself:

> My lord, the man I know.... But to say I know more harm in him than in myself, were to say more than I know. That he is old, the more the pity, his white hairs do witness it, but that he is, saving your reverence, a whoremaster, that I utterly deny. (1H4 II.iv.464–70)

What mock-king Hal, rehearsing his interview with his father, has denounced as scandalous "impediments" to the old ruffian's claims on the young prince, Falstaff denies or turns into virtues; all are swept into the accumulating rhythm of his iterative prose, splendidly varied at the moment of climax:

> No, my good lord, banish Peto, banish Bardolph, banish Poins, but for sweet Jack Falstaff, kind Jack Falstaff, true Jack Falstaff, valiant Jack Falstaff, and therefore more valiant, being as he is old Jack Falstaff, banish not him thy Harry's company, banish not him thy Harry's company—banish plump Jack, and banish all the world. (lines 474–80)

Shakespeare in Sonnet 116 ascends into poetry as though into a waking dream: one can follow him into it and feel the marriage of true minds without impediments; or, on reading it in relation to more troubled sonnets, one can glimpse under its surface what in Falstaff's waking dream is there for all to see. In the play we can, with Hal, enjoy the contradictions, which are, "like their father that begets them, gross as a mountain, open, palpable" (1H4 II.iv.225–26). "Dost thou hear me, Hal?" "Ay, and mark thee too, Jack" (II.iv.209–10). Instead of the tensions of anxious-pleading protestation, as in "Since my appeal says I did strive to prove/

The constancy and virtue of your love" (Sonnet 117), there is delightful release as we at once admire and dismiss Falstaff's excuses and evasions:

PRINCE HAL: Sirrah, do I owe you a thousand pound?

FALSTAFF: A thousand pound, Hal? a million, thy love is worth a million; thou owest me thy love. (III.iii.135–37)

In the Sonnets there is a queasiness about the latent self-love displaced onto the highborn young man:

Sin of self-love possesseth all mine eye,

. . . .

Methinks no face so gracious is as mine,

. . . .

But when my glass shows me myself indeed
Beated and chopped with tanned antiquity,
Mine own self love quite contrary I read;
Self so self-loving were iniquity.
    'Tis thee, myself, that for myself I praise,
    Painting my age with beauty of thy days. (Sonnet 62)

Falstaff's self-love is right out in the open, and at his most winning "plump Jack" has all the charm of a little child:

CHIEF JUSTICE: Do you set down your name in the scroll of youth, that are written down old with all the characters of age? . . . and every part about you blasted with antiquity? . . .

FALSTAFF: My lord, I was born about three of the clock in the afternoon, with a white head and something of a round belly.

(2H4 I.ii.178–80, 184, 187–89)

Self-disabling metaphor in the Sonnets is literalized in the drama—and yet does not daunt Falstaff:

Speak of my lameness, and I straight will halt (Sonnet 89)

A pox of this gout! or a gout of this pox! for the one or the other plays the rogue with my great toe. 'Tis no matter if I do halt, I have the wars for my color, and my pension shall seem the more reasonable. A good wit will make use of any thing. (2H4 I.ii.243–48)

The marvelous autonomy of Falstaff goes with his constant relaxation into physical gluttony, as against the strain on the sonneteer's psychic "gluttoning":

So are you to my thoughts as food to life,

. . . .

And by and by clean starvèd for a look;

. . . .

    Thus do I pine and surfeit day by day,
    Or gluttoning on all, or all away. (Sonnet 75)

On one side, the sonneteer is getting his comeuppance. Decrepit Falstaff takes delight in seeing his active Hal do deeds of youth in killing Hotspur: "Well said, Hal! to it Hal! Nay, you shall find no boy's play here, I can tell you" (*1H4* V. iv. 75–76). The merely vicarious enjoyment of manhood is explicit in "no boy's play here." A self-interest in love that seeks to leap over caste difference is made obvious in Falstaff; so also is overestimation of what artful wit can do across such difference: "I know the young king is sick for me. Let us take any man's horses, the laws of England are at my commandement" (*2H4* V. iii. 135–37). A resentment, potential in the Sonnets, at what belonging to a higher caste can do for someone actually mediocre is expressed and then rebuked as the Prince overhears Falstaff characterize him as "A good shallow young fellow. 'A would have made a good pantler, 'a would 'a' chipp'd bread well" (*2H4* II. iv. 237–38). Responding to Doll Tearsheet's question about Poins—"Why does the Prince love him so then?"—Falstaff speaks of roistering talents shared by Poins and the Prince: "gambol faculties . . . that show a weak mind and an able body, for which the Prince admits him" (*2H4* II. iv. 243, 251–52). "From me far off, with others all too near" echoes from Sonnet 61. As many have noted, Falstaff seems to carry a suggestion of Shake-speare. The buffoon's triumphant gluttonous and dramatic aggression is paid for by such playful self-mockery.

Sources of humiliation or helplessness for the Sonnets poet become resources of self-aggrandizement and (ultimately illusory) control for Falstaff.

> O for my sake do you with fortune chide,
> The guilty goddess of my harmful deeds,
> That did not better for my life provide
> Than public means which public manners breeds.   (Sonnet 111)

"I am Fortune's steward," Falstaff exalts when Pistol brings news of the old king's death: "Blessed are they that have been my friends, and woe to my Lord Chief Justice" (*2H4* V. iii. 130–31, 137–38). In the sonnet, "public means which public manners breeds" clearly refers to Shakespeare's gaining his livelihood in the theater:

> Thence comes it that my name receives a brand,
> And almost thence my nature is subdued
> To what it works in, like the dyer's hand.

Falstaff, for his public manners, receives one brand after another:

> SHERIFF: One of them is well known, my gracious lord, A gross fat man. . . .
> PRINCE: This oily rascal is known as well as Paul's.   (*1H4* II. iv. 509–526)

England is Falstaff's theater, and he takes heart that "Men of all sorts take a pride to gird at me" (*2H4* I. ii. 6).

Falstaff, within the plays, is always playing, freed by (and condemned to) a theatrical existence: "Out, ye rogue, play out the play, I have much to say in the behalf of that Falstaff" (*1H4* II. iv. 484–85). The poet, in writing the Sonnets, is freed and condemned in a different way to living by words and gestures, since it is by means of the poems that their author lives in his friend and his friend in him, as in Sonnet 81:

> When all the breathers of this world are dead,
>> You still shall live—such virtue hath my pen—
>> Where breath most breathes, ev'n in the mouths of men.

Such immediate consummation in utterance, as we observed in the chapter on the Sonnets, gives something like an immediate experience of immortality. We have a similar experience in the great speeches where Falstaff eludes morality and mortality: "What is honor?" "The better part of valor." But the dramatic context places the experience within limits controlled by the dramatist; with the Sonnets it is only by our assessment of the potentially conflictual relationships between poems that *we* can place—never fully satisfactorily—the event that is such a poem as Sonnet 81. One must add that from Morgann on down to Roy Battenhouse in his essay "Falstaff as Parodist and Perhaps Holy Fool," Falstaff has been seen as triumphing in an unqualified way, or a way that somehow transcends qualification.[5]

As he relishes his role at the beginning of *Part Two,* Falstaff makes a brag that can fit his author:

> The brain of this foolish-compounded clay, man, is not able to invent any thing that intends to laughter more than I invent or is invented on me: I am not only witty in myself, but the cause that wit is in other men.   (l. ii. 7–10)

Shakespeare of course was "the cause that wit is in other men" across the board, inventing all the parts for his fellows. There is good reason to feel uneasy in setting out to claim, as here, that Shakespeare is more in one part than in others. After all, as many have pointed out, Falstaff's role is compounded of several traditional roles: clown, fool, the Vice or Good Fellowship luring innocents to the tavern in the moralities, buffoon, Lord of Misrule, Carnival.[6] If there is Shakespeare in him, to be in everybody on stage was Shakespeare's professional job. One can add that, since Falstaff is a holiday figure, protagonist of saturnalian release, Shakespeare in animating him would be going on holiday—taking with him, as revelers do, his own everyday powers now heightened by being free to express otherwise inhibited attitudes. Moreover, Shakespeare's whole controlling dramatic construction is using Falstaff, along with Hotspur, Henry IV, and the rest, in the rhythm of the polarized action, to present the development of Hal as an inclusive royal nature. By design, the two parts of *Henry IV* are centered on the Prince, not Falstaff.

Although one must grant all this, and *gladly,* in the perspective of Shakespeare's whole development something more is going on: Shakespeare is acting out the Falstaff relationship to life in order to try to banish it—"I do, I will." The goal is to disinvest in the vicarious enjoyment of manhood in order to reinvest in Manhood itself. The exigencies of the whole development are encountered (beyond full control) in the unsatisfactoriness of the hero king who emerges from the process. Hotspur, in the scene just before the Boar's Head revels, exclaims "I could divide myself and go to buffets" (*1H4* II. iii. 32). Of course this is exactly what Hotspur cannot do. Shakespeare, however, is doing just such dividing, and while the divided parts are at play or at civil war, the drama has an inclusiveness which we can feel the Prince to be sharing from behind his circumspection. But the conclusion of *Part Two*, with its rejection of Falstaff, in effect tries for the simplification of such a sonnet as 110, which puts the "old offenses" of the poet behind in the renewed affiliation to the friend: "Then give me welcome, next my heav'n the best, / Ev'n to thy pure and most most loving breast." The play asks us to put Falstaff's perspective behind as we admire the heroic enterprise of King Henry V. Like "the star to every wand'ring bark" of Sonnet 116, the young king of *Henry V* becomes "this star of England" (Epi. 6), giving direction and inspiration to a whole nation that can be renewed in his presence, after having become mired in the old offenses of previous reigns. But in *Henry V*, without the full ironic interplay of perspectives that holds until the very end of *2 Henry IV*, we are back to such conflictual submission to an idealized figure as we have in the Sonnets.

"Ev'n at the Turning o' th' Tide"

The marvelous freedom of *Henry IV* depends on a redistribution outward of the aggression which in the Sonnets is so frequently turned inward on the poet. But it is striking that Shakespeare, in dealing for the first time with the transmission of heritage across tension between father and son, alters his sources to eliminate direct expressions of the Prince's hostile or defiant feelings toward his father. In the chronicles Hal and the large retinue he maintains burst in on the court dressed in strange, outlandish costume.[7] Shakespeare's Hal seeks other targets for hostile impulses engendered in a role and a bond that, by his own royal birth, are inescapable. In *The Famous Victories of Henry the Fifth*,[8] the Prince, until his sudden, unmotivated transformation, is a street bully who *does* undertake to abrogate the laws of England and to make one of his riotous companions a judge when he is crowned. This crude little play dramatizes the episode of Hal's striking the Chief Justice, an incident that is only referred to by Shakespeare in retrospect during the new Henry V's atonement with him at the close of *Part Two*. All explicit reference to the son's hostility is given to the father:

> PRINCE: I never thought to hear you speak again.
> KING: Thy wish was father, Harry, to that thought.   (*2H4* IV. v. 91–92)

The scene of atonement with the Lord Chief Justice makes explicit an orientation that will be developed (if with some strain) throughout *Henry V*: the young king's aggression is wholly a function of his commitment to the sacramental political role he now embraces. Confronted by the new king, the Chief Justice apprehensively recalls the rationale by which he had imprisoned the rebellious Hal:

> I then did use the person of your father,
> The image of his power lay then in me,
> And in th' administration of his law,
> Whiles I was busy for the commonwealth,

> Your Highness pleased to forget my place,
> The majesty and power of law and justice,
> The image of the King whom I presented.[9]   (*2H4* V. ii. 73–79)

Henry V responds by addressing the episode of striking the Chief Justice in a way that makes it part of an expectable pattern of youthful wildness contained politically within harmless limits—the pattern of the two Henry IV plays. He spells out, almost unctuously, the extension of filial commitment to a more general allegiance to authority and law, here embodied in the Chief Justice:

> There is my hand.
> You shall be as a father to my youth,
> My voice shall sound as you do prompt mine ear,
> And I will stoop and humble my intents
> To your well-practic'd wise directions.   (V. ii. 117–21)

This is pure Henry V, as we come to know him in the next play, always careful to keep righteousness on his side, consulting with the Archbishop of Canterbury about his title to France, denying that uncontrolled passion can have any part in his aggressive action, for "We are no tyrant, but a Christian king, / Unto whose grace our passion is as subject / As is our wretches fett'red in our prisons" (*H5* II. ii. 241–43).

When we see Hal at the outset of the Henry IV plays, the rebelliousness acknowledged in him only at the end is expressed by Falstaff:

> FALSTAFF: But I prithee, sweet wag, shall there be gallows standing in England when thou art King? and resolution thus fubb'd as it is with the rusty curb of old father antic the law? Do not thou, when thou art king, hang a thief.
> PRINCE: No, thou shalt.
> FALSTAFF: Shall I? O rare! By the Lord, I'll be a brave judge.
> PRINCE: Thou judgest false already. I mean thou shalt have the hanging of the thieves, and so become a rare hangman.   (*1H4* I. ii. 58–68)

As Ernst Kris pointed out in a pioneering psychoanalytic essay, "Prince Hal's Conflict,"[10] the Prince's problem is like Hamlet's in that he is in line to inherit from a usurper, but the Oedipal motive is repressed and displaced onto Falstaff, who both covets the power Hal will inherit when the father is dead and absorbs in his own person Hal's aggression toward a father. There is no need at this point to labor the aggressive tendency of Hal's wit in undoing Falstaff's pretensions, "dethroning" him at the Boar's Head during the extempore rehearsal of the interview with the king, enjoying a rhapsody of flyting about "that roasted Manningtree ox with the pudding in his belly, that reverent Vice, that grey Iniquity, that father ruffian, that vanity in years" (*1H4* II. iv. 452–54). The aggression becomes deadly in the lines of rejection: "I know thee not, *old man.*"

It is dizzying to reflect that in that final scene Shakespeare is dramatizing the kind of rejection which the poet fears in the Sonnets. He gives Falstaff, in his opportunistic eagerness—to see the new king and to control the impression he will make on him—language like the Sonnets:

> I will leer upon him as 'a comes by, and do but mark the countenance that he
> will give me.   (2H4 V. v. 6–8)

> But when your countenance filled up his line,
> Then lacked I matter, that enfeebled mine.   (Sonnet 86)

> But to stand stain'd with travel, and sweating with desire to see him, thinking
> of nothing else, putting all affairs else in oblivion, as if there were nothing else
> to be done but to see him.   (2H4 V. v. 24–27)

> For nothing this wide universe I call,
> Save thou, my rose; in it thou art my all.   (Sonnet 109)

> Being your slave, what should I do but tend
> Upon the hours and times of your desire?   (Sonnet 57)

Falstaff then calls out to the approaching king: "God save thy Grace, King Hal! my royal Hal! . . . God save thee, my sweet boy!" (V. v. 41, 43).

Of course, the patterns of "worship" in Shakespeare's society, peaking in the kind of courtier courtship lavished on Elizabeth, made common idiom of expressions somewhat like these—Shakespeare skillfully insists on the breach of decorum by Falstaff's inappropriately personal and possessive phrasing, climaxing in "sweet boy!" ("What's new to speak, what now to register, / That may express my love, or thy dear merit? / Nothing, sweet boy" [Sonnet 108].) Falstaff thinks he is calling out to Hal, but it is Henry V who is coming from his coronation. By showing Falstaff, before the king appears, calculating what effects he can hope to produce, Shakespeare demonstrates beyond any doubt how impossible, morally and politically, Falstaff would be as a royal favorite. It is all handled impeccably in social-historical perspective.

Such similarities between the Sonnets and Falstaff's language when he contemplates or addresses Hal also reflect the homogeneity of Shakespeare's idiom, his repertory of tropes and situations, regardless of whether they also reflect changing ways of investing himself in his art. To see them as surveyor's reference points in his development from work to work depends on having the whole territory in view, and on one's sense of their place in the dynamic whole of each work in which they appear. So we need to be aware of the role of the Chorus and its tension with the dramatic action in Henry V when we compare

> Behold, as may unworthiness define,
> A little touch of Harry in the night . . .

with Falstaff's great lie about the action at Gadshill, when "it was so dark thou couldest not see thy hand":

> By the Lord, I knew ye as well as he that made ye. Why, hear you, my masters,
> was it for me to kill the heir-apparent? Should I turn upon the true prince?
> Why, thou knowest I am as valiant as Hercules; but beware instinct—the lion
> will not touch the true prince.   (*1H4* II. iv. 223–24, 267–72)

Falstaff's lie, which Hal heartily enjoys seeing through, is a burlesque of the mystique
about magical royalty that undid Richard II, who imagined that the threat to his rule
would dissipate when the night-reveler Bolingbroke "Shall see us rising in our
throne, the east" (*R2* III. ii. 50). One find similar imagery, expressed with comparable seriousness, when the Sonnets celebrate the renewing presence of the friend.
In Sonnet 27, the young man, "like a jewel hung in ghastly night, / Makes black night
beauteous." "All days are nights" when the friend is absent in Sonnet 43, "And nights
bright days when dreams do show thee me."

On confronting Richard, even Bolingbroke will respond to the grandeur of the
king in terms of this imagery:

> See, see, King Richard doth himself appear,
> As doth the blushing discontented sun
> From out the fiery portal of the east,
> When he perceives the envious clouds are bent
> To dim his glory and to stain ...   (*R2* III. iii. 62–66)

Yet it is, of course, Richard's magical identification of himself with such metaphorical
equations that deflects him from full confrontation with political realities Bolingbroke knows how to manipulate. The same cluster of images is taken over by Hal
in the soliloquy in which he explains for the audience how he is going to make
Richard's imagery work, politically, by *using* his wildness and reformation:

> I know you all, and will a while uphold
> The unyok'd humor of your idleness,
> Yet herein will I imitate the sun,
> Who doth permit the base contagious clouds
> To smother up his beauty from the world,
> That when he please again to be himself,
> Being wanted, he may be more wond'red at
> By breaking through the foul and ugly mists
> Of vapors that did seem to strangle him.[11]   (*1H4* I. ii. 195–203)

By contrast, in the lines of the Chorus in *Henry V* about a magical sunlike presence
in the night, the royal mystique is again being used seriously. In following out Hal's
project to its heroic completion, with his "largest universal, like the sun, ... /
Thawing cold fear" among his soldiers, Shakespeare's search for idealized manhood
carries on in a heroic mode the effort of the Sonnets poet to live through the life
of his friend. It is essential to this project that Falstaff, and with him his ironic,
mocking perspective on the mystique of royalty, be left behind.

From the vantage point of Shakespeare's development, it is exactly right that he did *not* carry out the program, suggested by the epilogue for *Part Two,* to "continue the story, with Sir John in it, and make merry with fair Katherine of France, where (for any thing I know) Falstaff shall die of a sweat, unless already 'a be kill'd with your hard opinions." Certainly Falstaff was not killed in the audience's opinions, as contemporary allusions to his role, and its rehandling in *The Merry Wives of Windsor,* make clear. What we learn in *Henry V*—that "The King has kill'd his heart" (II. i. 88)—fits with the deeper levels of feeling underlying all the self-love and self-aggrandizement of his buffoonery, the level of feeling in the Sonnets:

> But do thy worst to steal thyself away,
> For term of life thou art assur'd mine,
> And life no longer than thy love will stay,
> For it depends upon that love of thine.   (Sonnet 92)

It is not so much that Falstaff loves Hal, but that Hal's love is for Falstaff the basis of his sense of self, however far he ranges in making himself a motley within the tavern world or sharking on Shallow in the country. On his side, Falstaff's love is as selfish *and* sincere as an infant's for its parent: "thy love is worth a million" in patronage, certainly, but also because "Thy sweet love rememb'red such wealth brings, / That then I scorn to change my state with kings" (Sonnet 29).

Sonnet 87 uses the poet's characteristic tendency toward self-effacement in an uncharacteristic reckoning with the prospect of losing the friend: "Farewell, thou art too dear for my possessing, / And like enough thou know'st thy estimate." At the end of *Part Two,* Falstaff finds that Henry V is too dear for his possessing, and very well knows his estimate. "Thus have I had thee as a dream doth flatter: / In sleep a king, but waking no such matter" (Sonnet 87) could serve to spell out the recognition we do not see banished Falstaff live to make. The poet, in the "farewell" sonnets that follow 87, can find consolation in the idea of dying if the young man abandons him:

> Thou canst not vex me with inconstant mind,
> Since that my life on thy revolt doth lie.
> O what a happy title do I find,
> Happy to have thy love, happy to die!   (Sonnet 92)

But here the escape into a fantasy of dying seems too easy: by introducing the logical extreme of the self-negating tendency in the Sonnets, Shakespeare pulls back from such troubling awareness of conflict as we find in many, far richer poems that surrender self-concern to extend the relationship. The effort in Sonnet 92 to bury in death the burden of exploration and understanding contrasts sharply with the powerfully resonant dramatization of the response to Falstaff's death in *Henry V.*

But Mistress Quickly's account of that death involves us in a strange, consenting fascination:

> Nay sure, he's not in hell; he's in Arthur's bosom, if ever man went to Arthur's
> bosom. 'A made a finer end, and went away and it had been any christom

child. 'A parted ev'n just between twelve and one, ev'n at the turning o' th' tide; for after I saw him fumble with the sheets, and play with flowers, and smile upon his finger's end, I knew there was but one way; for his nose was as sharp as a pen, and 'a babbl'd of green fields. "How now, Sir John? quoth I, "what, man? be a' good cheer." So 'a cried out, "God, God, God!" three or four times. Now I, to comfort him, bid him 'a should not think of God; I hop'd there was no need to trouble himself with any such thoughts yet. So 'a bade me lay more clothes on his feet. I put my hand into the bed and felt them, and they were as cold as any stone; then I felt to his knees, and so up'ard and up'ard, and all was as cold as any stone. (*H5* II. iii. 9–26)

Arthur's bosom, the turning of the tide, and the green fields, with or without Theobald's emendation from "a Table . . ." to " 'a babbl'd of green fields," make Falstaff almost a mythological figure. One could go on about him in *Golden Bough* language: a fertility spirit, a dying god, or a scapegoat.

Shakespeare keeps it all believably within the Hostess's idiom, right through to her characteristically modest way of describing the final failure of his potency, a theme picked up in the talk that follows:

NYM: They say he cried out of sack.
HOSTESS: Ay, that 'a did.
BARDOLPH: And of women.
HOSTESS: Nay, that 'a did not.
BOY: Yes, that 'a did, and said they were dev'ls incarnate.
HOSTESS: 'A could never abide carnation—'twas a color he never lik'd.
BOY: 'A said once, the dev'l would have him about women.
HOSTESS: 'A did in some sort, indeed, handle women; but then he was rheu-
matic, and talk'd of the whore of Babylon. (II. iii. 27–39)

The "mingled yarn" (*All's Well That Ends Well* IV. iii. 71) is beautifully woven here to include both Falstaff with Doll and the burlesque Puritanism in him that may go back to Oldcastle. The whole scene is an elegy, framed by the very unsavory life which, as Pistol says at the close of their previous scene, will go on:

PISTOL: His heart is fracted and corroborate.
NYM: The King is a good king, but it must be as it may; he passes some humors
and careers.
PISTOL: Let us condole the knight, for, lambkins, we will live. (II. i. 124–28)

The group turn to fresh fields and pastures new at the end:

BOY: Do you not remember, 'a saw a flea stick upon Bardolph's nose, and 'a
said it was a black soul burning in hell?
BARDOLPH: Well, the fuel is gone that maintain'd that fire. That's all the riches I
got in his service.
NYM: Shall we shog? the King will be gone from Southampton. (II. iii. 40–46)

The acceptance of death as a way out of the tensions of all-or-nothing relationship, eroticizing death within a seasonal rhythm, is the burden of one of the greatest of the sonnets. Like Mistress Quickly's elegy, Sonnet 73 culminates with warm life's yielding to the cold of the deathbed:

> That time of year thou mayest in me behold,
> When yellow leaves, or none, or few, do hang
> Upon those boughs which shake against the cold,
> Bare ruined choirs, where late the sweet birds sang.
> In me thou seest the twilight of such day,
> As after sunset fadeth in the west,
> Which by and by black night doth take away,
> Death's second self, that seals up all in rest.
> In me thou seest the glowing of such fire,
> That on the ashes of his youth doth lie,
> As the death-bed whereon it must expire,
> Consumed with that which it was nourished by.
>   This thou perceiv'st, which makes thy love more strong,
>   To love that well which thou must leave ere long.

"Fare well, thou latter spring!" Hal called out gaily after Falstaff's exit from their first scene together, "Fare well, All-hallown summer" (*1H4* I. ii. 158–59). He loves that well which he must leave ere long.

On Shakespeare's part: "Greater love hath no man than this, that a man lay down his life for his friends" (John 15:13)—or so vital a part of the life in him as animated Falstaff. To return to a significant point: the sacrifice of Falstaff's vicarious enjoyment of Hal within the Henry IV plays is made to permit vicarious realization of manhood by author and audience in admiring Henry V's "royalty of nature" (*Mac.* III. i. 49). The fundamental reason that Falstaff could not go on to help us make merry with fair Katherine of France is that in *Henry V* Shakespeare shifts to using the whole theater as an "oblation" (Sonnet 125) to its hero: in Henry V's world there is no place for Falstaff as, in his strange way, a steward of his excellence. Despite the program, the sacrifice does not entirely work. However admirable the civic or patriotic commitment animating the enterprise, King Henry V, "all shining with the virtues of success," in Empson's phrase,[12] is not adequate to the possibilities for manhood Shakespeare comes to envisage in tragedy.

NOTES

[1] C. L. Barber, *Shakespeare's Festive Comedy* (Princeton: Princeton University Press, 1959), pp. 192–221.

[2] *The Standard Edition of the Complete Psychological Works of Sigmund Freud*, trans. and ed. James Strachey et al., 24 vols. (London: Hogarth, 1953–74), vol. 18; see esp. 111–16.

[3] I am drawing here on Professor Neely's "Detachment and Engagement in Shakespeare's Sonnets: 94, 116, and 129," *PMLA* 92 (1977): 83–95, to which I am greatly indebted.

[4] *Shakespeare's Sonnets*, ed. with analytic commentary by Stephen Booth (New Haven: Yale University Press, 1977), p. 351.

[5] Maurice Morgann, *An Essay on the Dramatic Character of Sir John Falstaff* (London: T. Davies, 1777); Roy Battenhouse, "Falstaff as Parodist and Perhaps Holy Fool," *PMLA* 90 (1975): 32–52.

[6] See *Shakespeare's Festive Comedy*, pp. 67–73 for one consideration of these roles. See also J. Dover Wilson, *The Fortunes of Falstaff* (Cambridge: Cambridge University Press, 1943).

[7] See Geoffrey Bullough, ed., *Narrative and Dramatic Sources of Shakspeare*, 8 vols. (London: Routledge and Kegan Paul; and New York: Columbia University Press, 1957–75), vol. 4, pp. 179, 193–94, 216–17.

[8] Reprinted in *Sources*, vol. 4, pp. 299–343.

[9] The whole hopeful fusion of royal prerogative and constitutional law, which worked under Elizabeth and was to come apart under James, is invoked in Henry's reply to the Chief Justice, along with Shakespeare's respect for the institution of law and for the monarch as its sanction. The new king's response underscores the characteristically Elizabethan idea that he submits to the Justice voluntarily, that the monarch abides by law and Parliament by choice, with an absolute prerogative in reserve.

[10] Ernst Kris, *Psychoanalytic Explorations in Art* (New York: International Universities Press, 1952), pp. 273–88.

[11] William Empson, in his wonderful chapter on the Sonnets and *Henry IV*, observes that this is the same imagery as in Sonnet 33, "the earliest and most pathetic of the attempts to justify" the friend's infidelity: "Full many a glorious morning have I seen ... / Anon permit the basest clouds to ride / With ugly rack on his celestial face." Empson notes that the attitude of the sonnet is "turned backwards" in Hal's soliloquy: "the sun is now to free itself from the clouds by the very act of betrayal." *Some Versions of Pastoral* (London: Chatto and Windus, 1935), p. 100.

[12] *Some Versions of Pastoral*, p. 100.

Paul M. Cubeta

FALSTAFF AND THE ART OF DYING

Once the historical myths and dramatic concerns of *The Henriad* served by Falstaff's comic vision have been resolved by his legendary repudiation, Falstaff the character can no longer exist: "Reply not to me with a foolborn jest" (Shakespeare, *2H4* V. v. 55).[1] On that command to silence, the newly crowned king has destroyed his fool and jester. Falstaff could undergo a mock-magical death and resurrection at the end of *I Henry IV*, and he essentially "dies of a sweat" at the end of *2 Henry IV*, when he races recklessly to Westminster Abbey "to stand stain'd with travel, and sweating with desire to see" Hal newly crowned (V. v. 24–25). But Falstaff the man cannot be dismissed or lie forgotten in Fleet Prison, abandoned by king and playwright. The Shakespearean investment in the saving grace of that comic spirit in his Lancastrian world has been too great. And so in *Henry V* he redeems Epilogue's promise in *2 Henry IV* to continue the story "with Sir John in it" (Epi., 28) with a vividly realized, yet non-existent death scene, both comic and pathetic, private and demonstrated, dedicated to the spirit of Falstaff the man.

Never allowed securely to grasp this protean giant even when his comic imagination and ironic vision die, the audience participates in the immediacy and intensity of the deathbed scene but not by observing those who stand at Falstaff's bedside. Simultaneously the audience is kept at double distance from the mystery of Falstaff's dying thoughts. Instead of a sentimental farewell in the cold, pragmatic Lancastrian world, Shakespeare seeks instead a resolution in which tragedy and comedy, doubt and belief, clarity and confusion are bound in a manner historically appropriate, morally satisfying, and psychologically dazzling. The theatrical gamble of creating a character by not creating him, of giving him life by destroying him, yields the most memorable scene of the play.

To achieve the dense texture of this recollected deathbed scene, Shakespeare does not turn to his usual source for things even vaguely Falstaffian in *The Henriad—The Famous Victories of Henry V* (1598). In the life of Falstaff, Shakespeare has embodied rituals, folk tales, conventions, festivals as familiar to an Elizabethan

From *Studies in English Literature 1500–1900* 27, No. 2 (Spring 1987): 197–211.

audience as those he may now be suggestively recalling in the medieval and Renaissance tradition of *ars moriendi,* or the art of dying. To design a coherent structure and meaning to Falstaff's dying moments of introspection and memory, which appear as merely broken, delirious fragments, Shakespeare may also give Falstaff the occasion to attempt a private meditation on his life in the manner of a Renaissance meditation for Wednesday night.

Reported in an intensely moving yet uncertain retelling, Falstaff's mode of dying is as mysterious and as hauntingly perplexing as any circumstance in his life. The only words directly attributed to him, the great inventor of language, are "God, God, God!" (*H5* II. iii. 19). But what this punster, this parodist and unparalleled player with the rhythms of spoken language means or what tone the repetitions are spoken in is not ours to hear. The challenger of the moral, social, political, and religious values on which civilization rests dies with a word, the Word, on which pun cannot prevail. Like his heart, which Pistol avers, was "fracted and corroborate" (II. i. 124), the scene recollecting Falstaff's death is a kind of transitory memorial moment, broken, unfocused, contradictory, unchronological and impossible to recreate for even their listeners by his bedside mourners, who are then about to be swept up into events in France and propelled to their own deaths.

For the old man's allegedly delirious dying moments as told by a grieving companion whose control of the English language was never firm, Shakespeare needed some kind of intelligible inner structure not available to him in the limited theatrical possibilities of an undramatic scene of dubious recollection. All that is really necessary to complete the exposition of the Falstaff story is Pistol's opening declaration and exhortation, "for Falstaff he is dead. / And we must ern therefore" (*H5* II. iii. 5–6). The flexible strategies of the meditative exercises on *ars moriendi* allow Shakespeare the undergirding of a coherent traditional structure familiar to a Renaissance audience, with its fascination for deathbed scenes. Thus he can both shape rhetorically the dramatized design of the brief scene of companionable reminiscence and give meaning to the interior monologue and meditation of the dying Falstaff. Not rheumatic, as the Hostess suggests, he is also not incoherent, only seeming so in her narrative. In this shaky account, Shakespeare illuminates for his theater audience thoughts and intentions which even in happier times Falstaff could not always share with these companions. Yet Falstaff's voice must now be the Hostess's, hopelessly literal-minded and completely antithetical to his own.

Falstaff's mocking pledges of repentance, comically counterpointing Lancastrian political guilt, may at the hour of his death, no longer counterfeited, be transformed into another attempt at reformation. But this one is more ambiguous than those extending from Hal's first soliloquy promising to redeem the time to his father's dying plea for divine forgiveness: "How I came by the crown O God forgive me" (*2H4* IV. v. 218).[2] By prince or whore Falstaff is constantly reproached to repent, to remember his day of reckoning. His friends often sound as though they were repeating the conventional pieties of Thomas Lupset in his *Waye of Dyenge Well* (1541) or Robert Parsons's *The First Booke of the Christian Exercise, Appertayning to Resolution* (1582), in which chapter 8 is entitled "The daye of deathe

Of what opinion and feelinge we shalbe, touchinge these matters, at the tyme of our deathe,"[3] or Gaspar Loarte's *The Exercise of a Christian Life* (1579). The moral exhortations Loarte insistently makes are typical:

> take then a zelous and feruent desire to liue a new here after, and striue to get other new behauiours, & to liue far otherwise than thou hast done to-fore.... Eschewe al occasions of sinne, especially the companie of wicked men, but muche more of women, such as may prouoke thee to noughtines and geue thee loose and lewd example.... Thou must flye suche places where God is customably offended, as be dising houses, tauernes, dauncing schooles, and such like.... Thou must take hede of al excesse in eating, drinking, sleping and clothing, and indeuour thy self to obserue a mediocritie and temperance in eche of them.[4]

These books of Renaissance meditation, among others, Catholic and Protestant, published in numerous editions in fifteenth- and sixteenth-century England, all explored like good-conduct books the ways in which the devout or those whose faith was more fragile should prepare for a final reckoning.[5] The admonitions of sin, death, and judgment were so common as Renaissance homilies that an English audience could have warned Falstaff as well as Hal or Doll. "Live now as you will wish to have lived when you come to that sorrowful day" is the kind of exhortation that runs through Parsons's *First Book*. He would find a curious moral ally in Doll: "when wilt thou leave fighting a' days and foining a' nights, and begin to patch up thine old body for heaven?" (*2H4* II. iv. 231–33). Hal, newly crowned, is only more austerely puritanical in chastising the Falstaff he abandons: "Leave gormandizing, know the grave doth gape / For thee thrice wider than for other men" (V. v. 53–54).

For Falstaff, playing the penitent is a subject for infinite amusement. In plays which find their moral center in redeeming the time, repentance, reformation, and reckoning, Hal and Falstaff can counterpoint their pledges. "I'll so offend, to make offense a skill, / Redeeming time when men think least I will" (*1H4* I. ii. 216–17) is Hal's first promise to himself and to the audience as he rationalizes his manipulation of his tavern friends both to learn about the potential corruption of fleshly indulgence and to prepare for a public apotheosis in good time. The language may be spiritual, but the hours of study, more active than contemplative, are more for his brilliant political future than for the salvation necessary for his eternal life. For Falstaff, on the other hand, the language of moral reformation in *1* and *2 Henry IV* carries economic, not political or spiritual ambiguities. Hal, ironically amused, notes the rapidity with which Falstaff transforms his pledge to "give over this life, ... and I do not, I am a villain, I'll be damned for never a king's son in Christendom" (*1H4* I. ii. 95–97) into a plan to take purses at Gadshill: "I see a good amendment of life in thee, from praying to pursetaking" (102–103). Falstaff's instant moral defense is that it is "no sin for a man to labor in his vocation" (104–105). His pun on *vocation* as profession and religious conversion is echoed at Shrewsbury when Hal tells Falstaff to prepare for battle and say his prayers, for he "owest God a death" (V. i. 126). Falstaff's rejoinder picks up the homophonic pun on *debt*, as he is determined that this is not the day to prepare to die well or at all: " 'Tis not due yet. I would be loath to pay him before his day" (127–28). Let those who value honor do so. "A trim reckoning" (135). Playful language then can redeem all moral questions.

One of the deliberately unresolved mysteries of *The Henriad* is whether Falstaff does finally make a good end, for we have only the Hostess's not unbiased judgment that " 'A made a finer end, and went away and it had been any christom child" (*H5* II. iii. 10–12). An audience comes to this scene after another one of public confession and repentance so carefully orchestrated that the broken and uncertain fragments of Falstaff's only private meditation are made more resonantly convincing. Scroop, Cambridge, and Grey, trapped into confessing their treason and sentencing themselves to death, seem relieved that they have been caught. Each in turn thanks God for "the discovery of most dangerous treason" (II. ii. 162), asks for divine and monarchial forgiveness, and seem almost to parody the assertion of Lupset and others that in *ars moriendi* "this dyenge well is in effecte to dye gladlye":[6]

> CAM[BRIDGE:] But God be thanked for prevention,
> Which [I] in sufferance heartily will rejoice,
> Beseeching God, and you, to pardon me.   (158–60)

The traitors, "poor miserable wretches" (178), are borne off to their execution at the moment when Falstaff also dies, betrayed by his king, who, says the Hostess, "kill'd his heart" (II. i. 88). The perspectives of betrayer betrayed, parodied and balanced, continue as a Lancastrian legacy from the time of Bolingbroke and Northumberland in *Richard II.*

For a brief interlude, almost outside the time of *Henry V,* as Henry dispatches his traitors and exultantly moves to France "to busy giddy minds / With foreign quarrels" (*2H4* IV. v. 213–14), Shakespeare elusively distances the dramatic scene of Falstaff's death by recessing it into an interior moment, a scene-within-a-scene and then within that a memory-within-a-memory. Those last friends of Falstaff—Hostess, Boy, Pistol, Nym, and Bardolph—try to recapture Falstaff's deathbed hour as a last memory. But so equivocal is their disagreement that an audience cannot even be sure who was there besides the Hostess, the Boy, and Bardolph. Nym has heard another account of Falstaff's death: "They say he cried out of sack" (II. iii. 27). But who are these anonymous bedside witnesses whose story is as quickly challenged as are the contradictory reports of those who now botch the telling of their witnessed accounts? The distorted perspective of each seems finally to return the memory of Falstaff only to the security of the theater audience which can only intuit the manner of his death.

The design of the scene that is played is constructed from ambiguities of time, imagery, and theme inherent in the history plays: order/disorder, bawdy/sentimental, innocence/experience, youth/age, physical/spiritual, salvation/damnation, time/sea, life/death. Falstaff's dying like his living remains beyond precise description or adequate dramatization, imbedded in the structure of its telling. The

Hostess, as the primary witness, does not herself understand the import of her account. In the confusion, distancing, and failure of Falstaff's last story lies its dramatic achievement.

To the extent that there are facts, they suggest that an emaciated Falstaff developed a sudden sweat and a high fever and died shortly after midnight. Although delirious, he seemed aware that he was on his deathbed. He apparently saw a flea on Bardolph's nose and said it was a black soul burning in hell. He inveighed against sack and prostitutes whom he called devils incarnate. He talked about the Whore of Babylon. He fumbled with his sheets, smiled at his fingertips, apparently mumbled something about green fields, called out "God" three or four times. As his feet grew cold, he asked the Hostess for more bedclothes and died.

If Falstaff is making a determined effort to die well by attempting a deathbed repentance, it is one only his Maker could be sure of. No character has been advised more insistently to remember his end, nor promised more persistently to do so when the time was right. Yet at the moment of Falstaff's dying the Hostess urges upon him as a dubious theological comfort not to think of God: "I hop'd there was no need to trouble himself with such thoughts yet" (II. iii. 21–22). Her words express Falstaff's long-standing determination to postpone any day of spiritual reckoning. Nonetheless, Falstaff may be attempting a meditation in the Renaissance manner of *ars moriendi,* perhaps as broken and as incomplete as the narrated account of it. Whether spiritually efficacious or not remains beyond the limits of the play. But the dramatic, ritualistic, and psychological appropriateness of such a spiritual moment fulfills the design of Falstaff's creation and existence.

The paradoxical symmetry of Falstaff's life has always been mythic, not realistic,[7] as it embodies rituals, folk tales, and festivals. For a man who lives out of all time, the hours of his birth and death are recorded as nowhere else in Shakespeare. As he tells the Chief Justice, "My Lord, I was born about three of the clock in the afternoon, with a white head and something a round belly" (*2H4* I. ii. 187–89). Born allegedly an old, fat man, he dies "ev'n just between twelve and one, ev'n at the turnong o' th' tide" (*H5* II. iii. 12–13) like a "christom child," newly christened and now shrouded in his white baptismal clothes. From corrupted old age he moves in death to appearing as an innocent child, even as the play returns to the first time an audience saw Falstaff as he emerged at noon from bed in *I Henry IV*. The first mythic definition of Falstaff is reenforced in his death scene. It is, as Hal says, superfluous to ask Falstaff the time of day, for he has nothing to do with these symbols of order, political responsibility, or personal self-discipline. It is also superfluous to ask the Hostess how she could have been certain when high tide occurred on the Thames that last night. Like the fertility festival and the ritual games of the purged scapegoat, this moment is haunted by an aura of folklore and superstition. It was an old English belief, according to Sir James Frazer, held along the east coast of England that most deaths occur as the tide ebbs, a natural "melancholy emblem of failure, of weakness, and of death."[8] An audience would not have known which turning of the tide, or which twelve and one without a sense of the symbolic rightness that would remove the verbal ambiguity of the Hostess's sense of time and tide. The death of the dubiously legitimate king, Henry IV, who dies repentant in the Jerusalem Chamber as the Thames "thrice flowed, no ebb between" (*2H4* IV. iv. 125) parallels that of player-king Falstaff, who once mocked him for Hal's amusement in Eastcheap and now dies in Eastcheap no longer playing penitent. These balanced moments suggest again Christian rituals intertwined with folk tales, from the death of newly christened babies to those of kings and errant knights.[9]

If the Hostess, forgiving soul, believes that Falstaff is in Arthur's bosom, she is secure in her belief that Falstaff has not been judged and damned. It makes little difference whether she means the Christian heaven of Abraham's bosom as defined in Luke 16:22 or the pagan heaven of King Arthur's Avalon. And if Henry IV's belief in the prophecy that he would die in Jerusalem on his "voyage to the Holy Land, / To wash this blood off from my guilty hand" (*R2* V. vi. 49–50) can be accommodated by a quibble on Jerusalem Chamber, the Hostess's malapropism should be no less certain in its intent. Falstaff has always been more a practitioner of his view of *ars vivendi* than *ars moriendi*, so if the conduct of his life has been at best morally ambiguous, then its appropriate ending would be spiritually uncertain. Medieval and Renaissance meditative rituals serve both arts for him. At Shrewsbury he prefers catechisms on honor and comic resurrections that leave the body intact; rather than the grinning honor of dead Sir Walter Blunt, he declares, "Give me life, which if I can save, so" (*1H4* V. iii. 59–60). Salvation is a matter of preserving the body in time present. When at Eastcheap he promises, "I must give over this life, and I will give it over" (I. ii. 95–96), the words would suit a Puritan preacher better than does their context in the midst of battle. "But to counterfeit dying, when a man thereby liveth, is to be no counterfeit, but the true and perfect image of life indeed" (V. iv. 117–19).

One of Falstaff's most agile verbal games is that in his profane parody of the language of *ars vivendi* he plays a secular *ars moriendi*. As Hal tells Poins, "He will give the devil his due" (I. ii. 119). He constantly protests his fear of damnation, of being corrupted by Hal even if he were a saint; he delights in refuting the charge that he is "that villainous abominable misleader of youth, Falstaff, that old white-bearded Sathan" (II. iv. 462–64). He wishes, he says, that he could have been a puritan weaver so he could sing penitential psalms. He declares to the Chief Justice that he lost his voice "hallowing and singing of anthems" (*2H4* I. ii. 189–90). Whether he is playing Lord of Misrule, Antic, Miles Gloriosus, Comic Satan, or Corrupter of Youth, his archetypal roles make a travesty of the traditional posture of the penitent who must think of his sins and prepare for the hour of his dying. Robert Parsons indeed writes his *First Booke of the Christian Exercise* for readers "so carelesse, or so carnallie geeuen" that like Falstaff they would hardly do more than glance at his opening pages. He asks, therefore, only for their patience while he tries to persuade them of the error of their ways and so to move them to the "necessarie resolution, of leauinge vanities to serue God."[10] Falstaff knows Parsons's text—and Lupset's, Bunny's, and Luis de Granada's—and quotes them as liberally and as cavalierly as he does Scripture, whenever they accommodate his chameleon-like purposes of serving himself while pleasing a prince in whose earthly kingdom he has hopes of long-lasting reward. He will paraphrase a meditative counselor like Parsons to share a moment of self-mockery with his prince: "What are thow the better now to haue liued in credit with the world? in fauour of princes? exalted of men?"[11] No Renaissance leader of devotional meditation would have had the imagination to concoct for a deathbed repentance the moral inventory available to Falstaff: lying, cowardice, avarice, vanity, gluttony, drunkenness, sloth, thievery, misusing the king's press, fornication. But their ponderous spiritual guides would also have neglected to point out the love and loyalty, the wit and imagination, and the comic genius that redeem Falstaff's living.

If Falstaff's deathbed scene were simply to conclude a dissolute life as Hal, his brothers, or the Chief Justice would have it, Falstaff would fall to his prayers and seek the grace Henry urges in his repudiation of him—"How ill white hairs become a fool and jester!" (*2H4* V. v. 48). What for Luis de Granada is a metaphor of consequence for a wasted life has been Falstaff's whole reality in Eastcheap, but the Shakespearean dramatic moment of Falstaff's dying will not yield transparent spiritual conclusions to Luis de Granada's easy rhetorical questions:

> If a waiefaringe man, hauinge but one farthinge in his purse, shoulde enter into an inne, and placinge him selfe downe at the table, shoulde require of the host to bringe in Partridges, Capons, Phesauntes, and all other delicates, that maie be founde in the howse, and shoulde suppe with verie great pleasure, and contentation, neuer remembringe that at the last there must come a time of accompt: who woulde not take this fellowe, either for a iester, or for a verie foole? Now what greater folie or madnes can be deuised, than for men to geue them selues so looselye to all kindes of vices, and to sleepe so sowndlie in them, without euer remembringe, that shortly after at their departinge out of their Inne, there shall be required of them a verie strayt and particular accompte of all their dissolute and wicked lyfe?[12]

If Falstaff denies Luis de Granada's economic and moral premises, which are also at the heart of the Lancastrian political enterprises, his dying moments are brilliantly poised between accepting and rejecting those spiritual conclusions.

The undramatized scene of Falstaff's death has been ruthlessly anticipated in *2 Henry IV* as his voice modulates from robust, zesty parody to a genuine fear of encroaching death—"Peace, good Doll, do not speak like a death's head, do not bid me remember mine end" (*2H4* II. iv. 234–35). At his end he appears to be a shrunken, dying old man, no longer the maker and embodiment of vital language and consummate comic actor. No longer wittily supporting his role-playing as the devil incarnate, his language, incoherent and disconnected, is reduced to conventional religious platitudes, traditional pieties, and pleas for more blankets. No longer able to hide behind the fantasies of invented language, he cannot counterfeit kings of England nor play Lord of Misrule. He cannot turn diseases to self-serving commodity or spiritual utility. And he is no longer "the cause that wit is in other men" (I. ii. 10).

As a great performer in need of an audience, Falstaff has never before had an introspective or meditative moment which might be called personal. His soliloquies on honor in *I Henry IV* or on sack in *2 Henry IV* are essentially public moments, the comedian indulging himself with the theater audience rather than his stage audience. Only in a play in which he does not exist and on his deathbed does Falstaff have a ritualistic moment of meditation in which he is only partly aware of those around him and in which his mind turns inward and backward in memory.

Just before his death Falstaff may meditatively engage what Ignatius Loyola calls "seeing the spot," recalling the scene upon which one is meditating with the immediacy of actually being present in it.[13] This conventional "composition of place," which begins a meditation, would invoke the first of the "three powers of the soul"—memory, understanding, and will.[14] Falstaff may remember a romantic moment when he picked flowers in a green meadow, although the text remains as brilliantly insecure as the telling of the babbling. That lost innocence bears no resemblance to other memories recollected in Shallow's orchard of those nights when old classmates recall having heard the chimes at midnight. Other reminiscences are also unambiguous emblems of his life—sack and women; but those memories seem now touched with the recognition of some kind of moral or spiritual understanding, the second stage of the meditative process. Now Falstaff no longer cries out for sack but against it, and he calls the women of Eastcheap "dev'ls incarnate" (*H5* II. iii. 31–32). The Hostess's well-meaning denial, based on the fact that he "could never abide carnation" (33), was repudiated from the first when Falstaff admits that he would enjoy the sun only if it were "a fair hot wench in flame-color'd taffata" (*IH4* I. ii. 9–10). The identification of his whores with the Whore of Babylon may suggest that Falstaff is thinking of the Apocalypse in Rev. 17:3–6: "and I saw a woman sit upon a scarlet colored beast.... And the woman was arrayed in purple and scarlet colour." Or perhaps as a dubiously reformed Puritan he is attacking the Catholic Church, as Edmund Bunny would have him do in his meditation. The Hostess's possible pun on "rheum" for Rome—"but then he was rheumatic" (*H5* II. iii. 38)—may reinforce the allusion without clarifying Falstaff's "understanding." Seeing a flea land on Bardolph's nose may be only the last flicker of the endless jokes at his expense—"his face is Lucifer's privy kitchen" (*2H4* II. iv. 333)—or a deathbed prophecy of Bardolph's impending sacrilege and punishment.

Is Falstaff like Hal seeking a reformation that will glitter o'er his fault as he tries without parody to redeem the time? The fragmented and disconnected structure of his last words, the ambiguity of his observations, and the malapropisms of the Hostess deny resolution as Falstaff may drift to the third and final step in the meditative process, the engaging of the affections, or the will, which traditionally concludes with a colloquy. A meditation on *ars moriendi* would appropriately end in an invocation or prayer to God. And Falstaff calls out to God. But what does he mean? Is this only a feverish cry of fear? Is he trying to make an act of contrition and asking for divine forgiveness? Is this the cry of a man who believes that he has been abandoned by God—as by friend and king—in his last hour? Is one perhaps to hear an elusive echo of Christ's last words on the Cross, a moment Renaissance spiritual advisors urged for deathbed meditations; as, for example, Thomas More in *Four Last Things*: "But whan the poynt approched in which his sacred soule shold depart out of his blessed bodye, at that pointe he cryed loude once or twice to his father in heuen"?[15] Luis de Granada in his *ars moriendi* exercise for Wednesday night would be secure in his spiritual interpretation of this colloquy, but Shakespeare's audience is denied that certainty:

> And as well herein, as in the other things, thou hast to consider what great greiffe and anguishe of mynde the sycke person shall then abide in callinge to minde his wicked and synfull life: and how gladly he wishethe at that time that he had taken a better waie: and what an awstere kinde of lyfe he woulde then determine to leade, if he might haue time to doe the same: and how fayne he woulde then enforce himselfe to call vpon almightie God, and to desier him of helpe and succour. Howbeit the verie paine, greife, and continuall increasinge of his sickenes and death will scarcely permitte him so to doe.[16]

The Hostess is equally certain that she knows, but she urges Falstaff to get his mind off death and an afterlife. This, the only time any one tells Falstaff not to worry about his end, physical or spiritual, would be an ironic comfort, indeed, if Luis de Granada's precepts were attended to:

> The first stroke wherewith death is wont to strike, is the feare of death. Suerlie this is a very great anguishe vnto him that is in loue with his lyfe: and this forewarninge is such a great greife vnto a man, that oftentimes his carnall friendes doe vse to dissemble it, and will not haue the sicke man to beleue it, least it shoulde vexe and disquiet him: and this they will doe sometimes although it be to the preiudice and destruction of his miserable sowle.[17]

The Hostess's spiritual purposes may be a miscalculation, but this is her finest moment, not just in the innocence of her double entendres, the humor of her verbal blunders, or her sentimental recollecting of Falstaff's death. If ever there was a woman who had been sorely abused and put upon and "borne, and . . . been fubb'd off" (*2H4* II.i.34), it is she who has been victimized by Falstaff, who has indeed "handled" her most outrageously. Yet at the end she loves and comforts, forgives by forgetting. There is in her a Christian charity starkly missing in Falstaff's monarch. Her ministrations may also be reminiscent of those of Socrates' friends at the onset of the death of their companion, condemned as another alleged villainous, abominable misleader of youth and a threat to the established political order: "I put my hand into the bed and felt them, and they were as cold as any stone; then I felt to his knees, and so up'ard and up'ard, and all was as cold as any stone" (*H5* II.iii. 23–26). At the beginning of his "Remembrance of Death" in *Four Last Things*, Thomas More recalls Plato's account of Socrates' death in the *Phaedo*—"For some of the olde famous philosophers, whan thei were demaunded what facultie philosophy was, answerd that it was the meditacion or exercise of death"—and then urges us to "fantasy" our own death in a detailed vision that may bear resemblance to some of the Hostess's recollection: "lying on thy bedde, . . . thy nose sharping, thy legges coling, thy fingers fimbling, . . . and thy death drawyng on."[18] Even if Shake-speare is recalling More, the unintended bawdy is characteristically the Hostess's own in gesture and simile. Falstaff's stones are cold. Desire no longer outlives performance, as Poins once ridiculed the old man. And his nose, now as sharp as a pen, makes Falstaff's gloriously hyperbolic epithets of Hal—"you starveling, you eelskin, you dried neat's tongue, you bull's pizzle, you stockfish" (*1H4* II. iv. 244–45)—an inverted echo mocked by death, which has finally dethroned surrogate king and father.

The Hostess's vivid recollection of the approaching coldness of death suggests the unrelenting descriptions constantly set out by Loarte, Parsons, Bunny, and Luis de Granada as they urge one to meditate on the moment of dying with a calcu-latedly precise enumeration. If Shakespeare had their admonitions in mind, he has transformed the macabre and morbid into a bittersweet and humorous account worthy of Falstaff's vital comic spirit. He has detached the spiritual implications and left instead only the poignant corporeal reality, as the scene moves from meditation and remembrance to those who witness or learn of the event with limited under-standing and qualified affection. As Parsons lugubriously imagines the inevitable moment:

> Imagine, what the violent mortyfiinge of all the partes together will doe. For we see that first the sowle is driuen by death to leaue the extreamest partes, as the toes, feete and fyngers: then the legges and armes, and so consequent-lye one parte dyeth after an other, vntill lyfe be restrained onlye to the harte, which holdeth out longest as the principall parte, but yet must finallye be constrained to render it selue.[19]

Not so, however, with Falstaff. His heart was fracted and corroborate and killed first.

This final creating of a character thematically and dramatically dead at the end of *2 Henry IV* is thus theatrically and structurally achieved through a transformation of an *ars moriendi* meditation composed of the fragments of the disintegrating comic world of *The Henriad.* It is a memorial to a real and mythic character whose essential ambiguity remains as mysteriously allusive in dying as in living. The Shakespearean mode of dramatization is far more affective in its indirectness than any threatening exhortation of a Renaissance spiritual counselor. For us who are invited to meditate on Falstaff the loss of Falstaffian life leads to a diminution of theatrical richness. Consolation is not to be found in any recognition that Falstaff tried to die well.

In the Hostess's disjointed narrative it is possible that some in Shakespeare's audience might recall some of the popular block wood cuts of the *Ars Moriendi* that circulated in hundreds of editions and unknown numbers of copies throughout the fifteenth and sixteenth centuries.[20] In the Editio Princeps an emaciated Moriens lies naked in bed with a blanket pulled up to his waist and his arms extended over it. He is variously surrounded by friends, family, servants, doctors, and nurses as well as grotesque little demons.[21] Such an engraving precedes Luis de Granada's

Wednesday night meditation on *ars moriendi* in *Of Prayer, and Meditation*. To a Renaissance audience the realistic and the symbolic, the mythic or the allegorical could co-exist in art and could perhaps be recalled in this traditional mode as a model for the moment that Shakespeare is dramatizing through narration. The Hostess is surely an attentive nurse; Boy, a loyal young servant. Bardolph would have made a good devil; he has been advised of that often enough. Possibly at the end the shrunken Falstaff might, in addition to all his other mythic and traditional roles, unwittingly adopt that of Moriens. But whereas Moriens is shown to have died well as his soul, a young child, leaves his mouth and ascends, we are left only with the Hostess's sentimental assurance of Falstaff's "finer end."

The Hostess's lament brings only a brief truce to erstwhile companions who were at swordpoints earlier that evening. Falstaff's memory now yields to their economic self-serving calculation and suspicion even before the scene is over. By the day of Agincourt his name is forgotten. Swept up in the nationalistic fervor of war against France, this ironic band of brothers shogs off to turn a profit in a world where thievery and whoring have at least moral and mortal consequences. Nym and Bardolph are hanged by order of the King, and Nell dies disease-ridden "i' the spittle / Of a malady of France" (V. i. 82–83). And there is none to mourn their passing who would argue that they died well.

NOTES

[1] Quotations are taken from *The Riverside Shakespeare*, ed. G. Blakemore Evans (Boston: Houghton Mifflin, 1974).

[2] For a persuasive exploration of the parallelisms in the *Henry IV* plays and the two historical tetralogies, see Sherman H. Hawkins, "*Henry IV*: The Structural Problem Revisited," *Shakespeare Quarterly* 33 (1982): 278–301.

[3] The work of the English Jesuit Parsons was modified by the Puritan Edmund Bunny in *A Book of Christian Exercise* (1584), but with his admonitions on the Christian necessity for repentance in preparation for death virtually unchanged.

[4] Gaspar Loarte, *The Exercise of a Christian Life*, trans. James Sancer (pseud. Stephen Brinkley), (Rheims, 1584), pp. 8–10.

[5] When Caxton translated in 1490 the early fifteenth-century anonymous Latin *Tractus* as the *Ars Moriendi*, or the *Crafte of Dying Well*, he was making available a text that was to become immensely popular over the next two centuries. For a full discussion of the tradition of *Ars Moriendi* in England during the sixteenth century, see Nancy Lee Beatty, *The Craft of Dying: A Study in the Literary Tradition of the 'Ars Moriendi' in England* (New Haven: Yale Univ. Press, 1970), chs. 2 and 4. See also Louis L. Martz, *The Poetry of Meditation* (New Haven: Yale Univ. Press, 1954), pp. 135–44, and Sister Mary Catharine O'Connor, *The Art of Dying Well: The Development of the Ars Moriendi* (New York: Columbia Univ. Press, 1942).

[6] Thomas Lupset, *The Waye of Dyenge Well* (London, 1541), fol. 11ᵛ.

[7] *Morgann's Essay on the Dramatic Character of Sir John Falstaff*, ed. William Arthur Gill (London, 1912), p. 184.

[8] Sir James Frazer, *The Golden Bough* (New York: Macmillan, 1942), abridged edn., pp. 34–35. Noted in J. I. M. Stewart, *Character and Motive in Shakespeare* (London: Longmans, Green, 1949), p. 137.

[9] Philip Williams, "The Birth and Death of Falstaff Reconsidered," *Shakespeare Quarterly* 8 (1957):362.

[10] Robert Parsons, *The First Booke of the Christian Exercise* (Rouen, 1582), pp. 8, 9, 14, 25, and passim.

[11] Parsons, p. 107.

[12] Luis de Granada, *Of Prayer, and Meditation*, trans. Richard Hopkins (Paris, 1582), fol. 188ʳ. An English edition was published in London in 1592.

[13] "Thou must understand, that they are in such wise to be meditated, as though they happened euen

in that instant before thine eyes, in the selfe same place where thou art, or within thy soule: or otherwise imagining thou were in the very places where suche thinges happed, if haply this waies thou shalt feele better deuotion" (Loarte, p. 67).

[14] W. H. Longridge, *The Spiritual Exercises of Saint Ignatius of Loyola* (London: Robert Scott, 1919), pp. 52–57.

[15] *The Workes of Thomas More . . . wrytten by him in the Englysh tonge*, ed. William Rastell (London, 1557), p. 78.

[16] Luis de Granada, fols. 183^v–84^r.

[17] Luis de Granada, fol. 190^r.

[18] Rastell, pp. 77–78.

[19] Parsons, p. 102. Edmund Bunny's account (*A Book of Christian Exercise*, [London, 1584], p. 90) is essentially the same. Luis de Granada (fol. 184^r) is no less explicit in his urging our attention:

> Consider then also those last accidentes, and panges of the sicknes, (which be as it were messingers of death) how fearfull and terrible they be. How at that time the sicke mans breast panteth: his voyce waxeth hoarce: his feete begynnge to die: his knees to waxe colde, and stiffe: his nostrels ronne out: his eies sincke into his head: his countenance looketh pale and wanne: his tonge faultereth, and is not able to doe his office; finally by reason of the hast of the departure awaye of the sowle out of the bodie, all his senses are sore vexed, and troubled, and they doe vtterlie leese their force, and virtue.

[20] O'Connor, pp. 114–71. Of nearly 300 extant copies of block books, Sister Mary Catharine saw sixty-one of the *Ars Moriendi* in twenty-one printings from thirteen distinct sets of blocks. The series of eleven block prints depicting Moriens's deathbed temptations were printed in England by Wynkyn de Worde in the early sixteenth century and were copied and modeled with many adaptations in costume and character until Shakespeare's day, but always, as in the Wednesday night illustration in Luis de Granada's *Of Prayer, and Meditation*, with Moriens at the heart of each print in each set.

[21] In block cut I a demon with a long nose hooked upward leans menacingly over Moriens. In VIII there is a representation of the mouth of hell, signified by flames with three figures writhing in agony. In IX the long-nosed demon appears with another devil pointing to a cellar where a boy is stealing a jug of wine from one of four casks—memories of past pleasures now to be forsaken? In X a man extends a scroll to Moriens "Ne intendas amicis"—"Do not concern yourself with your friends," *The Ars Moriendi*, ed. W. Harry Rylands (London: Wyman and Sons, 1881).

CONTRIBUTORS

HAROLD BLOOM is Sterling Professor of the Humanities at Yale University and Henry W. and Albert A. Berg Professor of English at the New York University Graduate School. He is a 1985 MacArthur Foundation Award recipient, served as the Charles Eliot Norton Professor of Poetry at Harvard University (1987–88), and is the author of nineteen books, the most recent being *The Book of J* (1990). Currently he is editing the Chelsea House series Modern Critical Views and The Critical Cosmos, and other Chelsea House series in literary criticism.

MAURICE MORGANN (c. 1725–1802) held several offices in the British government prior to the American War of Independence, including positions as Weigher and Teller at the Royal Mint, Under-Secretary of State for American affairs under the Earl of Shelburne, and Secretary of the province of New Jersey. In addition to his essay on Falstaff (1777), he wrote *An Enquiry concerning the Nature and End of a National Militia* (1757), *Plan for the Abolition of Slavery in the West Indies* (1772), and other works. His commentary on Shakespeare's *The Tempest* (c. 1785–90) has been published posthumously in Daniel E. Fineman's edition of Morgann's *Shakespearian Criticism* (1972).

A. C. BRADLEY held professorships of Modern Literature at the University of Liverpool, of English language and literature at the University of Glasgow, and of Poetry at Oxford. *Shakespearean Tragedy* (1904) established him as the preeminent Shakespeare scholar of the early twentieth century and remains a classic of modern Shakespeare criticism. His *Oxford Lectures on Poetry* were published in 1909, and *A Miscellany* in 1929.

HAROLD C. GODDARD was head of the English department at Swarthmore College from 1909 to 1946. In addition to *The Meaning of Shakespeare* (1951), he published *Studies in New England Transcendentalism* in 1908, and edited a 1926 edition of the essays of Ralph Waldo Emerson.

PETER J. SENG is Professor Emeritus of English at Connecticut College in New London. He has written *The Vocal Songs in the Plays of Shakespeare* (1967) and has edited *Poems: Wadsworth Handbook and Anthology* (1961; with C. F. Main) and *Tudor Songs and Ballads from MS Cotton Vespasian A-25* (1978).

HAROLD E. TOLIVER, Professor of English at the University of California–Irvine, has written *Pastoral Forms and Attitudes* (1971), *Intimate Allusions: Explorations of Narrative Structure* (1974), *The Past That Poets Make* (1981), *Lyric Provinces in the English Renaissance* (1985), and *Transported Styles in Shakespeare and Milton* (1989). He has edited many anthologies with James L. Calderwood, among them *Perspectives on Drama* (1968) and *Essays in Shakespearean Criticism* (1970).

WILLARD FARNHAM was, until his death in 1981, Professor Emeritus of English at the University of California–Berkeley. Among his works are *The Medieval Heritage of Elizabethan Tragedy* (1936) and *Shakespeare's Tragic Frontier: The World of His Final Tragedies* (1950). He edited *Twentieth Century Interpretations of* Doctor Faustus (1969).

MICHAEL PLATT has written *Rome and Romans According to Shakespeare* (1976) and *Shakespeare's Christian Prince* (1987). He is a former fellow of St. Thomas More Institute in Fort Worth, Texas.

LEO SALINGAR is Fellow of Trinity College, Cambridge, and author of *Shakespeare and the Traditions of Comedy* (1974) and *Dramatic Form in Shakespeare and the Jacobeans* (1986).

BARBARA FREEDMAN is Professor of English at St. John's University (Collegeville, MN). She has written articles on *Twelfth Night* and *The Comedy of Errors*.

C. L. BARBER was Professor of English at the University of California–Santa Cruz until his death in 1980. *Shakespeare's Festive Comedy: A Study of Dramatic Form and Its Relation to Social Custom* was published in 1959, and two further works, *The Whole Journey: Shakespeare's Power of Development* (1986) and *Creating Elizabethan Tragedy: The Theater of Marlowe and Kyd* (1988), have been edited and completed by Richard P. Wheeler.

RICHARD P. WHEELER, Professor of English at the University of Illinois, has written *Shakespeare's Development and the Problem Comedies* (1981). He has edited and completed two works by C. L. Barber, *The Whole Journey: Shakespeare's Power of Development* (1986) and *Creating Elizabethan Tragedy: The Theater of Marlowe and Kyd* (1988).

PAUL M. CUBETA, Professor Emeritus of English at Middlebury College (Middlebury, VT), has edited *Modern Drama for Analysis* (1950; 3rd ed. 1962) and written articles on Marlowe and Jonson.

BIBLIOGRAPHY

Abrams, Richard. "Rumor's Reign in *2 Henry IV:* The Scope of a Personification." *English Literary Renaissance* 16 (1986): 467–95.

Ainger, Sir Alfred. "Sir John Falstaff." In *Lectures and Essays,* Volume 1. London: Macmillan, 1905, pp. 119–55.

Alexander, Franz. "A Note on Falstaff." *Psychoanalytic Quarterly* 2 (1933): 592–606.

Auchincloss, Louis. "Falstaff and Hal." In *Motiveless Malignity.* Boston: Houghton Mifflin, 1969, pp. 117–27.

Bailey, John. "A Note on Falstaff." In *A Book of Homage to Shakespeare,* edited by Israel Gollancz. Oxford: Oxford University Press, 1916, pp. 149–53.

Baker, Christopher. "The Christian Context of Falstaff's 'Finer End.' " *Explorations in Renaissance Culture* 12 (1986): 68–86.

Barber, C. L. *Shakespeare's Festive Comedy.* Princeton: Princeton University Press, 1959.

Barton, Anne. "Falstaff and the Comic Community." In *Shakespeare's "Rough Magic": Renaissance Essays in Honor of C. L. Barber,* edited by Peter Erickson and Coppélia Kahn. Newark: University of Delaware Press, 1985, pp. 131–48.

Bass, Eben. "Falstaff and the Succession." *College English* 24 (1962–63): 502–6.

Battenhouse, Roy. "Falstaff as Parodist and Perhaps Holy Fool." *PMLA* 90 (1975): 32–52.

Beck, Richard J. *Shakespeare:* Henry IV. London: Edward Arnold, 1965.

Bennett, Alan W. "Falstaff's Girth: Compass of Imagery." *University of Kansas City Review* 19 (1952–53): 51–56.

Biswas, Dinesh Chandra. "The Comic in *Henry IV.*" In *Shakespeare's Treatment of His Sources in the Comedies.* Calcutta: Jadavpur University, 1971, p. 199–232.

Bloom, Harold, ed. *William Shakespeare's* Henry IV, Part 1. New York: Chelsea House, 1987.

———, ed. *William Shakespeare's* Henry IV, Part 2. New York: Chelsea House, 1987.

Boughner, Daniel C. "Traditional Elements in Falstaff." *Journal of English and Germanic Philology* 43 (1944): 417–28.

———. "Vice, Braggart, and Falstaff." *Anglia* 72 (1954): 35–61.

Bowers, Fredson. "Theme and Structure in *King Henry IV, Part I.*" In *The Drama of the Renaissance: Essays for Leicester Bradner,* edited by Elmer M. Blistein. Providence: Brown University Press, 1970, pp. 42–68.

Bradbrook, M. C. *"King Henry IV."* In *Muriel Bradbrook on Shakespeare.* Brighton: Harvester Press, 1984, pp. 72–83.

Bryant, J. A., Jr. "Falstaff and the Renewal of Windsor." *PMLA* 89 (1974): 296–301.

———. "Shakespeare's Falstaff and the Mantle of Dick Tarlton." *Studies in Philology* 51 (1954): 149–62.

Burton, Philip. "Falstaff." In *The Sole Voice: Character Portraits from Shakespeare.* New York: Dial Press, 1971, pp. 78–94.

Carroll, William. " 'A Received Belief': Imagination in *The Merry Wives of Windsor.*" *Studies in Philology* 74 (1977): 186–215.

Cazamian, Louis. "The Humour of Falstaff." In *Essais en deux langues.* Paris: Henri Didier, 1938, pp. 111–29.

———. "The Supreme Achievement: Falstaff." In *The Development of English Humor.* Durham, NC: Duke University Press, 1952, pp. 240–52.

Charlton, H. B. "Falstaff." In *Shakespearian Comedy.* London: Methuen, 1938, pp. 161–207.

Dawtrey, John. *The Falstaff Saga*. London: G. Routledge & Sons, 1927.

Donaldson, E. Talbot. "Love and Laughter: *Troilus and Criseyde, Romeo and Juliet*, the Wife of Bath, and Falstaff." In *The Swan at the Well: Shakespeare Reading Chaucer*. New Haven: Yale University Press, 1985, pp. 119–39.

Draper, John W. *Stratford to Dogberry: Studies in Shakespeare's Earlier Plays*. Pittsburgh: University of Pittsburgh Press, 1961.

Empson, William. "Falstaff and Mr. Dover Wilson." *Kenyon Review* 15 (1953): 213–62.

Faber, M. D. "Falstaff behind the Arras." *American Imago* 27 (1970): 197–225.

Fiehler, Rudolph. "How Oldcastle Became Falstaff." *Modern Language Quarterly* 16 (1955): 16–28.

Fleissner, Robert F. "The Malleable Knight and the Unfettered Friar: *The Merry Wives of Windsor* and Boccaccio." *Shakespeare Studies* 11 (1978): 77–93.

Gehring, Wes D. "Fields and Falstaff." *Thalia* 8, No. 2 (Fall–Winter 1985): 36–42.

Giles, Henry. "Falstaff: A Type of Epicurean Life." In *Lectures and Essays*, Volume 1. Boston: Ticknor, Reed, & Fields, 1850, pp. 1–44.

Goodman, Alice. "Falstaff and Socrates." *English* No. 149 (Summer 1985): 97–112.

Gordon, George. "Morgann on Falstaff." In *The Lives of Authors*. London: Chatto & Windus, 1950, pp. 23–32.

Green, William. *Shakespeare's* Merry Wives of Windsor. Princeton: Princeton University Press, 1962.

Hapgood, Robert. "Falstaff's Vocation." *Shakespeare Quarterly* 16 (1965): 91–98.

Hardin, Richard F. "Honor Revenged: Falstaff's Fortunes and *The Merry Wives of Windsor*." *Essays in Literature* 5 (1978): 143–52.

Heath-Stubbs, John. "The Mythology of Falstaff." *Occult Observer* 1 (1949–50): 21–30.

Hemingway, Samuel B. "On Behalf of That Falstaff." *Shakespeare Quarterly* 3 (1952): 307–11.

Hinely, Jan Lawson. "Comic Scapegoats and the Falstaff of *The Merry Wives of Windsor*." *Shakespeare Studies* 15 (1982): 37–54.

Howe, Warren M. "The Rejection and Regeneration of Falstaff in *1 Henry IV*." *Rocky Mountain Review of Language and Literature* 34 (1980): 217–27.

Huebert, Ronald. "Levels of Parody in *The Merry Wives of Windsor*." *English Studies in Canada* 3 (1977): 136–52.

Hunt, Maurice. "Time and Timelessness in *1 Henry IV*." *Explorations in Renaissance Culture* 10 (1984): 56–66.

Hunter, Robert G. "Shakespeare's Comic Sense as It Strikes Us Today: Falstaff and the Protestant Ethic." In *Shakespeare: Pattern of Excelling Nature*, edited by David Bevington and Jay L. Halio. Newark: University of Delaware Press, 1978, pp. 125–32.

Huntley, Frank Livingston. "The Whole Comic Plot of Falstaff." In *Essays in Persuasion: On Seventeenth-Century English Literature*. Chicago: University of Chicago Press, 1981, pp. 12–21.

Kaiser, Walter. "Shakespeare's Falstaff." In *Praisers of Folly: Erasmus, Rabelais, Shakespeare*. Cambridge, MA: Harvard University Press, 1963, pp. 195–275.

Knowlton, E. C. "Falstaff Redux." *Journal of English and Germanic Philology* 25 (1926): 193–215.

Koller, Katherine. "Falstaff and the Art of Dying." *MLN* 60 (1945): 383–86.

Krieger, Elliot. *"Henry IV, Part One."* In *A Marxist Study of Shakespeare's Comedies*. New York: Barnes & Noble, 1979, pp. 131–38.

Landt, D. B. "The Ancestry of Sir John Falstaff." *Shakespeare Quarterly* 17 (1966): 69–76.

Levin, Harry. "Falstaff's Encore." *Shakespeare Quarterly* 32 (1981): 5–17.

Levin, Lawrence L. "Hotspur, Falstaff, and the Emblem of Wrath in *1 Henry IV*." *Shakespeare Studies* 10 (1977): 43–65.

McLaverty, J. "No Abuse: The Prince and Falstaff in the Tavern Scenes of *Henry IV*." *Shakespeare Survey* 34 (1981): 105–10.

Maginn, William. "Sir John Falstaff." *Bentley's Miscellany* 1 (1837): 494–508.

Mendilow, A. A. "Falstaff's Death of a Sweet." *Shakespeare Quarterly* 9 (1958): 479–83.

Monaghan, James. "Falstaff and His Forebears." *Studies in Philology* 18 (1921): 353–61.

Muir, Edwin. "Panurge and Falstaff." In *Essays on Literature and Society*. Rev. ed. Cambridge, MA: Harvard University Press, 1965, pp. 166–81.

Murry, John Middleton. "Falstaff and Harry." In *Shakespeare*. London: Jonathan Cape, 1936, pp. 170–87.

Newman, Franklin B. "The Rejection of Falstaff and the Rigorous Charity of the King." *Shakespeare Studies* 2 (1966): 153–61.

Nuttall, A. D. "*Henry IV*: Prince Hal and Falstaff." In *A New Mimesis: Shakespeare and the Representation of Reality*. London: Methuen, 1983, pp. 143–61.

O'Connor, Frank. "Falstaff and Hal." In *Shakespeare's Progress*. Cleveland: World Publishing Co., 1960, pp. 91–97.

Orkin, Martin P. "Sir John Falstaff's Taste for Proberts in *Henry IV, Part 1*." *English Studies* 65 (1984): 392–404.

Parrott, Thomas Marc. "The Falstaff Plays." In *Shakespearean Comedy*. New York: Oxford University Press, 1949, pp. 234–71.

Parten, Anne. "Falstaff's Horns: Masculine Inadequacy and Feminine Mirth in *The Merry Wives of Windsor*." *Studies in Philology* 82 (1985): 184–99.

Phelps, Charles Edward. *Falstaff and Equity: An Interpretation*. Boston: Houghton Mifflin, 1901.

Phillips, G. W. "Falstaff." In *Lord Burghley in Shakespeare: Falstaff, Sly and Others*. London: Thornton Butterworth, 1936, pp. 11–64.

Porter, Joseph A. *The Drama of Speech Acts: Shakespeare's Lancastrian Trilogy*. Berkeley: University of California Press, 1979.

Priestley, J. B. "Falstaff and His Circle." In *The English Comic Characters*. London: John Lane/The Bodley Head, 1925, pp. 69–105.

Prior, Moody E. "Comic Theory and the Rejection of Falstaff." *Shakespeare Studies* 9 (1976): 159–71.

———. "The Honor of Princes, Warriors, and Thieves: *1* and *2 Henry IV*." In *The Drama of Power: Studies in Shakespeare's History Plays*. Evanston, IL: Northwestern University Press, 1973, pp. 199–218.

Quennell, Peter. "John Falstaff: A Biography." In *Casanova in London and Other Essays*. London: Weidenfeld & Nicolson, 1971, pp. 187–98.

Quiller-Couch, Sir Arthur. "The Story of Falstaff." In *Notes on Shakespeare's Workmanship*. New York: Henry Holt, 1917, pp. 114–36.

[Radford, G. H.] "Falstaff." In *Obiter Dicta*, Volume 1, by Augustine Birrell. London: E. Stock, 1884, pp. 200–233.

Reese, M. M. "Falstaff." In *The Cease of Majesty: A Study of Shakespeare's History Plays*. New York: St. Martin's Press, 1961, pp. 292–305.

Rossiter, A. P. "Ambivalence: The Dialectic of the Histories." In *Angel with Horns and Other Shakespeare Lectures*. Edited by Graham Storey. New York: Theatre Arts Books, 1961, pp. 40–64.

Scoufos, Alice-Lyle. *Shakespeare's Typological Satire: A Study of the Falstaff-Oldcastle Problem*. Athens: Ohio University Press, 1979.

Sen Gupta, S. C. "Sir John Falstaff." In *Shakespearian Comedy*. Oxford: Oxford University Press, 1950, pp. 250–75.

Shirley, John W. "Falstaff, an Elizabethan Glutton." *Philological Quarterly* 17 (1938): 271–87.

Sider, John W. "Falstaff's Broken Voice." *Shakespeare Survey* 37 (1984): 85–88.

Siegel, Paul N. "Falstaff and His Social Milieu." In *Shakepeare's English and Roman History Plays: A Marxist Approach*. Rutherford, NJ: Fairleigh Dickinson University Press, 1986, pp. 86–92.

Small, Samuel A. "The Reflective Element in Falstaff." *Shakespeare Association Bulletin* 14 (1939): 108–21, 131–43.

Somerset, J. A. B. "Falstaff, the Prince, and the Pattern of *2 Henry IV*." *Shakespeare Survey* 30 (1977): 35–45.

Spargo, John Webster. "An Interpretation of Falstaff." *Washington University Studies* 9, No. 2 (April 1922): 119–33.

Speaight, Robert. "Mr. Priestley, Falstaff and the Establishment." *Month* 25 (1961): 152–59.

Spivack, Bernard. "Falstaff and the Psychomachia." *Shakespeare Quarterly* 8 (1957): 449–59.

Sprague, Arthur Colby. "Gadshill Revisited." *Shakespeare Quarterly* 4 (1953): 125–37.

Steadman, John M. "Falstaff as Actaeon: A Dramatic Emblem." *Shakespeare Quarterly* 14 (1963): 231–44.

Stewart, Douglas J. "Falstaff the Centaur." *Shakespeare Quarterly* 28 (1977): 5–21.

Stoll, Elmer Edgar. "Falstaff Again." In *From Shakespeare to Joyce*. Garden City, NY: Doubleday, 1944, pp. 205–34.

Taylor, Gary. "The Fortunes of Oldcastle." *Shakespeare Survey* 38 (1985): 85–100.

Thayer, C. G. "The Troublesome Reign of King Henry IV." In *Shakespearean Politics: Government and Misgovernment in the Great Histories*. Athens: Ohio University Press, 1983, p. 94–142.

Tolman, Albert H. "Why Did Shakespeare Create Falstaff?" In *Falstaff and Other Shakespearean Topics*. New York: Macmillan, 1925, pp. 1–13.

Torrance, Robert M. "Monarch of Make-Believe." In *The Comic Hero*. Cambridge, MA: Harvard University Press, 1978, pp. 111–43.

Walter, J. H. " 'With Sir John in It.' " *Modern Language Review* 41 (1966): 237–45.

Weiss, Theodore. "Now of All Humours: *Henry IV, Parts I and II*." In *The Breath of Clowns and Kings: Shakespeare's Early Comedies and Histories*. London: Chatto & Windus, 1971, pp. 260–97.

West, Gilian. "Falstaff's Punning." *English Studies* 69 (1988): 541–58.

Williams, Philip. "The Birth and Death of Falstaff Reconsidered." *Shakespeare Quarterly* 8 (1957): 359–65.

Wilson, Elkin Calhoun. "Falstaff—Clown and Man." In *Studies in the English Renaissance Drama*, edited by Josephine W. Bennett, Oscar Cargill, and Vernon Hall, Jr. New York: New York University Press, 1959, pp. 345–56.

ACKNOWLEDGMENTS

"The Twelfth Letter: To Sir John Falstaff of Caister in Norfolk" by James Branch Cabell from *Ladies and Gentlemen: A Parcel of Reconsiderations* by James Branch Cabell, © 1934 by James Branch Cabell. Reprinted by permission of Royal E. Cabell, Jr., Esq.

The Fortunes of Falstaff by J. Dover Wilson, © 1943 by Cambridge University Press. Reprinted by permission of Cambridge University Press.

"Falstaff and Smollett's Micklewhimmen" by Robert B. Heilman from *Review of English Studies* 22, No. 3 (July 1946), © 1946 by Oxford University Press. Reprinted by permission of Oxford University Press.

"The Creation of Falstaff" by John Middleton Murry from *John Clare and Other Studies* by John Middleton Murry, © 1950 by John Middleton Murry. Reprinted by permission of The Society of Authors as the literary representative of the Estate of John Middleton Murry.

An Approach to Shakespeare by D. A. Traversi, © 1956 by Doubleday & Company, Inc. Reprinted by permission of Doubleday, a division of Bantam Doubleday Dell Publishing Group, Inc.

"The Prince's Dog" by W. H. Auden from *The Dyer's Hand and Other Essays* by W. H. Auden, © 1962 by W. H. Auden. Reprinted by permission of Random House, Inc., and Faber & Faber Limited.

"The Sword in the Crown" by John Wain from *The Living World of Shakespeare: A Playgoer's Guide* by John Wain, © 1964 by John Wain. Reprinted by permission.

"Introduction" to *Shakespeare's Living Art* by Rosalie L. Colie, © 1974 by Princeton University Press. Reprinted by permission of Princeton University Press.

"Immenso Falstaff" by Vincent Godefroy from *The Dramatic Genius of Verdi: Studies of Selected Operas,* Volume 2, © 1977 by Vincent Godefroy. Reprinted by permission of Victor Gollancz Ltd.

"*Henry IV:* The Ascendance of the Lie" by James L. Calderwood from *Metadrama in Shakespeare's Henriad: Richard II to Henry V* by James L. Calderwood, © 1979 by The Regents of the University of California. Reprinted by permission of The University of California Press.

"Character: The Windsor Falstaff" by Jeanne Addison Roberts from *Shakespeare's English Comedy: The Merry Wives of Windsor in Context* by Jeanne Addison Roberts, © 1979 by the University of Nebraska Press. Reprinted by permission of the University of Nebraska Press.

"Falsifying Men's Hopes: The Ending of *I Henry IV*" by Edward Pechter from *Modern Language Quarterly* 41, No. 3 (September 1980), © 1980 by the University of Washington. Reprinted by permission of *Modern Language Quarterly.*

"Falstaff and the King" by Sukanta Chaudhuri from *Infirm Glory: Shakespeare and the Renaissance Image of Man* by Sukanta Chaudhuri, © 1981 by Sukanta Chaudhuri. Reprinted by permission of Oxford University Press.

" 'The Savage Yoke': Cuckoldry and Marriage" by Coppélia Kahn from *Man's Estate: Masculine Identity in Shakespeare* by Coppélia Kahn, © 1981 by the Regents of the University of California. Reprinted by permission of The University of California Press.

"Falstaff, Sancho Panza and Azdak: Carnival and History" by Jonathan Hall from *Comparative Criticism* 7 (1985), © 1985 by Cambridge University Press. Reprinted by permission of Cambridge University Press.

"Language: *Macbeth, Richard II, Henry IV*" by Terry Eagleton from *William Shakespeare* by Terry Eagleton, © 1986 by Terry Eagleton. Reprinted by permission of Basil Blackwell Ltd.

"Henry IV" by Harold C. Goddard from *The Meaning of Shakespeare* by Harold C. Goddard, © 1951 by The University of Chicago. Reprinted by permission of The University of Chicago Press.

"Songs, Time, and the Rejection of Falstaff" by Peter J. Seng from *Shakespeare Survey* 15 (1962), © 1962 by Cambridge University Press. Reprinted by permission of the author.

"Falstaff, the Prince, and the History Play" by Harold E. Toliver from *Shakespeare Quarterly* 16, No. 1 (Winter 1965), © 1965 by the Shakespeare Association of America, Inc. Reprinted by permission of *Shakespeare Quarterly.*

"Falstaff and the Grotesque" by Willard Farnham from *The Shakespeare Grotesque: Its Genesis and Transformations* by Willard Farnham, © 1971 by Oxford University Press. Reprinted by permission of Oxford University Press.

"Falstaff in the Valley of the Shadow of Death" by Michael Platt from *Interpretation* 8, No. 1 (January 1979), © 1979 by Queens College, © 1991 by Michael Platt. Reprinted by permission of *Interpretation* and the author.

"Falstaff and the Life of Shadows" by Leo Salingar from *Shakespearean Comedy,* edited by Maurice Charney, © 1980 by New York Literary Forum. Reprinted by permission.

"Falstaff's Punishment" (originally titled "Falstaff's Punishment: Buffoonery as Defensive Posture in *The Merry Wives of Windsor"*) by Barbara Freedman from *Shakespeare Studies* 14 (1981), © 1981 by The Council for Research in the Renaissance. Reprinted by permission of *Shakespeare Studies.*

"From Mixed History to Heroic Drama: The *Henriad"* by C. L. Barber and Richard P. Wheeler from *The Whole Journey: Shakespeare's Power of Development* by C. L. Barber and Richard P. Wheeler, © 1986 by The Regents of the University of California. Reprinted by permission of The University of California Press.

"Falstaff and the Art of Dying" by Paul M. Cubeta from *Studies in English Literature 1500–1900* 27, No. 2 (Spring 1987), © 1987 by William Marsh Rice University. Reprinted by permission of *Studies in English Literature 1500–1900.*

INDEX